THE GOLDEN KEY

A Study of the Fiction of George MacDonald

THE GOLDEN KEY

A Study of the Fiction of George MacDonald

BY ROBERT LEE WOLFF

New Haven: Yale University Press, 1961

Publication of this book has been aided by
grants from the Kingsley Trust Associ-
ation Fund established by the Scroll and
Key Society of Yale College; the founda-
tion established in memory of James
Wesley Cooper of the Class of 1865, Yale
College; and the Mary Cady Tew
Memorial Fund.

To my Mother and to the Memory of my Father

Preface

GEORGE MACDONALD's fiction has certain features that give it a compelling interest of its own: to students of comparative literature, of theology, of psychology, and of the Victorian Age; and even to the reader who is a student of nothing at all. C. S. Lewis once suggested what I mean:

> I believe there are two kinds of poetry. The commonest, and by wide human agreement the greatest, kind . . . communicates such experiences as all men have had, so that simple readers exclaim "How true," and classicists call it a "just representation of general nature," and realists say that the poet is stripping off the mask of convention and facing "the facts." But I must admit that there are also poems which seem to give me a new and nameless sensation, or even a new sense, to enrich me with experience which nothing in my previous life had prepared me for. . . . I do not find it in Homer, Sophocles, Chaucer, Spenser, Milton, or . . . in Racine: I find it seldom in Virgil, and only in the very latest works of Shakespeare; but I find it abundantly in Blake, in the early Morris, in Mr. De la Mare and Miss Sitwell, in Mr. Eliot, and even in Poe. I find it most of all in the prose work of George Macdonald [sic], whose literary competence is so often to seek that any of us could improve even the best passages very materially in half an hour.[1]

While I doubt that "any of us" could improve Mac-
Donald's best passages, Lewis has here vaguely said
something that this book tries to say more precisely.

This study deals primarily with MacDonald's fiction.
I have referred to his poetry, sermons, essays, and works
of literary criticism only when they proved helpful.

In using psychoanalysis, I have accepted the views set
forth in Leon Edel's admirable chapter in his recent
Literary Biography. But this book is not primarily literary
biography: I have put the emphasis on MacDonald's
writing, "as if it were, as indeed it is, a being no less
alive and contradictory than the man who created it." [2]
The reader will find that I have laid before him all the
data on which my own conclusions are based.

My thanks go first to Yale University, whose authorities
in the summer of 1959 invited me to give four "Harvard"
Lectures in New Haven in the spring of 1961, on the
subject of some forgotten Victorian novelists. From the
first, I intended to give one lecture on MacDonald; and
the original plan also called for submitting all four lectures for publication as a book. When I told my friend,
Chester Kerr, the Director of the Yale University Press,
that the MacDonald lecture had already become a book
all by itself, he said reflectively that it would be all right
not to submit the others: for this, and for many other
kindnesses, I thank him. The authorities at Harvard, dead
game as always, gave me leave to go to England and
Scotland during the month of May 1960, and the Harvard
Foundation for Advanced Study and Research helped
foot the bills. At the British Museum and the London
Library, and at the Brander Library in Huntly, Aberdeenshire, somewhat less frequented by scholars, I was received with great generosity.

My friend, Dr. Gregory Rochlin, a practicing analyst, with great kindness read *Phantastes* and *Lilith* at my suggestion, and has since read and discussed with me the manuscript of this book. He has saved me from all sorts of *gaffes* and has no responsibility for those that remain. Howard Mumford Jones, John Clive, Mrs. Alan Simpson, and Stuart Atkins read the manuscript in whole or in part, and made valuable suggestions. After the book was finished, Mrs. Simpson generously allowed me to read her own unpublished study of MacDonald's fairy-tales, written as an Oxford B.Litt. thesis some years ago; as a result I modified and improved my treatment of *The Princess and the Goblin* and *The Princess and Curdie*. Miss Carol Whiting gave me the refuge in which I wrote a large part of this book. Mrs. Florence Mintz, Miss Eve Altmann, and Miss Patricia Ford cheerfully and competently typed the various drafts. My friends and family have listened patiently to many long disquisitions on George MacDonald. To all of these go my warmest thanks.

Grateful acknowledgment is made to George Allen and Unwin for permission to quote from Greville Mac-Donald's books *George MacDonald and His Wife* and *Reminiscences of a Specialist* and to reproduce three illustrations from the former book. The H. Gernsheim Collection has kindly granted permission to reproduce the fourth illustration, George MacDonald with his daughter Lily.

R. L. W.

Cambridge, Mass.
December 1960

Contents

Illustrations

THE GOLDEN KEY

A Study of the Fiction of George MacDonald

CHAPTER 1

The Beginnings

Bury me, bury me lone
Where no dirge is sung and no music plays
In echoes around my sepulchral stone,
And the only funeral lays
Be the hollow moan, in its rocky caves
Of ocean awaking its thousand waves.

Bury me, bury me deep,
In some lonely cave on the wild sea's shore
There are none o'er my grave will seek to weep,
And the mad waves' tempest roar
Will soothe this spirit, when, shrouded in gloom,
It visits the strange and unrecked of tomb.*

GEORGE MACDONALD, 1844

I

As CHILDREN, many of us read George MacDonald's *At the Back of the North Wind* or *The Princess and the Goblin* and can still remember how appealing and yet how puzzling and disquieting we found the story of the London cabman's child who drove his father's white horse by day and adventured with the North Wind by night, or the story of the king's daughter whose splendid great-grandmother sat spinning in a tower room at the top of a long staircase that was often difficult to find,

* Unpublished verses, dated 28 September 1844; manuscript in a scrapbook now in the Houghton Library at Harvard.

while below in the earth the evil goblins tunneled away
in their effort to undermine the castle. Publishers keep
these tales in print, together with the sequel to the second,
The Princess and Curdie. Like the top of an iceberg, they
float in plain sight. Below the surface, however, lurks
the massive achievement of one of the most astonishing
—and almost completely forgotten—literary careers of
Victorian England.

Poet, myth-maker, novelist, allegorist, critic, essayist,
lecturer, and always a preacher, George MacDonald,
during forty-six active years from 1851 to 1897 wrote
well over fifty books. Of his twenty-five novels, thirteen
deal with Scotch themes, and twelve with English. In
addition to a long series of fairy-tales, he wrote two
romances for adults, one near the very beginning of his
career (*Phantastes,* 1858), the other near the very end
(*Lilith,* 1895), that form almost a new literary genre in
themselves. In their day his writings enjoyed immense
popularity, excited bitter controversy, elicited long articles in the serious critical journals, and brought him
fame—and, what is more remarkable, love—on both
sides of the Atlantic.[1]

At the height of his career, in the sixties and seventies,
MacDonald knew everybody. It was to MacDonald and
his family, in 1862, that their intimate friend Lewis Carroll diffidently gave the manuscript of *Alice;* the Mac-
Donald children's delighted reception of the story decided their "Uncle Dodgson" to publish it. John Ruskin
made MacDonald his closest confidant at the critical
moments of his anguished middle-aged courtship of the
young and beautiful Rose LaTouche. Frederick Denison
Maurice, whose preaching brought MacDonald into the
Church of England, in 1869 invited him to collaborate

in writing a book he was planning on the unity of the Church and its expression in the Sacraments. Ruskin and Maurice joined with Lord Houghton (R. Monckton Milnes), Charles Kingsley, Dean Stanley of Westminster, and others in supporting MacDonald in 1865 (without success) for the chair of Rhetoric and Belles Lettres at Edinburgh. At a party at MacDonald's house, Ruskin led off a "Sir Roger de Coverley" with Octavia Hill. Tennyson came and borrowed a Gaelic edition of Ossian in order to read the Latin translation. With Thackeray and Leslie Stephen, Leigh Hunt, G. H. Lewes, and others, Mac-Donald (though he thought *Vanity Fair* "awful") used to dine with Thackeray's publishers and one of his own, George Smith, of Smith and Elder. Attracted by Mac-Donald's first full-length book, Lady Byron had rescued him in 1857 from poverty, becoming the first of a long series of patrons. The Leigh-Smiths, one of whose daughters, as Madame Bodichon, founded Girton, introduced him to militant feminist circles. Matthew Arnold became a friend. So did the aged Crabb Robinson—who long ago with Coleridge had welcomed the German romantic Tieck to England. Dickens is said to have praised *Phantastes,* and a photograph survives—undated but surely before 1859—showing MacDonald with Dickens, Thackeray, Wilkie Collins, Trollope, Bulwer-Lytton, Carlyle, Froude, and Macaulay.[2] (See illustration on next page.)

In America, where MacDonald had a triumphant lecture tour in 1872, Emerson, Longfellow, Phillips Brooks, and Whittier received him warmly, and a delegation of deacons from one of the large Fifth Avenue churches begged him in vain to accept the pastorate of their church at a salary of $20,000 a year, a staggering figure in those days. Boston friends got up a special fund in token of their

dismay at the large sums he was losing through the piracy
of his books by American publishers. The young Richard
Watson Gilder, within a few months of his first meeting
with the MacDonalds, was calling them "Father" and
"Mommy." Later, Mark Twain came to visit MacDonald
in England, and remained a friend and admirer.[3]

Tall, broad-shouldered, and athletic in build, with
bright blue eyes and one of the biggest of all the big
Victorian beards—black in middle life, snow-white in his
old age—MacDonald loved horses and riding, and had
been a boxer in his youth, though persistent ill-health
kept him sedentary as he grew older. He had a strong
taste for finery, appearing on the streets of London or at
Delmonico's in New York in full Highland costume, dirk
and all, "with his Tartan plaid . . . fastened to the left
shoulder by the glimmering topaz in silver setting." At
other times, he wore waistcoats of his own design with
a long row of several dozen small buttons, usually gilt,
all but the top and bottom few left open over a soft white
shirt. A black velvet jacket, or a scarlet cloak, or a complete suit of white serge or white flannel dazzled the
beholder. A Chicago newspaper took gushing note of
". . . his diamond pins, jewelled shirt-studs, massive
watch-chain, daintily-shod feet, and Christ-like countenance." All his life MacDonald loved the flash of precious
stones; lady admirers once gave him an opal. In the
beauty of colorful clothes and jewels, as everywhere in
nature and in man, he saw God's loving hand. The
"Christ-like countenance" the Chicago reporter saw reflected a character that those who knew him *felt* to be
Christ-like. Men and women of all classes came to him
with their troubles. His devotees called him prophet and
seer and saint.[4]

As he grew old, he felt the decline in his powers, and

MacDonald with a group of contemporary writers

Front row: W. M. Thackeray, Lord Macaulay, Bulwer Lytton, Thomas
Carlyle, Charles Dickens
Back row: MacDonald, J. A. Froude, Wilkie Collins, Anthony Trollope

Louisa MacDonald with her children and Lewis Carroll, 1862

feared the falling-off of his great audience. Blow after
blow fell upon him, as family tragedies succeeded each
other in rapid succession. When he died, at eighty-one,
in 1905, he had written nothing for seven or eight years;
indeed, he had spoken scarcely a word for five, but had
withdrawn into silence and waited for death.[5] A number
of critics even then thought him neglected, and were
predicting that it might take several generations before
he would be rediscovered. As one perceptive American
lady admirer put it, calling him a "giant among today's
pigmies":

> He was to his own age shockingly liberal, and to
> ours he is amazingly orthodox. When another genera-
> tion or two shall have passed, certain religious peculi-
> arities will have become historic quaintness, and a
> fuller appreciation than he has yet had is awaiting
> him.[6]

Her prediction made in 1906 still awaits its fulfillment.

A few voices have always sung MacDonald's praises.
H. G. Wells admired *Lilith*. When MacDonald died,
G. K. Chesterton wrote in an obituary notice: "If we test
the matter by originality of attitude, George MacDonald
was one of the three or four greatest men of the nineteenth
century." Almost twenty years later, writing an introduction to Greville MacDonald's life of his father, Chesterton
hailed him as "St. Francis of Aberdeen," who had accomplished a "miracle of the imagination." And in his little
book on *The Victorian Age in Literature,* Chesterton
speaks of

> . . . George MacDonald, a Scot of genius as genuine
> as Carlyle's; he could write fairy-tales that made all
> experience a fairy-tale. He could give the real sense

that everyone had the end of an elfin thread that must at last lead them into Paradise. It was a sort of optimist Calvinism. But such really significant fairy-tales were accidents of genius.[7]

In 1924, the centennial of MacDonald's birth, a leading article in the *Times Literary Supplement* said of him:

> The author of *David Elginbrod* and *Robert Falconer* and *Alec Forbes* was a good novelist. The poet of the *Poems* and *The Diary of an Old Soul* was a true poet. The author of *The Golden Key* and of *Lilith* had a touch of genius . . . not yet has he been recognized as the man who did one sort of work better than anyone else has ever done it . . . the writing of what are commonly called his fairy stories.[8]

C. S. Lewis in 1946 compiled an anthology of prose passages from MacDonald's works, only one of a number which his devotees have put together, and in the preface declared:

> What he does best is fantasy—fantasy that hovers between the allegorical and mythopoeic. And this, in my opinion, he does better than any man . . . MacDonald is the greatest genius of this kind whom I know . . . The great works are *Phantastes*, the *Curdie* books, *The Golden Key*, *The Wise Woman*, and *Lilith*.

Lewis thinks much less well of the novels, as novels, but even in these he hails MacDonald as a "supreme preacher, as golden and genial as Traherne; but also as astringent as the *Imitation*." He tells of his own debt to MacDonald:

I have never concealed the fact that I regarded him as my master; indeed I fancy I have never written a book in which I did not quote from him. But it has not seemed to me that those who have received my books kindly take even now sufficient notice of the affiliation. Honesty drives me to emphasize it.

A copy of *Phantastes*, bought almost reluctantly thirty years before, had played the key role in beginning Lewis' own conversion: from its "morning innocence" and "a certain quality of Death, *good* Death" Lewis' imagination took the turn that led him in the end to faith: "what I learned to love in *Phantastes* was goodness." Again, in his autobiography (1955), Lewis tells the tale of buying *Phantastes* on a railway bookstall, and of the momentous changes it began in his spiritual life.[9]

W. H. Auden, writing an introduction to the 1954 reprint of *Phantastes* and *Lilith,* echoes Lewis:

> George MacDonald is pre-eminently a mythopoeic writer . . . In his power . . . to project his inner life into images, events, beings, landscapes which are valid for all, he is one of the most remarkable writers of the nineteenth century: *The Princess and the Goblins* [sic] is, in my opinion, the only English children's book in the same class as the Alice books, and *Lilith* is equal if not superior to the best of Poe.

Others, like Charles Williams and J. R. Tolkien, have paid MacDonald the even greater compliment of presenting his ideas in twentieth-century fantasies—often influenced by his creations—without explicit acknowledgment. We have a full and detailed biography by his son

Greville, based in large part on original correspondence. Yet, so far, nobody has written a critical assessment of MacDonald's books. In the midst of a Victorian revival they await their rediscoverer.[10]

On Christmas Day 1851, as the twenty-seven-year-old Minister of the Congregational Church at Arundel, Sussex, MacDonald published and gave to his friends as a gift his first literary work, a little pamphlet of twenty-six pages containing his own translation of *Twelve of the Spiritual Songs of Novalis* (Friedrich von Hardenberg, 1772–1801). The English verses often limp; inversions sometimes spoil them, but occasionally they reach the mystical heights of the German original, and always they reflect its intense piety. In a short preface MacDonald translated a few sentences from Tieck's brief notice of Novalis' life, those that record the death (1797) of Novalis' fifteen-year-old fiancée, Sophie von Kühn, his grief, his recovery, and the composition of the *Spiritual Songs*. "Had I not the distant hope," MacDonald began, "of one day offering the works of Novalis in an English garb to English readers, I should be tempted to extract more largely." [11]

Although he never realized the distant hope, the tragic figure of Novalis, who had died of tuberculosis at the age of twenty-nine (1801), continued to exercise a powerful attraction on MacDonald, himself tubercular and intensely preoccupied with death and with earthly and heavenly love. At least three times, MacDonald reworked his translation of *Spiritual Songs*. At Christmas 1873 he sent his friends a new and expanded version, as he said, "like a sheet of Christmas Carols." In 1876 and 1897 he printed revisions for wider circulation. Usually the revisions brought improvement, and the later versions show

a command of English versification almost equal to
Novalis' own control of German.[12] Yet this preoccupation with the *Spiritual Songs* is the merest symptom of
the young MacDonald's immense debt to Novalis. The
Spiritual Songs, after all, rank among Novalis' minor
works. His greater achievements—*Heinrich von Ofterdingen* and *Die Lehrlinge zu Saïs*—together with the
writings of other German romanticists, influenced Mac-
Donald's own early thought and writing to a degree that
nobody has yet realized.

However inauspiciously, the translation of the *Spiritual Songs* launched MacDonald on a literary career. The
deacons of the congregation at Arundel now suspected
that their minister was tainted with German theological
ideas. Moreover, he had affirmed that the heathen would
go to heaven, and not only the heathen, but even animals. So from a salary of 150 pounds per annum, small
enough in all conscience for a man with a wife and little
daughter, the deacons cut him down to about 115 pounds.
Had this been all, he might well have braved the hard-
ship. But various "annoyances" and "spiritual wickedness
in high places" forced him in May 1853 (aged twenty-
eight) to resign his pulpit.[13] He never had another. The
course of his future, though for a long time it would
prove uncertain, had in fact been decided.

II

Born at Huntly in Aberdeenshire on December 10, 1824,
George MacDonald took his descent from a branch of
one of the great Highland families. His great-grandfather's father and grandfather had fled from the massacre of Glencoe (1692), when the troops of Campbell of

Glenlyon slaughtered the MacDonalds. William, his
great-grandfather, Town's Piper of Portsoy, was out in
the '45, and escaped alive from Culloden's field (1746).
Charles Edward, his grandfather, born in the year of
Culloden, founded a thread-spinning factory at Huntly,
and was part-owner of the bleaching fields along the
River Bogie. Charles Edward's wife, George MacDonald's grandmother, born Isabella Robertson, was a fero-
cious Calvinist. She left the Parish Church and joined
that of the "Missionars," so-called because it early ad-
vocated the despatch of missionaries to the heathen. She
had nine children of her own, and adopted four beggar
children. One of her sons, Charles, in financial difficulty,
absconded to America, and two of his brothers, George
and James, though without obligation, assumed his enor-
mous debt of 6,000 pounds, paying an installment each
year of their lives. As the development of the Glasgow
spinning mills rendered the primitive thread factory un-
profitable, and the invention of chloride of lime wrecked
the bleaching business, George and James became tenant-
farmers of the great local landowner, the Duke of Gordon.

This George MacDonald, father of the author, married
in 1822 Helen MacKay, beautiful and well-educated,
who gave her husband six sons in ten years. Two died
in childhood. Four survived: Charles, our George Mac-
Donald, born in 1824, Alexander, and John Hill. In 1832,
when George MacDonald was eight, his mother died of
tuberculosis. All his life long he kept a single letter of
hers, written about himself to her mother-in-law, his
pious Calvinist grandmother, who, with others, had been
urging that she wean him, her baby son. Against her
will, she had complied:

But I cannot help my heart being very much grieved for him yet, for he has not forgot it: poor little fellow he is behaving wonderfully well as yet. He cryed desperate a while the first night, but he has cryed very little since, and I hope the worst is over now.

"Nearly a century old," wrote George MacDonald's son and biographer Greville in 1924, "is this letter with its pretty Highland English. It has lain in my father's cabinet with its secret nest of drawers, along with a golden brown lock of that mother's hair, and her wedding gift to her husband, a little silver-set seal with the name *George* engraved on its red stone; together also with little trifles belonging to those of his own children who had followed her to the grave." [14]

This letter offers us a clue to George MacDonald's character and writing that we shall find invaluable at almost every turn. His mother's death dealt him a wound that never healed. In his secret drawer there always lay the letter describing her reluctance to wean him, proclaiming the love that nobody else could give, and that he had forever lost. His father "could not make up for the loss." George MacDonald the elder "rarely caressed his boys: it was not in the fashion in those days to do so." "Sufficient discipline ruled the home. A look of displeasure from the beloved father was punishment for any sin, while his rebuke was awful indeed." A man of extraordinary courage, the father submitted to the amputation of his tubercular leg, refusing "the customary stupefying dose of whiskey." When a mob burned him in effigy during the potato famine of 1846 because they suspected that he had potatoes hidden in his barn, he first made them laugh by shouting that they had attached the wooden leg to the wrong hip of the effigy, and then proved to them that his barn was as bare as their own.[15]

Had severity and courage been the limit of the father's qualities, it would have been easier for the young George MacDonald to grow up openly acknowledging how badly he missed his mother, and how little of a substitute he found his father. But the elder MacDonald was also humorous, kind, and understanding. In an age and country where patriarchal power reigned unchallenged in most households, he gave his sons much freedom of choice. George MacDonald would later tell his children that his father had never refused him anything he had asked. When such paternal love and generosity and tolerance accompany paternal authority, filial love makes the natural filial resentments the more shameful, and a son must repress all the harder his rebelliousness and even his longing for the lost mother. With the repression there grows a deep sense of guilt. This tension we shall find repeatedly in MacDonald's writing: we shall find him constantly preoccupied with the relationships between fathers and sons, and shall, without forcing the evidence, we think, be able to show how his writing reflected his own predicament.

C. S. Lewis once hailed MacDonald's whole life as illustrating the operation of an "anti-Freudian" principle:

> An almost perfect relationship with his father was the earthly root of all his wisdom. From his own father, he said, he first learned that Fatherhood must be at the core of the universe. He was thus prepared in an unusual way to teach that religion in which the relation of Father and Son is of all relations the most central.

Yet we shall find it more complicated than that. You can throw nature out with a pitchfork, but she still keeps on coming back. George MacDonald tried hard to transform his love for his mother into love for his father, and to persuade himself that this was all he needed. But again and again we shall find him telling us, in terms so unmistakable that we confess our astonishment that Lewis should not have understood them, that fathers are not everything, that men want mothers as well. We shall find him feeling such guilt at what he regards as his own deficiencies in gratitude and affection toward his father that he will invent many imaginary ways—some of them utterly fantastic—for sons to show their fathers their love through acts of service and dedication, even when the fathers do not deserve it. It is in the paradox of a kind father who has deprived his son, George MacDonald, of the right to feel rebellious that we shall find one key to the son's books. MacDonald struggled all his life to conceal the guilt he felt so deeply, and to present a lovable demeanor to the world.[16]

By the time the senior MacDonald remarried, George was fifteen. His stepmother, of whom he grew very fond, found the boys courteous, forbidden by the rule of the house to speak Scotch at meals or in the presence of their elders, a prohibition that George obviously resented, as he shows in the many spirited defenses of his mother-tongue that stud his books. His childhood gave him also his love for the Scotch countryside. For all animals he developed affections far stronger than usual, even among Britons. He learned to admire the hunger for learning and the stanch self-respect that shone amidst the poverty and harshness of the Highland farmer's life. From the Huntly school, with its brutal schoolmaster, he proceeded at sixteen to Aberdeen, where, after a few months coaching, he won a bursary at King's College. He worked hard, but in spurts, with a strong interest in natural science, and a considerable ability in languages. He learned German easily and thoroughly, and hoped to go on to Giessen to study with von Liebig, in preparation for a medical career. Poor Scotch students in those days would usually earn enough in the fields during seven months of the year to pay their expenses during the five-month sessions of the college. But MacDonald, too poor to go to Germany and too unwell with pleurisy (they used to bleed his arm as a cure) for farm labor, took another sort of post.

In 1842 he "spent some months in a certain castle or mansion in the far North . . . in cataloguing a neglected library." Though his son Greville has lovingly assembled great detail with regard to just about every other episode in MacDonald's life, he could never identify this great house or find any documentation for the summer of 1842. Yet here, we can be sure, George MacDonald had some of the most important experiences of his life. He read widely in the English poets and discovered the German authors, chiefly the romantics, perhaps first through Carlyle's essays and translations, but soon enough through the originals.

And—no reader of his books can doubt it—he fell in love, with a girl somewhat older than he, a member of the family that owned the castle and the library. She led him on a certain distance, and then rejected him because she felt him to be of an inferior social class. Again and again in his writing we shall find George MacDonald recurring with pain to these crucial events of the mysterious summer of 1842, giving a different turn to each of his fictional accounts of the affair, striving to exorcise his own anguish and humiliation. No wonder his son could find no record of the summer: the fiction provides all that remains. MacDonald's disappointment taught him to feel bitter scorn (and, eventually, some pity) for the heartless jilts who appear so often in the libraries of his imaginary mansions. It enhanced his fierce pride in his own origin—he felt himself to be as gently born as anybody—and at the same time created a lasting distrust —even hatred—of rich noblemen, and of the false social values he had found in the girl in the library.

Back in Aberdeen, MacDonald, now eighteen, taught arithmetic in the Aberdeen Central Academy. Friends later remembered him at a charade party wearing huge disks of sliced carrot as buttons on an otherwise button-less bottle-green coat; or striding on a stormy night up and down the shore addressing poetry to the sea and the wind. His great friend and confidante, and possibly something more, was his cousin Helen MacKay, three years older than he, to whom he wrote some of his poetry. Later she remembered him in this period as deeply mournful and depressed; his favorite saying, she reported, was "I wis' we war a' deid." The Calvinist doctrine of the elect appeared to him intolerable; even as a child he "did not care for God to love me if he did not love everybody," a view he would later embody in his writings, and argue with much passion.

In 1845, aged twenty, he took his M.A. degree, and for the next three years he was tutor in the household of a difficult family in a London suburb. In 1846, his first published poem—a blank-verse effort called *David*—appeared anonymously in the *Congregational Magazine*. His cousin Helen MacKay having married a son of James

Powell, a well-to-do leather-factor of Welsh origin with
a fine house at Clapton, MacDonald soon found himself
welcomed as an intimate of the eight young people of the
family. It was a strict Congregationalist household but
by no means a joyless one. MacDonald promptly fell in
love with the fourth child and second daughter, Louisa,
two years older than he.

More and more feeling the call to the ministry, he
resigned his tutorship in the spring of 1848, and, with his
father's consent, went to study at Highbury College, one
of the five Congregational Theological Halls then in the
London area. Mr. Powell gave him permission to pay his
addresses to Louisa: "Though but a needy theological
student, with indifferent health and no *personal* ambition, whose father, a tenant-farmer in the impoverished
North, could give him no pecuniary help, he was yet
welcomed as son-in-law by this prosperous, stern dis-
ciplinarian, whose smile was not a ready one, who seldom petted his daughters, and who was yet curiously
jealous when any lover came between them." [17] Louisa's
mother, like the MacDonalds, had tuberculosis; no doubt
the match was in the highest degree inadvisable. Yet the
two young people loved each other, and their letters show
their passion through all their preoccupation with God
and with their own sins and unworthiness. When George
asked his fiancée to go to his cousin Helen, her sister-
in-law, and get back some notebooks full of verses he had
sent to her, Louisa showed some natural jealousy, especially as Helen declared she had burned some of the
poems because they "were for no eye but her own." But
the girls eventually reached an understanding.

MacDonald's father wrote him in an "old-fashioned
tone of parental advice, criticism, and admonishment:"

I hope you will by and by be in circumstances to pay off your small debts, and make conscience of never venturing on taking a wife before then. If you begin by thinking lightly of such a case, depend upon it the carelessness will increase until none but yourself and such as are in similar circumstances can paint the agony it will entail.

Mr. Powell too, after having heard George preach, felt free to criticize the life-like way in which he had read the Gospels, commenting that his "illustrious friend S. T. Coleridge" had long ago convinced him that "Scriptures should be delivered more as the Oracles of God than the opinions of man." At a sign of disgust from Mr. Powell, George shaved off his new beard. After he had served as "supply" minister for brief periods elsewhere, the Arundel Congregation invited him to become their regular minister (October 1850) at a salary of 150 pounds a year. Mr. Powell had agreed to pay their rent and to furnish their house as a wedding present. Louisa wrote in ecstasy over a new tea-caddy: "I know it will just suit you—it is so neat and elegant-shaped, with a likeness of York Minster at the top done in the coloured mother of pearl."

But in November 1850 came a severe hemorrhage. At the very beginning of his career, with marriage only a few weeks off, MacDonald found himself ordered by the doctors not to preach, to rest, and to take codliver oil. Mr. Powell tried to persuade Louisa to postpone the marriage; but she insisted that she must nurse George, and her father gave in. After four months convalescence, during which MacDonald wrote a five-act blank verse drama, they were married on March 8, 1851.[18]

As his wedding present to Louisa, George wrote a long

poem, "Love Me, Beloved," in which one sees the ever-present thoughts of death that obsessed him.

Love me, beloved; the thick clouds lower;
A sleepiness filleth the earth and air;
The rain has been falling for many an hour;
A weary look the summer doth wear;
Beautiful things that cannot be so;
Loveliness clad in the garments of woe.

Love me, beloved; I hear the birds;
The clouds are lighter; I see the blue;
The wind in the leaves is like gentle words
Quietly passing 'twixt me and you;
The evening air will bathe the buds
With the soothing coolness of summer floods.

Love me, beloved; for, many a day,
Will the mist of the morning pass away;
Many a day will the brightness of noon
Lead to a light that hath lost her moon;
And in joy or in sadness, in Autumn or Spring,
Thy love to my soul is a needful thing.

Love me, beloved; for thou mayest lie
Dead in my sight, 'neath the same blue sky,
Love me, O love me, and let me know
The love that within thee moves to and fro;
That many a form of thy love may be
Gathered around thy memory.

Love me, beloved; for I may lie
Dead in thy sight, 'neath the same blue sky;
The more thou hast loved me, the less thy pain,
The stronger thy hope till we meet again;

And forth on the pathway we do not know,
With a load of love, my soul would go.

Love me beloved, for one must lie
Motionless, lifeless, beneath the sky
The pale stiff lips return the kiss
To the lips that never brought love amiss;
And the dark brown earth be heaped above
The head that lay on the bosom of love.

Love me, beloved; for both must lie
Under the earth and beneath the sky;
The world be the same when we are gone;
The leaves with the same quiet tone sound on;
The spring come forth, and the wild flowers live,
Gifts for the poor man's love to give;
The sea, the lordly, the gentle sea
Tell the same tales to others than thee;
And joys, that flush up like the light of morn,
Irradiate hearts that are yet unborn;
A youthful race call our earth their own,
And gaze on its wonders from thought's high throne,
Embraced by fair Nature, the youth will embrace
The maid beside him, his queen of the race;
When thou and I shall have passed away
Like the foam-flake thou lookedst on yesterday.

Love me, beloved; for both must tread
On the threshold of Hades, the House of the dead;
Where now but in thinkings strange we roam,
We shall live and think, and shall be at home;
The sights and the sounds of the spirit land
No stranger to us than the white sea-sand,
Than the voice of the waves, and the eye of the moon,

Than the crowded street in the sunlit noon.
I pray thee to love me, belov'd of my heart
If we love not truly, at death we part;
And how would it be with our souls to find
That love, like a body, was left behind!

Love me beloved; Hades and Death
Shall vanish away like a frosty breath;
These hands, that now are at home in thine,
Shall clasp thee again, if thou are still mine;
And thou shalt be mine, my spirit's bride,
In the ceaseless flow of eternity's tide,
If the truest love that from mine can flow.
Pray God, beloved, for thee and me,
That our souls may be wedded eternally.[19]

Struck down suddenly by the disease that had killed
his mother and Louisa's mother, that had crippled his
father, and had destroyed Sophie von Kühn and Novalis
himself, MacDonald felt a revival of his youthful wish
that "we were all dead." The wish to join those who had
gone before and the assurance that death would lead to
new life he would already have found in Novalis too:
"Death is at the same time an end and a beginning," and
"The best among us, who have attained the spirit-world
during their lifetimes, only seem to die"; and even "Life
is only for the sake of death." And elsewhere: "Perfect
life is heaven . . . What we here call death is a conse-
quence of absolute life, of heaven . . . Hence the perpetual destruction of all imperfect life . . . Everything
must become heaven." [20] It would have been surprising
had MacDonald, in his first encounter with tuberculosis,
not felt the special bond that united him with the passionate and eager young Novalis, who had literally chosen

to die—or at least had pretended to choose to die—after the loss of his destined child bride. Death spared Mac-Donald, but the example of Novalis was ever before him.

After the resignation at Arundel, the MacDonalds faced a grim struggle against sickness and poverty. They went to Manchester, to be near A. J. Scott, a Presbyterian minister who had lost his license to preach because he opposed the Calvinist doctrine of the elect, and who had won the admiration of Carlyle, Ruskin, and others. In Manchester, MacDonald lectured a little, taught a little, and wrote a little. But frequent hemorrhages interrupted his work, and made it necessary to take long periods of rest and convalescence. He and his wife were often down to their last few shillings. Five children were born to them between 1852 and 1857. From Huntly, his father advised him to

> give over the fruitless game of poetry, and apply yourself to the preaching of the Gospel and the instruction of your people. A nervous temperament and a poetical imagination are too much for a frail clay tabernacle.

But George MacDonald replied:

> . . . why be troubled because your son is not like other people? Perhaps it is *impossible* for him to be. Does not the spirit of God lead men and generations continually on to new truths? [21]

In all societies the assumption of the priestly function creates in the life of the priest a major spiritual crisis, comparable to those induced by puberty or marriage. Primitive peoples regard it as one of the most solemn of

Man's undertakings, and feel that it should appropriately be accompanied by a period of withdrawal, rest, contemplation, even isolation, by way of preparation for the return to action, refreshed and competent. Though civilized societies hardly ritualize to this extent the preparation for priestly duties, hardly anybody will deny the solemnity of the act. I do not know of any study of the psychological consequences of failure in the priestly office, but it would seem reasonable to suppose that this would produce a severe shock, and one that the failed priest would have to explain to himself and to the world again and again.

For a Scot the problem would be especially difficult. In Scotland, as MacDonald knew very well indeed, the "stickit" minister, who had failed in the pulpit, remained forever afterwards as a mockery to his fellow-townsmen. To himself, to his anxious and affectionate but domineering father, and to the people of Huntly among whom he had grown up, George MacDonald was a "stickit" minister. Almost at once we find him beginning on the life work of turning this over and over in his mind, and accounting for it.

The only piece of fiction that survives from this period is a short story called "The Broken Swords," which he published anonymously in October 1854, only a year and a half after leaving Arundel. It tells, in strongly melodramatic language, of a sensitive and introspective boy, who shows cowardice as an officer on the battlefield and is disgraced, but, after many unhappy vicissitudes in other occupations, enlists as a private in his own former regiment and performs prodigies of valor. He dies defending the honor of a fleeing girl against a number of enemy soldiers who are chasing her, buying with his life enough time to enable her to throw herself over a cliff and die unstained.

The boy has been "a home-boy, the loved of his mother, the pet of his sisters," whereas MacDonald of course had been brought up among men: perhaps this in itself is significant camouflage of an intention to depict himself. His hero has too much "inner life . . . while other boys were acting, he was thinking." Irresolute, he yet has a "vivid imagination and a high sense of honour, nourished in childhood by the reading of the old knightly romances." But when you put such a youth into "a position where action is imperative, you have elements of strife sufficient to reduce that fair kingdom of his to utter anarchy and madness. Yet so little do we know ourselves, and so different are the symbols with which the imagination works its algebra, from the realities which those symbols represent," that the boy does not anticipate how little qualified he would prove for war. Though they break his sword after his disgrace, and though he plunges into a deep depression, takes a post as a factory workman in a town, and eventually loses the girl he falls in love with there, he keeps the pieces of the broken sword. When he dies honorably in the ranks, he breaks a second sword in defense of the purity of the fleeing maiden. The second broken sword redeems the first.[22]

Was not MacDonald saying that he had been temperamentally unfit to be a minister, and that his resignation at Arundel had arisen from his incapacity to be an officer, but that he would now prove himself as a humble worker for Christianity, and would gladly die in the ranks demonstrating his courage and devotion? Read in this way, "The Broken Swords" serves to put us on warning at the very beginning of MacDonald's literary career.

Much that we shall find in his writing we shall better understand if we think of the Arundel failure as a major blow to his pride. We add it now to the loss of his mother, to the problem of his father, to the love affair in the library, to his tuberculosis, his love of Novalis and the other Germans, and his detestation of doctrinaire Calvinism as one of the chief sources of his literary inspiration.

III

In 1855, after many rejections by publishers, Longmans accepted the verse drama, *Within and Without,* first written during the earliest attack of tuberculosis and polished since. Though reluctant, Louisa agreed to let her husband include "Love me, Beloved" among the many other lyrics that studded the play. Written in blank verse, *Within and Without* tells the story of Count Julian Lamballa, an Italian nobleman who has become a monk, but regrets his decision, feeling that after all an active life is the way to serve God. He escapes from the monastery, rescues Lilia, a lady he has loved in the past, from a wicked noble in whose power she is, stabs the villain, and elopes with her. This action occupies the first two of the five "Parts" of the play.

Part III opens five years later in London, where Julian and Lilia are living in poverty with their little daughter, Lily. Julian now knowns that he is on the right path to God: the very fact that he has become the father of a beloved child has awakened in him the true sense of the fatherhood of God. He has some menial post in a "counting-house." Lilia has taken work as music teacher to the daughter of Lord Seaford. She misunderstands Julian's preoccupation with the search for the love of God, and believes that he has stopped loving her, so that when Lord Seaford falls in love with her she is momentarily tempted. But she does not yield. She leaves Seaford's house, and on Hampstead Heath decides to purify herself by seeking God, and, when she has found Him, to write to Julian and tell him her whole story. Julian receives an anonymous letter telling him that Lilia has run off with Seaford; in anguish he searches for her in vain through Seaford's house, after knocking down the servant at the door. Alone, he finds his comfort in his little daughter, who wanders about with him in search of Lilia, but then sickens and dies. Exhausted and defeated, Julian himself dies also, with Lilia's letter of explanation unread; but at the last moment Lord Seaford has assured him of her innocence. In a dream, Lily leads Julian to the cottage where Lilia still is. He tells her that it had all been his own fault: "I made it possible to tempt thee, child." But calling herself "defiled and outcast," she assures him that "when I think of Him he looks like thee," and asks to be his slave.[23] Julian, Lily, and Lilia are reunited in heaven.

In this play, almost unreadable today, George MacDonald was explaining to Louisa Powell how it was that he could not love her so much loved he not God more. Indeed, he was seeking to explain to himself the relationship between earthly and heavenly love. Until he had come to feel that "the perfect love of man and woman is but offshoot of that love for God which bids them leave all lower ties to follow Him," MacDonald suffered at the apparent conflict between his love for Louisa and his love for God. Until she had come to understand and share his overriding concern with the divine Fatherhood, she had feared that his love for her was somehow lacking. Clumsily *Within and Without* deals with this problem, one which now seems impossibly far-fetched, yet full of pathos for the author and his wife.

If Julian and Lilia had ever really loved each other, an understanding word could at any moment have prevented their quite unbelievable tragedy: she could never even have thought of Seaford, nor could Julian have allowed himself to become so preoccupied with his search for God that he ignored her need for love. In a summary that MacDonald himself prepared for his publisher, he wrote

> From the different mental conditions of [Julian's] wife and himself a gulf gradually opens between them. She cannot sympathize with his absorbing hunger for individual communication with the source of life; and he is too engrossed to minister his share of the beautiful to a nature that can only exist on the favour of the world.

But he excuses neither Julian nor, by implication, himself:

> He who had been seeking good for the sake of personal perfection to a degree that interfered entirely with what he owed to her who was nearest to him, comes to feel the baseness of even such lofty selfishness as this, and abjures it and himself with it; confesses that less than all was too little to cast at the feet of his wife, in whom God was present in his eyes. Then he has leave to die.[24]

The whole play carrying his reassurance to Louisa ends for the lovers and their child in the death—and the re-

union after death—that MacDonald so often contemplated with longing as the greatest good; and echoes the
lyric, "Love me, Beloved," which he eventually inserted
in it. One need not, perhaps, be astonished at the excess
of Victorian morality that makes Lilia regard herself as
utterly befouled because, in her sorrow at Julian's apparent neglect, she had listened, even briefly, to the
urgent voice of Lord Seaford. Julian's casual violence,
however, is a surprise: he stabs the villain and briskly
wipes his dagger on the dead man's coat; and never,
throughout the play, does he express a word of regret for
an action at first perhaps a little hard to reconcile with
his "absorbing hunger for individual communication with
the source of life." But MacDonald puts the explanation
into Julian's mouth at the very moment of the stabbing:
" 'If men *will* be devils,' " he says, " 'They are better in
hell than here.' " [25] We shall later encounter again Mac-
Donald's doctrine, here only hinted at, that the wicked,
who perhaps would not repent on this earth, might just
as well go to hell in a hurry, and there start at once on the
repentance that would eventually lead to the salvation
of them all. Besides, MacDonald himself was a passionate
man, and never doubted the righteousness of a righteous
blow. So too Julian knocks down the porter who would
deny him entrance to Lord Seaford's house.

It is a measure of our distance from the Victorians that
Within and Without—with its long mawkish passages of
recitative—proved a decided literary success. The *Scotsman* said of it:

> This strange and original drama is full of the most
> exquisite poetry sustained at the pitch of sublimity
> with immense yet apparently effortless power . . .

A very remarkable production of intellect and heart united as perhaps they have seldom been before.

Charles Kingsley wrote MacDonald a letter approving it; though we have not its text, we may conjecture that Kingsley found Julian's escape from the monastery especially to his liking: he loathed clerical celibacy, and would surely have endorsed Julian's choice of an active life. Frederick Denison Maurice also wrote in praise. Lady Byron became deeply interested in the poem and its author: it took "a powerful hold on her." In MacDonald's own family, his father-in-law, the stern James Powell, was found reading it "with the tears streaming down his cheeks," while A. S. MacColl, brother of MacDonald's stepmother and a noted Shakespeare scholar, called it the finest poem to appear in twenty years. The publisher was much pleased with the sales.[26]

But of course the sales could not support the growing family. The scourge of tuberculosis, which had taken MacDonald's beloved brother Alec in 1853 at the age of twenty-six, killed his charming half-sister Isabella in 1855 at the age of fourteen, and visited MacDonald himself again and again. When he went back to Huntley to see his father, he wrote Louisa:

> I have been with my father to see Alec's grave, five miles away. He lies beside my mother and my two brothers. I thought—, oh, there is room for me between him and the wall. But I must be where you are, my own—only I should like if we could both be in that quiet country churchyard.

And after his sister had died, once more echoing Novalis:

> . . . death is only the outward form of birth. Surely it is no terrible thing that she should go to Alec. And

we can't be very long behind her. There is room for
us all between Alec and the wall in the churchyard.

To his father he quoted Schiller:

Schiller says—"Death cannot be an evil because it is
universal." God would not let it be the law of His
universe if it were what it looks to us.

However great his resignation, even his eagerness, death
persistently refused to visit him.

Borrowing a few shillings here, accepting a present
of a sovereign there, trying to paint a table for one of her
brothers in exchange for a promised fee of five pounds,
Louisa found life harsh indeed, especially when contrasted with that of her well-to-do relatives. George's father gave him all he could afford: "If fathers knew how
liberality makes their sons love them," MacDonald wrote,
"they would exercise it oftener." And, "Oh that fine old
man my father! He is the man to tell anything to. So
open and wise and humble and kind—God bless him."
There was more pother about George's beard, which he
had allowed to grow again: his conservative uncle James
opposed his preaching at Huntly because of it; but his
"noble old father told me that for his part I might let it
grow until I stuffed it into my trousers." Lady Byron,
whom he had never met, none the less offered to pay the
expenses of a winter in Algiers for him and his wife, and
there they went in 1857, leaving three of their children
behind with the Powells. The MacDonalds had begun—
and would always continue—to live in some measure at
least, on contributions from others, even in the later years
when his novels were bringing large prices.

MacDonald's attitude toward these funds that friends
were providing never varied. In 1857, with his tuberculosis still not arrested, he wrote from Algiers:

I shall do better by and by. If not, I hope He will
let me go very soon—for if I cannot provide for my
family, I would rather not add to the burden. At the
same time, some of what is given to me must be regarded in a very different light from charity in the
ordinary sense of the word. True, it would not be
offered to me if I did not require it; but if I contribute to make life endurable or pleasurable or
profitable, I do not see why I should be ashamed of
having been acknowledged in the way I need, any
more than if I were paid for keeping a merchant's
books.

And Lady Byron, first of his patrons, felt the same way
about it, writing, "I hope it is no disgrace to me to be
rich, as it is none to you to be poor," and "If I can do anything for you, you must understand, Mr. MacDonald, it is
rather for the public than yourself." Checks of twenty-
five or fifty pounds came in from her at regular intervals
until her death in 1860, and in her will she left MacDonald 300 pounds, which arrived at a moment when the
family had literally no money and not enough food in
the house. Later on, Ruskin, the Cowper-Temples (afterwards Lord and Lady Mount-Temple), and other well-
to-do friends gave him or left him money, prevailed on
the Queen to grant him a civil list pension of 100 pounds
a year, and raised purses to contribute to the cost of
building him his beautiful big house in Bordighera. But
he would not accept money if he felt it would put him
under obligations he would rather not incur. In a letter
of refusal to a wealthy woman he wrote:

I am not ashamed of taking money; if I were I would
not take it; neither do I wish the fact concealed that

> I have often accepted money with grateful and un-
> ending obligations . . . But . . . I could not have
> been sure that, at some time before long, when you
> were dissatisfied with something I had done, you
> would not have said something, in still continuing
> kindness I would not doubt, which would have made
> me sorry that I had ever been laid under obligation
> to you.[27]

During the stay at Algiers, MacDonald wrote steadily,
and completed a volume of poems, which he saw through
the press upon his return to England in April 1857.[28] The
most important poem is the long blank-verse narrative
called "A Hidden Life." This tells the story of a young
Scotch farmer, who reads "old tales of Scotland's war-
riors," chants "ancient tunes," and sings Burns' songs in
the field, proud of his labor. One day a beautiful lady
rides by; her saddle-girth slips; he repairs the damage,
and lifts her back into the saddle, not knowing how to
make a stirrup of his hands, but

> Around her waist he put his brawny hands,
> That almost zoned her round; and like a child
> Lifting her high, he set her on the horse;
> Whence like a risen moon she smiled on him,
> Nor turned aside, although a radiant blush
> Shone on her cheek, and shadowed in her eyes.

She thanks him, but he cannot muster speech to answer,
and she rides away, leaving him with the vision of her
as a gift. Daughter of a neighboring laird, she soon goes
off to the city, while he remains to savor and enjoy the
beauties of the countryside, to which the sight of her
beauty has opened his eyes. In winter he reads, and goes

to the nearby town at night to study mathematics and Latin; moved by his progress, his father sends him to college, "in that great northern city," where he works hard, and wins honors. Amid the dangers of the town the memory of the maiden's face serves to keep him pure, and his return to the farm each summer prevents his head from being turned by the respect and liking that the men and women of the city have come to feel for him.

After the end of the four-year term, he decides to return to be a farmer:

He knew his father's wish—it was his own.
"Why, should a man," he said, "when knowledge grows,
Leave therefore the old patriarchal life,
And seek distinction in the noise of men?

So, though the professors were

. . . ready at a word to speed him on
. . . towards any goal; . . .
. . . he took his books, what little of his cap and gown
    remained
And leaving with a sigh the ancient walls,
Within the old stony crown, unchanging, gray
Amidst the blandishments of airy spring,
He sought for life the lone ancestral farm.

Delighted, his father has prepared for him as a surprise a little study in the loft. And he resumes the seasonal round of labor and reading. On the farm, he is merciful to man and beast:

. . . no creature fled from him;
And when he slew, 'twas with a sudden death
Like God's benignant lightning. For he knew

That God doth make the beasts, and loves them well—
And they are sacred. Sprung from God as we,
They are our brethren in a lower kind;
And in their face he saw the human look.
They said: "Men look like different animals;"
But he: "The animals are like to men, ..."

Saddened at the news of wickedness and disasters from the cities, he none the less refuses to listen to philanthropists' protests that he is wasting his talents on the farm. He answers that in the city it would take many years for him to gain men's confidence, while on the farm he knows each individual with whom he deals and has established with them long-standing bonds of trust.

He often dreams of the maiden, but she never passes his way again. When he reads a romance, he thinks of her; he even thinks he will marry, but "never came the maid,/ Or never came the hour: he walked alone." She, however, has married "One of the common crowd," and is discontentedly living an idle fashionable life. After three years, during the heavy labor of a harvest season, in the midst of a thunder-storm, he sees a vision of her again in a flash of lightning.

"Ah me!" he said; "my dreams are come for me;
Now shall they have their time."

He has a dreadful fever, and after it has abated,

Before its time, a biting frost set in.
And gnawed with fangs of cold his shrinking life;
And the disease so common to the north
Was born of outer cold and inner heat.

Resigned, he waits for death, yet is sometimes tormented by doubts. As the tuberculosis is about to kill him, his father, earthly reflection of the heavenly Father, comforts him:

> "I think, my boy, death hath two sides to it—
> One sunny and one dark; as this round earth
> Is every day half sunny and half dark.
> We on the dark side call the mystery *death;*
> They on the other, looking down in light,
> Wait the glad *birth,* with other tears than ours."

Just before he dies, in his wish to be sure of the maiden's purity, he writes her a letter, to be delivered after his death, telling her how her beauty had served as his inspiration, and begging her "for God's sake be as beautiful / As that white form that dwelleth in my heart," and urging that she turn to God, "Doing the right in sweet unconsciousness." Then he dies, and the lady is seen to visit his grave and weep, and pluck a daisy or a blade of grass before she drives away.[29]

"A Hidden Life" is a fantasy, of a common type: "how-sorry-she'll-be-when-I'm-dead." It acquires a special flavor, however, because MacDonald has turned it into a special sub-species: "how-much-I-can-do-for-her-possibly-sinful-soul-by-playing-on-her-grief-after-I'm-dead." Additional melodramatic overtones are supplied by the circumstance that the noble ploughman and the lady have met only once and that she has never been allowed to know of his love for her. Is not MacDonald trying to deal in this poem with the shattering disappointment of the summer flirtation in the library, imagining how it might have been if the girl, who in real life had rebuffed him, had never even known of his love for her? How much

more nobly he would have come out of the affair had he
been able to keep silence until just before an edifying
death! The hero's father, youth, education at Aberdeen,
love of nature, and tuberculosis are all MacDonald's own.
Yet MacDonald had made the decision *not* to go back to
the farm, as indeed had all his brothers. Perhaps this was
preying on his conscience, and he tried to fancy what
might have happened had he been healthy enough to
labor on his father's acres.

The hero's belief that "animals are like to men" and
"They are our brethren in a lower kind" comes direct from
Novalis, who held that the order of creation ascended
from minerals through plants through animals to man,
each evolving upward into the next category, and man
himself destined to evolve toward God. Novalis in turn
probably derived this concept from the mystic Jacob
Boehme (1575–1624), whom he had carefully studied,
or possibly from Swedenborg. William Blake had long
before taken it from them, for example in the "Verses sent
to Butts":

> Each grain of Sand
> Every Stone on the Land,
> Each rock & each hill,
> Each fountain & rill
> Each herb & each tree,
> Mountain, hill, earth & sea,
> Cloud, Meteor & Star,
> Are Men Seen Afar.

Here Blake does not mention animals, but in *Vala* they
appear, while rocks do not:

As the seed waits, Eagerly watching for its flowers &
    fruit . . .

So Man looks out in tree & herb & fish & bird & beast . . .

Novalis' poem, *Es färbte sich die Wiese grün,* gives the whole hierarchy:

> The formless dust becomes a bush
> The tree takes on the likeness of a beast
> The beast itself will become a man . . .
> And in sum I saw that now on earth
> Human Beings will turn to Gods.

And elsewhere Novalis remarks: "I do not know why people always talk of humanity as something separate. Are not animals, plants, and stones, stars, and breezes also portions of humanity?" In the portions of his romance *Heinrich von Ofterdingen* that he did not live to complete, Novalis intended his hero to become successively a stone, a tree, a golden ram, and a human being, moving from each incarnation to the next as the result of a sacrifice.[30]

In "A Hidden Life" George MacDonald is using only part of this elaborate theory of evolution, taken from the German mystics and romantics: he limits himself to animals and men. But he found the entire system attractive, and we shall find him using other features of it in his later writings. Just as Novalis' disease and tragic love and death and his deep mystic piety had struck responsive chords in MacDonald, so the mystics' doctrine of evolution also appealed irresistibly to him, as a true lover of animals, eager to believe that the beasts share in man's higher attributes and will share his fate. These views had already cost him the pulpit at Arundel. In "A Hidden Life" he re-states them deliberately. And in the father's comments on death as birth, addressed in consolation to his son, we hear again the echo of Novalis.

At one moment, while awaiting death, the hero has the fancy that

> . . . behind those world-enclosing hills,
> There sat a mighty woman, with a face
> As calm as life, when its intensity
> Pushes it nigh to death, waiting for him,
> To make him grand forever with a kiss,
> And send him silent through the toning worlds.[31]

Who is the woman? Is she the spirit of death? Is she the hero's mother? Is she a vision of MacDonald's own? The poem does not help us much. But this is the first appearance of a figure whom we shall later come to know.

No reader of "A Hidden Life" can fail to think of Wordsworth: the form, the substance, remind one of "Michael" or "The Leech-Gatherer." In some sustained passages, such as the description of the harvest, Mac-Donald reaches Wordsworthian heights. Far quieter in tone, less "spasmodic," more credible than *Within and Without*, "A Hidden Life" deals not with monks, monasteries, knights, Italy, lords and ladies, and high-flown metaphysics, all of which were strange to MacDonald, but with Scotch farm life, the village scholar, the University of Aberdeen, the changing of the seasons, and the sudden sight of blood on a handkerchief, all of which he knew at first hand. He never again wrote any poetry so good.

CHAPTER 2

Phantastes, The Dream Romance

"To make the dream-story from which *Wonderland* was elaborated seem Freudian one has only to tell it."

WILLIAM EMPSON, *English Pastoral Poetry*

I

IN OCTOBER 1857 George MacDonald settled in Hastings with his family and began to write "a kind of fairy tale, in the hope that it will pay me better than the more evidently serious work." It took him "two months to write without any close work," and within two days of its submission to Smith & Elder they accepted it and gave him fifty pounds for the copyright. This was *Phantastes.* Always recognized as one of MacDonald's most important works, it has never before received any sort of serious critical examination, though kept in print for many years by Everyman's Library and republished most recently in 1954.¹ Just because *Phantastes* was, as its subtitle declares, "a faerie romance for men and women," its author could draw freely for inspiration upon the whole range of his reading. So, too, he could feel free to explore and reveal his own emotions behind the imagery of a story so remote from real life that even the members of his own family never regarded it as more than a delightful work of the imagination. Nor can we be altogether sure how many of the personal references that we think we see in it MacDonald inserted consciously.

The title comes from Canto VI of Phineas Fletcher's *Purple Island,* two lines of which appear misquoted on the half-title of the first edition:

> Phantastes, from their fount all shapes deriving,
> In new habiliments can quickly dight.
>> ("their fount" should read "the first")

Phantastes is the personification of the Fancie, the second of the three councillors in Fletcher's poem who control the castle of the mind. The first is Judgment, the third Memory:

> The next that in the Castles front is plac't,
> Phantastes hight; his yeares are fresh and green,
> His visage old, his face too much defac't
> With ashes pale, his eyes deep sunken been
>> With often thoughts, and never slackt intention:
>> Yet he the fount of speedy apprehension,
> Father of wit, the well of arts, and quick invention.

> But in his private thoughts and busy brain
> Thousand thinne forms, and idle fancies flit;
> The three-shap't Sphinx, and direful Harpyes train,
> Which in the world had never being yet:
>> Oft dreams of fire and water, loose delight;
>> And oft arrested by some ghastly sprite,
> Nor can he think, nor speak, nor move for great affright.

> Phantastes from the first all shapes deriving
>> In new habiliments can quickly dight;
> Of all materiall and grosse parts depriving,
> Fits them unto the noble Prince's sight;

Which soon as he hath view'd with searching eye,
He straight commits them to his Treasurie
Which old Eumnestes keeps, Father of Memorie.

In this passage Fletcher was directly inspired in part by
the "House of Alma" in Book II, Canto IX of Spenser's
Faerie Queene, and in part by Joshua Sylvester's *Divine
Weeke,* both deriving from Du Bartas and ultimately
from Ficino and the Neo-Platonists.[2]

MacDonald here suggests as strongly as Fletcher's context enables him to do that what follows is to be a work
of the imagination, stripping the fancies of his busy brain
of their grosser parts and reworking them into suitable
form for the reader to view and store in his memory. Yet
not many readers would know Fletcher well enough to
remember the full context of the poem from the single
couplet MacDonald gives, nor would many of them turn
to it for enlightenment. Thus the quotation on the half-
title is only a clue, and a partly concealed one, to the
author's intention.

Nor did he stop playing with his reader at this point.
On the verso of the halftitle is the following quotation
from Novalis, given in the original German, which few
English readers then or since can have understood. In no
edition has anybody bothered to translate it. All through
the years, since 1858, two important and misleading mis-
prints in the German have remained uncorrected. In the
1954 edition the quotation was omitted entirely. Moreover, in the edition of Novalis that MacDonald was using,
the editors themselves had made a major mistake in
transcription.

One can imagine narratives without coherence [*Zusammenhang*] but rather with association [*Associa-*

tion], like dreams; poems that are indeed good to hear and full of beautiful words, but also without any meaning and coherence [*Zusammenhang*], with at the most single stanzas comprehensible, like fragments of the most varied sort of things. This pure poetry can at best have an allegorical meaning in general, and an indirect effect like music. That is why Nature is so purely poetical, like the workshop of a sorcerer, of a physicist, like a nursery, a lumber- or store-room. . . .

A fairy-tale [*Märchen*] is like a dream-picture without coherence. A collection of wonderful things and events, for example a musical phantasy, the harmonic sequences of an Aeolian harp, Nature itself.

In a genuine *Märchen*, everything must be wonderful, mysterious, and coherent [*zusammenhängend*]; everything bustling, everything [*jedes*, not *jeder*, as in *Phantastes*] in a different way. All nature must be wonderfully mixed with the whole world of spirit; this is where the time of anarchy comes in, of lawlessness, freedom, of the natural state of Nature, the time before [*vor*, not *von*, as in *Phantastes*] the world . . . The world of the *Märchen* is the world that is entirely opposite to the world of the truth and is yet just as similar to it as is Chaos to the completed created universe [*Schöpfung*].[3]

The reader will observe at once that in the first of Novalis' remarks he calls for *no* coherence (*Zusammenhang*) in the narration, while, in the last, he seems to say just the opposite, and declares that all must be coherent (*zu-*

sammenhängend). This is not Novalis' inconsistency: he had written *unzusammenhängend*—*in*coherent—and his friends and editors Tieck and Schlegel had printed the opposite.[4] Novalis was consistent: incoherence and not coherence was to be the character of the *Märchen,* and this behest MacDonald—who apparently had not noticed or been troubled by this inconsistency—followed in *Phantastes.*

MacDonald omitted a sentence after the words "time before the world," in which Novalis says: "This time before the world reveals the fragmented traits of the period after the World [i.e. after creation] in the same way as the state of Nature is a distorted picture of the eternal kingdom [i.e. the new age]." And after the end of the portion quoted by MacDonald, Novalis continued:

> In the future world everything is the same as in the former world, and yet entirely different; the future world is the chaos of reason, a chaos that has permeated itself, that is both inside and outside itself. The true *Märchen* must at the same time be a prophetic representation, an ideal representation, and an absolutely necessary representation. The true teller of fairy tales [*Märchendichter*] is a seer of the future.

By omitting these passages, MacDonald declined to accept Novalis' cosmogony, of the past, present, and future worlds, and the theoretical relationship to them of the teller of fairy-tales. As a Christian, MacDonald presumably could not openly embrace these views, nor perhaps did he wish to claim to be a seer of the future.

The climate of literary discussion in Victorian England in 1858, when *Phantastes* appeared, differed completely from that of early romantic Germany, sixty years earlier. In 1795, immediately after the appearance of Goethe's *Märchen,* in *Unterhaltungen deutscher Auswanderten* (published in Schiller's magazine, *Horen*), the critics—A. W. Schlegel, Tieck, and Novalis himself, among others—had embarked on a debate as to what a *Märchen* was and ought to be. Novalis maintained that a novel (*Roman*) should properly flow into a *Märchen,* and Schlegel agreed with him, citing Novalis' own *Heinrich von Ofterdingen* as an example.[5]

In order to beguile and attract a mid-Victorian audience into accepting as much as he intended to feed them of German romanticism, MacDonald had to jettison its wilder claims. Indeed, the omissions of the passages quoted gave him, paradoxically enough, far more freedom to attempt what the passages prescribed than he could have retained had he quoted them in full. He preferred not to let his readers in England suspect that he was setting himself up as a seer of the future, or that he wanted his "faerie romance for men and women" to be in any sense a prophetic representation. Only if he refrained from making the claim could he leave himself the scope to make the effort.

Phantastes, then, we learn from the Novalis passages omitted as well as those included, was to be a *Kunstmärchen,* one of those fairy-tales in which a sophisticated artist makes use of the folklore materials and naive effects of the *Volksmärchen,* or popular fairy story, to create what was, when Goethe founded it, virtually a new genre. MacDonald owed a large debt to the *Kunstmärchen* in general and to Novalis in particular. The form of *Phantastes*—mingled prose and verse, with many interpolated songs sung by the characters—reminds one of *Heinrich von Ofterdingen.* But though we shall discover in *Phantastes* much inspiration and many borrowings from Novalis and E.T.A. Hoffmann, and other German romantic writers, we shall also find that some of the episodes, some of the allegory, some of the tempo remind us of Shelley's *Alastor*, of the *Faerie Queene*, of *The Pilgrim's Progress*. And much of the romance reflects MacDonald's own personal sorrows, and his own outlook on life and death.

The narrator, Anodos, on his twenty-first birthday, receives the keys to his father's secretary, which has stood undisturbed since his father's death many years before. At once he thinks he may learn his father's personal history. He soon discovers a secret compartment, in which there is a packet of papers, and on its threshold suddenly sees a tiny beautiful woman, who tells him she is about to grant him a wish. When he doubts that a being so small can do so, she jumps to the floor and becomes a full-sized woman. Drawn to her irresistibly, he reaches out for her. But she says that if he touches her she will hurt him; and "besides a man must not fall in love with his grandmother, you know." She is two hundred and thirty-seven years old. She reminds him that he had expressed the wish to find the way to fairyland, and promises that he will do so on the next day. She tells him to look into her eyes; when he complies he is filled with longing, remembering that his mother had died when he was a baby. He has a brief vision of a sea like moonlit fog, and goes to bed. While thinking, between waking and sleeping, of all this, he becomes conscious that the marble basin in the corner of his room is overflowing onto the flowered carpet, whose flowers are now waving in the breeze; in fact, he is out of doors before he can be dressed. He follows a path into the woods.

Anodos is now in fairyland. The preliminaries to his arrival there have sounded some of the keynotes of the entire work. The hero's name is presumably Greek, meaning "pathless": he has not found his way in life. At the earliest opportunity, he looks into his father's secret place, and finds a beautiful woman there. The woman whom a father keeps secret from his son would ordinarily be the father's wife, the mother. The attraction Anodos feels for the woman is clearly sexual; instantly, however, she warns him off with the words "a man must not fall in love with his grandmother, you know"; she is using the incest taboo to prevent his touching her. Anodos remembers his mother's death as soon as he looks into her eyes. She is not, however, his lost mother; perhaps this would have been too crudely close to George MacDonald's own wish; the fairy is his grandmother instead.

Quite possibly the substitution (and the warning) were suggested to MacDonald by the title of Thomas Haynes Bayly's otherwise irrelevant farce-comedy, *You Can't Marry Your Grandmother*, which often was played at the Olympic Theater in London during the period. By making her a fairy, rather than a human being, MacDonald has gained more freedom to indulge his fantasy. Does not the setting remind one strongly of George MacDonald's own desk, with its secret compartment, containing (alas!) not the beautiful lost ancestress in person, but only the letter in which she laments the need of weaning him?

Anodos is partly of fairy ancestry; this must mean that in the past one of his mortal ancestors has married a fairy, no doubt one of those elemental spirits (*Elementargeister*) whom the German romantics loved so much, like Undine, for example, la Motte Fouqué's enchanting heroine (1809). MacDonald himself once wrote that he considered *Undine* the best of all fairy-tales, and his publisher, George Smith, coupled it with *Phantastes* as "unique" in literature. Denizens of earth, air, fire, and water—goblins, sylphs, salamanders, and undines—each of the different types of elemental spirits inhabited its own element or Chaos, and all craved marriage with mortals—the legend ran—so that they might acquire immortal souls.

Fouqué himself had gone back to Paracelsus (Theophrastus Bombast von Hohenheim, 1495–1541) for the lore of his elemental spirits, and Paracelsus himself, though quite original in many ways, had only been adapting the beliefs of the Neo-Platonists of the second and third centuries, transmitted to the Renaissance by Michael Psellus, their eleventh-century Byzantine disciple. But one did not need to go to Paracelsus direct; E.T.A. Hoffmann (1776–1822), for example, had learned all he needed to know about elemental spirits, who appear in several of his tales, from the peculiar novel of the Abbé de Montfaucon de Villars, *Le Comte de Gabalis* (1670).[6]

MacDonald has handled the transition from Anodos' room to fairyland with extraordinary delicacy and skill: the spring that flows, quite naturally—and maternally —from the basin, the flowers in the carpet that begin to wave in the breeze, the ivy foliage of the old oak dressing table that is transformed into real ivy—all this carries the real dream-conviction with it. Again, MacDonald has given us a clue from Novalis. As epigraph to this chapter (II) of *Phantastes,* he uses a quotation from *Heinrich von Ofterdingen* in the original and in his own translation: " 'Where is the stream?' cried he, with tears. 'Seest thou

not its blue waters over us?' He looked up, and lo! the
blue stream was flowing gently over their heads." Novalis'
hero, Heinrich, is dreaming about his beloved Matilda.
He is struggling in vain in a blue river to save her after
her boat has begun to be sucked in by a whirlpool; he
loses consciousness, and when he awakes it is on dry land,
in a strange country, *where flowers and trees speak to
him.*

We never learn what they say, because Matilda suddenly catches up with him, and it is then that he asks
where the river is, and that she tells him it is floating
over them. "Where are we?" he asks, and she tells him
they are "with their fathers," and will remain there forever. He wakes just as she is telling him a wonderful
secret word.[7] So in Heinrich's dream, he and Matilda are
dead; they have joined their fathers under the water,
Novalis' primal element and, in his view, the source of
all life. So too, MacDonald, who longed for death as
Novalis did, suggests by quoting this passage that Anodos' flowing stream is the river of death, and that the
strange country into which he has passed, in which, as
we shall see, *flowers and trees will indeed speak to him,*
is in some degree a land of death.

Anodos' sudden realization of the transformations in
his room reflects the half-world on the borderline between
waking and sleeping in which dreams come, and which
has engaged the attention of every serious author of
fantasy, Poe's "mere points of time, where the confines of
the waking world blend with those of the world of
dreams." Poe himself may well be echoing E.T.A. Hoffmann's preoccupation with what he calls the "delirium"
of the transitional moment between wakefulness and

sleep; while Hoffmann had read G. H. Schubert's *Symbolism of the Dream* (*Symbolik des Traumes*, 1814), and *Aspects of the Night-side of the Natural Sciences* (*Ansichten von der Nachtseite der Naturwissenschaften*, 1808) and noted Schubert's scientific interest in just this point. In a passage that MacDonald used as epigraph to the last chapter of *Phantastes*, Novalis remarks "Our life is no dream, but it ought to become one and perhaps it will," and this idea MacDonald made a favorite of his own.[8]

II

Anodos' adventures in fairyland are doubly difficult to analyse: they are entirely episodic, and dream-episodes at that. One may, however, distinguish certain major themes: the tree-spirits, who dominate the early part of his stay; the shadow, appearing soon after the disappearance of the tree-spirits and dominating the rest of the narrative; the sojourn in the palace of the fairy queen, the search for the spirit of the earth, and, throughout, a steady series of commands disobeyed, and of erotic frustrations. The landscape varies greatly, but the whole tale conveys an impression of extreme sadness and longing for death, which alone will bring the satisfactions that life denies.

As he enters the forest, Anodos meets a country maiden, who is speaking aloud to herself words of warning to him:

> "Trust the Oak, and the Elm, and the great Beech. Take care of the Birch, for though she is honest she is too young not to be changeable. But shun the Ash and the Alder; for the Ash is an ogre—you will know

him by his thick fingers; and the Alder will smother
you with her hair if you let her near you at night."

He finds a warm welcome in a cottage, where the mother
of the girl who has warned him recognizes him as, like
herself, of fairy blood. She is terrified of the Ash tree, but
avoids his question as to the danger to be expected from
it. In her cottage Anodos reads in an old book a tale of
Sir Percival in rusty armor; just as he reaches a point
where the damsel of the Alder tree is beguiling Percival,
the horrid shadow of the Ash tree's fingers passes across
the cottage blind and interrupts his reading: the woman
explains that though Ash tries to kill with fright, she is
protected in her cottage by the Oaks. She tells him also
about flower-fairies, "of the same race" as the tree-fairies.

Anodos visits the garden at night, and sees a carnival
of these flower-fairies, playing and singing, holding a
mock funeral for a primrose, and teasing the cat by pick-
ing sparks out of her fur with thorns and pins. As he starts
on his journey again, the flowers mock him, calling:
"Look at him! Look at him! He has begun a story without a beginning, and it will never have any end. He!
He! He! Look at him!" He fears the Ash, and does not
know how he will attack. When the awful shadow of the
Ash's hand appears again in the moonlight, Anodos lies
down in it, and looks back to try to make out Ash's features; they are horrible, like those of a vampire, or a
corpse, with greedy eyes. In a headlong flight across the
forest, through a rainstorm, he falls at the foot of a tree.
With Ash's hand only three feet from his face, Anodos
feels "two large soft arms thrown around" him from behind; and "a voice like a woman's" reassures him.

This is the voice of the great Beech tree, which he

soon hears saying: " 'I may love him, I may love him; for he is a man, and I am only a beech tree!' " The arms around him are "those of a woman . . . above the human size and largely proportioned."

> "Why do you call yourself a beech tree?" I said.
>
> "Because I am one," she replied, in the same low, musical murmuring voice.
>
> "You are a woman," I returned.
>
> "Do you think so? Am I very like a woman then?"
>
> "You are a very beautiful woman. Is it possible you should not know it?"
>
> "I am very glad you think so. I fancy I feel like a woman sometimes. I do so tonight—and always when the rain drips from my hair. For there is an old prophecy in our woods that one day we shall all be men and women like you. Do you know anything about it in your region? Shall I be very happy when I am a woman?"

When he tells her he is twenty-one, she says " 'Why, you baby!' " and kisses him. She also explains that Ash wants to bury Anodos at the foot of his tree because

> ". . . he has a hole in his heart that nobody knows of but one or two; and he is always trying to fill it up, but he cannot . . . I wonder if he will ever be a man. If he is, I hope they will kill him!"

As a charm against the Ash, she now offers Anodos some of her hair, saying " 'You men have strange cutting things about you.' "

> As gently as I could, I cut with a knife a long tress of flowing, dark hair, she hanging her beautiful head over me. When I had finished, she shuddered and

breathed deep, as one does when an acute pain,
steadfastly endured without sign of suffering, is at
length relaxed.

She ties the hair around him, singing a sweet song, embracing him, and wrapping him in delight, until he awakens wearing a girdle of beech leaves under a superb
beech tree. Its "great boughs . . . hung drooping round
me. At my head arose its smooth stem, with its great
sweeps of curving surface that swelled like undeveloped
limbs." He embraces it and kisses it goodbye.[9]

Although the country maiden has mentioned six trees
to Anodos (Oak, Elm, Beech, Birch, Ash, and Alder),
we never meet Elm or Birch, and hear of Oak only as
the protector of the cottage against Ash. Ash, Beech, and
Alder are the only trees that play a part in the story, an
evil male and two females, one good, the other evil. The
flower-fairies, though MacDonald lovingly describes them
at length, play only a minor role. In this way MacDonald
is embroidering on the merest hint given by Novalis in
the dream of Heinrich von Ofterdingen. Novalis never
got around to telling his readers what the flowers and
trees said when they spoke to Heinrich; MacDonald
builds the whole first portion of *Phantastes* by imagining
how flowers and trees might speak. The flowers remind
one also of the *Märchen* of Hyacinth and Rosebud in
Novalis' *Lehrlinge zu Saïs:* though these children are
human, they have flower names, and all of nature loves
Hyacinth. The rose creeps round him and twines herself
in his hair; the ivy caresses his brow; the violet first tells
the strawberry in confidence of Hyacinth's love for Rosebud, and the gooseberry scratches him because of it. The
flowers' mocking of Anodos is reminiscent of the way

the birds, in Hoffmann's *Golden Pot,* mock the hero, the
student Anselmus, in the mysterious forest-like study of
the archivist-salamander Lindhorst. We know that Mac-
Donald had been rereading *The Golden Pot* with great
admiration immediately before he wrote *Phantastes,* and
Greville MacDonald thought that his father had been
directly influenced by the story, an idea accepted but
not explored by at least one student of Hoffmann's influence abroad.[10]

It is the trees, so far Ash and Beech, that most engage
our attention. The male is the enemy, the good female
the protector. Ash personifies greed and cruelty. Beech
is female love; Anodos' encounter with her is an erotic
delight for both of them, as the quoted passages should
amply show; but she regards him as a baby because he is
only twenty-one, which allows an element of maternal
love and protection (the girdle of hair or beech leaves) to
attenuate what would otherwise be altogether a sexual
adventure. Does not the talismanic girdle of hair remind
one of the "golden brown" lock of MacDonald's mother's
own hair that he kept in the secret compartment with her
letter about weaning him?

The prophecy foretelling that trees will become people
echoes once more that evolutionary theory of the earlier
mystics which Novalis had adopted, and MacDonald had
already put into the mouth of the hero of "A Hidden
Life." But in the mystics' hierarchy, trees were destined
to become animals before they achieved human nature.
Perhaps the Beech tree, who knows very little about the
prophecy anyhow, simply has not heard that she must
pass through an animal phase. Yet this seems highly improbable, because MacDonald so clearly delineates her
physical and emotional humanity—and femaleness. It

seems more likely that he intended Beech to be a hama-
dryad, and thus for the moment only to echo the evolutionary theory of the German mystics while returning
to the ancients for his main imagery.

Some lines of *Within and Without,* when Lord Seaford
is trying to make love to Lilia on a beautiful evening,
lend color to this supposition:

Twas on such nights . . .
The poets of old Greece saw beauteous shapes
Sighed forth from out the rooted-earth-fast trees,
With likeness undefinable retained
In higher human form to their tree-homes
Which fainting let them forth into the air,
And lived a life in death till they returned.
The large-limbed, sweepy-curved, smooth-rinded beech
Gave forth the perfect woman to the night;
From the pale birch, breeze-bent and waving, stole
The graceful slight-curved maiden, scarcely grown . . .
The broad-browed oak, the stately elm, gave forth
Their inner life in shapes of ecstasy.

The fantasy of tree-beings is widespread in literature,
from Ovid to Joyce Kilmer: among the many transformations into trees in the *Metamorphoses,* one thinks especially of Phaeton's sisters, of Daphne, of Philemon and
Baucis. MacDonald, who used a few lines from Shelley's
Alastor as epigraph to the first chapter of *Phantastes,*
had of course read the description of the forest there,
where

                                    The oak
        Expanding its immense and knotty arms,
        Embraces the light beech.

and no doubt knew as well Coleridge's "huge broad-breasted old oak tree" in "Christabel," as well as Wordsworth's elaborately sexual attack on the glade in "Nutting." Metaphors drawn from humanity seem almost inevitable for a poet dealing with trees.[11]

Continuing on his way, Anodos, while resting in a grotto in the forest, sees "a strange time-worn bas-relief" on a rock, which represents Pygmalion waiting for his statue to come to life. Then he notices that the rock on which he himself has been lying is really moss-covered alabaster. When cleaned this reveals a beautiful marble woman reposing inside the alabaster block:

> I thought of the Prince of the Enchanted City, half marble and half a living man; of Ariel; of Niobe; of the Sleeping Beauty in the Wood; of the bleeding trees; and many other histories.

He wonders how to awaken her; a kiss does not reach her; remembering Orpheus, he tries to awaken her in song, urging her to wake. This liberates her. With a "slight crashing sound," she bursts from the stone, and glides away into the forest; she is "found, freed, lost!" a little like Alastor's vision who is "Lost, lost, forever lost," when he wakes. Anodos hastens in pursuit. In the forest he encounters a knight, like Sir Percival in rusty armor. Sad and shameful, he tells Anodos that the Alder woman had beguiled him as she had beguiled Percival; and that now nothing can cleanse his rusty armor except the blows of knightly encounter.

Warned once more against the wiles of the Alder, Anodos hears the sweet voice of a woman saying "It is your white lady." He takes her hand; something distresses him, as he senses that she is not what he thinks her, but she is beautiful, and he accepts her invitation to her grotto. Here she keeps her face always toward him; he lies down at her feet. She tells him a strange story, which he cannot remember, but it entrances him. "What followed I cannot clearly remember." But when he wakes, at dawn, she has disappeared, and he sees at the mouth of the cave

> a strange horrible object. It looked like an open coffin set up on one end; only that the part for the head and neck was defined from the shoulder-part. In fact it was a rough representation of the human frame, only hollow, as if made from decaying bark torn from a tree. It had arms, which were only slightly seamed, down from the shoulder blade by the elbow, as if the back had healed again from the wound of a knife. But the arms moved, and the hands and fingers were tearing asunder a long silky tress of hair. The thing turned round—it had for a face and front those of my enchantress, but now of a pale greenish hue in the light of the morning, and with dead lustreless eyes.

Anodos' girdle of beech leaves is gone; the woman now turns him over to the Ash tree, who enters the cave, and is about to seize Anodos, when the sound of axe blows is heard, and Ash shudders and retreats.

> The other walking Death looked at me once, with a careless dislike on her beautifully molded features; then, heedless any more to conceal her hollow deformity, turned her frightful back and likewise vanished. . . . I lay and wept. The Maid of the Alder-Tree had befooled me—nearly slain me—in spite of

all the warnings I had received from those who knew
my danger.

Attributing his rescue to the knight, Anodos begins to
consider the question, "How can beauty and ugliness
dwell so near?" At a farmhouse, a handsome matronly
woman greets him as "boy," comforts him when he bursts
into tears, and feeds him. He tells her the story of his
adventure, and she explains about the Alder-maiden:

> ". . . she would not look so beautiful if she did not
> take means to make herself look more beautiful than
> she is. And then, you know, you began by being in
> love with her before you saw her beauty, mistaking
> her for the lady of the marble—another kind alto-
> gether, I should think. But the chief thing that makes
> her beautiful is this: that though she loves no man,
> she loves the love of any man; and when she finds
> one in her power, her desire to bewitch him and
> gain his love (not for the sake of his love either, but
> that she may be conscious anew of her own beauty,
> through the admiration he manifests), makes her
> very lovely—with a self-destructive beauty, though;
> for it is that which is constantly wearing her away
> within, till, at last, the decay will reach her face, and
> her whole front, when all the lovely mask of nothing
> will fall to pieces, and she will be vanished for
> ever." [12]

As the first main group of Anodos' adventures, those
with the trees comes to an end, he has had two more
sexual encounters: with the marble lady whom he has
awakened with a song, and who has vanished, but whose
pursuit carries the story on; and with the Alder-maiden,

who has been able to beguile him, despite all the warnings he had received. Not only has she seduced him, but she has deprived him of the maternal girdle of beech leaves-hair which alone protected him against Ash. She and Ash have been in league all along.

There can really be no doubt as to what has taken place. Victorian prudishness has made it necessary to have Anodos forget exactly what happened, and the scene is not nearly so erotic as that with the Beech tree, where the language is orgasmic. But the Alder-maiden must have slept with Percival, with the knight in rusty armor, and with Anodos: why else would they be so ashamed? No mere listening to beguiling stories would account for their later revulsion.

The mythical and fairy-tale inspiration of the marble lady is duly indicated by MacDonald himself; we know too that as a boy he had been much impressed with the marble statue of a nude goddess in the garden of a nobleman at a small Scotch port, probably Cullen.[13] The knight with the rusty armor is a Spenserian character introducing mediaeval trappings and the concepts of chivalry into a story already thoroughly eclectic: these will become more important in the later portions of *Phantastes*. The Alder-maiden, however, besides being a wicked tree-spirit, represents MacDonald's second effort to come to grips with his own grave disappointment at the hands of the heartless girl of the library in the great house. A flirt, needing conquests to feed her confidence in her own beauty, she has been hollow all along. In "A Hidden Life" he had been able to handle the theme only by making the lady inaccessibly distant and ignorant of her swain's admiration, and so he had preserved the hero's dignity. Now, in the form of allegory, he comes closer to his own experience, and allows the hero to sin and feel shame. And in the diagnosis of the Alder-maiden offered by the matronly comforter who mothers Anodos when it is all over, he shows his preoccupation with the jilt: the decay working within her will eventually destroy her beauty completely. One can still detect his own vindictiveness and chagrin.

The matron who has been soothing Anodos has warned him that her husband does not believe in the creatures of fairyland. This jolly peasant is so normal, so benevolent and hearty, that Anodos begins to wonder if he has not been imagining all his adventures. He believes in fairyland again, however, when the farmer's daughter reminds her father that her mother is descended from the princess who was turned into a white cat by the wicked fairy; and the farmer, laughing, remembers that his wife has indeed jumped out of bed and frightened a mouse away by mewing like a cat. The farmer also warns Anodos against a neighboring ogress. His hostess tells Anodos that his room faces "southward toward the open country," where the strange creatures never show themselves. The view of the ordinary vegetable garden convinces him that he no longer believes in fairyland; he is not anxious to go on with his adventures. But when he sees the little girl's room, built of the stones of a ruined abbey, with a view of the forest, "a gush of wonderment and longing flowed over my soul like the tide of a great sea. Fairy Land lay before me, and drew me towards it with an irresistible attraction." Anodos sets off again.

The theme of the tree-spirits has been exhausted. MacDonald plans to introduce a new one, for which this rather tedious interlude is of major importance. For the first time, to some degree as a result of his disappointments, but more under the impact of the matter-of-fact peasant, Anodos has begun to feel "almost certain that Fairy Land was all a delusion of my brain." But when he comes near his hostess or her daughter, he feels differently (the little girl tells him in the morning that "A white lady has been flitting around the house all night"). And the view from the child's room into the forest wins him back once more. This wavering between belief and disbelief strongly reminds us of Anselmus, hero of Hoffmann's *Golden Pot*, who finds himself torn between the real world of Dresden and his bourgeois love Veronica, who wants to be a Frau Geheimrath, and—on the other hand—the dream world of myth, poesy, and Serpentina, daughter of the salamander, the elemental spirit who doubles as the archivist Lindhorst.

While the tension that Hoffmann achieves between the two worlds strikes the reader as extraordinarily skillfully managed, MacDonald's attempt at imitation fails. Hoffmann's Anselmus is in Dresden, and experiences the transformation of everyday things by his imagination, thus coming and going from and into another world. But MacDonald's Anodos is *inside* fairyland the whole time; we know that he must complete his journey; so his conflict is not a real one. The two views from the two windows of the farmer's house are *both* views of fairyland, no matter what the author or the farmer may say to convince the reader or Anodos that the one window looks onto the real world. (And all they can say—lamely—is that the "creatures" seldom come there.)

Moreover, Hoffmann and MacDonald are both on the side of the imagination, of poesy, of fairyland (Hoffmann, indeed, is joining in the Romantics' attack on the dullness of the late *Aufklärung*); but while Hoffmann successfully persuades the reader that Anselmus' occasional temporary preferences for Veronica and the real world are stodgy and unworthy of him, and that adventure and excitement and the high realization of human potentialities lie with Serpentina, MacDonald has made his fairyland so unattractive and frightening, and filled it so full of such disagreeable experiences for Anodos that he has not persuaded us that it stands for poesy and the bursting of the bonds of everyday conventional life. Indeed, MacDonald's farmer's stout refusal to believe in the "creatures" is positively attractive, while Hoffmann's burghers of Dresden are as dull as he intended them to be. One can hardly believe in Anodos' "gush" of longing to go on exploring the land where he has so far met with nothing but terror and sexual frustration. The suggestion that the kind matron is really a were-cat, the mention of a white lady that flits around all night, and the warnings against the longtoothed ogress hardly add to the attractions of the place.

III

Anodos now finds a hut in the forest, where a woman is reading by lamplight. Though he has a vague misgiving, "an irresistible attraction" makes him enter. She reads aloud from her book:

> "So, then, as darkness had no beginning, neither will it ever have an end. So, then, it is eternal. The negation of aught else, is its affirmation. Where the light cannot come, there abideth the darkness. The light doth but hollow a mine out of the infinite extension of the darkness."

Despite her warning not to do so, Anodos now opens a door to a cupboard. From the back of it, a dark figure comes running to join him, and becomes his own black shadow. He is horrified, and the woman tells him:

> "It is only your shadow that has found you . . .
> Everybody's shadow is ranging up and down looking
> for him. I believe you call it by a different name in
> your world; yours has found you, as every person's
> is almost certain to do who looks into that closet,
> especially after meeting one in the forest whom I
> dare say you have met."

She looks at him, and he sees her long, shining teeth; he has wandered into the hut of the ogress, against whom the farmer had warned him. Disregard for *her* warning has now brought him this black shadow, brighter in the sunlight, and arousing Anodos' dislike.

The shadow now dominates Anodos' wanderings. Flowers on which he has lain lift their heads when he gets up; but those on which the shadow has fallen wither; it emits rays of darkness that depress his heart and even darken the face of the sun. As he passes a cottage, a lovely fairy child emerges holding two wondrous toys,

> the tube through which the fairy-gifted poet looks
> when he beholds the same thing everywhere; the
> other that through which he looks when he combines
> into new forms of loveliness those images of beauty
> which his own choice has gathered from all regions
> where he has travelled.

When the shadow touches these, they become a mere multiplying glass and a kaleidoscope and the charming child "a commonplace boy with a rough broad-brimmed hat." Anodos now meets the rusty-armored knight for the second time; he is less sad and his armor has been partly cleansed by the mighty deeds he has now performed. The knight has no shadow; he has not entered the dark house.

Though they travel together for two days, Anodos does not tell him his story; the shadow makes Anodos distrust him; indeed, Anodos himself is now beginning to enjoy the shadow; saying to himself:

> In a land like this, with so many illusions everywhere, I need his aid to disenchant the things around me. He does away with all appearances, and shows me things in their true colour and form. And I am not one to be fooled with the vanities of the common crowd. I will not see beauty where there is none. I will dare to behold things as they are. And if I live in a waste instead of a paradise, I will live knowing where I live.

But now he meets a little girl with a crystal globe, her plaything and her greatest treasure; she asks him to touch it very gently; it vibrates harmonically, increasingly so as he touches it. When the shadow touches the globe, it begins to waver with inward light and to shoot out flashes. Anodos touches the globe again, but this time he will not let go in spite of the maiden's entreaties, and he breaks it, a black vapour rising from it. She is disconsolate, and a storm separates them. In the village to which he comes next, the appearance of the inhabitants changes focus according to their distance: a pretty girl provokes him to try to kiss her; when he does, she suddenly turns hideous; he starts back, she laughs at him, and runs away.[14]

With the introduction of the shadow, MacDonald has embarked on his new theme. It reminds the reader at once of Adalbert von Chamisso's charming *Peter Schlemihl*

(1814); but there the hero, in the real world, finds he cannot get along *without* his shadow, and must seek to reclaim it from the devil, to whom he has unwittingly sold it. Anodos, on the contrary, is in fairyland; and the shadow he has acquired is not an earthly shadow ("'You call it by a different name in your world,'" the ogress has told him); moreover, he seeks not to find a shadow but to lose it. So MacDonald has turned the symbolism of *Peter Schlemihl* upside down and enabled himself to deal allegorically and in an original way with one of the oldest and most frequently recurring folklore and literary themes.

The shadow is, ordinarily, a special form of *Doppelgänger*. Ringing the changes on Chamisso's theme, E.T.A. Hoffmann had transformed the lost shadow into a lost reflection in a mirror, in *The Story of the Lost Reflection* (*Die Geschichte vom verlorenen Spiegelbilde*), his tale of Erasmus Spikher, third of the *Adventures of St. Sylvester's Night* (*Abenteuer der Sylvesternacht*, 1815). Here the lost reflection becomes a double and pursues the protagonist, as it does in Hans Andersen's *Shadow*. From the giant in Goethe's *Märchen* (1795), whose shadow is so powerful at sunrise and sunset and so weak at noon, to Stevenson's "little shadow that goes in and out with me," who ". . . Sometimes shoots up taller like an india-rubber ball,/ And he sometimes gets so little that there's none of him at all," and Barrie's shadow of Peter Pan that Wendy must sew back onto its master, poets and storytellers have played with the theme, sometimes lightly, but seldom without the uncanny sense of the shadow as a special kind of second personality.

The *Doppelgänger* proper appears even oftener: in Hoffmann's horrifying *The Devil's Brew* (*Elixiere des Teufels*, 1816), and *Die Doppeltgänger* (1822), in his

Kater Murr (1820, 1821), *Prinzessin Brambilla* (1821), and other works, all of which MacDonald had read. And Hoffmann himself, in his constant fascination with the theme of a second ego, especially in *Kater Murr,* was surely following the lead of Jean Paul Richter, whose Schoppe, in *Titan* (1800–1803), to take only one example of many, is terrified lest his self appear to him, cannot bear to look into a mirror, and wonders who he really is. MacDonald had read *Titan* too—as well as Chamisso and Hoffmann—and uses one of its many references to the ego as an epigraph to a later chapter of *Phantastes.*

After Goethe had bade farewell to Friederike, he actually met his own double on horseback, dressed in clothes which he himself would not wear until eight years later on the return journey. Maupassant's double came and sat opposite him at his writing table. Tieck, von Arnim, Brentano, Fouqué, and Heine, among the Germans, dealt with the theme of the *Doppelgänger.* Poe's *William Wilson* (1839), Dostoevsky's *Double* (1846) and *Brothers Karamazov* (1880), Mark Twain's *The Facts Concerning the Recent Carnival of Crime in Connecticut* (1876), Maupassant's *Horla* (1887), Stevenson's *Dr. Jekyll and Mr. Hyde* (1886) and *Markheim* (1887) testify to the lasting attraction of the theme in other countries before and after MacDonald wrote *Phantastes.* Examples abound in folk-literature also: the double signifies death, and inspires an ambivalent reaction of fear and hate, on the one hand, and of love, on the other. The Narcissus of myth becomes the Dorian Gray of art. Perhaps the closest analogy to the mournful *Stimmung* of Anodos and his shadow is to be found in Alfred de Musset's poem, *La Nuit de décembre* (1835):

Partout où j'ai voulu dormir,
Partout où j'ai voulu mourir,
Partout où j'ai touché la terre,
Sur ma route est venu s'asseoir
Un malheureux vêtu de noir
Qui me ressemblait comme un frère.

But Anodos' shadow has—for the moment at least—chiefly an allegorical meaning. From the ogress' first explanation that people who have had the kind of experience that he has had with the Alder-maiden usually find their shadows, it is clear that the shadow represents pessimistic and cynical disillusionment, the worldly-wiseness that destroys beauty, childish and naive pleasures, the delights of friendship and love; it is the foe of innocence, of openness, of optimism, of the imagination. He has got the shadow as the indirect result of his seduction by the Alder-maiden. The cupboard where he finds it, the house of darkness where the cupboard door is, and the ogress-proprietress who reads from the book of darkness are more difficult to identify. But the passage the woman reads from her book represents the negation of all Mac-Donald's belief about good and evil, love and disillusionment, light and darkness; if one exactly reversed it, and maintained that darkness but hollowed a mine out of the infinite extension of light, and evil out of the all-pervading goodness, one would come close to the core of Mac-Donald's own views. The episode of the little maiden's globe can easily be interpreted sexually: the breaking of a bowl or pot is a symbol universally understood, and the girl's preference for gentle treatment is entirely clear. Yet here too the poetic interpretation is also possible:

Anodos may have shattered an illusion, not a maiden-head.[15]

Anodos now traverses a rocky desert region, peopled by goblins, who mockingly offer him gold and jewels, until they notice his shadow, and then cease teasing him, out of pity and contempt. These are elemental spirits of the earth, and worth noting because MacDonald was to make much use of them later. Anodos finds a little stream, which gradually broadens out into a wide river; on its banks, he feels "a gush of joy," and sees roses all around him. He now for the first time expresses a new wish:

> And my heart fainted with longing in my bosom. Could I but see the Spirit of Earth, as I once saw the indwelling woman of the beech-tree, and my beauty of the pale marble, I should be content. Content! Oh, how gladly would I die of the light of her eyes! Yes, I would cease to be, if that would bring me one word of love from the one mouth.

Earth is Mother Earth, and Anodos yearns—as Mac-Donald yearned—to find his mother, who will speak the one word of love. Finding a boat by the side of the river, he steps in, and floats gently along, through sleep and waking, noticing the beauty of the reflections—lovelier than the originals—and commenting that "all mirrors are magic mirrors. The commonest room is a room in a poem when I turn to the glass."

The stream now wafts him in his boat to a white marble fairy palace on a lawn, glimmering in the moonlight. He disembarks, enters a courtyard where a fountain plays, and goes into a great marble hall, where he senses that others are present but cannot see them, because "Since my visit to the Church of Darkness, my power of seeing the fairies of the higher order had gradually diminished until it had almost ceased." He feels the presence of a woman who loves him. Down a great hall, he finds a room, with his name, "Sir Anodos," on the door. He is magically and invisibly fed, and in the morning finds a new suit by his bed. The sight of his shadow, even though faint, arouses the hope that the Queen of Fairy Land will give him a shadow of light to devour the shadow of darkness.

Exploring the palace, he finds one whole courtyard whose floor is a great basin, filled with water; his "irresistible desire" leads him to plunge in; once under water he finds that the basin extends like a sea in all directions, and he can see submarine wonders. In the palace, where he spends many days, he vaguely begins to discern the forms of persons, but he never comes close to them, nor does he ever meet the Queen herself. On the third day, he discovers the library, and thereafter spends part of each day there: whatever book Anodos reads, he himself is projected immediately into his reading: if it is metaphysics, he seems to be making the discoveries and presenting them; if travels, he himself becomes the traveller; if history or fiction, he is the chief actor. Two of the wonderful stories he reads he decides to reproduce; they are inserted in the narrative at this point.[16]

Water has suddenly begun to play a major role in Anodos' adventures: the beautiful river on whose bosom he is cradled to the fairy palace, and the miraculous fountain and basin. For the first time since the overflow of the basin in his own bedroom had signalized his first entry into fairyland—where trees and flowers speak, as in the underwater afterworld of Heinrich von Ofterdingen's dream—Anodos encounters the maternal ele-

ment *par excellence,* and it laps him around. Harshness
for the moment has passed; there is somebody in the
palace who loves him; even the shadow is scarcely visible;
everything is refreshing and beautiful and comfortable,
and the delicious uterine water-experiences symbolize
the change.

We are listening to echoes of the "Neptunist" theory
of the universe popularized in early romantic Germany
by Novalis' famous teacher of mineralogy, Abraham
Gottlob Werner: water was the original primal substance
from which all others derive: "the white blood of the
mother," as Novalis calls it in *Heinrich von Ofterdingen.*
Novalis had found the same idea in Boehme:

> Sweet water is the primordial principle of nature.
> . . . . nothing exists if it is not water, whether it is
> flesh . . . or a plant of the earth, metal, or stones;
> water is the nucleus and the heart of everything.

All men, Novalis felt, should adore and venerate water;
the slaking of thirst, all our agreeable sensations, sleep,
and waking are tidal. When we return to the new golden
age, we shall again experience union with this primal
substance.

But the Neptunist theory itself only reflects the universal association of water images with motherhood;
Swinburne's longing for the waves in *The Triumph of
Time* ("O fair green-girdled mother of mine,/ Sea, that
art clothed with the sun and the rain,/ Thy sweet hard
kisses are strong like wine,/ Thy large embraces are keen
like pain./ Save me and hide me with all thy waves. . . .")
or Matthew Arnold's river Oxus, longing for the "dash of
waves" and "His luminous home of waters," in *Sohrab
and Rustum,* echo what MacDonald's Anodos is feeling,

and in the same spirit, that combines a longing for a close relation to his mother with a longing for death and surcease.[17]

When Anodos calls the ogress' hut where he got his shadow the "Church of Darkness," he confirms the view that she and her book stand for an anti-religion, whose doctrines are those of the true religion of light turned inside out. Since his visit there, he says his powers of seeing the fairies "of the higher order" have diminished. Yet Anodos has so far met only tree- and flower-fairies, not a single fairy "of the higher order" except perhaps his own grandmother, who started the whole adventure, but whom he met outside fairyland. Despite MacDonald's inconsistency, what he means is important: he is saying that the shadow—disillusionment and suspicion and intellectual questioning—spoils the poetic power of the imagination.

This is what Hoffmann was saying in *The Golden Pot*, but it is also the general war cry of the German romantics against the intellectuals of the Enlightenment. Novalis, MacDonald's inspiration throughout *Phantastes*, repeatedly voices this point of view: with regard to his personal life, he remarks that

> . . . my intelligence developed bit by bit and imperceptibly substituted itself for my heart. Sophie returned to my heart its lost throne. Perhaps her death may once more restore power to the usurper . . . but perhaps the invisible world and its force, up to now dormant in me, will save me.

Elsewhere he states it simply: "The heart is the key of the world and of life." And the converse: "Thought is only a dream of feeling, a feeling that has died, a pale gray feeble life." With regard to literature, he declares: "If poesy wants to reason and argue, it is no longer poesy." In Klingsohr's phantasmagoric *Märchen* in *Heinrich von Ofterdingen,* Novalis makes of Intellect an evil scribe, destructive and vicious, who writes steadily, but most of whose writings are erased in the bowl of tears, or truth, into which Sophie dips them. Whenever a few drops of poetic truth touch the scribe, ciphers and geometric figures drop from him, and he collects these and hangs them around his neck as ornaments.

And in the *Märchen* of Hyacinth and Rosebud, Hyacinth's idyllic contentment in his love for Rosebud is broken by the learned old man from foreign parts with the strange book that awakens his longing for wisdom, for "the Mother of all Things, the Veiled Virgin," Isis. When he finds her after an arduous quest, and lifts her diaphanous veil, he discovers that she is Rosebud after all. For the German romantics the battle against what they regarded as the cold and dead rationalism of the *Aufklärung* was a real fight; for George MacDonald more than half a century later and in another milieu, it had less meaning. Yet he, too, deeply distrusted the intellect as the foe of the imagination, and he is voicing this feeling when he has Anodos' shadow diminish his power to see fairies "of the higher order." [18]

The name "Sir" Anodos on the door prompts Anodos to remark that he has no right to knighthood; he also refers to his own castle: this represents a revival of the Spenserian mediaeval images already introduced in the person of the knight in rusty armor. The delights of the palace derive from the general treasury of fairy-tale material. The library is the magic room in the Scottish country house, where the gates of the imagination had

first been flung open for MacDonald himself. Anodos'
identification of himself with the protagonist of whatever
he reads, his discovery of himself in the books, reminds
us of Heinrich von Ofterdingen's discovery of himself in
the pictures in the ancient Provençal book in the hermit's
cave. But while the romance that Heinrich has stumbled
upon—which relates a poet's life and praises all aspects
of poesy—symbolizes the novel of *Heinrich von Ofterdingen* itself, and both, ironically enough, remain un-
finished, Anodos' discovery of himself in books apparently
has no particular meaning.

IV

Turning now to the two stories that Anodos read in the
library of the fairy palace, we find that the first, introduced in verse, is a myth of a distant planet, older than
the earth and further from the sun, where each season
lasts for many earthly years, and children born in winter
may never live to know spring. Here, children are found,
not born:

> A maiden, walking alone, hears a cry: for even there
> a cry is the first utterance; and searching about, she
> findeth, under an overhanging rock, or within a
> clump of bushes, or it may be, betwixt gray stones
> on the side of a hill, or in any other sheltered and
> unexpected spot, a little child.

She takes it home, and it is hers. Since the nature of the
child is determined by the conditions of the weather and
the nature of the place where it is to be found, maidens
usually search only at propitious moments. No maiden
may have more than one. The men have arms, but the

women have wings, colored differently according to the seasons and conditions of their birth. There the water gives back no reflection, but the heavens do.

When an earth-dweller explains how children are born on earth, the people of the other planet show deep emotion:

> A great light shone in the eyes of one maiden, who turned and walked slowly away, with her purple and white wings half dispread behind her. She was found, the next morning, dead beneath a withered tree on a bare hill-side some miles inland.

Among them death comes from

> an indescribable longing for something, they know not what . . . When a youth and a maiden look too deep into each other's eyes, this longing seizes and possesses them: but instead of drawing nearer to each other, they wander away, each alone, into solitary places, and die of their desire. But it seems to me, that thereafter they are born babies upon our earth: where if, when grown, they find each other, it goes well with them; if not, it seems to go ill.

The account ends with the story of a maiden born near the end of autumn, who lives in perpetual winter; she sets out on a pilgrimage to find spring elsewhere on her planet, and after much weary travel finds a single snowdrop and dies.

This melancholy little fantasy seems to be original with MacDonald. He skillfully conveys the limbo-like atmosphere of the other planet, where the glorious colors of the women's wings alone shine out. The description of the rocks, clefts, and bushes where the children are found suggests that "discovery" on that planet is not after all so different from birth on this one; but MacDonald certainly intended to make this the great distinction between the two worlds. It is a mournful place indeed, where love between the sexes leads to death, where birth is unconnected with love, and where the mere news of the sexual connection as it exists on earth is enough to bring on the death-dealing longing in a maiden. Only the rebirth on earth of those who die of frustration on the other planet mitigates the hardness of their lot; but though Anodos says he believes this to be true, he is not sure; and even if they are born again here, it is only if they find each other that happiness can be theirs in this world. In all this, I find little reminiscent of any other literary work, though the moon-world in Klingsohr's *Märchen* may possibly have suggested the possibility of life on other planets. We shall find in *Lilith* echoes of this planet, and students of C. S. Lewis' fantasy novels may well discover that this story of MacDonald's has influenced him.

The second of Anodos' stories has, according to its preface, a double meaning: on the one hand, it shows that two souls, loving each other, and longing to come nearer, do, after all, but behold each other as in a glass darkly; on the other, it illustrates the way in which "Faerie" invades the world of men. Cosmo von Wehrstal, a serious student at the University of Prague, maintains an interest in occult books; he has curious instruments and a skeleton in his room, as well as a dried bat and other peculiar things. He is very imaginative, and makes up stories about the people he sees; indeed, he is a "poet without words." An antique dealer consents to sell him a curious carved mirror for a quarter of the original asking price, on condition that he give the dealer the first chance to buy it back if he ever wishes to dispose of it. As Cosmo is taking it away, the dealer says to himself: "Sold for the sixth time . . . I wonder what will be the upshot of it this time. I should think my lady had enough of it by now."

The mirror reflects Cosmo's room; in the reflection all commonness has disappeared: it has turned nature into art. As Cosmo muses on this theme, ending with the wish " 'I should like to live in *that* room if I could only get into it,' " the door in the reflected room opens, and a woman in white glides in, her back to Cosmo, and lies down on the couch; she is lovely, as she turns her face towards him, but it shows "suffering and dislike, and a sense of compulsion, strangely mingled with beauty." He decides that she cannot see him, but notices that she shows repugnance at the sight of the skeleton. She falls asleep, he sits dreaming of blessedness. When he looks up again, she is gone. He moves the skeleton and some of his other curios, so that she will not be offended by them if she comes back.

Each night thereafter she returns, sleeps, and "without opening her eyes; . . . she passed from the room with the gait of a somnambulist."

> Cosmo was now in a state of extravagant delight. Most men have a secret treasure somewhere. The miser has his golden hoard; the virtuoso his pet ring; the student his rare book; the poet his favourite haunt; the lover his secret drawer; but Cosmo had a mirror with a lovely lady in it.

He determines to transform his room into a boudoir for her, and she shows her appreciation, but there is always sorrow mingled with her pleasure. One night, in full

evening dress and diamonds, she seems to notice Cosmo
and blush; suddenly he imagines that she has a lover;
she looks sorrowful and weeps, and leaves earlier than
usual.

The next night, and for six nights, she fails to come,
while Cosmo suffers agonies. He determines to bring
her back by magic, and procures the "ingredients . . .
scarcely fit to be mentioned" that he needs for his spell.
She returns to the mirror, seeming to beg him not to call
her, but he continues with his magic, and in a moment she
enters the real room. She tells Cosmo she is the slave of
the mirror until she shall be disenchanted, that she has
come more because of his longing than because of his
spells, and that (until the mirror is destroyed) she does
not know whether she can love him. She begs him to
break the mirror, but warns him that they may not meet
again; he hesitates; but when he nerves himself to hit out
at the mirror with the pommel of his sword, he misses
his mark, and is struck by lightning. Upon finding that
both the lady and the mirror have vanished, he has a
brain fever that lasts for weeks.

On his recovery, he tries to find the mirror again. The
dealer from whom he bought it has "a laughing sneer"
on his face, but will not admit that he knows anything
about it. Cosmo now accepts all invitations, hoping to
hear some news, and one night at a party learns of the
strange malady of the Princess von Hohenweiss, who has
been ill for more than a year, after giving offense to an
old woman-servant; the illness is associated with the loss
of an antique mirror. Soon afterwards, however, he hears
that one of the greatest rakes of the court, von Steinwald,
has been seen emerging from the antique dealer's. Seeking an opportunity to break the mirror, Cosmo decides

to mingle with the guests at a party at von Steinwald's house. The scene shifts to the princess' house. In a trance, she suddenly cries out *"Cosmo!"*, wakes, and thanks him for freeing her, and rushes out into Prague. On a bridge, she meets Cosmo, who begs to know if she is free; she tells him she is, and is his forever; but he falls dead, the blood welling out between his fingers: he has broken the mirror, but von Steinwald has killed him.[19]

This short story—very effective in itself—seems out of place in the library of the fairy palace. Dealing as it does with Prague, a real city, and with earthly people who have real names, it suits less well with the supernatural *mise-en-scène* of fairyland than does the myth of the distant planet. MacDonald would have been well advised to omit it from *Phantastes* and to publish it separately. Although its themes are not as original as those of the myth of the other planet, MacDonald shows originality and flexibility in his treatment of them. In *Das verlorene Spiegelbild* (1815), E.T.A. Hoffmann had used a mirror as the essential prop, but his hero, Erasmus Spikher, was deliberately modeled on Chamisso's *Peter Schlemihl* and had sold his reflection out of love for a devilish woman, Giulietta: thus the mirror image here, as we have seen, is only a special kind of *Doppelgänger*. In MacDonald's story of Cosmo, however, the mirror holds its interest not because it fails to reflect the hero but because it magically reflects the heroine, who is not there. We have been prepared for the story by Anodos' musing, as he floats down the stream toward the fairy palace, on the superiority of the reflection to the original object, and by his conclusion that all mirrors are magic.

As for Cosmo's princess, she is what the nineteenth century called a somnambule: she has been mesmerized;

her entire behavior, her trance, her mood combining compulsion and sorrow proclaim it. No single theme appealed to Hoffmann more: his early story, *Der Magnetiseur* (1814), introduces, in Alban, a fiendish hypnotist who takes complete control of Maria, sister of a university friend, and brings catastrophe upon the entire family. Alban, Hoffmann hints, is a reincarnation of a mysterious Danish major who had enslaved Maria's father in his own youth; in another story, *Der Elementargeist* (1821), the major reappears in Irish guise, as a wicked mesmeriser named O'Malley. In *The Uncanny Guest* (*Der unheimliche Gast,* 1819), *The Deserted House* (*Das öde Haus,* 1817), *Kater Murr* (1820, 1821), to name only a few stories, Hoffmann explores mesmeric phenomena.

And behind Hoffmann, again, stands Novalis, and Heinrich von Ofterdingen's refutation of his father's famous matter-of-fact statement that "dreams are only froth" ("Traüme sind Schaüme"). Speaking for Novalis, Heinrich proclaims that on the contrary dreams are gifts from heaven to guide us on our way. Hoffmann at first intended to call *Der Magnetiseur* "Traume sind Schaüme," and only later changed his mind. The story begins with a discussion between the Baron and his son Ottmar, exactly parallel to and surely based on that between Heinrich von Ofterdingen and his father. Thus the defense of dreams in *Der Magnetiseur* Hoffmann took from Novalis; he also introduced the theme of mesmerism, drawn chiefly from the manual of C.A.F. Kluge, *Attempt at an Account of Animal Magnetism as a Cure* (*Versuch einer Darstellung des animalischen Magnetismus als Heilmittel,* 1811). In *Phantastes,* the insulted woman-servant who had cast a spell on Cosmo's princess is a mesmerist modeled after those in Hoffmann. MacDonald never gives any details of her operations, but the theme remained attractive to him, and he was to return to it, as we shall see, in *The Portent* and in *David Elginbrod*.[20]

V

Having recounted the two stories he found in the library of the fairy palace, Anodos returns to his own adventures. Exploring the palace at night, he discovers several splendid marble halls; in one, a series of white marble statues stands about on black pedestals; he feels that on his arrival they have just sprung back into their pedestals after the dance. That night he dreams that he is quick enough to find the statues still dancing; in the room, but standing still on her pedestal, is the white marble lady whom he had awakened in the cave and then lost. Slowly a dark shadow hides her: his own, he asks himself in horror, which he has not seen for days? Then he wakes up. He later manages to surprise the statues, but when he comes up to his lady's pedestal, he can see only the indistinct outlines of her feet. What song, he asks himself, should he sing "To unveil my Isis, if indeed she was present unseen"? He takes a harp, still quivering, from one of the other statues, and sings:

> And while I sang, I did not feel that I stood by a statue . . . but that a real woman-soul was revealing itself by successive stages of imbodiment, and consequent manifestation and expression.

> Feet of beauty, firmly planting
>   Arches white on rosy heel!
> Whence the life-spring, throbbing, panting,

Pulses upward to reveal!
Fairest things know least despising;
  Foot and earth meet tenderly:
'Tis the woman, resting, rising
  Upward to sublimity.

Rise the limbs, sedately sloping,
  Strong and gentle, full and free;
Soft and slow, like certain hoping,
  Drawing nigh the broad firm knee.
Up to speech! As up to roses
  Pants the life from flower to flower,
So each blending change discloses
  Nearer still, expression's power.

Lo! fair sweeps, white surges, twining
  Up and outward fearlessly!
Temple columns, close combining,
  Lift a holy mystery.
Heart of mine! what strange surprises
  Mount aloft on such a stair!
Some great vision upward rises,
  Curving, bending, floating fair.

Bends and sweeps, and hill and hollow
  Lead my fascinated eye;
Some apocalypse will follow,
  Some new world of deity.
Zoned unseen, and outward swelling,
  With new thoughts and wonders rife,
Queenly majesty foretelling,
  See the expanding house of life!

Sudden heaving, unforbidden
  Sighs eternal, still the same—
Mounts of snow have summits hidden
  In the mists of uttered flame.
But the spirit, dawning nearly,
  Finds no speech for earnest pain;
Finds a soundless sighing merely—
  Builds its stairs, and mounts again.

Heart, the queen, with secret hoping,
  Sendeth out her waiting pair;
Hands, blind hands, half blindly groping.
  Half inclasping visions rare;
And the great arms, heartways bending;
  Might of beauty, drawing home;
There returning, and re-blending,
  Where from roots of love they roam.

Build thy slopes of radiance beamy,
  Spirit, fair with womanhood!
Tower thy precipice, white-gleamy,
  Climb unto the hour of good.
Dumb space will be rent asunder,
  Now the shining column stands
Ready to be crowned with wonder
  By the builder's joyous hands.

All the lines abroad are spreading,
  Like a fountain's falling race.
Lo, the chin, first feature, treading,
  Airy foot to rest the face!
Speech is nigh; oh, see the blushing,
  Sweet approach of lip and breath!

Round the mouth dim silence, hushing,
  Waits to die ecstatic death.

Span across in treble curving,
  Bow of promise, upper lip!
Set them free, with gracious swerving;
  Let the wing-words float and dip.
Dumb art thou? O Love immortal,
  More than words thy speech must be;
Childless yet the tender portal
  Of the home of melody.

Now the nostrils open fearless,
  Proud in calm unconsciousness,
Sure it must be something peerless
  That the great Pan would express!
Deepens, crowds some meaning tender,
  In the pure, dear lady-face.
Lo, a blinding burst of splendour!—
  'Tis the free soul's issuing grace.

Two calm lakes of molten glory
  Circling round unfathomed deeps!
Lightning-flashes, transitory,
  Cross the gulfs where darkness sleeps.
This the gate, at last, of gladness,
  To the outward striving *me:*
In a rain of light and sadness,
  Out its loves and longings flee!

With a presence I am smitten
  Dumb, with a foreknown surprise;
Presence greater yet than written

Even in the glorious eyes.
Through the gulfs, with inward gazes,
　　I may look till I am lost;
Wandering deep in spirit-mazes,
　　In a sea without a coast.

Windows open to the glorious!
　　Time and space, oh, far beyond!
Woman, ah! thou art victorious,
　　And I perish, overfond.
Springs aloft the yet Unspoken
　　In the forehead's endless grace,
Full of silences unbroken;
　　Infinite, unfeatured face.

Domes above, the mount of wonder;
　　Height and hollow wrapped in night;
Hiding in its caverns under
　　Woman-nations in their might.
Passing forms, the highest Human
　　Faints away to the Divine:
Features none, of man or woman,
　　Can unveil the holiest shrine.

Sideways, grooved porches only
　　Visible to passing eye,
Stand the silent, doorless, lonely
　　Entrance-gates of melody.
But all sounds fly in as boldly,
　　Groan and song, and kiss and cry
At their galleries, lifted coldly,
　　Darkly, 'twixt the earth and sky.

> Beauty, thou art spent, thou knowest
>   So, in faint, half-glad despair,
> From the summit thou o'erflowest
>   In a fall of torrent hair;
> Hiding what thou hast created
>   In a half-transparent shroud:
> Thus with glory soft-abated,
>   Shines the moon through vapoury cloud.

This song achieves the effect it describes, and lifts the veil. And no wonder! Few poems so explicitly and thoroughly erotic can exist in English. Pausing at the knee, the veil rises past thighs and the "holy mystery" between them, belly (expanding house of life), and breasts. Hands and arms appear; and then the poet describes, with imagery reminiscent of the metaphysical poets, the chin, mouth, nostrils, eyes, forehead, hair, and ears. The detail, the passion, and the ambiguities of the language describing the beauties of the face strongly suggest an "upward displacement" of sexual interest. The reader cannot decide whether he is more surprised to find a poem comparable to Carew's *Ecstasy* embedded in a mid-Victorian romance or to consider that nobody at the time or since, among the thousands of readers who have found *Phantastes* fascinating, has apparently thought this worthy of comment.

Frustration follows at once upon Anodos' success: his white lady becomes a statue again as soon as he stops singing, but she is at least visible. He seizes her in his arms, and lifts her from the pedestal; but she springs away, writhing, with the cry " 'You should not have touched me!' " and disappears behind a pillar. When he follows, he discovers a heavy oaken door, with a sign on it saying "No one enters here without the leave of the Queen," but of course he bursts through in pursuit of the lady, and finds himself on a waste windy hill. The palace has disappeared. Great stones stand about. A white figure gleams past him, wringing her hands, and crying, " 'Ah, you should have sung to me; you should have sung to me!' " and vanishes, apparently into a great hole in the earth. Anodos sits down and weeps.[21]

One cannot suppress a feeling that the white lady is being unreasonable. Anodos *had* sung to her, and said a good deal more than most gentlemen say to a lady whom they have met only once before. What more was there to sing? Naturally, in his impetuosity he violated both the "Touch Not" rule and the "Do not enter" rule. The authorities of fairyland seem rather more exacting than those of most societies. Like Cosmo, Anodos has successfully broken the spell that holds his white lady—indeed he has done it twice—and for a second time he has lost her, again like Alastor. When MacDonald has Anodos refer to her as Isis, and speak of unveiling her, he is remembering Novalis' Hyacinth. But whereas Hyacinth's encounter with Isis is a triple triumph—he unveils her, she proves to be Rosebud, and she falls into his arms, thus reconciling the emotions with the search for knowledge—Anodos' victory in raising his lady's veil with his song proves doubly hollow. The white lady is not Isis—intellect or wisdom—for the moment that role is played by the shadow. Nor is she Rosebud—fulfilled erotic love—since she continues to elude her lover. The strength of the entire episode lies in the successful dream-like quality of Anodos' behavior in the palace—he even has a dream within his dream—and in the extraordinary boldness of his song.

Frustration of his passionate desire leaves Anodos steeped in gloom. He continues his travels, this time descending into a chasm down a spiral staircase into the abyss, and then along a horizontal underground passageway in the rock, which grows wider and brings him into "an underground country, in which the sky was of rock, and instead of trees and flowers, there were only fantastic rocks and stones." Here more goblin creatures mock him. They actually sing tauntingly the very song that Anodos has sung to raise the veil of the white lady, and then surround him shouting " 'You shan't have her; you shan't have her; he! he! he! She's for a better man; she's for a better man; how he'll kiss her! how he'll kiss her!' " A spark of nobility awakens in him and he answers " 'Well, if he is a better man, let him have her.' " Instantly the goblins withdraw from his path. As he proceeds, he meets a little elderly woman, who taunts him with not having a pretty girl to walk with, saying, " 'Strange that one can never have what one would like best.' " Suddenly she turns beautiful, and begs him to stay with her; when he draws back, she turns hideous again, and threatens that he will never see the White Lady again; he turns away, pursued by her mocking laughter, frustrated again.[22]

Here MacDonald draws briefly upon one of the richest storehouses of the German romantics, the underground world. At the copper mines of Falun in Sweden in 1719, workmen recovered the well-preserved corpse of a miner who had been buried forty-nine years earlier. His fiancée was still alive, and was the only one to recognize the body. G. H. Schubert told the story in his *Aspects of the Night-side of the Natural Sciences* (*Ansichten von der Nachtseite der Naturwissenschaften,* 1808), which the romantics all knew. A second inspiration for the romantics' devotion to mines and mining-lore came from the teaching of the mineralogist Abraham Gottlob Werner at Freiburg. Werner's pupil, Novalis, who was professionally connected with the administration of the salt mines of which his father was director, introduced into *Heinrich von Ofterdingen* a gentle old miner who tells his life story, praising his profession and taking Heinrich to explore underground caves. The old miner says of his own journeys underground:

> In many places I saw myself as in a magic garden. All that I gazed upon was made of the rarest and most finely wrought metals. In the beautiful tresses and branches of silver hung glittering, ruby-red, transparent fruits; and the heavy-laden shrubs stood on crystal ground of inimitable workmanship.

Novalis is here stressing the beauty and richness, rather than the sombreness of the world underground, but his image of the garden of rock clearly underlies MacDonald's own. Ludwig Tieck's story *Der Runenberg* (1803) also deals with the strange fascination of treasures under the earth; its hero's encounter with the mysterious oversize beautiful naked female spirit, who is also the hideous *Waldweib,* and his sensations may also have inspired MacDonald: Anodos' adventure, longings, and excitements are very similar.

Closest of all to *Phantastes* here, however, is E.T.A. Hoffmann's powerful tale, *The Mines at Falun* (*Die Bergwerke zu Falun,* 1819), whose hero, Elis Fröbom, a sailor,

returns to Sweden from a voyage to find his beloved
mother dead. Grief-stricken, he cannot take part in his
shipmates' celebration of their return, nor does a prostitute bring him any comfort. He meets an old miner, who
tells him of the glories of a miner's life in much the same
terms as Novalis' miner in *Heinrich von Ofterdingen:* to
him it is like a garden:

> He wandered through the mine-shafts as along the
> paths of a magic garden. The stone came to life; the
> fossils were in motion, the wondrous Pyrosmalith, the
> Almandin shone; in the light of the pit-lanterns the
> rock-crystals glittered and flashed in brilliant con-
> fusion.

Elis' original distaste for burrowing in the ground like a
mole is replaced by a violent urge to do so. That night
he dreams that he visits the mines, and sees a vision of
a mighty woman, the queen of the mine; the sight of her
face melts his whole personality into the stone of the
mine itself.

At Falun, he becomes a miner, and falls in love with
Ulla, the daughter of the mine manager, who returns his
love. But now there begins a struggle between his love
for Ulla, and the claims of the mine queen, voiced by the
old miner who is actually a magician in her service. Terrible foreboding, which he cannot share with Ulla, grips
Elis: he is sure that if he mentions the queen he will turn
to stone; he babbles of the treasures of the mountain;
his changed aspect frightens Ulla. He claims that only he
can understand the secret signs that the queen has placed
in the rocky clefts. On the wedding morning itself, Elis
insists on going to the mine, to get for Ulla a precious
stone, the cherry-red Almandin. She begs him not to

go; but, deathly pale, he insists, and is caught in a great cave-in. Fifty years later his body is found, and the aged Ulla is the only one who can identify him.

As the prostitute did not so neither can Ulla really cure the depression which seizes Elis after he loses his mother. Working in the interior of mother earth becomes his substitute for his mother. His love for Ulla is treachery to the personification of mother earth, the maternal queen of the mine. Unlike Novalis' Isis, the mother of all, who, when discovered, is really also the beloved Rosebud, the queen of the mine does not turn out to be Elis' true love Ulla, and the story is a tragedy. Elis' effort to bring back the treasure of the queen to Ulla as a wedding present ends in his death.[23]

Similarly Anodos has lost his mother; from the very beginning of his adventures he has met with frustration in each of his many sexual encounters. From the initial warning, "a man must not fall in love with his grandmother, you know," voiced by the beautiful female who launches him on his adventures, through the episode of the Beech tree, who, though maternal and female, is after all a tree, through the deceit of the beguiling Aldermaiden, the meeting with the girl whose face becomes ugly when he accepts her invitation to kiss her, and the two vain disenchantments of the white lady—the second amidst the most sensual circumstances—down to the girl with the bowl and the ugly underground woman who taunts him and turns beautiful and then ugly again, there is no fulfillment for Anodos. Is not this because, like Elis, he is seeking his mother, and one may fall in love with one's mother even less than with one's grandmother?

The teasing of the goblins who warn Anodos that he will never succeed in obtaining the white lady's love because a "better man" will be kissing her instead bears

out this interpretation. Is not the better man the father,
the rival who wins when the son loses? The "spark of
nobleness," in Anodos (as in all children, who know that
the yearning for their mothers can never really be fulfilled), recognizes that this must be so. "Let him have
her," he says sadly in the end, and the goblins stop teasing
him. Thus the underground mine scenery, here only
briefly hinted at, though later to be used extensively by
MacDonald in *The Princess and the Goblin* and *The
Princess and Curdie,* is by no means the only link that
binds *Phantastes* to *Die Bergwerke zu Falun.* The whole
configuration of the stories has much in common: both
heroes are suffering primarily from the loss of and longing
for their mothers. Unlike Elis, however, Anodos has not
found Ulla; except for the wicked Alder-maiden, whose
seduction is defilement, all he has found are women
whom he may not touch.

Quite apart from the German romantics' specific devotion to mines and mining, we are in a more general way
reminded of the universal literary use of huge hollow
mountains, underground caverns, and passageways, with
all their overtones of symbolism, going back both to the
classical and the ancient Semitic religious traditions
(Plato's *Phaedo,* Seneca, *Gilgamesh*) and finding expression, for example, in *Paradise Lost* and *Kubla Khan.*
MacDonald usually included such underground episodes
in his fairy-tales. We shall encounter them in "The Castle,"
in "The Golden Key," in the *Princess* books, and elsewhere.

VI

Drearily, Anodos continues his travels underground
until the path brings him out onto the shore of a wintry

sea. Deciding that he will not be tortured to death, he plunges into the sea.

> A blessing, like the kiss of a mother, seemed to alight on my soul; a calm, deeper than that which accompanies a hope deferred, bathed my spirit. I sank far into the waters, and sought not to return. I felt as if once more the great arms of the beech-tree were around me, soothing me after the miseries I had passed through, and telling me, like a little sick child, that I should be better tomorrow.

As he rises to the surface, he finds—as Alastor found under other circumstances—a little boat floating nearby, and scrambles in. He floats along, covered with a purple velvet cloth (a pall, surely), resting, as the stormy northern sea changes to a balmy southern one. When he looks down,

> . . . I floated above my whole Past. The fields of my childhood flitted by; the halls of my youthful labours; the streets of great cities where I had dwelt; and the assemblies of men and women wherein I had wearied myself seeking for rest . . . at times, a beloved form seemed to lie close beneath me in sleep; . . . and the arms would heave upwards, as if in dreams they sought for a satisfying presence . . . In dreams of unspeakable joy—of restored friendships; of revived embraces; or love which said it had never died; of faces that had vanished long ago, yet said with smiling lips that they knew nothing of the grave; of pardons implored, and granted with such bursting floods of love, that I was almost glad that I had sinned—thus I passed through this wondrous twilight. I awoke with the feeling that I had

been kissed and loved to my heart's content; and found that my boat was floating motionless by the grassy shore of a little island.

Anodos jumps ashore. The island

rose nowhere more than a few feet above the level of the waters, which flowed deep all around its border. Here there seemed to be neither tide nor storm. A sense of persistent calm and fulness arose in the mind at the sight of the slow, pulse-like rise and fall of the deep, clear, unrippled waters against the bank of the island. . . .

Knocking on the door of a cottage, he hears "the sweetest voice I had ever heard" bidding him enter. Over a pot cooking on the fire there bends "a woman-face, the most wonderful, I thought, that I had ever beheld." She is old, but her eyes are young. She bids him welcome.

A wondrous sense of refuge and repose came upon me. I felt like a boy who has got home from school miles across the hills, through a heavy storm of wind and snow. Almost, as I gazed on her, I sprang from my seat to kiss those old lips. And when, having finished her cooking, she brought some of the dish she had prepared, and set it on a little table by me, covered with a snow-white cloth, I could not help laying my head on her bosom, and bursting into happy tears. She put her arms round me saying, "Poor child; poor child!"

As he continues to weep, she feeds him, "like a baby," with food he cannot identify, and then sings wonderful ballads to him. "While she sung, I was in Elysium, with the sense of a rich soul upholding, embracing, and over-

hanging mine, full of all plenty and bounty. I felt as if
she could give me everything I wanted; as if I should
never wish to leave her, but would be content to be sung
to and fed by her, day after day, as years rolled by."
Anodos falls asleep.

MacDonald's own words render comment superfluous:
after another water voyage full of mother images, Anodos
has found the mother that he and George MacDonald
have longed for in vain, the mother whom Alastor also
invokes: "Mother of this unfathomable world!/ . . . my
heart ever gazes on the depth of thy deep mysteries . . .
though ne'er yet / thou hast unveiled thy inmost sanctu-
ary,/ Enough from incommunicable dream . . ./ Has
shone within me. . . ." While Anodos cannot identify
the food she gives him, perhaps because George Mac-
Donald did not want to raise to consciousness his mother's
letter, we may surely guess that it was milk. Anodos sets
down one of the ballads she sings to him, the song of Sir
Aglovaile, who rides through the churchyard and sees
a female ghost who sings

> Alas, how easily things go wrong!
> A sigh too much, or a kiss too long.
> And there follows a mist and a weeping rain,
> And life is never the same again.
>
> Alas, how hardly things go right!
> 'Tis hard to watch on a summer night,
> For the sigh will come, and the kiss will stay,
> And the summer night is a winter day.

These little verses have charmed all readers and are sometimes even singled out as MacDonald's most memorable
work. The ghost proves to be Aglovaile's lost love Ade-

laide, who has died at the death of her child; he loves her again, and she allows him to sit by her side, but warns him not to touch her; but of course one night he forgets the warning, and loses her again, forever. The close association of love and death, the graveyard atmosphere, and the sexual frustration of the lovers who may not touch reflect MacDonald's own preoccupations.

When Anodos wakes, he finds the woman weeping, and expressing various degrees of distress as she faces in turn the four doors of the cottage, one in each wall; then she sits spinning by the fire, and singing "a low strange song, to which the hum of the wheel made a kind of infinite symphony." When Anodos proposes to explore the island, and to go out at the door by which he had entered the cottage, she warns him that he will not see what he expects to see, and shows him a mark on the palm of her hand which he is to look for whenever he wishes to come back to her. As soon as he leaves the cottage, he finds himself back on the fields of his father's house, in his childhood, playing with his brothers happily; he and one of his brothers have a disagreement before going to bed, and the next morning the brother is drowned. Weeping bitterly, and feeling that he has had the same experience before, Anodos rushes from the house, sees the mark on the door of a barn, but has forgotten its meaning; he enters the barn, and finds himself back in the old woman's cottage. She comforts him with a song. He then tries the second door.

This time he is in a lordly hall, where a lady sits waiting. She is his marble lady, but is not waiting for him. Indeed, Anodos is invisible: he casts no reflection in a nearby mirror. The knight of the rusty armor enters; it is he for whom the lady has been waiting; his armor is

now perfectly clean, and they embrace. Then they talk
about Anodos. Although the knight appreciates Anodos'
twice saving her from enchantment, he thinks Anodos
"may yet perish of vile fear." The lady thanks the knight
for saving Anodos from the Ash tree, and admits that
she loves him, but far less than she loves the knight.
Anodos speaks aloud, and accepts his role as moon rather
than sun; he thinks they hear him. The knight and lady
then withdraw into a bedchamber: on its very door
Anodos sees the mark, and in agony dashes the door
open. Back in the cottage again, he hears the woman
singing of the need to give love. Then he goes out at the
third door.

He finds himself in a crowded street, where he recognizes a former love, from a time before his visit to fairyland. He tries now to avoid a meeting by rushing into a
house; it proves to be the girl's own; but when he goes
to her room, he finds himself in a church, and discovers
the girl's marble effigy on a tomb. He then discovers his
own family burial vault, and calls out to the dead to take
pity on him. He is kissed and his hand grasped in the
dark. Spying the mark on the great slab that covers the
entrance to the vault, he grasps the ring, and finds himself back in the cottage. Again the old woman sings to
him; he sleeps, and when he wakes she tries to prevent
him from going out through the fourth door, calling him
"my child." He disobeys, but remembers nothing after
going out of the door until he wakes from a dead faint in
her arms.

She bathes his head and face and hands "in an icy cold,
colourless liquid, which smelled a little of damp earth,"
which restores him. She explains that she has had to go
through the fourth door, that of the Timeless, to find him,

since otherwise he could never have come back; and that
as a result the waters will not rise and bury her cottage for
a year, although she can keep them out by burning fuel
steadily, and she has enough. Therefore, Anodos must
go. She begs him to remember in any future sorrow that
"the old woman in the cottage, with the young eyes . . .
knows something, though she must not always tell it, that
would quite satisfy you about it, even in the worst moments of your distress." She leads him out; they embrace;
he feels "as if I were leaving my mother for the first time,
and could not help weeping bitterly. At length she gently
pushed me away, and with the words, 'Go my son, and do
something worth doing,'" leaves him.[24]

From each of the four doors of the cottage, leading
respectively to past sadness and regret, to frustration in
love, to dismay and death, and to "the Timeless," Anodos
has come back to receive comfort at the hands of the
mother. She is clearly not only his mother, but mother
earth, "the spirit of earth" whom he had earlier expressed
the wish to see. The damp-earth-smelling restorative is
enough to make this perfectly clear. She is the same
female personage as that glimpsed in fancy by the hero of
"A Hidden Life," "the mighty woman" who sits waiting
quietly to "make him grand forever with a kiss." A mythical creation of MacDonald's own, she will reappear in
all of MacDonald's most important fairy stories, with her
spinning wheel, her fire on the hearth, her youthfulness
despite her age. It is *Phantastes*, however, that introduces
her for the first time.

The mark on her palm, reappearing on the door of
Anodos' father's barn, on the door of the bedchamber of
the knight and the white lady, and on the slab that covers
the entrance into the burial vault of Anodos' family, re-

minds one of the secret signs which the queen of the
mine in *Die Bergwerke zu Falun* has placed in the clefts
of the earth, and which only Elis Fröbom can read. This
is the mark that brings the son back to the mother; it is
no surprise that it should be found on the door of the
parental bedchamber, from which he is excluded in his
wretchedness, or on the family tombs: the grave is the
way back to mother earth, and also, for a Christian, to the
reunion with those who have gone before, in Anodos'
case, as in MacDonald's, his mother.

The episode of the second door reveals who the white
lady is: a mortal, the love of the knight in armor, whom
we now identify as the better man about whom the goblins had taunted Anodos. Why should she prefer the
knight to Anodos, who rescued her twice? The knight,
we know, has been unfaithful to her with the Alder-
maiden, but this now seems forgotten, since his good
deeds have cleansed his rusty armor. Gone also, is all the
allegorical significance that the white lady seemed, in
her earlier appearances, to have. But if we remind ourselves that *Phantastes* is a dream, we shall realize that the
knight is the father, "the better man," and that the white
lady was all along forbidden to Anodos-Oedipus. And
we shall perhaps not mind too much the loose ends of
plot or the unexplained details.

Anodos' experiences in the hut are most successful as
dream literature: the sudden changes of scenery as he
goes through the doors, the sense that his brother's drowning has happened before (guilt at wishing for the death
of a sibling rival?), the reappearance of elements from
other parts of the story, such as the mirror (which this
time has no reflection in it, and is therefore now the
reverse of Cosmo's magic mirror, but the same as that in

Hoffmann's *Das verlorene Spiegelbild*), the transformation of the girl's chamber to a church, all carry real dream conviction. It is Anodos' disobedience to the woman's command—only one of those innumerable disobediences of his that arise from his desire, and that keep the story moving—that brings upon him the fate of having to leave her, and brings upon her punishment, too, for having braved the timeless to rescue him. Like a mother, she reluctantly sends him off to do great deeds: the knight doubted Anodos' capacity to perform them at all. This lachrymose, buffeted, frustrated young man must, now that he has found his mother, stand on his own feet.

VII

On the top of a hill Anodos finds a tower where two brothers are busy forging a sword and armor; they explain that their father is the king of the country, and that long ago three giants had appeared there. At first regarded as harmless, the giants gradually had rebuilt their castle, created uneasiness, and finally become terrorists, taking knights and ladies prisoner, and executing them when threatened. A "lonely woman of wisdom" has told the king's sons that a third brother will join them against the giants; she has shown them Anodos' face in a magic mirror and explained that, though he is weeping, "Past tears are present strength." The maternal spirit has thus known all along that Anodos was on his way to her, and that she would send him on to join the preparations against the giants. The king's sons have sad premonitions that they will not survive the combat to come. Anodos forges himself a suit of mail and sings to the princes as they work together.

When the preparations are complete, they make ready for the fight itself, rejecting horses, since they believe, "with Sir Gawain, that, though mare's sons might be false to us, the earth would never prove a traitor." When the giants actually come, they catch the youths unarmed, but Anodos kills his giant, and the other giants kill the two princes but themselves are killed in doing so. Looking behind him, Anodos now sees his shadow. He summons the neighboring peasants, takes the keys from the giants' corpses, liberates their prisoners, and takes the dead brothers' corpses to the capital. Here the bereft king makes a trophy of the useless armor they had forged, generously knights Anodos, and receives him warmly, but Anodos keeps seeing his shadow during the round of gaiety in the capital and determines to go to visit the city where the lady of the elder brother lives.

We have now been plunged back into Spenserian atmosphere, and suspect that the three giants, at first tolerated and then seen to be wicked, may have some allegorical meaning. The long-prepared defensive armor in the end proves useless, and only the weapons of offense have value. Evil comes, MacDonald is saying, at a moment when our guard is down. We must rely on our impulse of the moment to be a good one. The chthonic theme continues, as the princes rely on the earth rather than on horses. The shadow, however, now seems to have quite lost its original meaning; it is now little more than a kind of conscience or self-consciousness: so long as Anodos is actively doing good deeds it does not obtrude itself upon his attention, but as soon as he relaxes for a moment or gives thought to himself it reappears.

Warned by a youth that the forest is enchanted, Anodos none the less rides on into it. His shadow disappears, and he begins to think very well of himself, comparing himself to Galahad. He sees approaching him a splendid knight, and he recognizes that the knight is wearing the same armor and riding the same horse as he himself. He sees his own face reflected in the knight's steel breastplate, and above it, the knight's own face is also his own. He admires this double, but is sure that he ought to fight him, and yet cannot bring himself to the attack even after the other has scornfully refused to let him pass. Instead, when the double haughtily commands him to follow, Anodos humbly obeys, and, cowed, is led to a dreary tower in the forest, where the knight makes him dismount, sends his horse off into the forest with a blow, and orders him to enter the tower and "take your companion with you." The knight vanishes; Anodos sees that the shadow has reappeared. They are locked in the tower together alone.

When moonlight enters the prison and touches him, it sets him free, but when day comes he finds himself with the shadow imprisoned once more. Each night it is the same. Yearning for freedom, once he dreams of a happy return to his own castle, and hears a woman singing; the song tells him of Mother Earth's kindness to her children and her love for them, and urges him to "Go forth to her from the dark and the dust,/ And weep beside her, if weep thou must;/ If she may not hold thee to her breast,/ Like a weary infant that cries for rest;/ At least she will press thee to her knee,/ And tell a low, sweet tale to thee,/ Till the hue to thy cheek, and the light to thine eye,/ Strength to thy limbs and courage high / To thy fainting heart, return amain,/ And away to work thou goest again./ From the narrow desert, O man of pride,/ Come into the house, so high and wide."

He opens the door, unable to say why he had not done so sooner, and recognizes the singer as the girl whose globe he had once broken. She explains that she now sings songs wherever she goes, comforting people and delivering them. She leaves, and Anodos feels a great gulf between them because "She was uplifted, by sorrow and well-doing, into a region I could hardly hope ever to enter." Leaving the tower behind, Anodos casts off his armor, and proceeds through the wood with only an axe: he is too lowly for knighthood; and determines to be a squire:

> Then first I knew the delight of being lowly; of saying to myself, "I am what I am, nothing more." "I have failed," I said, "I have lost myself—would it had been my shadow." I looked round: the shadow was nowhere to be seen. Ere long, I learned that it was not myself, but only my shadow, that I had lost. I learned that it is better, a thousand-fold, for a proud man to fall and be humbled, than to hold up his head in his pride and fancied innocence. I learned that he that will be a hero, will barely be a man; that he that will be nothing but a doer of his work, is sure of his manhood. In nothing was my ideal lowered, or dimmed, or grown less precious; I only saw it too plainly, to set myself for a moment be-side it. Indeed, my ideal soon became my life; whereas, formerly, my life had consisted in a vain attempt to behold, if not my ideal in myself, at least myself in my ideal. Now, however, I took, at first, what perhaps was a mistaken pleasure, in despising and degrading myself. Another self seemed to arise, like a white spirit from a dead man, from the dumb and trampled self of the past. Doubtless, this self

must again die and be buried; and again, from its
tomb, spring a winged child; but of this my history
as yet bears not the record. Self will come to life
even in the slaying of self; but there is ever something deeper and stronger than it, which will emerge
at least from the unknown abysses of the soul: will
it be as a solemn gloom, burning with eyes? or a
clear morning after the rain? or a smiling child, that
finds itself nowhere, and everywhere? [25]

Anodos' encounter with his double in the forest marks
another transformation of the shadow. It has been a
special form of *Doppelgänger* all along; now it becomes
the double itself, not merely a shadow image, of the
hero. When the shadow disappears, the knight appears;
when the knight in turn disappears, the shadow reappears. Yet MacDonald shows no serious or sustained interest in the problem of double personality that had fascinated so many writers, Hoffmann and Jean Paul among
them. Instead, he is using their device for mere allegory
and sermonizing. The shadow, which began as the intellectual skepticism that withers the imagination, and
which later became conscience or consciousness of self,
has now become personal pride, or a misconception of
one's true role in the world. Anodos is unwilling or unable to fight this aspect of himself when he meets it face
to face; it confines him with itself (in the form of the
shadow); and it is not until the singing girl addresses
him as "man of pride" and urges him to come out into
the world that he is able simply to open the door of the
tower prison and walk out. Now he knows he is not
Galahad and admits to himself that the trappings of
knighthood are not for him; he has conquered pride, and

his shadow vanishes. Humility and a recognition of his true role in the world have made him "sure of his manhood." He will henceforth be "nothing but a doer of his work."

Here, I think, one may venture to read autobiography into *Phantastes*. Had not George MacDonald thought of himself with pride as a minister, as a Galahad doing good deeds in the world, and had not his misfortune in the ministry brought him low and led him to see that this was not his true role? Instead, through suffering and poverty, and despite the failure of his own society to understand him, he had come to think of poetry and writing as his work. His new self, the winged child, had sprung from the old. But at the moment when he wrote *Phantastes*, in 1858, he was still almost unknown, though thirty-four years old, and burdened with heavy responsibilities. Had he not, like the hero of "The Broken Swords," lost his sword as an officer and accepted that of an enlisted man? Had he not, like Anodos, laid aside his armor and set off through the forest armed only with an axe? Read in this light, this episode of *Phantastes* becomes both revealing and moving.

Anodos next encounters a mounted knight dragging the body of a dragon; it is the knight of the soiled armor, the successful lover of the white lady; although the knight apparently recognizes him, he accepts him as his squire, but they do not speak of their earlier meetings. As they continue on their way, the knight tells him of a girl who had been collecting butterfly and moth wings to make herself a pair of wings on which to fly away to her own country. Just as she had been about to get some wings from most beautiful butterflies, she found herself thrown down and trampled upon by creatures of whom the forest was full: men of wood, without joints at knees or elbows, without noses or mouths. When the knight went to help her, he discovered that no matter how often he dismembered them with his sword, the pieces went on trampling the girl; only when he turned them upside down and stood them on their square heads did he render them immobile and harmless. This interpolated story has a touch of the comic: it delighted contemporary readers of *Phantastes:* the butterfly wings clearly stand for the wings of poetic imagination; the little wooden blockheads that try to prevent the girl from getting them no doubt stand for the literary critics, or the philistine public, who need to be upended before their pernicious activities can be stopped.

Anodos' love for the knight grows, and he determines that "'If I cannot be noble myself, I will yet be servant to his nobleness.'" Here, as later in MacDonald's novels, the son enters the service of the father. In the forest, they come upon a clearing, where ranks of white-robed sword bearers are solemnly awaiting something. Though the knight thinks it is surely something good, and expects to hear the voice of a prophet, Anodos suspects that something is wrong. Six of the men escort a youth to a throne on a platform on a slope; on the throne sits a majestic figure. After kneeling at its foot, the escorts open a door in the pedestal and push the youth in, although he shrinks back; the crowd sings; Anodos' master, the knight, is full of reverence and awe. "Incapable of evil himself, he could scarcely suspect it in another." (Forgotten, apparently, is the fact that long ago the Alder-maiden had forced the knight too to sin.) Anodos, how-

ever, suspects something "worse than the ordinary
deceptions of priestcraft." As the men proceed to escort
a girl to the pedestal, Anodos mounts the platform, and
tears the image from the throne, with a sound of the
breaking of rotten wood. From the hole in the pedestal
a great wolf leaps, which grapples with Anodos; he fixes
his hands on its throat, determined to throttle it, and the
crowd closes in, shouting with anger; he feels no blow,
but loses consciousness.

Here the very nobility of the knight stands him in ill
stead; he is ready to believe in the holiness of a vile cult
because of its trappings and because he cannot imagine
evil. Though only a squire, not fit for knighthood, Anodos
has the keenness of vision to see the youth shrink as the
pedestal opens, and summons up the boldness and daring to challenge the fiend directly. Though George Mac-
Donald was not worthy to be a minister, he seems to be
saying, at least he could show the worthy ones some of
the wickedness of priestcraft, even if he should die in the
attempt. Humility has its own pride. The Galahads of
this world are unfit for certain tasks that need doing. The
hero of "The Broken Swords," Anodos, and George Mac-
Donald must perform these tasks. And one is to expose
the seamy side of religious observance.

Anodos is dead. He lies in his coffin, and the knight
and the white lady weep over him; the knight tells her
how nobly Anodos died, and how he had killed the
monster.

> Now that I lay in her bosom, the whole earth, and
> each of her many births, was as a body to me, at
> my will. I seemed to feel the great heart of the
> mother beating into mine, and feeding me with her

own life, her own essential being and nature. I heard the footsteps of my friends above, and they sent a thrill through my heart.

He rises into a single large primrose that grows by the edge of the grave. His lady plucks it, puts it in her bosom, and kisses it. But the flower soon withers, and he forsakes it, his spirit floating on a cloud. Anodos has learned "that it is by loving, and not by being loved, that one can come nearest the soul of another," and he determines that when his senses return he will go back to earthly life "with the love that healeth." As he reaches this resolve, he is once more conscious of life.

He finds himself on a hillside above his own castle. To his delight, he has "only the natural shadow that goes with every man who walks in the sun." His sisters welcome him with joy: he has been gone twenty-one days. Can he, he asks himself, translate the experiences in fairyland into terms of his daily life? "I, who set out to find my Ideal, came back rejoicing that I had lost my shadow." He often thinks of the wise woman in the cottage, and when sad or perplexed feels that he will return to the place again; he looks about for the mystic red mark and reminds himself that this will lie upon his tomb. He will find it again and be glad. A few days ago, resting under a great ancient beech tree at the edge of his field, after helping his reapers, he has heard the leaves of the beech whispering that "a great good is coming" to him, and the sound reminded him of the voice of the old woman in the cottage; he thinks he sees her face among the leaves. And he knows that good is coming to him "that good is always coming; though few have at all times the simplicity and the courage to believe it.

What we call evil, is the only and best shape, which, for the person and his condition at the time, could be assumed by the best good." [26]

And here *Phantastes* ends. As in "A Hidden Life," the hero enjoys the fantasy of the lady he has loved weeping over him after his noble death, and this time even plucking him in the form of a primrose after he has returned to mother earth, in the tomb. Back to real life after his prolonged dream-adventure, Anodos takes with him the lesson of giving love. His shadow, whatever its manifold meanings have been, is lost. MacDonald uses as epigraphs for his last chapter both the quotation from Novalis, "Our life is no dream; but it ought to become one, and perhaps will," and the lines from Chaucer's *Pardoner's Tale:* "And on the ground, which is my modres gate,/ I knocke with my staf, erlich and late,/ And say to hire, Leve mother, lat me in." The reunion with mother earth, though now interrupted by the return to life, will come again: on Anodos' tomb there will be the mystic red mark that will bring him back to the wise woman of the cottage. Nor is it coincidence at the end that the wise woman's voice speaks and shows her face from the leaves of the beech tree. All the images of motherhood: the earth, the beech tree, and the wise woman herself come together harmoniously at the end of life, for which the lugubrious Anodos waits, knowing that evil as such does not exist but is the shape that good seems to take for those who are not brave and simple. From the experience of his own life, and the manifold sorrows that have dismayed him, MacDonald preaches his sermon, as much to himself as to his reader, and patiently waits to see the red mark on the tomb.

CHAPTER 3

Fancy and Imagination

> Struggling in my father's hands,
> Striving against my swadling bands,
> Bound and weary, I thought best
> To sulk upon my mother's breast.

WILLIAM BLAKE, "Infant Sorrow"

I

AFTER *Phantastes,* there began a period of false starts and frustrations that lasted down to 1863, when *David Elginbrod,* the first of MacDonald's novels, found a publisher. The only significant survival of these years 1858 to 1862 is *The Portent,* a supernatural story. But with the publication of *David Elginbrod,* MacDonald plunged into a productive period of steady writing that lasted almost to the end of his career in the 1890's. His novels, of course —to which we shall turn in Chapters 4 and 5—form the bulk of his output. But, especially at first, he wrote many fairy-tales as well. Here we shall be examining *The Portent* and the fairy-tales, "works of fancy and imagination," as MacDonald himself called them, when he reissued in 1871 all that he had so far written. They number fifteen and include his most celebrated work.

The shorter ones came out in groups: four in *Adela Cathcart* (1864), a collection of stories held together within the framework of a feebly-plotted novel; two more in *Dealings with the Fairies* (1867), in which three of the *Adela Cathcart* stories were reprinted; and three more for the first time in the ten-volume *Works of Fancy and Imagination* (1871), in which *Phantastes, The Portent,* and the shorter fairy-tales were reprinted. *At The Back of the North Wind* appeared serially in 1868–1869, and as a book toward the end of 1870; *The Princess and The Goblin* serially in 1870–1871, and as a book in 1872. The last three—*The Wise Woman, The Princess and Curdie,* and "Photogen and Nycteris"—belong respectively to 1875, 1877 (book publication late 1882), and 1879 (book publication 1882).[1] As this publication schedule shows, MacDonald gradually abandoned the writing of fairy-tales. In the early eighties, he gave it up altogether; he returned to it only once more, at the very end of his writing career, with *Lilith* (1895). We shall be dealing in this chapter, then, wholly with work published during the years 1858–1882.

Greville MacDonald has chronicled the course of his father's family and professional life during this quarter of a century. In 1859, still suffering from ill health, and distracted from his writing by frequent lecture engagements, George MacDonald moved to London, and accepted a professorship of English literature at Bedford College. The family grew steadily: when *Phantastes* appeared in 1858, there were already five children; six more were born in the next nine years. The early sixties were crowded with the new friendships in London's literary world, with a full schedule of lecturing, and with the first travel abroad. In 1865 came the failure to obtain the chair at Edinburgh; in 1868 an honorary LL.D. from Aberdeen; in 1869 the editorship of a children's magazine published by Alexander Strahan, *Good Words for the Young*, at a high salary to begin with, but bringing with it many problems and lasting only four years.

By 1867, the family was established in a handsome house in Hammersmith, "The Retreat," later William Morris' "Kelmscott House." Prosperity grew, but never quite as fast as money worries. The years 1872–73 saw the American tour. The brief period that followed in 1873–74 Greville MacDonald regards as the culmination of success, energy, and happiness. But in 1875 tuberculosis struck the MacDonalds' second daughter, Mary Josephine, and MacDonald himself was ill again. The family abandoned "The Retreat," for fear that the Thames was unhealthy. Migration began once more, and financial problems loomed ever larger. "Greatly to the dismay of all our relatives and of many long-tried friends," Louisa MacDonald now decided to produce in public and for money *Pilgrim's Progress* and the other plays that had been such a success in private family theatricals. George MacDonald himself disliked the enterprise, but he felt he must humble his pride and allow his wife to do the work that God had given her to do.

So, although the family made its first trip to Italy in 1877, and soon afterwards settled there, eventually in a fine house they built in Bordighera, the MacDonalds returned to England as a family acting troupe every summer until 1887. MacDonald himself participated in the performances, whose star was his eldest daughter Lily, a beautiful and talented actress. She had wanted to go on the stage professionally, but her parents had refused to allow it, after hearing from the American actress Charlotte Cushman how dangerous the life was for a young girl. Poor Lily lost her fiancé as the result of the family plays: a rich relative threatened to disinherit him unless she would stop acting in public. She refused the ultimatum and remained a spinster for the rest of her short life. Mary Josephine died of tuberculosis in 1878 as did Maurice, a son of fourteen, in 1879.[2]

When we turn back to 1858 and consider the sterile years down to 1862, we conclude that MacDonald had poured so much into *Phantastes* that it left him written out. Quite possibly the death of his father (August 24, 1858), while *Phantastes* was still in the press, created a mixture of sorrow and guilt and inferiority so strong as to make writing difficult. This is suggested by a letter of October 15, 1858, to his stepmother, in which MacDonald wrote: "I dreamed last night I saw my father. I felt I loved him so much and was clinging to him, when to my surprise I found he was so much taller than I that I did not reach his shoulder. There is a meaning in that, is there not?" The theme of his next literary effort is in itself suggestive, and so is its failure. It was a play, entitled "If I Had a Father," later many times revised but never produced, and not even published until twenty-three years later in a collection of short stories.[3]

Even if we could be sure what elements in the published version we might safely ascribe to the MacDonald of 1859, we could never regard the piece as more than an ill-advised potboiler. In it, a Colonel, who has served many years in India, returns to England. Wishing to make up to his son for past neglect, he enters his service in disguise as his valet. The son, a sculptor, has adopted a beggar girl, whom his aunt has educated and chaperoned, and who has now grown beautiful. The sculptor falls in love with her too late, because she has agreed to marry another man, but all works out well in the end. George

Smith, who had published *Phantastes,* advised MacDonald to turn "If I Had a Father" into a novel. This he did in *Seekers and Finders,* which he himself eventually decided not to publish. His sons Greville and Ronald endorsed the decision, and later wisely destroyed the manuscript.[4] The father in service to the son was a theme close to MacDonald's heart, and one which he would later vary by reversing the roles.

On 27 December 1859, Monckton Milnes commended MacDonald to Thackeray, who had just undertaken the editorship of the *Cornhill,* with George Smith as publisher:

> I heartily wish you would employ MacDonald, the author of "Phantastes" and "Within and Without." He is a man of very fine fancy, high education, and good taste. He would write you some poetical prose that would be sure to be good.[5]

The first version of *The Portent* accordingly appeared in the *Cornhill* for May, June, and July 1860. The portent itself is the noise of a horse, galloping with the characteristic sound of a loose shoe; it had first been heard in the dim past, when a Campbell, jealous of his brother's success with the girl they both loved, had forced his brother's horse over the edge of a cliff, and had then died himself, together with the girl, in a mad wild ride in the mountains. The narrator-hero, a remote descendant, learns from his old nurse of the evil that the sound always portends for the family.

He takes a post in England as tutor in the family of Lord Hilton. Lady Alice, the stepdaughter of Lady Hilton, is a strange girl, treated almost as if she were mentally deficient. She can read to herself but not aloud, has a musical voice but cannot sing, glides gracefully in her walk but cannot dance. Yet Campbell finds her remarks near genius in their originality. One night he discovers Lady Alice in a haunted chamber walking in her sleep; the portentous hoofbeat sounds at their encounter. He brings her to his room. When she wakes, her initial anger fades after she learns that they both hear the sound of the portent. By pure will-power Campbell succeeds in bringing her to his room again in her sleep, but she makes him promise not to repeat the experiment. They fall in love; he begins to teach her along with his other pupils, and finds her apt, but Lady Hilton forces her to give up the lessons. Now Alice in turn summons Campbell by will-power to the haunted room; he discovers that they were born and that their mothers died at the same time.

Before they can put into effect their plan to flee together, they hear the portentous hoofbeat at one of their meetings. Lord Hilton and some servants burst into the room; Campbell is wounded, and comes to his senses lying out on the moor. He enlists, fights at Waterloo, where he is wounded, and on his way through Brussels after the battle thinks he hears Alice's cry and sees her face at a window, but the building proves to be an insane asylum, and she is not there. He looks for her in vain; at Hilton Hall he cannot bring her to him by exercising his will in the old way, even by sitting in their haunted chamber, which he enters by stealth. Until he finds her, his soul "is but a moon-lighted chamber of ghosts; and I sit within, the dreariest of all. When she enters, it will be a home of love; and I wait—I wait." [6]

Readers of *Phantastes* will recognize Lady Alice as a somnambule like Cosmo's Princess von Hohenweiss, inspired like her by Hoffmann. Mesmerism plays its part, as man and woman summon each other by will-power alone. Poe-like in its suggestion that both hero and heroine suffer from hallucinations, fast-moving, with hardly a superfluous word, the *Cornhill* version of *The Portent* is a first-rate little Victorian ghost story. Unfortunately, MacDonald later added a good many new episodes, gave it a happy ending, and published it in book form in 1864. We now follow in detail Campbell's search for Alice. He returns to Scotland; the old nurse with the second sight reveals that Alice is at Hilton Hall after all. Campbell finds Alice mad, and re-lives with her every episode of their earlier romance until he brings her back to sanity. They are again on the point of flight when the portent sounds, and the Hiltons burst in; but this time, as Campbell hesitates, Alice fortunately seizes a Malay creese, and gets them away to safety, marriage, and happiness. Clumsy and contrived, the new material substitutes banality, coincidence, and longwindedness for economy and tragedy.

Yet into this revision, MacDonald put something of himself. Before Campbell falls in love with Lady Alice, he receives permission from Lord Hilton to catalogue the library. He finds a "perfect set of the poets."

> I began to nibble at that portion of the collection which belonged to the sixteenth century; but . . . found nothing, to my idea, but love poems without any love in them, and so I soon became weary. But I found in the library what I liked far better—many romances of a very marvellous sort. . . . I likewise came upon a whole nest of the German classics. . . . I found in these volumes a wealth inexhaustible.

Later on, after he has fallen in love with Lady Alice,

> One day, in listless mood, I took up a volume, without knowing what it was, or what I sought. It opened

at the *Amoretti* of Edmund Spenser. I was on the
point of closing it again, when a line caught my eye.
I read the sonnet; read another. I found I could
understand them perfectly; and that hour the poetry
of the sixteenth century became an open well of
refreshment, and the strength that comes from
sympathy . . . this old fantastic verse . . . proved
an intellectual nexus between my love and my
studies, or at least a bridge by which I could pass
from the one to the other.[7]

Here, MacDonald takes us back to that summer of
1842, when the library revealed its treasures to him, and
the lady in the end denied him her own. In the revision
of *The Portent*, he handles the episode more directly and
with fewer layers of protection between him and the
facts. Love and literature come to the hero, as they had
to MacDonald, simultaneously. But he was not yet able
to face the treachery of the girl in his own past: Lady
Alice truly loves Campbell and remains loyal to him. The
very choice of Campbell—the name of the family tradi-
tionally the MacDonalds' desperate enemies—seems significant camouflage. But the peculiar Lady Alice is not
yet a portrait of MacDonald's early love.

Despite the Hoffmann-esque somnambulism and mesmerism, the story strikes strong Scotch notes. The loving descriptions of Scotch scenery in the early portions
of the novel, the "second sight" of the nurse, the portent
itself, testify to MacDonald's own first discovery of the
inspiration he might find in his native land. Though
Campbell once quotes MacDonald's favorite saying of
Novalis: "Our life is not a dream; but it may become a
dream, and perhaps ought to become one," we can none

the less view *The Portent* as marking the beginning of a gradual emancipation from the German romantics. It occupies a transitional place between the fairy-tales and the Scotch novels.

II

Of the four *Adela Cathcart* fairy-tales, two—"The Light Princess" and "The Cruel Painter"—owe much to Hoffmann. In "The Light Princess," the wicked witch at the royal christening deprives the infant of her gravity: the princess floats toward the ceiling and must be pulled down; the servants play ball with her. She grows to the age of seventeen, laughing at everything, even at her mother's tears or the victories of her father's enemies. Only when she swims in the beautiful lake on whose shores her palace stands does she recover her gravity, and then only in the physical sense. A wandering prince hears her laugh, and mistakes it for a scream, "for the hatching of a real hearty laugh requires the incubation of gravity." He learns of her plight and begins to join her for regular swims. But the wicked old princess summons up a white snake of darkness, which she takes through underground caves to a chamber through whose roof the snake sucks away the lake's water; further enchantments dry up all sources of water in the kingdom.

"The poor princess nearly went out of the little mind she had." In despair at the interruption of their swims, the prince enters the palace service as a bootblack. The king learns that the situation can be saved only if a man can be found who will plug with his body the hole through which the water is running out, and so die by drowning as it flows in again. The prince volunteers to be the martyr, provided that the princess will stay with him, feeding and comforting him from a boat until the waters close over his head. Quite unmoved, she listens to him singing as the water rises around him, gives him a "long sweet cold kiss" as it reaches his chin, and begins to feel strange only when it rises to his mouth and nostrils. At the very last moment, she shrieks with agony, tugs him free, and saves his life. The enchantment is broken; she can actually fall to the floor for the first time. Rains refill the lake; the prince and princess are betrothed. The moral: "no girl is worth anything till she has cried a little."

Some psychoanalysts would no doubt have a field day with this story: one may regard as obvious symbols the white snake, the underground caves, the sucking of the lake water through the hole, the plugging of the hole by the prince's body, the lake itself, the delicious swims, and perhaps even the act of bootblacking to which the prince resorts when temporarily deprived of his love. Were the servants who tossed the weightless child in the air playing with the phallic maiden? Who can be sure?

What does seem clear, however, is that MacDonald was inspired by the *Märchen* of King Ophiuch and Queen Liris in Hoffmann's *Prinzessin Brambilla* (1821). Hoffmann's king is always sad: rationalism has entered his kingdom and destroyed intuition, the only way by which man may come into contact with nature. To cheer him up, his advisers have married him to Princess Liris, who is perpetually laughing, a laughter without depth, just like that of MacDonald's light princess. But husband and wife do not love each other. Eventually a magician gives them the magic lake of Urdar, in whose surface they may see themselves with detachment: both can now laugh, he at his solemnity and she at her frivolity: their laughter is now true and deep. Urdar is the saving sense of humor. In the sequel, it dries up by enchantment, but is eventually restored.

MacDonald has discarded the sombre king and kept only the eternally laughing princess. But her laughter— even at matters that should produce tears—does not, as in Hoffmann, symbolize comedy without self-understanding; it means only that she has never had to consider anybody else, or experienced grief or pain or love, has never had to "cry a little." Nor is MacDonald's lake the lake of Urdar: it is not a mirror surface in which to examine one's ego; it is not the sense of humor; it is just a body of water to swim in, which the princess enjoys because it restores her physical sense of gravity. She is otherwise just as superficial and inconsiderate in the lake as out, although MacDonald is not entirely consistent here: the prince likes the princess much better when she is submerged. MacDonald's story makes of Hoffmann's materials just a nice little sermon, based essentially on a pun: *gravity* in English has two meanings, and this gave MacDonald the opportunity to consider what would happen if a girl without spiritual gravity also lacked physical gravity.

In addition to his usual attack on the deadness of the *Aufklärung,* and his plea for intuition as against intellect, Hoffmann was commenting on the relationship of art to life, and especially of dramatic representations on the stage (the subject of *Die Prinzessin Brambilla*) to actuality. Most of this MacDonald throws away, although he pokes fun at both materialists and spiritualists in the king's College of Metaphysicians, who are consulted about solving the princess' problems. Yet the very luxuriance of Hoffmann's imagery, his repetitions, his elaborate psychology, his repeated abstractions, overburden his *Märchen* and make it a bore, while MacDonald's simple sustained good humor and his agreeable imagery make his sermon palatable.

"The Light Princess" was a favorite with his children, and he read it aloud with great success to other audiences, from a manuscript with the pages gummed together into a long scroll. In the punning that the King and Queen exchange—as possibly in the gravity theme itself—one may perhaps catch an echo of Lewis Carroll, " 'It is a good thing to be light-hearted.' " " 'It is a bad thing to be light-headed.' " " ' 'Tis a good thing to be light-handed.' " " ' 'Tis a bad thing to be light-fingered.' " " ' 'Tis a good thing to be light-footed . . . in fact it is a good thing altogether to be light-bodied.' " " 'But it is a bad thing altogether to be light-minded.' " [8]

"The Cruel Painter" takes us back to Prague, scene of Cosmo's adventures as read by Anodos in the library of the fairy palace in *Phantastes*. The hero is another student, Karl von Wolkenlicht, strong and handsome but somewhat effeminate, who falls in love with Lilith, the most beautiful girl in Prague, daughter of a painter named Teufelsbürst ("Devil's Brush"). Teufelsbürst hates mankind and always paints human beings suffering some sort of torture, with his beautiful daughter in the background, entirely indifferent to what is going on: ". . . when the red blood was trickling drop by drop from the crushed limb, she might be seen standing nearest, smiling over a primrose or the bloom on a peach."

Welcoming the opportunity to "hold the heart of the youth in his hand and wring it and torture it to his own content," Teufelsbürst accepts Karl as a resident pupil, who shares the studio while the painter paints his beautiful indifferent daughter "in every variety of costume that could best show the variety of her beauty." He adds to the terror by drugging his pupil and by discoursing about his late neighbor, Mr. Kunz, who has become a vampire. The strain tells on Karl, who faints so completely one evening that his master thinks him dead. Lilith now begins to pity and love him.

Teufelsbürst puts what he believes to be Karl's dead body into a plaster cast, "a huge misshapen nut with a corpse for a kernel," but is interrupted by a terrible thunderstorm, and leaves the studio. Karl bursts the cast under the drugged illusion that *he* is now a vampire; but a visit to Lilith's room cures him. Her father, however, catches sight of him crawling along the roof of the house after he has left Lilith's window, and is convinced that he must be a vampire. So Karl begins a program of terrorizing Teufelsbürst: he returns to live with his fellow students, but steals into the studio by night, reassembles the pieces of the cast, and fills it with old metal; later he sprinkles red wine on it to make the painter think the vampire is actively eating. He also alters Teufelsbürst's pictures. In one, the painter

> had represented poor Wolkenlicht as just beginning to recover from a trance, while a group of surgeons, unaware of the signs of returning life, were absorbed in a minute dissection of one of the limbs. At an open door, he had painted Lilith passing, with her face buried in a bunch of sweet peas.

Karl now changes it so that

> the face of one of the group was now turned towards that of the victim, regarding his revival with demoniac satisfaction, and taking pains to prevent the

others from discovering it. The face of this prince of
torturers was that of Teufelsbürst himself. Lilith had
altogether vanished, and in her place stood the dim
vampire reiteration of the body that lay extended on
the table, staring greedily at the assembled company.

After these and other pranks have reduced Teufelsbürst almost to madness, Karl appears one morning and
calmly announces that he has been away for a few days,
so that the painter comes to think the whole affair has
been an illusion of his own. His morbid tastes now change;
he paints a portrait of Karl "without evil or suffering,"
and then one of Lilith and one of both. Reformed, he
accepts Karl as his son-in-law. Many years later, Karl reveals the whole truth to Teufelsbürst, at a moment when
the painter is "lying on the floor of a room in Karl's ancestral castle, half-smothered in grandchildren."

Essentially, this story is a *fabliau:* the student overcomes the father's devices for protecting his daughter and
wins her in the end. MacDonald has taken some of the
theme from Hoffmann's *Der Artushof* (1816), in which
a painter with a beautiful daughter also accepts the
young hero as an apprentice. But in Hoffmann's story the
father has been warned that he will die when his daughter accepts a lover; so he has dressed her as a young
man and painted her so skillfully in masculine dress that
the hero has almost fallen in love with the youth before
he knows that it is really a girl. In "The Cruel Painter"
there is no sexual ambiguity about Lilith, who is a beautiful girl from the first; but MacDonald, for reasons that
escape us, has transferred the effeminacy to Karl, who
plays a wholly masculine role, but whose fellow students
call him "Lottchen," the diminutive of Charlotte.

Hoffmann's painter is not cruel, but does suffer from delusions and thinks that a blank canvas is his masterpiece. His flight from the hero is undertaken to preserve his life: he is a father who cannot survive the loss of his daughter to another man. MacDonald's painter, on the other hand, is purely sadistic. The *grand guignol* of his paintings and of his teasing exhibition of Lilith to the increasingly frustrated Karl seems to be MacDonald's own invention, and is surprisingly precise and effective; but one cannot believe in Teufelsbürst's transformation —solely as the result of a series of scares—into a man without evil who romps on the floor with his grandchildren.

MacDonald manages clumsily the introduction of the supernatural element, breaking into his narrative to summarize the outbreak of vampirism. He rejects his own supernatural touches so that he deprives them of their effectiveness as literary devices, even though his only purpose was to suggest how belief in such phenomena render a man vulnerable. In the *Adela Cathcart* version, the narrator of "The Cruel Painter" reveals to his audience that he got the idea of the vampire from Henry More's *An Antidote against Atheism.* But the one trick that More's revenant did *not* play on his victims was to bite them or suck their blood. So it is MacDonald who has introduced this detail. When Lilith is awakening to her love for Karl, and thinks he may be a vampire, she feels jealous lest he may have bitten some other girl: he has not bitten her. The vampire's bloodletting here clearly can be made to stand for defloration.[9]

"The Giant's Heart" represents a different genre, much closer to true folklore; it tells of the vengeance taken by two children, Buffy-Bob and his sister Tricksey-Wee, on a wicked giant who catches children, plants them in his garden, grows them like radishes, and eats them. The brother and sister wander into the giant's house, and from their hiding place in a broom see him pop into the pot over the fire one of the little boys he had been planning to use for seed. But his wife, an amiable giantess who has warned the little boy and girl, knows that her husband only likes boys crisp; so she throws the cooked one out of the stew with a ladle, "as if he had been a black-beetle that had tumbled in and had the worst of it." The hiding children also overhear the giant telling his wife that he has recently changed the place where he keeps his heart, leaving it in a distant eagle's nest at the top of a mountain. They escape, determined to find the heart and destroy the giant.

The owl does not help them find the way, but they wheedle the answer out of the lark by assuring her that they intend no mischief. At the foot of the mountain, they assist a spider, who in exchange gives them some spider juice to drop onto the heart when they find it, to shrink it down small enough to carry. The spiders also help them up the mountain and molest the eagle, who leaves her nest. Tricksey-Wee drops the spider juice on the heart, hears the giant screaming for pain in the distance, gives it another touch of the juice when it starts to grow, squeezes it until the giant agrees to take home all the children he has stolen, and pinches it again until he gives up the last child and promises never to carry off another. But he rushes at them as they are about to give the heart back to him; so Buffy-Bob stabs the heart, and "the giant fell dead at the feet of little Tricksey-Wee, who could not help being sorry for him after all."

" 'What a horrid story,' " says one of the children in

Adela Cathcart, who has listened to "The Giant's Heart."
It is indeed full of terrifying and cruel ideas and images
—from the eating of children to the agony of the giant,
which is prolonged by the little girl's savage tricks with
his heart. One thinks of Teufelsbürst's wish to hold
Karl's heart in his hand and torture it. The saccharine
Victorian fairy-names given the children cannot conceal
from the reader the fact that they are vicious little sadists,
and liars too: they obtain vital information from the un-
suspecting lark only by telling her the exact opposite of
the truth. Tricksey-Wee's final wave of pity for the giant
she has been delightedly torturing goes well with the
rest of her character. In *Adela Cathcart* MacDonald gives
the story a moral: one of the listening children, "a darling
little blue-eyed girl," thanks the narrator:

> "Thank you, dear Mr. Smith. I will be good. It was a
> very nice story. If I was a man, I would kill all the
> wicked people in the world. But I am only a little
> girl, you know; so I can only be good."
>
> The darling did not know how much more one
> good woman can do to kill evil than all the swords
> of the world in the hands of righteous heroes.

The children planted as radishes may well be a reminiscence of Hoffmann's vegetable story *Die Königsbraut*
(1821), with its carrot-monarch and other edible characters. But the chief inspiration for "The Giant's Heart"
comes not from Hoffmann, but from a story of the
folklore-type classified by specialists as that of the "external soul": a personage keeps his soul, or his heart,
outside his body. The theme appears in all of the folk
literatures of the world, and has met with rich variety

of treatment. The two versions known to me that come closest to MacDonald's are a Norse tale, "The Giant Who Had No Heart in his Body," and a North German tale, "The Man Without a Heart." Both had been translated into English and made widely available in popular collections in the 1850's, less than a decade before MacDonald wrote his own story; so that he may easily have read either or both.

These two are very close to each other: instead of eating children, the giant's (or man's) crime is that he has turned to stone the six eldest sons of the king and their brides, giving the seventh son a chance to rescue them. The youngest son helps a raven, a salmon, and a wolf (Norse), or an ox, a boar, and a griffin (German); and they in turn help him when it comes to finding the giant's heart, which is in an egg, in a duck, in a well, in a distant church (Norse), or in a bird, inside a church on an island (German). In each case it is a girl who lives with the giant who cajoles him into revealing where the heart is hidden. In both versions the hero and heroine squeeze the heart a good deal after they have got it, but the nasty spider juice is MacDonald's own invention. In the Norse version, the hero flatly promises to save the giant's life if he will bring the stone men and women back to life, and then calmly breaks his promise. MacDonald alters this detail by having his giant make a treacherous lunge at the children, which excuses their final despatch of him. But things we can quite easily accept when they are told of Norse or German folks heroes, we find less palatable when we are asked to believe them of nice little nineteenth-century English children. MacDonald's version of "The Giant's Heart" must be voted nauseous.[10]

"The Castle," called "a parable," is indeed a transparent one: "When or how it was built no man knew; nor could anyone pretend to understand its architecture . . . the whole might be constructed on some higher principle of architecture than they yet understood." Nobody has ever seen all of it; some parts are always wrapped in mist; the inhabitants are always finding new rooms, or new staircases, or endless successions of vaults and passages going deep into the huge mountain below. At the foot of the cliff is a deep lake, into which a flight of steps descends. The large family of brothers and sisters who live in the castle have never seen their father, but his coming is some day expected. Meanwhile they are expected to obey their eldest brother. But he wants them to seek the highest, and they find it distasteful; so when he orders them not to give a great party in the reserved state apartments, they chain him in the cellar and invite the guests indiscriminately. During the dance an earthquake and a great storm disrupt the festivities; the eldest brother reappears, and reasserts his authority. With the subordination to him comes increase of freedom. They recognize their brotherhood, sing a hymn to fatherhood, start to aspire upward, and await the coming.

A few ambiguities remain to trouble us: is there any political moral? Does acceptance of *temporal* authority really mean salvation? If it is only *spiritual* authority that is to be accepted, and the elder brother is indeed Christ, who are the unworthy guests invited to the party, for whom apparently there can never be any salvation at all? Who is the eldest sister, who is always opposed to the rebellion against the authority of the brother? She is beautiful and silent, loves her brother, but thinks him stern because he never changes his mind. "The Castle" is a sermon, with just enough cloudiness to keep the con-

gregation talking after church. The chief interest it has
for us is that the scene anticipates that of *The Princess
and the Goblin,* where we shall find a more finite castle,
but still one possessing mysterious corridors, stairways,
and towers, resting on a mountain that is tunneled full
of passages.[11]

With these four tales from *Adela Cathcart,* we may for
convenience group "Cross Purposes" (1867), on the whole
a failure, which none the less has certain aspects of interest. The queen of the fairies kidnaps two mortal children, the squire's daughter, Alice, "a pretty, good-natured
girl, whom her friends called fairy-like and others called
silly," and the son of a poor widow, Richard. In fairyland,
although Alice at first has some compunction about the
difference in their status, she none the less falls in love
with Richard, and he with her. But when they escape,
and find that it is still the same day and they are back
in their village, they separate at once: fairyland, Mac-
Donald is saying, is the only place for a successful love
affair across class lines. He hints also that Alice is not
very bright: he will develop later his mystical sense of
the special sanctity of slow-witted or idiot children.

Alice's passage into fairyland is also interesting, when
one remembers her namesake, and the intimacy between
MacDonald and Lewis Carroll. When the fairy Peaseblossom comes to take her from her bed, Alice finds

> that she was no bigger than the fairy; and when she
> stood up on the counterpane, the bed looked like
> a great hall with a painted ceiling. As she walked
> towards Peaseblossom, she stumbled several times
> over the tufts that made the pattern. But the fairy
> took her by the hand, and led her towards the foot of

the bed. Long before they reached it, however, Alice saw that the fairy was a tall, slender, lady, and that she herself was quite her own size. What she had taken for tufts on the counterpane were really bushes of furze, and broom, and heather, on the side of a slope.

Here MacDonald imitates Lewis Carroll in the size-change of the little girl, managing to catch her twice as she shrinks, first to the size of Peaseblossom, and then to the appropriate size *relative* to Peaseblossom in her new incarnation. The dislocation and changes in size so characteristic of Lewis Carroll, and the source of so many comments by psychologists, are much less frequent in MacDonald's stories: only Anodos' grandmother and North Wind expand or contract, and both are supernatural, not human beings. The skill with which MacDonald manages the transition from the real bedroom to fairyland is as great as Carroll's own. But of course he does not owe this to Carroll: before the two met, and four years before *Alice* was written, MacDonald had got Anodos out of his bedroom and into fairyland with similar success.[12]

III

The first part of "The Carasoyn," published as "The Fairy Fleet, an English Mährchen," belongs to the year 1866. A motherless Scotch shepherd boy, Colin, who does the housework for his father, diverts the course of the burn near their house, so that, instead of flowing into the barnyard and becoming muddy before it can continue on its way, it actually passes right through the house it-

self. One night the fairy fleet appears on the stream inside the cottage, and the fairies disport themselves. A
changeling whom they have stolen, a little girl, begs Colin
to rescue her; so when the queen of the fairies offers him
a wish as a reward for having made the brook so much
pleasanter, he asks for the little girl. Angry, the queen
tricks him into promising first to bring her a bottle of
carasoyn, a "kind of wine that makes people happy,"
although she already has everything that she can possibly want.

To help him on his quest for the carasoyn, Colin seeks
an old woman who lives in a hut on the moor, who can
be found only when the seeker is already lost. She is
blind and spins by the fire; she has a wonderful hen who
gathers the wool for spinning from the flowers in the
field. She tells him that he must dream three days without working, work three days without dreaming, and
then work and dream for three days together. Then

> The old woman took the wool, and fastening it on
> her distaff, began to spin, giving the spindle a twirl,
> and then dropping it and drawing out the thread
> from the distaff. But as soon as the spindle began to
> twirl, it began to sparkle all the colours of the rain-
> bow, that it was a delight to see. And the hands of
> the woman, instead of being old and wrinkled, were
> young and long-fingered and fair, and they drew out
> the wool, and the spindle spun and flashed, and
> the hen kept going out and in, bringing wool and
> swallowing the seeds, and the old woman kept tell-
> ing Colin one story after another, till he thought
> he could sit there all his life and listen. Sometimes
> it seemed the spindle that was flashing them, some-

times the long fingers that were spinning them, and
sometimes the hen that was gathering them off the
heads of the long dry grass and bringing them in
her beak and laying them down on the floor.

When the wonderful spinning of stories stops, Colin finds
that he has already fulfilled the first part of his task: he
has dreamed for three days without working.

The three days work without dreaming he accom-
plishes in the forge of a humpbacked smith, a goblin,
with goblin children and assistants. The goblins have
been ordered to lift Cumberstone Crag a yard higher
and send a flue under Stonestarvit Moss. To help perform this engineering job, Colin must make crowbars
and wedges, giving blow for blow with the smith. The
smith tells him how to make a trench, and wait for the
growth of a magic vine, whose grapes will contain the
carasoyn for the fairy queen. This is his three days of
mixed working and dreaming: the happiest he has ever
known, for he understands the entire growth of the wonderful grapes.

It is not until the next summer that the fairy queen
returns; she accepts the carasoyn. Colin holds fast to the
little changeling, as she is transformed into various animals and birds. When the queen draws the cork from
the carasoyn bottle, the wine runs out,

and a strange odour filled the cottage. The queen
stood shivering and sobbing beside the bottle, and
all her court came about her and shivered and sobbed
too, and their faces grew ancient and wrinkled. Then
the queen bending and tottering like an old woman,
led the way to the boats, and her courtiers followed
her, limping and creeping and distorted.

Weeping, the fairies board their boats and float away. Colin has his little girl, who stays with him and his father. She takes over the housework, and when he grows up and has been to college, he and she are married.[13]

Here the first version of the story ends. It is by far MacDonald's most successful fairy-tale since *Phantastes*. He has kept to a minimum folklore themes such as the changeling and her repeated transformations into animals at the end, and has skillfully worked them into the framework of a basically original tale. We recognize the old woman in the hut, who can be found only when one is lost: we have met her in *Phantastes* as the earth-mother, who comforts Anodos in the little cottage on the island. Here, too, she is a mother. Like Anodos, Colin is motherless; we do not learn directly that he yearns for a mother; but why else should he divert the stream so that it flows into the cottage? The symbolism speaks out. The old woman's blindness is new: she explains that she sees better without eyes than other people with them. The earth-mother in *Phantastes* also had a spinning wheel, but this time it is the thread of poesy and imagination that comes off the flashing spindle; the old woman is telling marvellous stories, and Colin is dreaming the entire time without working. Three days are over before he can realize it: the earliest of MacDonald's dream-like experiments with time-distortion, which begin with this story. The goblin smiths are new too, with their hard heads, their bad manners, and their tunneling away at the mountain. All of these personages are beautifully realized preliminary sketches for some of MacDonald's most famous characters in *The Princess and the Goblin:* Colin himself for Curdie the miner-boy, the old woman for the fairy grandmother, and the good goblins for their wicked successors.

A proper combination of imagination and hard labor: sometimes pure imagination, sometimes pure labor, sometimes a mixture of the two—as in real life—brings success to Colin: he gets the carasoyn. Although the queen of the fairies says that it makes people happy, she admits from the first that she knows nothing about it, and her wish for it is likened to that of a spoiled child for something unknown. When the old woman hears that the queen has asked for the carasoyn, she tells Colin, "You shall carry the silly queen her bottle of carasoyn. But she won't like it when she gets it, I can tell her." And the effect on the fairies is as devastating as it is surprising. The uncorking of the bottle may be viewed as the symbol of defloration, which always leads to trouble and grief. The fairies are already quite vicious; so that it cannot be primal innocence they are losing when the bottle is uncorked. Is our moral simply that when one allows one's greed to get the better of one, one is obviously asking for disillusionment, old age, and sickness? In the end, Colin gets the woman he needs: it is a wife, not a mother; but this is the substitute that most men have to put up with. All in all, "The Fairy Fleet" is really very good.

In adding a sequel, and publishing it as the last part of the story, MacDonald committed a major lapse in taste. Years later the fairies take their revenge on Colin and his wife by stealing their youngest child: Colin does nothing about this for seven years, but when the fairies come and sing that they have cut off the baby's cheek and chin and ear, and put out his eye, and salted the pieces down in the kelpie's pool, so that the child has only a hole to

put his porridge in, Colin rouses himself to action. He has
nine days, or the child will be lost permanently. Once
again he finds the old woman by getting lost. She is still
blind: "Where her eyes should have been there was nothing but wrinkles." He greets her as "mother." Seven of his
nine days pass in listening to her stories. Once again he
seeks goblin help, this time from cobblers—who want to
dismember him, and use the parts to make shoes—from
whom he must obtain a lump of wax and an awl. At the
kelpie's pool, the fairies offer him horrors instead of his
own child:

> a huge sea-slug, a horrid creature like a lump of
> blubber . . . a blue lobster . . . a spider-crab . . .
> a whelk . . . a dreadful object . . . very like a baby
> with his face half eaten away by the fishes, only that
> he had a huge nose like the big toe of a lobster.

He uses the awl to let the water out of the pool, and
the wax to draw a line over which the fairies may not
pass, and thus recovers his child from a cave at the bottom of the pool, ten years old, but retarded to the age he
had been at his capture, three. The child recovers. He has
not really been tortured or dismembered. The spirit of
the second portion of the story is altogether different
from that of the first. The fairies and goblins have always
been mischievous; but they are now sadistic. Colin has
always been dreamy, but he is now passive and incompetent. The old woman has always been blind, but she
is now terrifying. We are back to the savagery of "The
Giant's Heart." The story has been spoiled.[14]

But the next major fairy-tale, "The Golden Key," is
probably MacDonald's very best. He had experimented
with his own mythic creations, and had come to feel a

sureness in handling them. A little boy, living near the borders of fairyland, hears from his aunt about a golden key at the end of the rainbow. She tells him that long ago his father, now dead, had found it, but cannot say what it was like or what he did with it. The boy sets out into the wood; without difficulty he sees the rainbow, with beautiful forms moving in the colors. He sleeps on a bed of moss for the night. In the morning, there is the little golden key, its handle set with sapphires, lying on the moss near his face. The reader is surprised; the quest seems accomplished, the story over. Not at all: ". . . the pretty thing was of no use to him yet. Where was the lock to which the key belonged?"

Meanwhile, nearby, a little girl, the daughter of a merchant, has been left with servants who neglect and ill-use her. They call her Tangle because of the state of her hair. Disliking untidiness, the fairies of the forest frighten the child. She runs off into the forest. Here a curious guide takes over. It is

> made like a fish, but covered, instead of scales, with feathers of all colours, sparkling like those of a humming-bird. It had fins, not wings, and swam through the air as a fish does through the water. Its head was like the head of a small owl.

It saves her from the frightening clutch of a tree, and finally swims ahead of her through the air into a cottage, and then into a pot cooking over the fire. Here a beautiful woman greets the child. She is thousands of years old, asks to be called grandmother, and is completely at home in the humble cottage, though she looks "as if she had just put off quantities of diamonds and pearls." Three whole years have already passed since Tangle ran away.

The old woman bathes her in a pond full of the strange
feathered fish, dresses her in a fine new dress like her
own (but both are barefoot), and for supper serves her
the messenger air-fish who of his own accord had flown
into the pot. Grandmother explains that

> "In fairyland the ambititon of the animals is to be
> eaten by the people; for that is their highest end in
> that condition. But they are not therefore destroyed.
> Out of that pot comes something more than the dead
> fish, you will see."

After Tangle and grandmother have eaten the fish, there
rises from the pot a "lovely little creature in human shape"
with white wings.

Tangle spends a day outside; grandmother has disappeared. The cottage, whose walls are covered with
moss, has no windows; the doors open only from inside.
But at night a light appears inside, a door opens, and
grandmother welcomes Tangle back. The wisest mes-
senger-fish has now been chosen to fetch the boy from
the foot of the rainbow, and when they arrive at the cottage, this fish too flies directly into the pot. The youth
with him has outgrown his garments; his face is ruddy
with health; and in his hand he carries the sparkling
golden key. He is called Mossy "because he had a favourite stone covered with moss, on which he used to sit
whole days reading" and his companions said that "the
moss had begun to grow upon him too."

When Grandmother sees that Mossy has the golden
key, she makes him take her chair, and despite his protests waits upon him like a servant: it is her pleasure to
do so. To find the keyhole for the golden key is Mossy's
work; she cannot help him. But Tangle is to go along.

Mossy is delighted, but Tangle does not wants to leave her grandmother. Again, the fish is eaten, the winged human figure comes from the pot and is sent out into the dark. Grandmother tells Tangle that "No girl need be afraid to go with a youth that has the golden key," and asks her to be sure to request the Old Man of the Sea to supply more fish for the tank. If Tangle and Mossy lose each other on their travels, each is to go right ahead. They leave hand in hand. But in his right hand Mossy holds the key.[15]

The little boy, like his father long ago, finds his phallus as a child, but does not know where to find the lock to which it belongs. This he must do by himself and without help. The mossy bed on which he sleeps, the moss on the stone on which he reads as he grows older, and which gives him his name when it eventually grows on him, is surely the pubic hair of maturity. So is the moss on the outer walls of grandmother's cottage, the female organ with no windows, with doors which only grandmother herself may open. Grandmother we have met in *Phantastes* and in "The Carasoyn": as she says, she is never allowed to keep her children long, but sends them out into the world with work of their own to do. She respects Mossy for having the phallus and enjoys waiting on him, as a woman who admires virility and knows that it may be trusted: no girl need be afraid to go with a man who has the golden key. Tangle, whose disorderly hair—the symbol of her own sex—is rearranged, and who is cleansed and made sweet and feminine by grandmother, shows a maiden's first hesitation to leave girlhood and go with a man, but later casts a glance at him, and thinks she will enjoy the the experience.

Here is a rough psychoanalytical interpretation of the

story up to this point. If this were all, we should perhaps
derive a certain interest from observing that even the
pre-Freudian and supposedly repressed Victorians, when
they wrote myth and fairy-tale, reverted to the essential
sexual symbols, but would we not find the story banal? We
must read "The Golden Key," however, at other levels:
the key may stand for the poetic imagination, for warmth
and kindness, for religious faith, for love: any or all of
these are talismans which a man may not fully know how
to use, but whose mere possession makes it safe for a
woman to accompany him. The quest, which we had
thought finished when Mossy found the key, or when its
possession brought him to the cottage and to Tangle, is
just beginning.

The bird-fish-messengers play the role that the old
woman's hen plays in "The Carasoyn." They are the helpful animals, the familiars of the good witch, and do her
work. But they also evolve into a higher state: from the
animal to the human, as the Boehme-Novalis-MacDonald
theory of evolution prescribed. Their evolution is accomplished by being eaten, itself an annihilating experience,
but the one they crave more than any other. Just as
Novalis in the unwritten part of *Heinrich von Ofterdingen* intended each step of his hero's evolution upward
from a stone to a man to be accomplished by a sacrifice,[16] so sacrifice attends the advance of the bird-fish.
An eating sacrifice never lies very far from the surface of
a Christian's imagination. The fish in the tank assemble
in council to choose the wisest among them as a messenger, and by that token as a candidate for being cooked,
eaten, and transfigured: it is wisdom that qualifies one for
the advance to the next stage. Just what constitutes the
superiority of the angel state over the fish-bird state we

do not learn; can it be the mere possession of a human form?

The dream-like passage of time MacDonald handles beautifully. The reader must be warned that it is passing much more quickly than the external narrative would imply: to Tangle it has seemed to take only a day to make her way through the forest to grandmother's house. A tree with drooping branches has held her as in a trap, and pressed her closer and closer to the trunk, giving her great distress (like Ash), but that has been her only adventure: it too we may interpret as a sexual one. In fact, however, she was only ten when she ran away from home; but she is thirteen and more now. It comes as a surprise to her to hear from grandmother that the day had been three years long, but Tangle has reached puberty; as readers, we are now alert to the fact that time is passing fast. So, when Mossy appears, we have been prepared to learn that he is wearing outgrown clothes, and that he is a strong youth instead of the little boy we left. He arrives one whole day after Tangle; so if three years pass every day, she must be sixteen and he perhaps a few years older when they set out.

They journey now through a forest, where the squirrels and old moles give them food, but the bees refuse them honey. And thence they emerge onto rising treeless ground, along a narrow path between rocks, on into a dark narrow gallery cut in the rock, and out onto a precipice, where a path winds down to a wide circular smooth sandstone plain surrounded on all sides by mountains,

> everywhere crowded with shadows. It was a sea of shadows. The mass was chiefly made up of the shadows of leaves innumerable, of all lovely and

imaginative forms, waving to and fro, floating and
quivering in the breath of a breeze whose motion
was unfelt, whose sound was unheard. No forests
clothed the mountain-sides, no trees were anywhere
to be seen, and yet the shadows of the leaves,
branches, and stems of all various trees covered the
valley as far as their eyes could reach.

Shadows of birds, wonderful forms, half bird half human,
gambolling children, "loveliest female" shapes, occasional
profiles of unspeakable beauty and grandeur, lovers, fathers and sons, sisters, wild horses—all cross the plain as
shadows. Half-way across, Mossy and Tangle rest, and
find each other in tears. Each is longing for the country
from which the shadows fall. They hope the golden key
may be the key to it. After their rest, they continue to
cross the plain, the shadows gathering as evening comes
on.

How long they were in crossing this plain I cannot
tell; but before night Mossy's hair was streaked with
grey, and Tangle had got wrinkles on her forehead.

Suddenly, Tangle finds that she has lost Mossy's hand.
The man and woman have now together made the
whole journey of human life, through the forest of their
youth, where some of their acquaintances are generous
and some are not (by the time they leave the forest they
are very fond of each other, and Tangle is not in the
least sorry that grandmother has sent her away with
Mossy), on into the difficulties of middle life—symbolized by the climb, the dark gallery, and the descent
of the mountain—and out onto the plain of the later
years, where the intimations of paradise, the Platonic

shadows of real things, invisible but of heavenly beauty, lie ever thicker around them, deepening as they advance. Tired, and with tears in their eyes, they long to go where the shadows come from; and then, now that both are old, they are suddenly no longer hand in hand. One of them has died. The sad, inevitable separation has come, the separation MacDonald had dwelt upon when he wrote "Love me, Beloved" almost twenty years before.

We do not know which has died, but surmise that it was Tangle, since it is her adventures we follow first. After initial despair, she remembers that Mossy has the golden key and will be safe and that she must go on. She climbs a path that takes her to a door in the mountainside. When she is terrified to enter, her former air-fish, now an angel, an aeranth, lights her way through the mountain and down onto the seashore. Across the sea she sees the foot of a great rainbow. She meets the Old Man of the Sea, who says he cannot show her the way up to the country from which the shadows fall, but promises to send her to the Old Man of the Earth, who is older than he is, and who may be able to help her. He also takes her to show her his fish through an undersea window; but he has none that are ready for her grandmother yet. He refers to grandmother as his daughter, and explains that he needs more time to prepare the fish than she does. After giving Tangle a soothing and reviving bath, the Old Man of the Sea shows her the way down a long winding stair in the rock to a cave, in which a beautiful youth who looks from behind like a very old man sits entranced at a vision he is looking at in a silver mirror. This is the Old Man of the Earth.

He too cannot help her reach the land whence the shadows fall, but he shows her the way to the oldest man of all, the Old Man of the Fire: she must pass through an underground river.

> Then the Old Man of the Earth stooped over the floor of the cave, raised a huge stone from it, and left it leaning. It disclosed a great hole that went plumb-down.
>
> "That is the way," he said.
> "But there are no stairs."
> "You must throw yourself in. There is no other way."

Tangle waits what seems like a minute to her but is really a whole year. Then she jumps. The river sweeps her downward into almost unbearable heat. As it runs shallower and then stops, she has to continue on foot; but the stair ends at a rude archway in "all but glowing rock." Through it she falls exhausted into a cool mossy cave. Its floors and walls are covered with moss—green, soft, and damp. A little stream spouts from a rent in the rock, and falls into a basin of moss. Suddenly she has a marvellous sense that she is

> in the secret of the earth and all its ways. Everything she had seen or learned from books; all that her grandmother had said or sung to her; all the talk of the beasts, birds, and fishes, all that had happened to her on her journey with Mossy, and since then in the heart of the earth with the Old man and the older man—all was plain; she understood it all, and saw that everything meant the same thing, though she could not have put it into words again.

In the corner of the cave is a little naked child, playing with balls of various colors and sizes, which he disposes in strange figures upon the floor beside him. Tangle realizes that she does not yet understand everything, and she watches him arrange and rearrange the patterns for what seems like seven hours but is seven years. Finally she asks him where the Old Man of the Fire is, and he tells her that it is he. He does not smile; his face has the "awfulness of absolute repose," and love shines in his eyes. He is the oldest man of all and can help everybody. She bursts into tears, and he shows her how to cross the blazing desert, first touching her so that she will not suffer from the heat. He takes an egg from under a stone; a snake emerges from the egg, and grows, and Tangle follows it, after a last vision of the marvellous Child.

We return now to Mossy; he is very old. His possession of the golden key enables him at once to recognize the Old Man of the Sea. While he lies in the Old Man's bath, he sadly remarks that he has never found the keyhole for the golden key, and does not know why he keeps it. But the bath rejuvenates him; his grey hairs have gone.

> "You have tasted of death, now," said the Old Man.
>
> "Is it good?"
>
> "It is good," said Mossy. "It is better than life."
>
> "No," said the Old Man: "it is only more life."

Because he has the golden key, Mossy can walk right across the water to the rainbow. He crosses the sea for many days on foot, and on the other side he finds a path that leads up a precipice to a smooth rock with a little sapphire-bordered keyhole in it. He has found it. He inserts the key and the door opens. Down a flight of stairs, he comes into a splendid hall in the rock; here Tangle is waiting for him, as she has been for seven years. "Her face was beautiful like her grandmother's, and as still and peaceful as that of the Old Man of the Sea." To her he resembles all the three Old Men, but is still her own old Mossy.

> She had a hundred questions to ask him, and he a hundred more to ask her. They told each other all their adventures, and were as happy as man and woman could be. For they were younger and better, and stronger, and wiser, than they had ever been before.

In a pillar in the hall, a second keyhole appears; the golden key opens a door onto another staircase; the key then vanishes. Mossy and Tangle are inside the rainbow, with other beautiful beings, on their way to the country whence the shadows fall.[17]

In death, life continues. Tangle and Mossy follow separate paths toward reunion and the door into the rainbow that leads to paradise. The topography is clear: both visit the Old Man of the Sea; but Tangle has to get to the foot of the rainbow through the bowels of Mother Earth, via the visits to the other two Old Men, and thence across the desert in the wake of the snake; while Mossy, by virtue of his possession of the golden key, can walk directly away from the Old Man of the Sea and across the sea itself to the foot of the rainbow, where the first keyhole is, without visiting the Old Men of Earth and Fire. The golden key gives Mossy the power to walk on the water; it makes him Christ-like. Why has he this advantage over

Tangle, except that he is a man? He has an instrument which she has not. Without it she cannot open the lock, and must reach the vestibule to the rainbow by another route. No doubt MacDonald also sensed that to make Mossy repeat the entire journey to all three Old Men would have been a bore and a delay. The golden key itself, love, faith, the power of the imagination—what we please—has two last phallic moments, once when Mossy, as an old man, wonders in brief disillusion what it is for anyhow and why he has always kept it, and again when it disappears after opening the door into the rainbow: the phallus will not be needed in paradise, where there will be no marrying or giving in marriage.

MacDonald's golden key reminds one of the key that Mephistopheles gives to Faust in the dark gallery; at first Faust calls it "Das kleine Ding," but, after Mephistopheles has warned him against undervaluing it, it swells in his hand, grows hot, and shoots out sparks, imagery we cannot fail to recognize as physiological. Moreover, it is the key with which Faust is to touch the glowing tripod in the realm of the Mothers. And when the Old Man of the Earth tells Tangle that there "is no other way" except to hurl herself directly into the mouth of the pit, we hear MacDonald echoing Mephistopheles' celebrated answer when Faust asks him the way: "Kein Weg! Ins Unbetretene,/ Nicht zu Betretende. . . ."

Tangle's journey—perhaps a Jungian "night journey under the sea" that must precede a "renewal of life"— gives MacDonald a chance at cosmological paradox: the older the Old Men are, the younger they are: the Old Man of the Sea, seeming old at first, is really middle-aged; the Old Man of the Earth, who is older, and at first looks old, is really a youth; while the Old Man of the Fire, the oldest of all, who alone knows the way to paradise and says that he sometimes goes there, the possessor of the secrets of the universe, is a child. This expresses Mac-Donald's profound belief that child-like qualities are eternal, the most marvellous and mysterious of all, a view that Vaughan, his favorite seventeenth-century poet, shared with Wordsworth and with many of the Victorians.[18]

Moreover, since death, as the Old Man of the Sea declares, is simply more life, MacDonald subtly makes it a mirror-image of life rather than a mere repetition. The further one goes in life the older one gets; after death, the process is the other way, at least with regard to the climactic progression from one of the Old Men to the next. The divine child, who radiates love, is, of course, a Christ-symbol. As Tangle looks back at him for a last glimpse, "He stood alone in the midst of the glowing desert, beside a fountain of red flame that had burst forth at his feet, his naked whiteness glimmering a pale rosy red in the torrid fire." The geometrical figures into which he arranges the balls were suggested to MacDonald by those very different figures in Klingsohr's *Märchen* in *Heinrich von Ofterdingen:* we know this, and do not have to infer or suggest it, because MacDonald himself inserted a footnote at this point in "The Golden Key," which reads "I think I must be indebted to Novalis for these geometrical figures." [19] Footnotes shatter the mood in a story like this, but at least the indebtedness is clear.

Tangle's journey is arduous indeed, requiring of her the highest courage. Down she moves through the subterranean passages, canals, and rivers, growing hotter all the time, until, exhausted, she reaches, through a burning archway, a damp and mossy cave: can we escape the genital symbolism of her voyage? And when she has reached the womb, what she finds there is a child: which is what one would expect. Why should she have had to suffer so much more than Mossy? Perhaps MacDonald is saying that woman's lot is suffering. She does get to the vestibule to paradise seven years earlier, but this seems to be because she died first. Once the two are reunited, there is something of a letdown; all they can do, alas, is talk like any other husband and wife who have been separated and tell what they have done since last they met. We are prepared to believe that they are younger and stronger and wiser and better, but we do not know, and MacDonald's imagination cannot cope with, the place to which they are going: it is only the land whence the shadows fall, of unimaginable beauty; and we have the same objections to it that are always raised to such vague concepts of heaven: will it not be rather a dull place?

Tangle's encounter with the Old Man of the Sea and her meeting with the aeranth throw a little more light on the evolutionary processes of these beings. In order to be promoted to grandmother's tank, and thus to become air-fish, the fish belonging to the Old Man of the Sea have to pass through an evolution of their own: no doubt in wisdom. It takes a long time; indeed, it has taken Tangle her entire lifetime to get to the Old Man and ask for the fish; and no new ones are yet ready. Once they are air-fish, however, it apparently takes them less time to deserve to become aeranths. The duty of an aeranth—at least of the only one we see—is to act in the world of death as a guide in the same way that the air-fish act in fairyland. What may be its further upward evolution we do not learn.

All in all, in richness and variety of imagery, kept well in hand, in suggestiveness and pathos, in brevity and point, in simplicity and beauty of language, "The Golden Key" is a little masterpiece, the best thing MacDonald ever did.

IV

Of all MacDonald's works, *At the Back of the North Wind* has remained the best-known, delighting and disturbing generation after generation of children. It takes place in two worlds, the real world of everyday Victorian London, and the dream-world of the imagination of Diamond, the coachman's son, named after his master's beautiful white horse. With equal matter-of-factness, and no change of pace, MacDonald narrates the events that take place in both worlds; so that the dream world seems a natural extension of the real world. He does not tell us that Diamond is dreaming whenever he sees North Wind, whether by night or by day. We are here not dealing with an explicit transfer from the world of reality to the world of dreams, as in *Phantastes* or the *Alice* books, which are purely dream narratives. For adults, *At the Back of the North Wind* is like Hoffmann's *Golden Pot:* as if falling asleep, almost without warning, we pass from one world to the other, and at times the two worlds are fused. No doubt this is one of the reasons why the book gives children the shivers.

In the real world, Diamond sleeps in a loft over the stable in the grounds of his father's master, Mr. Coleman, a kind man with a kind daughter. Diamond meets a miserable waif of a crossing-sweeper, a little girl named Nanny, and does what he can to help her. He goes for a visit to the seaside, visits a toy shop, goes to the beach with his mother, and has a severe illness. The Colemans are ruined through speculation, and Miss Coleman's fiancé is lost at sea in a wreck of one of their merchant ships that also shatters the family fortunes. Out of work, Diamond's father buys a four-wheeler cab and manages to acquire Old Diamond, the horse. The family has to live in a mews. Diamond rescues the baby next door; its father is a drunkard and beats his wife, but Diamond's gentle kindness launches him on the road to repentance. When Nanny is ill, Diamond makes a dangerous excursion into a desperate slum, where he is nearly stripped of his clothes by the predatory women who live there. He meets a kind man, an author named Mr. Raymond, who helps him get Nanny into a hospital.

When Diamond's father is sick and cannot work, Diamond himself drives the cab. He becomes a general favorite of the stablemen and cabdrivers of London. Miss Coleman's lover has survived the shipwreck after all; he comes home, and it is Diamond, as cabdriver, who brings him to the humble house where the Colemans now live. A baby girl is born to Diamond's parents. Diamond, who has always enjoyed making poems and singing songs to his little brother, welcomes her with the famous sentimental verses, "Where did you come from, baby dear?" Mr. Raymond offers Diamond's father the use of another horse while he travels abroad. Nanny too comes to live with them; this is very expensive. But when Mr. Raymond returns, he has married a charming woman, and offers Diamond's father a post as his own coachman. They all move to Kent, and Diamond becomes a page in the household, and a friend of the narrator, a tutor who lives nearby. Diamond has a nest in a beech tree. Diamond dies.

In the dream world, at the very beginning of the story North Wind makes a window into Diamond's bed by blowing through a knothole. She is a beautiful woman, who warns him at once that she will vary in size. Though she asks him to accompany her, she has vanished by the time he gets downstairs, and he wanders onto the lawn of the Coleman's house, and is eventually rescued. Everybody thinks he has been walking in his sleep. On her second visit, North Wind takes Diamond for a walk along the river and carries him behind her in a nest made of her hair while she "sweeps" out London. He gets a splendid aerial view of the city; and it is then he sees Nanny for the first time, and asks North Wind to put him down to help her. So the two worlds fuse; Diamond escorts Nanny through London for the rest of the night, and she will not believe what he tells her about North Wind.

In mid-summer, North Wind appears to him in the garden, during the day, very tiny, and tells Diamond that she has to sink a ship that night. She takes him along, but while she sinks the ship (Mr. Coleman's ship), she leaves Diamond in a cathedral on a high ledge, where he learns to walk alone, goes to sleep, and hears the Apostles in the stained-glass windows talking, and wakes up in his own bed: there has been a severe windstorm in the night. At the toy shop, North Wind appears to him blowing a tiny windmill. He tells her that he wants to go to the country at her back; she answers that this is very difficult to do; since the country is at her back, she cannot get there herself, but must sit on the doorstep, facing out, and listen to the voices inside.

This is the moment of Diamond's illness. That night
North Wind blows him aboard a little northbound yacht,
arranges his transfer to a German vessel, sets him down
on a northward-moving iceberg, and joins him there, only
to leave as the south wind, blowing the berg north, makes
her faint. He is on the way to North Wind's house, and
finds her on the doorstep, sitting as if dead on an icy ridge,
waiting until she is wanted. To get to the country at her
back, he must walk right through her:

> When he reached her knees, he put out his hand to
> lay it on her, but nothing was there save an intense
> cold. He walked on. Then all grew white about him;
> and the cold stung him like fire. He walked on still,
> groping through the whiteness. It thickened about
> him. At last, it got into his heart, and he lost all sense.
> I would say that he fainted—only whereas in com-
> mon faints all grows black about you, he felt swal-
> lowed up in whiteness. It was when he reached
> North Wind's heart that he fainted and fell. But as
> he fell, he rolled over the threshold, and it was thus
> that Diamond got to the back of the north wind.

The narrator now intervenes to declare how hard this
part of the story is to tell, because by the time Diamond
got back from the country at the back of the north wind,
he had forgotten much about it, and he found it hard
to tell what he could remember. Other people have been
there, an Italian named Durante (Dante), and a Scotch
peasant girl, Kilmeny, who came back from it for a visit
to her friends: and MacDonald now quotes "the shepherd who tells her story," who is James Hogg, the Ettrick
Shepherd (1770–1835):

Kilmeny had been she knew not where,
And Kilmeny had seen what she could not declare;
Kilmeny had been where the cock never crew,
Where the rain never fell, and the wind never blew;
But it seemed as the harp of the sky had rung,
And the airs of heaven played round her tongue,
When she spoke of the lovely forms she had seen,
And a land where sin had never been;
A land of love and a land of light,
Without sun, or moon, or night;
Where the river swayed a living stream,
And the night a pure and cloudless beam:
The land of vision it would seem,
And still an everlasting dream.[20]

It is not hot, or cold; nobody talks; nothing is wrong or
right; there is beautiful music.

So the land where Diamond is, at the back of the
north wind, is a kind of limbo. It is clearly not paradise,
but one of the way stations. When you want to know
about anybody there, you climb a tree and wait to see
what happens. Diamond looks for his mother, and sees
her crying; then the land shrinks as if it were a map, and
he steps across the whole country, and finds North Wind
again. She flies him southward and home. His absence
seems to him to have lasted for years, but only seven days
have passed: here is another of MacDonald's dream-like
distortions of time. When Diamond comes to himself,
his mother is there; he has been very ill, and she had
thought him dead. He has, an adult reader can see, been
to death's door and come back again. In an earlier story,
"The Shadows," [21] MacDonald had told of an artist, sick
almost to death, and of the way the shadows in his room,

flickering in the firelight, become personages and take
him with them on two long night journeys flying over
England and Scotland and the sea, to Iceland, where they
hold a kind of conventicle and report on what they have
been doing. "The Shadows" is a kind of preliminary sketch
for what later became a major theme of *At the Back of
the North Wind*.

After this episode, North Wind reappears three times
more. Once she takes Diamond to the stable to hear a
dialogue between Mr. Raymond's lazy horse, Ruby, and
the good horse, Old Diamond. A second time, near the
very end of the story, she dances with Diamond in an
attic, and talks to him again:

> "Please, dear North Wind," he said, "I am so happy
> that I'm afraid it's a dream. How am I to know that
> it's not a dream?"
>
> "What does it matter?" returned North Wind.
>
> "I should cry," said Diamond.
>
> "But why should you cry? The dream, if it is a
> dream, is a pleasant one, is it not?"
>
> "That's just why I want it to be true . . . it's for
> you, North Wind: I can't bear to find it a dream
> because then I should lose you. You would be nobody
> then, and I could not bear that. You ain't a dream,
> are you, dear North Wind? Do say *No*, else I shall
> cry, and come awake, and you'll be gone for ever."

She also explains that the country he had visited had
been only a picture of the country at the back of the
north wind, and that the real one is much more beautiful,
and that he may see it very soon. On her last visit, she
takes him out at night, and he sings a comforting song to
a lady who is sorrowing at an open window. North Wind

takes Diamond back to revisit his old stable and the Coleman's old house; but although he anticipates this with great pleasure, he finds it a letdown: the spirit has left it with the people. A few days later, everybody thinks that Diamond is dead. But the narrator knows that he has gone to the back of the north wind.

Whatever her size, North Wind has beautiful eyes, long deliciously fragrant hair, and a splendid bosom, to which she often clasps Diamond. She is usually tender and affectionate with him; on one occasion she settles with him into the nest at the top of the beech tree, and "placed him on her lap, and began to hush him as if he were her own baby, and Diamond was so entirely happy that he did not care to speak a word." He loves her dearly, and in this capacity she has the motherly qualities of MacDonald's mythic grandmother or earth-mother. (The location of Diamond's nest in a beech tree is also no accident.)

But North Wind also has her "work" that she must do. Once she transforms herself into a grim wolf and terrifies an incompetent nursemaid who has been drinking and frightening the baby in her charge; the next day the nurse's employers will discharge her. In "The Shadows," the shadows do the same sort of thing, terrifying a potential murderer into not committing the crime he intends, reproving a neglectful mother, and the like. Sometimes North Wind takes care of a bee caught in a blossom. Sometimes she sinks great ships, and people think her cruel; but

"I can do nothing cruel, although I often do what looks cruel to those who do not know what I am

really doing. The people they say I drown, I only
carry away to—to—to—well, the back of the North
Wind."

She does not know how she gets her assignments; she just
does what she must do. East Wind has told her that "it
is all managed by a baby," but North Wind does not know
whether or not to believe it.

By now we feel ourselves at home in the MacDonald
mythology. Evil is only the shape that good takes if we
but knew it. And a baby is in charge: this is the divine
child who was the Old Man of the Fire in "The Golden
Key," the Christ-symbol.

> "People," [says North Wind at another time,] "call
> me by dreadful names, and think they know all about
> me. But they don't. Sometimes they call me Bad
> Fortune, sometimes Evil Chance, sometimes Ruin;
> and they have another name for me which they think
> the most dreadful of all."
>
> "What is that?" asked Diamond, smiling up in her
> face.
>
> "I won't tell you that name. Do you remember
> having to go through me to get into the country at
> my back? . . . You were very near knowing what
> they call me then."

North Wind does not tell Diamond what it is, but the
reader will of course know that it is Death. But just as
she is not any of the other things they call her, North
Wind is not precisely Death either: she is a divine
motherly messenger, with a wind's work to do. But the
death of which she sometimes does the work, is the good,

the welcome death of *Phantastes* and "The Golden Key,"
the death that is a reunion with the cosmos and mother
earth, the death that is not to be feared but sought.

Diamond is preternaturally good: he loves everybody,
and is always eager to help, simple, and kind. It comes as
a surprise to the reader when Nanny, the realistic little
crossing-sweeper,

". . . tapped her forehead in a significant manner,"
when talking to Mr. Raymond, and

"the cabbies call him God's baby," she whispered.
"He's not right in the head you know. A tile loose."
Still Diamond, though he heard every word, and
understood it too, kept on smiling. What could it
matter what people called him, so long as he did
nothing he ought not to do? And besides, *God's baby*
was surely the best of names.

Diamond is a Christ-like child, then, God's baby (his
father's name is Joseph, his mother's Mary) whom people
think silly—not Mr. Raymond who thinks him a genius,
but those of coarser clay like Nanny and the cabmen—
a model of divine simplicity, who does not care what
people say of him, who lives only for others, who is indeed
too good for this real world, which he must leave. We
shall encounter heroes like him in several of MacDonald's
novels.

The real world, in *At the Back of the North Wind,* is a
tough place indeed. When North Wind first talks to Diamond, through the knothole before he has ever seen her,
he asks her " 'Why don't you make a window into Mr.
Dyves's bed? . . . he must have a nicer bed than I have,
though mine is *very* nice, so nice that I couldn't wish a
better.' " And North Wind answers " 'Nobody makes a

window into an ash-pit . . . It's not the bed I care about; it's what is in it.'" Mr. Dyves (who is not a character in the book and is never mentioned again) is clearly *Dives*, the rich man, and MacDonald has nothing good to say of the rich, except for Mr. Raymond. North Wind tells Diamond that "'every man ought to be a gentleman and your father is one,'" and when Nanny has been ill in this hospital she is like a lady: "she might have had a lady and a gentleman for a father and mother"—radical doctrine indeed for the late 1860's in England.

Nanny's guardian, Old Sal, is a drunken wretch, who forces the child to turn over all her earnings as a crossing-sweeper, and will not get out of bed late at night to let her in to their squallid cellar, but keeps her out in the cold wind. Policemen are always moving Nanny on, just as they had done with her literary ancestor, little Jo, the crossing-sweeper in *Bleak House:* her cry is the same as his, "'They're always at it.'" She and Diamond have to take a nap in a barrel, huddled together for warmth. Nanny explains to Diamond why she does not commit suicide.

> "When I think of it, I always want to see what's coming next, and so I always wait until next is over. Well! I suppose there's somebody happy somewheres. But it ain't in them carriages. Oh my! *how* they *do* look sometimes—fit to bite your head off!"

The drunken cabman, shamed by Diamond's kindness to his baby, stays away from pubs for a week, "hard as it was to avoid it, seeing a certain rich brewer had built one, like a trap to catch souls and bodies in, at almost every corner he had to pass on his way home." [22] The roughness of the slum-dwellers is matched by the bullies

among the cabmen who do not know Diamond, and by
the street toughs who beat up crossing-sweepers. Diamond, we are told, remains pure, despite the foul language of the stablemen. One wonders how many of the
Victorian parents who made *At the Back of the North
Wind* such a success by giving it to their children knew
what incendiary material was in it. Novels of social in-
dignation were by no means rare in the late 1860's, but
they were seldom, like *At the Back of the North Wind,*
books ostensibly for children, tricked out in lavishly gilt-
stamped cloth, with a little girl on the front cover looking
out of a window in the moon.

There are three interpolated fairy-tales in *At the Back
of the North Wind:* Diamond and Nanny each has a
dream, and Mr. Raymond tells the story of "Little Daylight," often afterwards reprinted separately. Diamond
dreams of falling asleep in a rose garden, and being summoned to the sky by children's voices calling from behind
the surface of the stars. The way up (as so often) proves
to be a way down: via a staircase leading into the earth:
of turf and moss, "a nice stair, so cool and soft—all the
sides as well as the steps grown with moss and grass and
ferns." At the foot he emerges onto a hillside, where the
naked little boy-angels greet him. They dig for stars in the
hillside; when they dig them up, they look through the
star-holes down to earth again: this is how they had called
Diamond in the first place. When one finds a color he
likes, he throws himself through the star-hole into space.
There are no little girl-angels, but the captain of the little
boys tells Diamond that he believes the little girls come
around later and polish the stars they have dug up. This
cloying little fantasy reintroduces the familiar theme of
a passage through mother earth providing the way to

heaven, forewarns us that Diamond is to die, and illustrates once more the futility of trying to make life in heaven seem amusing even for a child.

Nanny dreams that the moon descends to her while she is in a summerhouse in a garden, and that a little old man steps out of a door in the side of it and summons her in. Inside, the moon is a charming little house with blue windows and white curtains and the mistress of the place looking out of one of them; it takes off from the grounds, and Nanny and the old man look back at the earth through the windows. Her work is to keep the windows polished. The moon is full of passages, and at the end of one Nanny listens at a door, and hears a hum: my lady's bees, that collect honey from the stars. While cleaning the windows on the outside of the moon, Nanny climbs into the room where the bees are kept and accidentally lets them out, contrary to orders. The lady of the moon is angry, and says that Nanny won't do, that she is only fit for the mud; and she wakes up pulling at a ring she has been loaned by a kind visiting lady at the hospital; the moon-lady says she has stolen it. This dream, with its cruel touches of orders disobeyed and frustration, suggests that Nanny herself fears that she is not ready for the peaceful motherly interior of the moon, with its attendant lady, and that she has the guilt feelings of the poor: she is fit only for mud, she has stolen the ring.

Mr. Raymond's story of "Little Daylight" tells of the princess at whose christening the wicked fairy requires that she sleep all day; the good one balances it by allowing her to be awake all night; the wicked one condemns her to wax and wane with the moon; the good one provides that when a prince shall kiss her, not knowing the truth, she will be released from the enchantment. When the prince does kiss her, in her wretched waning phase, he murmurs "Mother, mother! Poor mother!"; her lips are withered. After the kiss she is young and beautiful at once. To an ordinary fairy-tale of the enchantment-at-the-christening and the loathly-lady type, MacDonald has added two elements: the nature-myth that has the princess waxing and waning and the prince's kissing her out of filial pity, which turns into something quite different. Very similar to "Little Daylight" in some respects, though much longer and more developed, is the last fairy-tale MacDonald wrote, "The History of Photogen and Nycteris, a day and night Mährchen," in which there is not only a night-blooming princess but a day-blooming prince.[23]

Although *At the Back of the North Wind* has strikingly original features, it is much too long: MacDonald, one feels, did not quite know how to bring it to an end— a serious fault in his fiction generally—and there are many dull moments and oversentimentalities that prevent its reaching the level of his very best work. Yet it is unique among his stories for its combination of realism and fantasy. After completing it, he wrote purely in one vein or the other, but never in both within the framework of the same tale.

V

Second only in reputation and popularity to *At the Back of the North Wind,* and a better work of art, is *The Princess and the Goblin.* Princess Irene, eight years old, when the story begins, lives in a "large house, half castle half farmhouse" on the side of a mountain quite far from her father's capital. Her mother is dead. In the caverns under the mountain lives a race of goblins, who—the legend runs—had long ago been people, but who went underground because of their discontent with the laws of the kingdom, and who had now evolved into hideous, clever, mischievous gnomes with very hard heads and very soft feet. They have grotesque and horrible domestic animals, the product of a peculiar evolutionary process. For fear of the goblins the princess may never venture out at night. On a rainy day, Irene runs upstairs and along a corridor and up some more stairs into a tower she has never seen before, and finds a beautiful old lady, also named Irene, her great-great-grandmother, spinning; she keeps pigeons and eats their eggs, and has her crown in her bedroom. The princess' nurse will not believe in her existence, and when Irene tries to find her grandmother's stair again she cannot.

A miner's boy named Curdie, about twelve years old, rescues the princess and the nurse when they stay out too late one afternoon and the goblins begin to frighten them. As an experienced worker underground, Curdie knows that the goblins cannot bear singing, and he makes up short rhyming verses extempore to keep them off. The nurse will not allow the princess to give him the kiss she has promised him as a reward for his kindness and bravery. Curdie listens unseen to a meeting of goblin strategists underground: they intend to flood the mine but only if some other plan of theirs is frustrated. He keeps trying to overhear what this is, and eventually the goblins capture him: they wall him in, and plan to leave him there to starve, although the savage goblin queen would prefer to throw him to the beasts.

Meanwhile, Irene's father the king has visited her. He does not know about the grandmother, and the princess concludes that she was only a dream, but one moonlit night she wakes from the pain in a pricked finger and finds her way back up the stairs: she would have found grandmother sooner if she hadn't come to think it had been a dream. Great-grandmother is spinning spider-webs, which her pigeons bring her from over the sea; she works only on moonlit nights, and she is spinning the thread for Irene. She shows Irene her beautiful bed-room:

> It was large and lofty and domed-shaped. From the centre hung a lamp as round as a ball, shining as if with the brightest moonlight, which made everything visible in the room, though not so clearly that the princess could tell what many of the things were. A large oval bed stood in the middle, with a coverlid of rose-color, and velvet curtains all around it of a lovely pale blue. The walls were also blue—spangled all over with what looked like stars of silver.

Grandmother heals her sore hand, invites her to spend the night with her, and tells her that " 'if that light were to go out, you would fancy yourself lying in a bare garret, on a heap of old straw, and would not see one of the pleasant things round about you all the time.' " The prin-cess wakes up in her own bed next morning. She is to come back in a week.

When the night comes, one of the horrible goblin crea-tures jumps in at the open window; the princess' faith in her grandmother's reality fails her, and she rushes out onto the mountain side. But from there she catches sight of her grandmother's lamp, and finds her once more. This time, the bedroom is almost transformed, and what she had taken for a huge bouquet of roses on a low stand against the wall was in fact a fire which burned in the shapes of the loveliest and reddest roses, glowing gorgeously between the heads and wings of two cherubs of shining silver. And when she came nearer, she found that the smell of roses, with which the room was filled, came from the fire-roses on the hearth. Her grandmother was dressed in the loveliest pale-blue velvet, over which her hair, no longer white, but of a rich gold colour, streamed like a cataract, here falling in dull gathered heaps, there rushing away in smooth shining falls . . . It flowed from under the edge of a circle of shining silver, set with alternated pearls and opals. On her dress was no ornament whatever, neither was there a ring on her hand, or a necklace or carcanet about her neck. But her slippers glimmered with the light of the Milky-way, for they were covered with seed-pearls and opals in one mass. Her face was that of a woman of three-and-twenty.

Grandmother tells Irene that she has the gift of seeing the great lamp, and hopes that one day everybody will have it. She gives the princess an opal ring and a small ball of the thread she has spun; then she purifies the thread in the fire of roses, and puts it away in a cabinet; she has fastened the end of the thread to the ring:

If you ever find yourself in any danger . . . you must take off your ring and put it under the pillow of your bed. Then you must lay your forefinger, the same that wore the ring, upon the thread, and follow the thread wherever it leads.

When her nurse sees the ring, she tells Irene she has had
it a long time, but remarks that it is glowing unusually
brightly.

Frightened by the sound of a cat-and-dog-fight, Irene
follows her grandmother's counsel. The thread leads her
along a stream-bed into the mine, and finally to a pile of
stones underground; it goes into the pile: on the other
side Curdie is imprisoned. She moves the stones, and sets
him free and, still following the thread, leads him back to
the castle garden. Curdie is astonished at her having
found him and baffled at her success in following the passages in the mine by the use of a thread he cannot see or
feel. When they get back to the castle, the thread takes
the princess, and the princess takes Curdie, up the stairs
to her grandmother's room.

Though grandmother is there, Curdie cannot see her,
or the fire of roses, or the blue bed, or the lamp: all he
sees is

> a big bare garret-room . . . a tub, and a heap of
> musty straw, and a withered apple, and a ray of
> sunlight coming through a hole in the middle of the
> roof and shining on your head. . . .

Nor can he hear her talking to her grandmother; all he
hears is the cooing of pigeons. He is hurt at what he takes
to be the princess' making game of him; she is troubled
that he cannot believe her. Grandmother reassures her:
in time he will understand. The thread is magically returned to Irene, and her ring too, for use another time.
Grandmother gives her a refreshing bath that makes her
blissful.

When Curdie gets home and tells his story, his mother
persuades him that there may be some things he cannot

see. Long ago she herself had been saved from the goblins by one of the white pigeons that belonged to the grandmother, and by the great lamp. Curdie now thinks the goblins are intending to undermine the castle and steal the princess, in order to marry her to their own prince. On one of his exploring trips, he is wounded by one of the royal guards and brought into the castle in a fever to recuperate. Nobody will believe his warnings about the goblins. But they are by now right under the castle and dig their way into the wine cellar. Curdie tries to get up from his bed and hold them off, but for a time he can only dream that he is awake. Grandmother comes to his room with her ointment and heals him. He rushes downstairs to find the goblins already in the house; they have swarmed in and overpowered the guards. Curdie gets the guards on their feet again; he teaches them to sing and to stamp on the goblins' feet. He disperses the invaders, but the princess has disappeared. Suddenly Curdie finds the thread, which leads him back to his own house. There the princess is, in the care of his mother; the thread has brought her there also. He is now convinced she has been telling him the truth. Irene is restored to her father, who sees to it that Curdie gets the kiss she had promised him long ago.

In the end, the goblins let loose the torrent underground, but Curdie's prompt action saves the entire royal household, and grandmother sends a pigeon to assure them of her own safety. The king takes the princess away, and Curdie returns to his parents; the king promises to send his mother a red petticoat. The goblins are either drowned, or leave the country, or change in character, becoming like Scotch brownies.

While we recognize the goblins as *Elementargeister,*

and realize that debt that MacDonald owed to Novalis and Hoffmann for his interest in mines and mining, we none the less find *The Princess and the Goblin* altogether fresh and original. The goblins are more complex than those in *Phantastes* or in "The Carasoyn," suggesting the greedy, cunning side of our own human nature tunneling away in the secret subterranean chambers of the sub-conscious and always threatening to take possession of the castle of our minds, unless we, like Curdie, remain on our guard against them, with the aid of our higher selves, which dwell like grandmother in the lofty towers of our personalities. MacDonald's own mythological crea-tion, the grandmotherly goddess, is a complete success, perhaps better realized than any of the many counter-parts that had preceded her. She is less lachrymose and much less sentimental than Anodos' earth-mother; beauti-ful, not blind and somewhat repellant, like the old woman in "The Carasoyn"; not so solemn and cosmologically symbolic as the grandmother in "The Golden Key"; not so supernatural as North Wind. Her pigeons bring her the stuff she spins with, as the hen Jenny does in "The Cara-soyn," but what she spins is more complicated than the thread of poesy, although it is that too.

The thread that takes the princess to Curdie's rescue and leads both her and him to the miner's cottage after the catastrophe of the goblin invasion is also the thread of faith or love. It is the princess' substitute for the golden key. The princess has suspended disbelief; she believes that her grandmother exists; she believes that she must put herself unquestioningly in her grandmother's care, and follow where the thread leads her. Curdie cannot at first see anything in the tower room; he has not suspended disbelief and yielded to poetic rather than literal truth;

he has no faith; he cannot see the thread. But his mother shakes his literal-mindedness, and at the end the thread comes to him; he has not yet seen the grandmother, but he believes in her. All the imagery connected with the grandmother is beautiful and soothing: MacDonald has realized her gentle power and her charm. Yet she has character; she does more than spin and tell stories; she heals and refreshes. Her lamp and her pigeons, her spinning wheel and her heavenly chamber combine into a harmonious vision of benevolence.

Despite the ugliness of the goblins, and the savagery especially of the goblin queen, there is very little horrible in *The Princess and the Goblin*. A child reader feels that the forces of evil exist, but knows they can be surmounted. Cruelty is limited to stepping on the goblins' tender feet, or to the threat that Curdie will be starved to death. The hideous goblin beasts are not very frightening; they are, however, with the air-fish-aeranths of "The Golden Key," the most explicit example since "The Hidden Life" of MacDonald's Boehmian-Blakeian-Novalisian evolutionary theories. He says of them:

> No one understands animals who does not see that every one of them, even among the fishes, it may be with a dimness and vagueness infinitely remote, yet shadows the human: in the case of these, the human resemblance had greatly increased; while their owners had sunk toward them, they had risen toward their owners.

The concept of a *two*-way evolution: the degeneration of people into beasts, in addition to the transformation of beasts into people, is something that MacDonald had never made explicit before, although when North Wind frightened the drunken nurse she had taken the shape of a wolf, because, she explained, the shape of a wolf was growing inside the nurse. We shall soon find this concept even more thoroughly worked out.

Even in this fairy-tale we find a little social comment: Curdie is a self-respecting "noble" miner's boy, who is respectful but not awed by princess or king. Both of them treat Curdie as a friend without embarrassment or tension. The nurse, on the other hand, though she loves the princess, has the servant-class attitude that Curdie is socially inferior to her mistress and does what she can to prevent her giving him his well-deserved kiss. The princess is thoroughly child-like; but she is not unbelievably good like Diamond; she has her pride, and MacDonald has so charmingly realized her various conversations and conflicts and reconciliations with her nurse that even a twentieth-century adult reader enjoys them. She has also her fully developed conception of honor: princesses keep their words.

George MacDonald himself, while he was writing *The Princess and the Goblin,* felt it to be "the most complete thing I have done." We share this view. Ironically enough, in view of the book's later success, Alexander Strahan, the publisher of *Good Words for the Young,* was worried about the failure of the magazine to make money, and attributed it in part to "too much of the fairy element" in the stories that MacDonald was writing for it.[24]

The Wise Woman (1875) is a sad falling-off. It concerns two horrid children, one a princess, Rosamond, and the other, Agnes, a shepherd's daughter. Both suffer from the illusion that they are Somebody. Rosamond is greedy and selfish, is never satisfied with her toys, is cruel to her pets, and has a terrible temper. Agnes, though poor, has been spoiled by her parents' admiration for her; they quote her every remark as if it were memorable. There is nothing to choose between the folly of the two sets of parents or the nastiness of the children: "What is there to choose between a face distorted to hideousness by anger, and one distorted to silliness by self-complacency?" Both are taken in hand by the wise woman, a figure we already know very well indeed. She tames Rosamond, at first by terror: "For when people will be naughty they have to be frightened, and they are not expected to like it." But though the wise woman makes her work, starves her, and allows her by magic to be substituted for Agnes, the cure is far from complete. The great shepherd dog terrifies her "almost to death," and is very rough with her, but she comes to love him. Her disobedience persists even though it leads her into a dangerous bog and exposure to savage beasts, and only after three attempts in the wise woman's "mood chamber" and two failures does she show even the faintest consideration for others. Her regeneration, however, finally gets under way.

Agnes is even worse. The wise woman puts her into a hollow sphere, where she has to make her own acquaintance, but she is just as smug when released. She escapes by magic into the royal palace, sure that she will be welcomed there as the lost princess, but instead is made a scullery maid and roughly treated. Her parents are summoned; the king and queen interrogate them fiercely. The servants bring in Agnes, "white as death and mean as sin": she has been planning to profit by her knowledge of Rosamond's whereabouts. At the end, the wise woman intervenes, blasting the king and queen with blindness;

while she condemns the shepherd family to have Agnes back; she puts Agnes' father into a deep sleep; so that only the mother is now responsible.

The wise woman, who ought always to be all-successful, has not altered Agnes at all, after all her efforts, and has only partly reformed Rosamond. Instead of the benevolence of all her predecessors in MacDonald's gallery of mother-goddesses, she has cruelty as her only weapon: frightening and hurting the children, blinding the parents or putting them to sleep, although with her supernatural knowledge she has known for years of their troubles and weaknesses, and has done nothing about them. Yet MacDonald seems to feel that these are proper methods, and somehow that her wisdom has succeeded. Instead of the simple paraphernalia of lamp, spinning wheel, and pigeons or hen or air-fish, the wise woman has an elaborate addition to her doorless cottage, where pictures are hung, into which the children both step by crossing the frame; the hollow sphere, the mood-chamber, all her complicated devices prove ineffectual. Grandmother has lost her power; she can do nothing now but strike out cruelly, and her blows do not achieve their purpose. The story makes the social statement unusual for MacDonald, that the poor are sometimes even worse than the rich. One can hardly believe that the same man wrote *The Wise Woman* and *The Princess and the Goblin*.[25]

The Princess and Curdie shows him regaining the power of *The Princess and the Goblin* but not its mood. It begins where *The Princess and the Goblin* leaves off, and opens with a rhapsody on the glories of the mountains and the mines that might have come straight from Novalis or Tieck or Hoffmann:

> But the inside [of the mountains], who shall tell what
> lies there? Caverns of awfullest solitude, their walls
> miles thick, sparkling with ores of gold or silver,
> copper or iron, tin or mercury, studded perhaps
> with precious stones—perhaps a brook, with eyeless
> fish in it, running, running ceaseless and cold and
> babbling, through banks crusted with carbuncles
> and golden topazes, or over a gravel of which some
> of the stones are rubies and emeralds, perhaps dia-
> monds and sapphires . . . all waiting to flash, wait-
> ing for millions of ages. . . .

But Curdie is becoming commonplace without the pressure to do great deeds. He thoughtlessly shoots a pigeon
with his bow and arrow, and then, in remorse, fearing
that it may be one that had belonged to the princess's
grandmother, he runs up the tower stair of the castle and
finds her, in one of her very old phases, spinning. She
rebukes him for his thoughtless act: " 'Whoever does not
mean good is always in danger of harm,' " she tells him,
and " 'When people don't care to be better, they must be
doing everything wrong.' " This is Curdie's first interview
with grandmother, but soon she appears to Curdie and
his father Peter in the mine itself, young and beautiful,
and this time dressed in green velvet, with emeralds as
her ornament.

She explains to them that they are of royal blood, and
Curdie is to accept a mission for her. He visits her tower
again, and she has him thrust his hands and arms into the
fire of roses. It hurts, but it makes him sensitive, and gives
him a remarkable gift. Henceforth, when he grasps a
man's hand, he will be able to tell what sort of beast the
man is becoming:

"Have you ever heard what some philosophers say
—that men were all animals once?"

"No, ma'am."

". . . all men, if they do not take care, go down
hill to the animal's country; . . . many men are
actually, all their lives, going to be beasts . . . it
is always what they *do*, whether in their minds or
in their bodies, that makes men go down to be less
than men . . . the change always comes first in their
hands—and first of all in the inside hands, to which
the outside ones are but as gloves. They do not
know it . . . you will . . . feel the foot of the beast
he is growing, just as if there were no gloves made
like a man's hand between you and it."

Grandmother introduces to Curdie a hideous beast,
a kind of combination dog, dragon, snake, and bear,
named Lina, who is attending on her; when she gives
Curdie her paw, she has the hand of a human child.
Curdie's mission is to go to the royal court.

He crosses a blasted heath: Lina joins him, arriving
from the air, sent as an emissary from grandmother to
accompany him on his journey. They pass through a
forest, where Lina conquers forty-nine grotesque creatures each uglier than she. They follow a river valley,
until they come to the capital city of Gwyntystorm, rising
on a cliff above the stream. It once had mighty fortifications, but these have been neglected:

No man pretended to love his neighbour, but every
one said he knew that peace and quiet behaviour
was the best thing for himself, and that, he said, was
quite as useful, and a great deal more reasonable.

The city was prosperous and rich, and if anybody was not comfortable, everybody else said he ought to be.

The very decay of the fortifications the inhabitants regard as the best proof of their prosperity:

> Commerce and self-interest, they said, had got the better of violence, and the troubles of the past were whelmed in the riches that flowed in at their open gates. Indeed there was one sect of philosophers which taught that it would be better to forget all the past history of the city, were it not that its former imperfections taught its present inhabitants how superior they and their times were, and enabled them to glory over their ancestors.

In Gwyntystorm almost everybody is unfriendly. To do a favor for a baker Curdie takes up his miner's mattock, and breaks a stone over which the baker always trips. A fragment shatters the window of a barber shop, and the barber instantly demands to be paid: as Curdie gives him the money he finds that the barber's hand is a monkey's paw. Butchers' dogs attack Lina, who kills two of them, and the butchers demand to be allowed to kill her in revenge. The entire town is frightened of the beast, and the inn closes its doors. A nice old woman with a little grandchild opens her house to them: "because she never gossiped or quarreled, or chaffered in the market, but went without what she could not afford, the people called her a witch. . . ." Barricaded in the house, Lina escapes, but Curdie is put into prison: ". . . the people of Gwyntystorm always gave themselves an hour of pleasure after their second breakfast, and what greater

pleasure could they have than to see a stranger abused
by the officers of justice?" Curdie cannot reconcile conditions in Gwyntystorm with the nobility of the princess'
father the king, whom he had known.

He begins to understand when Lina makes her way
back to him, and he digs their way out of the cell, and into
the wine cellar of the royal palace next door. The servants
are drunk; the place is dirty and full of rats: the hands
of the servants reveal that they are turning into oxen,
pigs, or other animals. Upstairs Curdie meets the princess,
now nine or ten; she tells him that the king has been desperately ill for a year, but the illness has been kept secret.
The doctor who is in charge of the king has a hand like
the belly of a creeping thing; he is drugging the king with
bad wine, and Curdie manages to substitute good, and to
procure good bread. In fact the royal officials have con-
spired to take over the kingdom, but the king recovers
enough to refuse to sign papers without reading them.
The decay of the whole kingdom and its principles had
made the king despondent and led to his illness. Among
the thieving, quarrelsome bestial servants Curdie finds
one honest serving maid, whom he enlists on his side.
Lina helps him and marshals the dreadful beasts she has
conquered to make war on the villains.

The revenge is savage: as the doctor is about to give
the king another draft of poison, Lina with one "scrunch,
. . . crushed the bone" of his leg "like a stick of celery."
The beasts with delight inflict upon the servants positively
scatological punishment:

> . . . the scorpion kept grabbing at their legs with
> his huge pincers, a three-foot centipede kept screw-
> ing up their bodies, nipping as he went . . . they

were bespattered with the dirt of their own neglect;
they were soused in the stinking water that had
boiled greens; they were smeared with rancid drip-
ping; their faces were rubbed in maggots; I dare
not tell all that was done to them.

All these beasts had once been people: one, a round ball-
shaped object, had been "a gluttonous alderman whom
nature had treated homoeopathically." Having routed the
servants, the beasts clean up the palace, and Curdie
manages to thwart the conspirators: the leg-serpent coils
around the chamberlain's bed and squeezes and bites
him, leaving him in a crushed cage that had been the
bedstead. Another villain is wrapped around and around
in the web spun by a gigantic spider. The leg-serpent
moves against the clergy of Gwyntystorm: one of them
who is preaching on the text "every one should take care
of that One. Honesty is the best policy" is snatched from
the pulpit by the leg-serpent, and goes mad: "in his par-
oxysms he jabbered sense."

Curdie finances a counterblow by summoning miners
to work on the rich ore that lies beneath the capital.
Grandmother appears (the loyal housemaid was she all
along), and heals the king by putting him into the fire of
roses. The king, a loyal officer, Curdie, and the beasts
destroy the Gwyntystorm legion of butchers, dogs, and
disloyal former guardsmen; and then, with the aid of
thousands of grandmother's pigeons, they rout an invad-
ing force from the neighboring kingdom, suborned by
the wicked chamberlain, Curdie's father Peter arriving
for the *coup de grâce*. None but men whose hands are
human may now run the government; the gold in the
ground gives the kingdom its fortune. Lina disappears

into the fire of roses. Grandmother stays on in the palace.
Irene and Curdie are married.

But this grim book is not allowed to close on a tradi-
tional note of joy.

> The old king died and they were king and queen.
> As long as they lived, Gwyntystorm was a better
> city, and good people grew in it. But they had no
> children, and when they died the people chose a
> king. And the new king went mining and mining in
> the rock under the city, and grew more and more
> eager after the gold, and paid less and less heed to
> his people. Rapidly they sunk towards their old
> wickedness.

He chips away at the pillars that support the city to get
more and more gold, and eventually brings the whole
city down:

> The cries of men and the shrieks of women went up
> with its dust, and then there was a great silence.
> Where the mighty rock once towered, crowded with
> houses and crowned with a palace, now rushes and
> raves a stone-obstructed rapid of the river. All around
> spreads a wilderness of wild deer, and the very name
> of Gwyntystorm has ceased from the lips of men.

The Princess and Curdie, MacDonald's last sustained
effort at a fairy-tale, shows him in an apocalyptic mood,
striking out at what he hates, and convinced that evil
triumphs in the end. Not even goodness serves to set
things right. Why should Irene and Curdie not have had
children? Only because MacDonald wanted to destroy
Gwyntystorm. What has happened to the power of grand-

mother, presented in the early chapters in the mine in all her glory as the "Mother of Lights," an extraordinary phrase for MacDonald, who often refers to God as the "Father o' lichts"? Why should she have been powerless against the new evil? Suddenly even the mother-goddess has become ineffectual. In *The Wise Woman* the children stay wicked despite her. In *The Princess and Curdie,* the last and most delightful of his great mother-goddesses simply vanishes. We never hear what happens to her or why she has not intervened to combat wickedness.

Even if the book had ended with the marriage of the princess and Curdie, it would still have been a savage satire on human nature. The hideous beasts, like Lina, who was once "a woman that was naughty, but is now growing good," are all now on the side of good: they are growing more human again, so much so that in fact they are far better than people who retain human shape but are becoming beasts and are on the side of evil. Those on the way up are better than those on the way down, a profoundly depressing way of saying that animals are really better than human beings. This is the ultimate transformation that MacDonald makes in the mystic theory of evolution that he took from Novalis.

In the descriptions of the people of Gwyntystorm and their beliefs and behavior, MacDonald is satirizing the England of his day. In all that he wrote, this is almost his only piece of direct political comment. He obviously believes that the high tide of prosperity has caused England to forget its defenses, and that the money-grubbing selfishness of individual Englishmen will one day lead them to ruin. As often, the best people are the poor: the old woman who takes Curdie in when he is being persecuted by the others and Curdie's own parents. Grandmother says to Peter that it is she who has kept him poor, because

> Things come to the poor that can't get in at the door
> of the rich. Their money somehow blocks it up. It
> is a great privilege to be poor, Peter,—one that no
> man ever coveted, and but a very few sought to
> retain, but one that yet many have learned to prize.[26]

But Curdie and his family must also be given royal blood, to make him eligible for the princess. The punishment meted out to the wicked, with all its revolting imagery, somehow must have satisfied the violent aggressions in MacDonald, often in his novels, as we shall see, also directed against servants as a breed, but never so roughly as here.

Early in the book, before Curdie leaves home for Gwyntystorm, he is stopped at the open gate of the king's castle by an insolent housekeeper who shows him the great house key as the symbol of her authority and tries to bar his way into the house because he is "an out-of-doors labourer." Here MacDonald is reverting to the parable of "the castle": the dwelling itself is the house of the king (God); the insolent housekeeper trying to exclude the poor is the church; the grandmother, to whom Curdie eventually wins his way, is a partial revelation of divine grace. Yet, as so often in MacDonald, the allegory dissolves: the king himself, when we meet him, is not God but a helpless, sick old man.

The joyfulness of *The Princess and the Goblin* has evaporated, and the charged, enchanted atmosphere that enveloped that book, and deprived even its ugly goblins of their power to frighten, has been replaced by a choking pessimistic gloom, in which, even when the forces of evil fly in disorder, it is only to regroup and triumph in the end. *The Princess and Curdie* is not a children's book in any ordinary sense. The princess of the earlier tale, with her preoccupations with her toys, her walks, her nurse, her responses to the beauties of the world, and her child-like dignity, now plays almost no role. She is a helpless little girl, waiting for a rescue that proves both temporary and illusory. MacDonald wrote like a man in despair, not resigned, but angry with an anger he felt to be futile.

CHAPTER 4

Three Theological Novels

". . . it is in exactly the same sense in which we pity
a man who has missed the whole of Keats or Milton that
we can feel compassion for the critic who has not
walked in the forest of Phantastes or made the acquaintance of Mr. Cupples in the adventures of Alec
Forbes."

G. K. CHESTERTON, Introduction to *GMDW*

"*Alec Forbes* . . . is very enjoyable, and the character of Annie Anderson one of the most delightful I
have ever met with in fiction. The Scotch dialect, too,
is pleasant enough when one gets a little used to it."

LEWIS CARROLL, *The Diaries of Lewis Carroll*, entry
for January 16, 1866

I

AN AMERICAN CRITIC, writing in 1870 on George Mac-
Donald as "The New Novelist," begins by quoting Frederick Denison Maurice on the importance of novels as a
reflection of men's minds: "All social harmonies and social
contradictions may come forth in the relations of fathers
and children, husbands and wives, brothers and sisters,
masters and servants." Scornfully dismissing Dickens as
one who now arouses only "faint antiquarian interest"
because he has not felt the new currents of the age, he
goes on to describe the age as he sees it:

It is especially a theological age. Its Trollopes and Oliphants must tell us of the Church and her influence upon society—upon her own servants at the altar. Colenso, Darwin, Ecce Homo and essays and reviews have taken the place of Brougham and Macaulay. . . . Never since the close of the Thirty Years War have the politics of Europe been so largely mixed up with questions of religion. Never since the days of Paracelsus have the contacts and antagonisms of science and theology been so keenly felt. The generation has been permeated by the thought of Carlyle, Hare, Arnold, and Ruskin; it has learned in some measure the lesson of earnestness. . . .

He hails MacDonald as presenting "man as the son of a Father in heaven, prospering in his life while he respects that relation and the other human and divine relations that grow out of it, ruining his life and its good by living as if under the restraints of no spiritual household." Though MacDonald may "excite lively dissent by his particular views," and though he may be "preachy," God is real to him, and human life illuminated by his presence, and even the "preachy" passages are "thoughtful studies of human life," not "devout platitudes." Also, he adds, he is the best portrayer of the Scots since Scott.[1]

Let us now make the effort to return to the age in which these novels were written, when the issues with which they dealt literally transcended life and death, since they involved man's salvation. Of the twenty-five or more novels that MacDonald wrote—the count depends on whether one includes as novels certain non-fairy-tales written primarily for children—three in particular emerge as the bearers of his message: *David Elginbrod, Alec*

Forbes of Howglen, and *Robert Falconer.* All belong to
the sixties; all are strongly Scotch in theme. In their own
day these three made MacDonald's reputation for good
or ill, and in ours we find them still the cornerstones of
his achievement as a novelist-theologian.

One evening, probably in 1862, "at an informal supper
of oysters," George MacDonald heard Manby Smith, a
journalist, recite a Scotch epitaph he had read somewhere: "Here lie I, Martin Elginbrodde;/ Hae mercy o'
my soul, Lord God;/ As I wad do, were I Lord God,/ An'
ye were Martin Elginbrodde." Much excited, MacDonald
got Smith to repeat the verses. He later called them the
"germ" of his first novel, *David Elginbrod.* Smith and
Elder and several other London publishers rejected the
manuscript. Finally, a friend of the MacDonalds showed
it to Miss Mulock, who pressed her own publishers, Hurst
and Blackett, to accept it. They paid MacDonald ninety
pounds and published it in 1863.[2] It was the last time
he had difficulty in placing a book.

David Elginbrod has many faults. Disjointed, long-
winded, didactic, with an elaborate plot whose clumsy
mysteries the author himself robs of their effect by flat-
footedly explaining them away at once, it understandably
frightened the publishers. Yet, with all its irritating qualities, it bears the marks of a struggling original talent,
striving within the same novel to combine both the Gothic
and the realistic genres.

In the first book of three, the scene is laid in Scotland,
on the estate called Turriepuffit. Mr. Glasford, the laird,
and his wife have employed as tutor for their sons Hugh
Sutherland, a young man, poor but of an ancient family,
on holiday from the University of Aberdeen. In the fir-
wood on the estate, early in spring, Hugh meets Margaret

Elginbrod, daughter of the laird's estate manager, David, and his wife Janet. Hugh lends Margaret Coleridge's *Poems,* discusses with her and her father the moral problems posed by *The Ancient Mariner,* reads Scott and Wordsworth with them, and teaches them mathematics. The laird's wife objects in vain to Hugh's spending his time with people so humble and discharges Margaret, who has been a maid in the laird's house. Hugh helps with the harvest. He almost becomes one of the Elginbrod family, and David builds him a study of his own, as a lean-to against their cottage. When Margaret is lost in the snow, Hugh finds her, and saves her life. Are they in love? MacDonald says he does not know. Hugh returns to Aberdeen, where the jollity of the life and the pressure of his work lead him almost to neglect writing to David. Finished at the University, he obtains a post as tutor to a family in Sussex; Margaret becomes a lady's maid.

This first book, pastoral and slow-moving, pausing long for detailed descriptions of the fir-wood and the estate in all seasons, reminds the reader of Mrs. Oliphant's first novel, *Passages in the Life of Margaret Maitland,* (1848). MacDonald vividly hits off Scotch country life: the laird who cannot see the beauty of the poppies that grow in the wheat field; the young farm boys who taunt Hugh when he shoulders his scythe because they resent him as a gentleman and are jealous of his success with Margaret; the homely interior of the Elginbrod cottage, with Margaret's bed in the main room, hot potatoes and warm milk as the chief fare eaten with a horn spoon, and the iron lamp holding the burning pith of a rush. The characters ring true: the laird's wife, descendant of a cheating merchant, who has brought a good dowry but is ill-bred; Janet Elginbrod, sharp and brusque, a bit intolerant of all the attention her husband and daughter give to books and learning; and above all David Elginbrod himself.

Earnestly though clumsily, MacDonald, in *David Elginbrod,* is trying to portray his ideal of a noble untaught sage. Within two pages of the story's opening, David says his morning prayer, strong and simple; before Hugh's book-learning he shows "the true humility that comes of worshipping the truth," though Hugh himself "at first did not know that there are many other educations besides a college one. . . ." Although MacDonald shows the reader David's superiority on every occasion, he insists on telling him about it also:

> David was one of those of whom is the kingdom of Heaven. There is a childhood into which we have to grow, just as there is a childhood which we must leave behind; a childlikeness which is the highest gain of humanity, and a childishness from which but few of those who are counted among the wisest among men have freed themselves in their imagined progress toward the reality of things.

In appearance, David is splendid:

> His carriage was full of dignity and a certain rustic refinement; his voice was wonderfully gentle, but deep; and slowest when most impassioned. He seemed to have come of some antediluvian breed; there was something of the Titan slumbering about him. He would have been a stern man, but for an unusual amount of reverence that seemed to over-flood the sternness, and change it into strong love.

His love he shows in his relations with Margaret, whom he gently shields from her mother's rebukes, and in his warmth toward Hugh, the stranger, in whom he recognizes a kindred spirit. When David talks about questions of religion, a "seer-like look" comes over his face,

> and the tears had gathered in his eyes and dimmed their blue. A kind of tremulous pathetic smile flickered about his beautifully curved mouth, like the glimmer of water in a valley, betwixt the lofty acquiline nose and the powerful but finely modelled chin. It seemed as if he dared not let the smile break out, lest it should be followed instantly by a burst of tears.[3]

David has been brought up on the driest possible diet of Scotch Calvinism. On the shelf of the lean-to study that he builds for Hugh, he ranges the few books he has of his own (besides the Bible, which he reads twice a day, from the Old Testament in the morning and the New at night). These books he had inherited from his mother. Probably few nineteenth-century readers of *David Elginbrod* could recognize the titles; now, a hundred years later, they seem to have vanished wholly from our consciousness. Yet just as the character of David Elginbrod clearly reflects MacDonald's idealized memory of his own father, so this little library, which had belonged to David Elginbrod's mother, reflects MacDonald's childhood memories of his own father's mother, the severe and terrifying "Missionar" Calvinist, Isabelle Robertson MacDonald, and of her favorite reading. To run one's eye over David Elginbrod's bookshelves, and to identify and examine each book, noting MacDonald's scornful distaste, takes one at once into the narrow world of his boyhood.[4]

First comes ". . . Boston's *Fourfold State*, in which the ways of God and man may be seen through a fourfold

fog; . . . ." This is *Human Nature in Its Fourfold State,
Of Primitive Integrity, subsisting in The Parents of Mankind in Paradise; Entire Depravation, subsisting in The
Irregenerate; Begun Recovery, subsisting in The Regen-
erate: And Consummate Happiness or Misery, subsisting
in All Mankind in the Future State. In Several Practical
Discourses By the eminently pious and learned Mr.
Thomas Boston, late Minister of the Gospel at Ettrick.*[5]
Boston (1676–1732) dwells lovingly upon the torments
of hell-fire, and urges his readers to consider that these
agonies last forever.

Then follows

> Erskine's *Divine Sonnets,* which will repay the
> reader in laughter for the pain it costs his reverence;
> producing much the same effect that a Gothic ca-
> thedral might, reproduced by the pencil and from
> the remembrance of a Chinese artist, who had seen
> it once; . . . .

This is *Gospel Sonnets; or, Spiritual Songs, in Six Parts.
I. The Believer's Espousals. II. The Believer's Jointure.
III. The Believer's Riddle. IV. The Believer's Lodging.
V. The Believer's Soliloquy. VI. The Believer's Princi-
ples. Concerning Creation and Redemption, Law and
Gospel, Justification and Sanctification, Faith and Sense,
Heaven and Earth,* by the late Rev. Mr. Ralph Erskine
(1685–1754), Minister of the Gospel, at Dunfermline.[6]
Can MacDonald be right: will Erskine really make us
laugh? Let us look only at three stanzas of "Thy Maker
is thy Husband," a long poem on Isaiah 54:5 in "The
Believer's Jointure":

> Yea, thou excell'st in rich attire
> The lamp that lights the globe;

> Thy sparkling garment heav'ns admire,
> > Thy Husband is thy robe.

> This raiment never waxeth old,
> > 'Tis always new and clean;
> From summer heat, and winter cold,
> > Thy Husband can thee screen.

> All who the name of worthies bore
> > Since Adam was undrest,
> No worth acquir'd, but as they wore
> > Thy Husband's purple vest.

We are told that "In dreary days, when religion was dull, dry and negative, [the Gospel Sonnets] secured a welcome and a home for those doctrines of grace which were the supreme concern of both brothers," [7] but we are hard put to it to imagine how religion could ever have been duller, dryer, or more negative than the (so-called) sonnets themselves.

Next on David Elginbrod's shelves stands ". . . *Drelincourt on Death*, with the famous ghost-hoax of Defoe, to help the bookseller to the sale of the unsalable; . . . ." This is *The Christian's Defence against the Fears of Death with Seasonable Directions How to Prepare Ourselves to Die Well, written originally in French by the late Reverend Divine of the Protestant Church of Paris, Charles Drelincourt, Translated into English by Marius D'Assigny, B.D.* To the work of Drelincourt (1595–1669), the publishers have prefaced without attribution Defoe's famous "True Relation of the Apparition of one Mrs. Veal, the next Day after her Death, to one Mrs. Bargrave, at Canterbury, the Eighth of September, 1705," even now anthologized occasionally as an early ghost

story. The publishers add "Which apparition recom-
mends the perusal of Drelincourt's Book of Consolations
against the Fears of Death." [8] We sympathize with Mac-
Donald's jibe that this was done to sell the otherwise unsalable, but note that many editions of Drelincourt's
hundreds of pages of dreary prose were sold *without* the
Defoe anecdote.

There follows ". . . the Scots Worthies, opening of
itself at the memoir of Mr. Alexander Peden; . . . ." This
is *Biographia Scoticana; or a Brief Historical Account of
the Lives, Characters, & Memorable Transactions of the
Most Eminent Scots Worthies, Noblemen, Gentlemen,
Ministers, and Others, Who testified or suffered for the
Reformation in Scotland During the Sixteenth and Seven-
teenth Centuries With an Appendix, Containing a short
Historical Account of the Wicked Lives and Miserable
Deaths of Some of the Most Bloody Persecutors in Scotland,* by John Howie, of Lochgoin.[9] Mr. Alexander
Peden, whose life David Elginbrod's mother (and George
MacDonald's grandmother) had liked so much, was a
seventeenth-century divine. Accused "by a young woman,
as being the father of a child, which she was with" he
prayed for divine guidance; the real father confessed,
and the girl later committed suicide on the spot where
Peden had prayed. Ousted from his pulpit by the Restoration (1660), he laid so powerful an injunction upon the
door of his pulpit that it never would open until another
Presbyterian minister appeared after the Revolution of
1688. Imprisonments, miracles, exiles, conversions, and
true prophecies of doom stud Mr. Peden's edifying life
as duly recorded by his hagiographer; his command of
abuse still impresses a reader: one opponent he calls the
"devil's rattle-bag," another a "railing Rabshakeh." There
was much here for MacDonald to enjoy.

Next comes ". . . the *Pilgrim's Progress,* that wonderful inspiration, failing never save when the theologian *would* sometimes snatch the pen from the hand of the poet, . . .", a tribute expressing MacDonald's old affection for Bunyan, diluted only by disagreement with his theology. And finally, *"Theron and Aspasio; Village Dialogues;* and others of a like class. To this must be added a rare edition of Blind Harry." The first of these is *Theron and Aspasio; or, a Series of Dialogues and Letters upon the Most Important and Interesting Subjects,* by James Hervey, A.M. (1714–1758), rector of Weston-Favel in Northamptonshire. Hervey deals with some of the same subjects as Boston or Erskine: Christ's righteousness, a man's need of acceptance by the Redeemer before anything he does may be considered a good work, the inflexibility of the divine law, and the depravity of human nature. But he dilutes the dose by casting his work in the form of a dialogue between two gentlemen, Theron and Aspasio, in Theron's country house. As he tells us himself, a dialogue enables the reader to turn "back a curtain and . . . overhear, by a kind of innocent and imaginary stealth, the debates, which pass in the recesses of privacy." Moreover, Theron and Aspasio go for walks in the beautiful gardens, sit in a well-furnished library, examine paintings, and visit a summerhouse; they discuss duelling, the reading of the classics, earthquakes, and other subjects; they write each other letters during an interruption of the dialogues; and Hervey's own learning, chiefly Ciceronian and Miltonian, pervades the whole book.[10]

Village Dialogues, between Farmer Littleworth, Thomas Newman, Rev. Mr. Lovegood and Others, by the Reverend Rowland Hill, A.M. (1744–1833) is still easier to read.[11] The character of the leading protago-

nists is revealed in their names: others besides those in
the title (and many more) include Squire Worthy, Dick
Heedless, Squire Bluster of Revel-Hall, Madam Flirt the
milliner, Mr. Goodenough the schoolmaster, and Parson
Dolittle, the defender of the old ways against the evangelical fervor that the author preaches. The villagers discuss such interesting subjects as the slave trade, proper
and improper marriages, the evils of seduction, conjugal
fidelity, and the progress of a rake, as well as the dangers
of Socinianism and Antinomianism and the doctrine of
justification. Though often flat, the dialogues are laced
with humor, and written with some pungency in the language of every day, in order to attract the ordinary
reader. MacDonald does not comment on these works,
but they must have made a pleasant change from those
of the Scotch Calvinists.

Not so pleasant, of course, as "Blind Harry," which
is the favorite fifteenth-century middle Scots poem (the
sole MS is dated 1488), *The Actis and Deidis of the Illus-
tere and Vaileand Campioun Schir William Wallace
Knight of Ellerslie* by Henry the Minstrel, commonly
known as Blind Harry. Its modern editor tells us that
"next to the Bible" it was "probably the book most frequently found in Scottish households." [12] It passed through
more editions than any other Scotch book written before the period of Burns and Scott: only one copy survives of the edition of 1570, and the seventeenth-century
editions are all scarce; probably David Elginbrod's "rare
edition" was one of these.

David tells Hugh Sutherland that his mother had given
him a kind of "scunner" against these books by making
him read them on Sundays. He shows him another volume that has long been in his family: this he cannot

read; it is the first edition (1612) of Boehme's first book, *Aurora*, (*Morgenroth in Aufgang*), that mystical tract that so appealed to MacDonald. On the flyleaf is the signature of Martin Elginbrod; and David tells Hugh that at Aberdeen he has found the gravestone of Martin: the epitaph of course is the one MacDonald had heard from Manby Smith, the "germ" of this novel: "Here lie I, Martin Elginbrodde:/ Hae mercy o' my soul, Lord God;/ As I wad do, were I Lord God,/ And ye were Martin Elginbrodde." To Hugh at first this seems irreverent, but David has come to think of it as

> jist a darin' way, maybe a childlike way, o' judgin', as Job micht ha' dune, the Lord by himsel'; an' sayin', 'at gin he, Martin Elginbrod, wad hae mercy, surely the Lord was not less merciful than he was. . . . He felt 'at the mercy in himsel' was ane o' the best things; an' he cudna think 'at there wad be less o't i' the father o' lichts, frae whom cometh ilka guid an' perfeck gift.

Here MacDonald is by implication contrasting Boehme's mysticism and David Elginbrod's own confidence in the love of God, together with that of his ancestor Martin, with the stern doctrines of the Scotch Calvinists as exemplified in the books of such men as Boston and Erskine. Even though David cannot read Boehme, he is a true disciple. As epigraph to the chapter in which Hugh and Margaret are reading Wordsworth, and the girl's deep sensitivity to the divine in nature is awakening, MacDonald uses a passage from Boehme's *Aurora:* "When the Soul is kindled or enlightened by the Holy Ghost, then it beholds what God its Father does, as a

Son beholds what his Father does at Home in his own House." [13]

But MacDonald also attacks his Calvinist opponents head-on, beginning with Sunday morning's service at the kirk:

> One grand aim of the reformers of the Scottish ecclesiastical modes, appears to have been to keep the worship pure and the worshippers sincere, by embodying the whole in the ugliest forms that could be associated with the name of Christianity. It might be wished, however, that some of their followers, . . . had left the object of worship, as represented by them, in the possession of some lovable attribute. . . . The cause of this degeneracy they share in common with the followers of all other great men as well as of Calvin. They take up what their leader, urged by the necessity of the time, spoke loudest, never heeding what he loved most; and then work the former out to a logical perdition of everything belonging to the latter.

And into the mouth of David Elginbrod, who has been invited to be an elder of the kirk, but who has declined with "a queer smile," MacDonald puts an answering blast against the minister's sermon, which has apparently dealt with Justification by Faith and Imputed Righteousness.

Impatient with any but direct contact between the individual human being and his God, David does not deny the doctrines themselves, but—sometimes over the objections of his wife, Janet—boldly puts forth his simple faith that was also MacDonald's:

> ". . . that man, and that man only, is justifeed, wha pits himself into the Lord's han's to sanctifee him.

Noo! an' that'll no' be dune by pittin' a robe o' richteousness upo' him, afore he's gotten a clean skin aneath't. As gin a father cudna bide to see the puir scabbit skin o' his ain wee bit bairnie, or his prodigal son either, but bude to hap it a' up before he cud lat it come near him! Ahva!"

To this Hugh Sutherland protests:

"But you don't think . . . that the minister intended to say that justification left a man at liberty to sin, or that the robe of Christ's righteousness would hide him from the work of the Spirit?"

And David answers:

"Na; but there *is* a notion in't o' hidin' frae God himsel'. I'll tell ye what it is, Mr. Sutherlan'; the minister's a'richt in himsel', an' sae's my Janet here, an' mony mair; an' aiblins there's a kin' o' trowth in a' 'at they say; but this is my quarrel wi' a' thae words an' words an' airguments, an' seemilies as they ca' them, an' doctrines, an' a' that—they jist haud a puir body at airm's lenth oot ower frae God himsel'. An' they raise a mist an' a stour a' aboot him, 'at the puir bairn canna see the Father himsel', stan'in' wi' his airms streekit oot as wide's the heavens, to tak' the worn crater—an' the mair sinner the mair welcome —hame to his verra hert. Gin a body wad lea' a' that, an' jist get fowk persuâdit to speyk a word or two to God him lane, the loss in my opingan, wad be unco' sma', and the gain verra great." [14]

It is not that David denies that sinners will be, indeed must be, punished. In a later discussion with Hugh, he makes this very clear: Hugh says to him:

"But you seem to me to make out that God is nothing but love."

"Ay, naething but love. What for no?"

"Because we are told he is just."

"Would he be lang just if he didna lo'e us?"

"But does he not punish sin?"

"Would it be ony kin'ness no to punish sin? No to use a' means to pit awa' the ae ill thing frae us? Whatever may be meant by the place o' meesery, depen' upo't, Mr. Sutherlan', it's only anither form o' love, love shinin' through the fogs o' ill, an' sae gart leik something verra different thereby. Man, raither nor see my Maggy—an' ye'll nae doot 'at I lo'e her—raither than see my Maggy do an ill thing, I'd see her lyin' deid at my feet. But supposin' the ill thing ance dune, it's no at my feet I wad lay her, but upo' my heart, wi' my auld arms aboot her, to haud the further ill aff o' her. An' shall mortal man be more just than God? Shall a man be more pure than his Maker?" [15]

Hell's misery as another form of love; punishment as a reflection of God's concern: David here echoes the lesson that Anodos had learned in *Phantastes:* "What we call evil, is the only and best shape, which, for the person and his condition at the time, could be assumed by the best good." And in contemplating what his own response would be to the idea of Margaret a sinner, and inferring from it what attitude God himself takes to His children's derelictions, David triumphantly echoes Martin Elginbrod's epitaph. The twentieth-century reader may well feel no real issue here. But George MacDonald's contemporaries felt it, as we shall see, and his Calvinist opponents heaped scorn upon him.

Perhaps the single greatest fault of *David Elginbrod* as a novel is that David himself disappears from the story after the end of this first part. His spirit, as MacDonald tells us repeatedly, dominates the work, and brings its beneficent influence to bear on the lives of the characters, but of David himself we see no more. The scene now shifts to Arnstead in Sussex, the great country house of Mr. Arnold, a rich widower, for whose son Harry Hugh Sutherland is engaged as tutor. Mr. Arnold's niece, Euphrasia (Euphra) Cameron, lives with him, and has been acting as teacher to Harry, a frail, nervous indoor boy who compulsively steps on every third diamond in the carpet. We recognize him as neurotic; MacDonald calls him diseased in mind as well as in body.

Hugh soothes Harry and allays his fears, stops his drinking wine and permits him only one dinner a day, persuades him to lay aside the dull book, takes him for walks and rides, builds for him a shelter in the wheat in the barn and a tree-house, and arouses his interest in learning by showing him a compass and telescope and surveying instruments and telling him stories about the Romans. Soon Harry is begging to learn geometry, geography, and Latin. As epigraph for Sutherland's system, MacDonald uses Jean Paul Richter's statement

> It is not the intention of sportive instruction that the child should be spared effort, or delivered from it; but that thereby a passion should be wakened in him, which shall both necessitate and facilitate the strongest exertion.

And MacDonald himself remarks that "Things themselves should lead to the science of them," [16] which would not have displeased John Dewey. From this account of

Hugh's dealings with Harry—in a very popular novel—
some Victorian parents no doubt got new ideas about
educating their children. MacDonald is preaching, but
he is preaching indirectly by demonstration rather than
by exhortation.

Euphra, half Scotch, half Bohemian, is MacDonald's
siren of the library, bent on making the tutor fall in love
with her. "Twenty-four or thirty-two or any age between" she is dark, with a "tawny" skin, fully conscious
of her own charms, joining Hugh and Harry on their
rides mounted on a white mare that provides "just the
right pedestal" for her own charming figure in a black
velvet riding habit "well-fitted, with a belt of dark red
leather, clasping a waist of the roundest and smallest,"
and a black hat with a single white feather. She never
lifts her dress to show her feet, but we later learn that
they are beautiful. She has a beautiful voice and sings
"The Flowers of the Forest" and other favorite Scotch
songs to Hugh. However, her "slyness" is so "tempered
with archness, that, if discovered, it might easily pass
for an expression playfully assumed." When she and
Harry go for a walk, she speaks to a primrose:

> "Is it not a little pet?—all eyes—all one eye staring
> out of its curtained bed to see what *ever is* going
> on in the world.—You had better lie down again: it
> is *not* a nice place."

Coyly she tries her ring on Hugh's finger, and lets
him slip it back on hers. She is cross when he seems to
enjoy riding with Harry alone. With calculation she
calls Hugh by his first name; he calls her by hers, and
squeezes her hand.

He never dreamed that she was exercising her skill upon him. What could be her object in bewitching a poor tutor? Ah! What indeed?

Perhaps, what enslaved Hugh most, was the feeling that the damsel stooped to him, without knowing that she stooped. She seemed to him in every way above him. She knew so many things of which he was ignorant; could say such lovely things; could, he did not doubt, write lovely verses; could sing like an angel . . . ; was mistress of a great rich wonderful house, with a history; and, more than all, was or appeared to him to be—a beautiful woman. It was true that his family was as good as hers . . . and the same pride made him despise his present position, and look upon a tutor's employment as—as—well as other people look upon it; as a rather contemptible one in fact, especially for a young, powerful, six-foot fellow.[17]

Euphra asks Hugh to help her with her Dante; he knows no Italian, but sets himself at once to learn; within two weeks he can explain the passage that had been troubling her. She is duly impressed, and reveres his learning; they embark on competitive translations; he begins to neglect Harry. Euphra has got his full attention.

Can we doubt that MacDonald is now at last recalling as she actually was the charmer who had dealt him such a blow in his own early youth? Not the unattainable laird's daughter of "A Hidden Life," not the mythological figure of the wicked Alder-maiden in *Phantastes* with her hollow back, not the strangely feeble-minded but loving Lady Alice of *The Portent,* but Euphrasia Cameron of *David Elginbrod,* a good deal older and far more ex-

perienced than the innocent Hugh Sutherland, a real
woman and not a type or an exaggeration, dark and
flirtatious, comes closest to the temptress who had so
dreadfully wounded MacDonald.

Reverting to the Hoffmannesque theme which he had
used in the story of Cosmo in *Phantastes* and in *The
Portent,* MacDonald makes Euphra a somnambule, mes-
merised by a wicked villain named Funkelstein, who
embraces her as he pleases when he has put her into a
trance. ("She had yielded to his will once. Had she not
done so, he could not have compelled her; but, having
yielded, she had not strength sufficient to free herself
again.") [18] No wonder she had assured the primrose that
the world was *not* a nice place. Admitted to Arnstead,
Funkelstein holds séances. A ouija-board produces David
Elginbrod's signature; various eerie manifestations occur, but most of them are immediately explained away.
Among the clumsiest is an ostensible "apparition" of
Margaret Elginbrod, which turns out to be Margaret
herself, now living in the household as maid to one of
the guests. Though they remain under the same roof for
many weeks, Hugh never realizes that she is there. David
Elginbrod has died, and Margaret is in mourning. Feeling malaise at the disappearance of the novel's one
memorable character, MacDonald says of David that "his
name will stand as the name of my story for pages to
come . . . because the influence of that ploughman is
the salt of the whole . . . when the story is wound up
it will be in the presence of his spirit." [19]

Funkelstein steals both a splendid crystal ring, now
part of the Arnold family jewels, but once the property
of a seventeenth-century Lady Euphrasia (who is re-

ported to lie unquiet in her tomb), and a diamond ring that belongs to Hugh. His love for Euphra blighted by his discovery of the power that the villain wields over her, Hugh goes off to London to try to earn his living by writing, and to look for Funkelstein. He gives Euphra —now crippled by a carriage-accident—the name of David Elginbrod, of whose death he is still unaware, in the hope that David may be able to reassure her as to the role of God in human affairs. In the end Hugh catches up with Funkelstein and obtains the crystal ring once more; this he restores to Euphra. His own ring, however, is gone, and Funkelstein evades the punishment due him. Euphra has an edifying death; with God's help, vouchsafed her through the agency af Margaret, who tells her about David; she conquers Funkelstein's influence; he can no longer summon her, and she is cured both of her somnambulism and of her discontent.

In catching Funkelstein, Hugh has the invaluable assistance of a man named Robert Falconer, whom he meets by chance in London. Falconer lives a noble life of knight-errantry among the poor; one day he spends in the cell of a condemned man at Newgate, the next he is off to soothe the deathbed of a man succumbing to typhus.[20] It is Falconer who explains to Hugh that Funkelstein wants the otherwise valueless Arnold crystal ring so that he may use it for crystal-gazing. Falconer also gives what would surely be MacDonald's own explanation for the phenomenon of the ouija-board: the spirits who produced David Elginbrod's signature are

The canaille of the other world . . . low miserable creatures that so lament the loss of their beggarly

bodies that they would brood upon them in the shape
of flesh-flies, rather than forsake the putrefying
remnants.

And he suggests that

Perhaps the wretched beings may want another
thousand years damnation because of the injury
done to their character by the homage of men who
ought to know better.

In winding up his novel, MacDonald uses Falconer to
clear up all remaining mysteries, and to comment in the
spirit of David Elginbrod himself on their implications.[21]

In *David Elginbrod*, MacDonald draws upon the
memory of his days in the pulpit at Arundel to deliver a
blow at the lower-middle-class shopkeepers he particularly detested. For a time, Hugh gives lessons to the nasty
children of a grocer named Appleditch, whose wife, a
penny-pinching shrew, spoils her children, treats Hugh
with disdain, and is determined to make a minister out
of her abominable son. The children are "those unpleas-
ant little immortals, whose earthly nature sprang from
a pair whose religion consisted chiefly in negations, and
whose main duty seemed to be to make money in small
sums, and spend it in smaller." The grocer and his wife
belong to "that class of humane parents who consider it
cruel to inflict any corporal suffering upon children, except they do it themselves and in a passion." Mrs. Appleditch objects to Hugh's growing a beard, as the critical
had objected to MacDonald's; one of the little Apple-
ditches is made to boast that he has five bags of gold in
the Bank of England, as a little boy at Arundel had
actually done; and when Harry comes to fetch Hugh in

a carriage, and Mrs. Appleditch sees that he has wealthy friends, she at once changes her manner.[22]

Again, in dealing with a London footman, Hugh shows some of MacDonald's own sensitive kind of snobbery, the fear of being snubbed by an inferior:

> Hugh had fixed him with his eyes before he began to explain his wishes. He had found out that this was the best way of securing attention from inferior natures, and that it was especially necessary with London servants; for their superciliousness is cowed by it and the superior will brought to bear on theirs. It is the only way a man without a carriage has to command attention from such.

Delighted with this, the *Athenaeum* reviewer of *David Elginbrod* referred to it satirically as "practical mesmerism" and went on (in a generally favorable review) to make fun of it:

> Stare hard at the housemaid before you ask her to dust the room; quell the cook with a glance if you wish the dinner to be properly dressed; but, above all, take care to *"cow the superciliousness"* of the footman if ever you expect him to open the door, or put some coals on the fire, when you desire him to do so.[23]

Yet some readers whose experience is limited only to the descendants of the Victorian English servant may perhaps sympathize a little with MacDonald.

Throughout the novel, MacDonald reports on the life of the church and the sermons delivered. In the Sussex countryside, the pompous Mr. Arnold tells his evangelical guest, Mrs. Elton, of his satisfaction with his clergyman:

". . . I assure you, Mrs. Elton, he is quite a respectable preacher, as well as clergyman. He is an honour to the cloth. . . . He is no Puseyite either . . . though he does preach once a month in his surplice."

"I am afraid you will not find him very original, though," said Hugh. . . .

"Original! . . . Really I am bound to say I don't know how the remark applies. How is a man to be original on a subject that is all laid out in plain print —to use a vulgar expression—and has been commented upon for eighteen hundred years and more?"

"Very true, Mr. Arnold," responded Mrs. Elton. "We don't want originality, do we? It is only the gospel we want. Does he preach the gospel?"

"How can he preach anything else? His text is always out of some part of the Bible."

"I am glad to see you hold by the Inspiration of the Scriptures, Mr. Arnold," said Mrs. Elton, chaotically bewildered.

"Good heavens! Madam, what do you mean? Could you for a moment suppose me to be an atheist? Surely you have not become a student of German neology." And Mr. Arnold smiled a grim smile.

"Not I, indeed!" protested poor Mrs. Elton, moving uneasily in her seat; "I quite agree with you, Mr. Arnold."

"Then you may take my word for it, that you will hear nothing but what is highly orthodox, and perfectly worthy of a gentleman and clergyman, from the pulpit of Mr. Penfold. He dined with us only last week."

For Mr. Arnold the church teaches men "to respect their superiors, and lead hard-working lives." When Sunday does come, Mr. Penfold delivers a sermon which MacDonald assures us he had bought for eighteen pence, proving that God is no respecter of persons, "a mark of indubitable condescension in the clergyman, the rank in society which he could claim for himself being duly considered." But, unfortunately, in his church the gentry, their servants, and the ordinary parishioners sit in three different places, and "all on the left of the pulpit were expected, as often as they stood up to sing—which was three times—to turn their backs on the pulpit, and so face away from the chancel where the gentry stood." Death, the clergymen assured them, lowers the rich to the level of the poor and raises the poor to the level of the rich, and "those who neglect the gospel-scheme, and never think of death and judgment—be they rich or poor . . . shall be damned. Glory be to the Father and to the Son, and to the Holy Ghost." Mr. Penfold's church itself has been plastered over and made generally ugly by modern restoration and innovation.[24]

In London, Mrs. Elton goes to a fashionable church. The many ladies who frequent it, "conscious that they had wandered from the fold, were waiting with exemplary patience for the barouches and mail-phaetons of the skies to carry them back without the trouble of walking." The vicar's sermon calls their attention to the fact that Queen Victoria herself,

the ruler over millions diverse in speech and in hue, to whom we all look up with humble submission, and whom we acknowledge as our sovereign lady—

even as she is, adds by her homage a jewel to his
crown; and hailing him as her Lord, bows and renders
him worship. Yet this is he who comes down to visit,
yea, dwells with his own elect, his chosen ones, whom
he has led back to the fold of his grace.

Hugh says to Falconer: "'Mr. ———— is quite proud
of the honour done his master by the queen,'" to which
Falconer answers: "'I do not think that his master will
think so much of it; for he once had his feet washed by
a woman that was a sinner.'" [25]

There is, however, one London preacher of whom
Falconer (and his creator MacDonald) deeply approve.
One Sunday Falconer takes Hugh to hear him.

> . . . from the communion-table rose a voice vibrat-
> ing with solemn emotion, like the voice of Abraham
> pleading for Sodom. It thrilled through Hugh's heart.
> The sermon which followed affected him no less,
> although, when he came out, he confessed to Fal-
> coner that he had only caught flying glimpses of its
> meaning, scope, and drift.

Hugh asks Falconer how the preacher can remain in the
church: he is known to have heterodox views, and Falconer answers that the preacher looks for the eternal
and divine in the confession of the Church of England,
with all its man-made faults, and loves the divine substance of it. This preacher

> trusts in God so absolutely that he leaves his salva-
> tion to him—utterly, fearlessly; and, forgetting it, as
> being no concern of his, sets himself to do the work
> that God had given him to do. . . . He believes
> entirely that God loves, yea *is* love; and, therefore,

that hell itself must be subservient to that love, and
but an embodiment of it. . . .

Falconer disapproves strongly of those who patronize
him, and, while praising his heart, deny his judgment;
these are the intellectuals, the theologians, "anxious for
their own salvation" who can "contemplate with calm-
ness the damnation of a universe," not realizing that God's
love will in the end prevail against hell itself.

This was intended as a portrait of Frederick Denison
Maurice, the celebrated "broad-churchman," whose influence had prevailed on MacDonald himself to enter the
Church of England. Maurice's connection, Augustus Hare,
long afterward remembered how he

> maundered over his own humility in a way which—
> even to a child—did not seem humble, and he was
> constantly lost mentally in the labyrinth of religious
> mysticisms which he was ever creating for himself.
> In all he said as in all he wrote, there was a nebulous
> vagueness. . . . When he preached before the Uni-
> versity of Cambridge to a church crowded with
> undergraduates, they asked one another as they
> came out, "What was it all about?"

Ruskin too calls Maurice "puzzle-headed," but "in his
Bible reading as insolent as any infidel of them all."
Matthew Arnold spoke of Maurice as "always beating
the bush with great emotion but never starting the hare."
Lord Mountstuart Duff, after hearing him thirty or forty
times, had "never carried away one clear idea, or even
the impression that he had more than the faintest conception of what he himself meant." "Like eating pea soup
with a fork," said Aubrey De Vere; and Jowett gathered

from one of Maurice's sermons that "today was yesterday and this world the same as the next." No doubt, some of the confusion at least arose from Maurice's effort to strike a balance between opposed views, to synthesize in the true Hegelian sense, between theses and antitheses all passionately held by some of his audience.[26] But the cloudiness that so many disliked George MacDonald (and many others) positively admired. Once again Mac-Donald proclaims the superiority of the heart to the mind: he feels that it does not matter whether Sutherland has understood what Maurice was saying, or even whether there was anything particular to understand in Maurice's sermon. And here too he voices for the first time one of his own most controversial theological opinions: that hell is not eternal, but will in the end be submerged in God's love.

David Elginbrod, even to a reader easily bored with Scotch rural life and too sophisticated for the flummery of mesmerism, in this way incidentally provides a kind of tour of the mid-Victorian Scotch and English religious scene. As everywhere in his writing, MacDonald uses the experiences of his characters as an opportunity to preach his own views: in the person of David Elginbrod, with his modification of the doctrine of justification by faith; in the person of Falconer, with his interpretation to Sutherland of F. D. Maurice's attitude toward eternal damnation; and, on one occasion, even in the person of young Harry Arnold, Hugh's former pupil: Harry cannot bear a homily read to him by Mrs. Elton on the doctrine of the elect; he cries out "'I don't want God to love me, if he does not love everybody,'" bursts into tears, and leaves the room. This cry had been Mac-

Donald's own in childhood, and we shall hear it again.[27]

At the end of *David Elginbrod,* Hugh returns to Turriepuffit to ask Janet Elginbrod to forgive him for his neglect of David; there he finds Margaret, and they tell each
other of their love. As epigraph for the last chapter Mac-
Donald uses the last lines of Novalis' *Märchen* of Hyacinth
and Rosebud: "He stood before the heavenly Virgin.
Then lifted he the light, shining veil and—Rosebud sank
into his arms." Hugh Sutherland's whole pilgrimage since
leaving Turriepuffit had been in search of something that
had been there for him all the time: Margaret was Isis and
Rosebud both. Again, in the high moments of his characters' lives—even in a Scotch story whose mainspring is
the attack on Calvinism—MacDonald turns to Novalis.

II

In *Alec Forbes of Howglen* (1865),[28] the scene is
Huntly, which MacDonald calls Glamerton, and Aberdeen, which he does not name. He wanted to call the
novel *The Little Grey Town,* but his publishers rejected
the title "as not conforming with the then fashionable
nomenclature in fiction." [29] His characters never leave
Scotland. Almost every last trace of German romantic influence has disappeared. A reader coming fresh to *Alec
Forbes* would never suspect that its author had read
Boehme, Novalis, or Hoffmann. Moreover, MacDonald
avoids many of the technical mistakes he made in *David
Elginbrod: Alec Forbes* does not fall apart because important characters vanish from the scene; instead they
remain and grow and develop. When the hero goes off
to the University, the author manages to follow his ad-

ventures there while simultaneously keeping his reader
in touch with the fortunes of those left behind in Glamerton. *Alec Forbes* is all of a piece.

The plot shows little sign of inventiveness. Alec Forbes,
an agreeable boy, active and brave, befriends and cham-
pions a much younger orphan girl, Annie Anderson, who
boards at the house of the mean-spirited shopkeeper
Robert Bruce, and attends the Glamerton town school
under its savage master, Murdoch Malison. From her
girlhood she worships Alec, who takes punishment for
her, names his boat for her, and saves her life in a great
flood. When Alec goes to the University, he meets and
falls in love with a distant cousin of his own, Kate Fraser,
niece of a professor. She is a charming girl, a devotee of
Byron, a romantic who has been brought up by a nurse
from the Shetlands who has told her Scandinavian tales
all day. She responds to nature in all its moods, and has
come to believe that women must give up everything for
love. She is fond of Alec, whose house she visits in Glamerton, but she falls in love with a fellow student of Alec's,
his sworn enemy, Beauchamp, The MacChattachan, a
handsome aristocratic villain who goes about in full Highland dress. Beauchamp makes love to Kate, using Shelley
as his weapon, and Alec, desperately jealous, takes to
drink and bad habits. Exposed as the man who has foully
tried to stab Alec and throw him into the river, Beauchamp has to leave the University. True to her principles
and mad with despair, Kate drowns herself; Alec fails to
save her. After a long illness and a trip to Greenland as
doctor on a whaler, he comes home to Glamerton to find
that Annie Anderson has grown up, and that they love
each other.

All this repeats the pattern of *David Elginbrod:* a nice,

rather callow, young man leaves behind him the girl he really ought to love, has an unhappy love affair with somebody else, and returns in the end, chastened, to the right woman. Even though Kate is no Euphra, no somnambule, no flirt, no incarnation of MacDonald's own youthful flame, she is just as truly in the power of the wicked Beauchamp as Euphra in that of Funkelstein. The clumsy machinery, however, has disappeared, and human passions fanned by Shelley have replaced mesmerism. Moreover, Margaret Elginbrod, when Hugh Sutherland first left her, had already grown into the woman he would later love, so that one may fairly call him blind; while Annie Anderson, when Alec Forbes leaves home, is only a little girl, whom one cannot blame him for not loving. It is not the main story, or even the protagonists, that make *Alec Forbes* an arresting novel, but MacDonald's picture of Scotch life and character.

MacDonald faces squarely the grimness of Glamerton. He opens the story at Annie's father's funeral—" 'Gin ony o' ye want to see the corp, noo's yer time,' " says the carpenter before nailing shut the coffin upstairs—and soon Annie's dour aunt is giving the child's small capital to the penny-pinching Robert Bruce to use, in exchange for letting Annie sleep in a wretched attic full of rats, and feeding her bad porridge and "sky-blue milk." " 'O God,' " Annie prays at night, " 'tak care o' me frae the rottans (rats),' " and in answer to her prayer the cat arrives, and the horrid rustling stops. The school brings its torments of dullness, as Annie is "condemned to follow with an uncut quill, over and over again, a single straight stroke set her by the master," or to give "Scripture proofs" of the various assertions of the shorter catechism: to the question " 'What doth every sin deserve?' "

she answers "'A lickin'.'" [30] Violence reigns; the master
brutally beats his victims, and Alec, intervening for Annie,
pushes him into the fireplace, where he burns his hand.
In his savagery, the schoolmaster actually cripples one
wretched youngster; but then reforms, makes friends with
his victim, takes him to the seaside, and finally dies in a
vain effort to save him from drowning.

But there are pleasures too. In the winter, the boys
pile all the snow they can find in front of Bruce's windows; he thinks the whole town has been buried. They
climb onto roofs and put turfs over the chimneys; they tie
the town animals nose-to-tail in a grotesque procession;
they go skating. Alec and his friend Curly make a boat,
with Annie watching from a deep pile of shavings, recit-
ing ballads to them, and occasionally retreating to the
smithy to warm up. On its maiden voyage, the boat is
whirled over the dam, and when the sluice is suddenly
closed, to save her, the resulting flood causes a millstone
to explode, endangering the men at the mill, and infuriat-
ing the miller. As the seasons follow each other at Glamerton MacDonald catches their rhythm, in his disciplined
descriptions of the changes in the sky and the landscape:
the northern lights flickering over the icy earth, the river
in flood, brawling against the bridges, the heat and beauty
of the harvest-time, and the dismal endless rains of autumn.

His people talk as people must have talked, with a
good deal of freedom in their speech, some of it astonishing for a novel of the prudish sixties. Bruce's biting
dog they call a damned bitch. A farmer's wife tripped
up by a rope held across the road complains to a shopkeeper:

> ". . . doon I cam' o' my niz . . . and mair o' my legs oot o' my coats, I doobt, than was a'thegither to my credit."
>
> "I'm sure ye can hae no rizzon to tak' shame o' your legs, gude wife," was the gallant rejoinder; to which their owner replied with a laugh:
>
> "They warna made for public inspection, ony gait."
>
> "Hoot! Hoot! Naebody saw them. I's' warrant ye didna lie lang." [31]

Peter Whaup the Smith, George MacWha the carpenter, Tibbie Dyster, the blind woman, whom Annie befriends and cares for, and who dies in the flood, James Dow ("Dooie"), Annie's father's former farm manager, who cherishes her as much as his means permit, Mrs. Forbes, Alec's mother, a lady, who loves Annie from the first, but hopes for a better match for her son, the parsimonious Aunt Meg, never able or willing to give in to her love for Annie because she fears what it may cost her, these form a gallery of genuine portraits.

But it is those who are connected with worship at Glamerton whom we remember longest. Greatly modified now are the slashing direct attacks on the Scotch Calvinists that characterized *David Elginbrod*. At Glamerton the minister of the parish church (the muckle kirk) is Mr. Cowie, a good and gentle man, but the sect of the Missionars, uncompromising in its Calvinism, has much strength. George MacWha, the carpenter, who is "a bit o' a Protestan', though . . . nae Missionar," finds the "muckle kirk does weel eneuch for him," as he tells his friend Thomas Crann, the stone-mason, a dedicated Missionar. Crann answers him with scorn:

"What get ye there but the dry banes o' morality,
upo' which the win' o' the world has never blawn to
pit life into the puir disjaskit skeleton. Come to oor
kirk, an' ye'll get a rousin', I can tell ye, man."

The Missionars, Crann declares, are not forced to swallow

". . . ony jabble o' luke-warm water that's been
standin' i' the sun frae year's en' to year's en', jist
because the patron pleases to stick a pump intil 't
an' ca't a well o' salvation."

Overhearing this conversation, and feeling sure that
Thomas Crann has a secret ("'Nane but them that has
the speerit can ken the speerit,'" Crann has said as he
leaves the carpenter's shop), Annie goes to the Missionar
church on Sunday, where she hears a visiting preacher, a

thin-faced cadaverous man, with a self-severe saintly
look, one to whom religion was clearly a reality,
though not so clearly a gladness, one whose opinions
—vague half-monstrous embodiments of truth—
helped to give him a consciousness of the life which
sprung from a source far deeper than his consciousness could reach.[32]

The sermon deals with the eternal hell-fire to which the
wicked who forget God shall be given over. Sure that she
is one of the wicked, Annie is terrified; she identifies
Murdoch Malison, the cruel schoolmaster, with the God
of the sermon, and in deep trouble goes to Mr. Cowie of
the parish church to ask for comfort. She explains that she
cannot help forgetting God at times, and he tries to reassure her:

"You haven't forgot your father, have you, Annie?" said he.

"I think aboot him most ilka day," answered Annie.

"But there comes a day, now and then, when you don't think much about him, does there not?"

"Yes, sir."

"Do you think he would be angry with his child?"

"Deed no, sir . . . he wad say: 'Let alane the lassie. She'll think aboot me the morn—time eneuch.' "

"Well, don't you think your Father in heaven would say the same?"

"Maybe he micht, sir. But you see my father was my ain father, and wad mak' the best o' me."

"And is not God kinder than your father?"

"He canna weel be that, sir. And there's the Scripter!"

"But he sent his only Son to die for us."

"Ay, for the eleck, sir," returned the little theologian.

Poor Mr. Cowie. Unable to deal with this question, he bursts into Scotch himself, and lamely tells her:

"Gang ye hame, Annie my bairn . . . and dinna trouble yer heid aboot election and a' that. It's no' a canny doctrine. No mortal man could ever win at the boddom o' 't. I'm thinkin' we haena muckle to do wi' 't. Gang hame, dawtie, and say yer prayers to be preserved frae the wiles o' Sawtan. There's a sixpence to ye."

It is actually a shilling and symbolizes his own love for Annie, but he has not really helped her with her problem, and is greatly discomfited. MacDonald tells us that had

Annie gone to Mr. Brown, the Missionar preacher, she
would have found him kind also, but "rather inclined to
gloat over" her "unhappiness as the sign of grace be-
stowed and an awakening conscience." How much more
effective it is in a novel to show the well-meaning Calvinist held captive by his cruel doctrine in a touching human
situation than to attack the doctrine in a counter-ser-
mon! [33]

Still disturbed, Annie now calls on Thomas Crann himself. Can a person have a chance even if she does sometimes forget God? No doubt, he answers.

> "The nations that forget God are them that
> dinna care . . . them that were never called, never
> chosen. . . ."
>
> "But hoo's a body to ken whether she be ane o'
> the elec'?"
>
> "That's a hard matter. It's no' needfu' to ken't
> aforehan'. Just lat that alane i' the mean time."
>
> "But I canna let it alane. It's no for mysel' either
> a'thegither. Could *ye* lat it alane, Thomas? . . . ."
>
> "Ye hae me there, lassie. Na, I cudna lat it alane.
> An' I never did lat it alane. I plaguit the Lord nicht
> an' day till he loot me ken. . . . Ye maun haud at
> it, lassie. . . . An' gin the Lord hears you, ye'll ken
> ye're ane o' the elec', for it's only his own elec' that
> the Lord dis hear."

Crann tells Annie of his own great religious experience:
how he spent the whole night in a bog of peat moss, praying to the Lord for grace, not daring to move; how he
came home and went to bed for three days, doing no
work, fearing damnation, taking no nourishment but a
little milk and water; and how, on the fourth day,

"I gaed to my work wi' my heid swimmin' an' my hert like to brak for verra glaidness. I *was* ane o' the chosen."

To Annie's natural question " 'But hoo did ye fin' that oot, Thomas?' " he answers only " 'Get a sicht o' the face o' God . . . It's all in the speerit. When ye see't ye'll ken't.' "

Deeply unsatisfactory though this is for Annie, and unsatisfactory as MacDonald feels it, much though he disagrees with the harshness of Calvinism in general and the Missionar doctrine in particular, he has now found the art to make it credible. Crann, the stonemason, with all his uncompromising downrightness, is deeply kind. Affectionately, he takes Annie home. Anxiously he inquires into the state of his fellow townsmen's souls. He believes in the future redemption of Alec Forbes, despite Alec's fight with the schoolmaster and many scrapes:

"He jist wants to be weel shaken ower the mou' o' the pit. He maun smell the brumstane o' the everlastin' burnin's. He's nane o' yer saft buirds (boards) that ye can sleek wi' a sweyp o' yer airm; he's a blue whunstane that's hard to dress, but anes dressed it bides the weather bonnie. I like to work upo' hard stane mysel'. Nane o' yer saft freestane, 'at ye cud wi' a knife, for me."

Though Crann is poor, he prays to be delivered from the love of money and puts into the plate far more than he can afford. As he comes to know Annie better and observes her kindness to the poor blind woman, Tibbie Dyster, he grows sure in his own mind that Annie is of the elect and tells her so, much to her delight. We see

him in the round, crusty, forbidding, the prisoner of a
cold and fiercely uncomfortable doctrine, yet in his grim
way a mystic, full of love, a saint. With true art, with
a restraint for which he had in no earlier writing evinced
the capacity, MacDonald *shows* us Thomas Crann rather
than telling us about him. This is no caricature, this is a
man.[34]

Less skillfully and less convincingly, MacDonald deals
with the schoolmaster, Murdoch Malison. He shows us
Malison boring and beating and crippling the children
in the school, and tells us that "there were other modes
of punishment of which the restraint of art would forbid
the description, even if it were possible for any writer
to conquer his disgust so far as to attempt it."

> Justice, according to his idea, consisted in vengeance.
> And he was fond of justice. He did not want to punish
> the innocent, it is true; but I doubt whether the
> discovery of a boy's innocence was not a disappoint-
> ment to him.

The sentimental reconciliation with the boy Malison has
lamed for life hardly reclaims him; so MacDonald must
explain him, must tell the reader rather than show him:

> There is not to be found a more thorough impersona-
> tion of his own theology than a Scotch school-master
> of the rough old-fashioned type. His pleasure was
> law, irrespective of right or wrong, and the reward
> of submission to law was immunity from punish-
> ment. He had his favorites in various degrees, whom
> he chose according to inexplicable directions of feel-
> ing ratified by "the freedom of his own will." These
> found it easy to please him, while those with whom

he was not primarily pleased found it impossible to please him.

No wonder Annie identifies him with the Lord of the Missionar sermon; he had done so himself.

> . . . in aggravation of the . . . feeling . . . that [his pupils] were not only the natural enemies of the master, but therefore of all law, theology had come in and taught him that they were in their own nature bad . . . with the badness for which the only set-off he knew or could introduce was blows. Independently of any remedial quality that might be in them, these blows were an embodiment of justice; for "every sin," as the catechism teaches, "deserveth God's wrath and curse both in this life and that which is to come." The master therefore was only a co-worker with God in every pandy he inflicted on his pupils.

But not all of this explanation, not even Malison's death in a good cause, can reconcile us to his brutality. Here MacDonald is too kind to Malison, and too hard on Calvinist theology. "Murder" Malison's sadism had deeper roots. So, no doubt, did the sudden sentimental friendship for the little boy he had crippled. No modern reader will hold Calvinism solely responsible for the schoolmaster's atrocities or accept MacDonald's explanation either as reasoning or as art. In *Alec Forbes,* we do not yet suspect that MacDonald himself may enjoy the beatings the schoolmaster inflicts. But we shall later have cause to think so.

Interestingly enough, Malison, who cherishes ambitions to become a minister, fails at preaching when he tries in the pulpit, and disgraces himself: he is a "stickit minister," and, to the laughter of many of the congregation, he steals from the pulpit feeling "much as Lady Godiva would have felt had her hair or her heroism proved unworthy of confidence." Despite all their reasons to hate him, the school-children sympathise with Malison in his moment of shame. Led by his little crippled victim, they put flowers on his desk, and touch his heart. He has turned defeat into victory. Because of Mac-Donald's own thwarted career in the pulpit, this episode of the "stickit" minister takes on especial meaning. Malison deserves the jeers of the mockers, but his very failure has taught him humility, as MacDonald believed his own had done.[35]

Best of all is Cosmo Cupples, the little weazened scholar who occupies the garret at the top of Alec Forbes' lodging house in Aberdeen, learned in all the disciplines, a poet, but a slave to alcohol. He stays sober all day, but as soon as he comes home at night, out comes the whiskey bottle, and he drinks himself slowly to sleep. He helps Alec with his Greek, mathematics, and chemistry, and acts as his adviser in the series of conflicts with Beauchamp. He warns Alec never to try drink. In despair at his discovery that Kate loves Beauchamp, Alex comes to Cupples' room, and finds him in a drunken sleep. He picks up the whiskey bottle to console himself:

> The *elixir mortis* flowed gurgling from the narrow neck into the tumbler which Mr. Cupples had lately emptied. Heedless and reckless he nearly filled it, and was just lifting it to his lips, when a cry half molded into a curse rang from the bed, and at the same instant the tumbler was struck from his hand.

It flew in fragments against the grate, and the spirit rushed in a roaring flame of demoniacal wrath up the chimney.

"Damn you!" half-shrieked, half-panted Mr. Cupples in his nightshirt, at Alec's elbow, still under the influence of the same spirit . . . "damn you, bantam! ye've broken my father's tumbler. De'il tak' ye for a vaigabon'! I've a guid min' to thraw the neck o' ye!" . . .

"Gin ye touch that bottle again, faith I'll brain ye and sen' ye into the ither warl' withoot that handle at least for Sawtan to catch a grip o' ye by . . ."

But Alec disregards Cupples' advice, and begins to drink with a group of wild companions. Drink leads to worse, at first only hinted at:

Vice grew upon vice. There are facts in human life which human artists can not touch. . . . Mothers have to know such facts of their sons, and such facts of women like themselves.

But the news of Alec's dissipation gets home to Glamerton, and there one of the townsfolk speaks right out to his wife: Alec has fallen into the hands of ". . . thae coorse jawds that hing aboot i' the gloamin'!" One night, Cupples himself appears on the threshold of a "low public house, which had a second and worse reputation." He tries to argue the drunken Alec out of going in:

"Alec, ye'll wiss to God ye hadna, whan ye come to marry a bonnie wife."

"Wife!" he cried, "there's no wife for me. Haud oot o' my gait. Dinna ye see I hae been drinkin'? And I winna be contred."

Finally, furious at being "made a laughter to the women," Alec knocks his friend down and strides past him into the house. Remorse overcomes Alec the next morning, and when Mr. Cupples—badly injured—forgives him and urges him to give up the drink, so that he may make a scholar of him, Alec answers

> ". . . gin I try to brak through the drinkin', I maun haud oot ower the smell o't; and I doobt . . . ye wadna hae the chance o' makin' muckle o' a scholar o' me in that case."
>
> "Bantam," says Mr. Cupples solemnly, "I sweir to God, gin ye'll gie ower the drink and the lave o' yer ill gaits, I'll gie ower the drink as weel. I hae naething other to gie ower. But that winna be easy."

Meanwhile a child in Glamerton who has overheard her parents talking of Alec's derelictions goes to Mrs. Forbes to report that "they" have got hold of Alec and are torturing him. "They"

> ". . . stand aboot the corners o' the streets, mem, in muckle toons, and they catch a haud o' young lads, and trail them awa' wi' them, and they jist torment the life oot o' them. They say they're women; but I dinna believe that. It's no possible. They maun be men dressed up in women's claes."

In alarm, Mrs. Forbes comes to the city, to find Alec hard at work. Mr. Cupples tells her that Alec has reformed, and she is

> reassured but not satisfied. . . . She felt that Alec had outgrown his former relation to her, and had a dim perception that her pride had prevented them

from entering upon a yet closer relationship. It is their own fault when mothers lose by the *growth* of their children.

To Mrs. Forbes, Mr. Cupples seems a dirty vulgar little man. She cannot understand Alec's affection for him, or realize how bad a time he has seen Alec through.[36]

Throughout this series of episodes MacDonald avoids the sentimentality to which he often yields elsewhere, and so makes his treatment far more than a mere temperance tract. Though he emphasizes the perils of alcohol, he makes Alec Forbes' sudden addiction to it seem entirely credible. Moreover, instead of merely raising pious hands in horror at Alec's seeking out prostitutes, or hinting at things too vile to mention, as so many Victorian novelists preferred to do, MacDonald actually takes his reader to the threshold of a brothel, where he hears the mocking laughter of the women. In making Mr. Cupples, himself an alcoholic, draw the line at whoring (he calls the house itself the mouth of hell, and adds: " 'Eh, man! to think nae more o' women nor that!' "), MacDonald has nicely distinguished between a deadly sin and an even deadlier. Most nineteenth-century novelists, had they got as far as the threshold, would have had Alec's conversion take place then and there. Not so MacDonald. In a supremely realistic moment, he makes his hero knock down poor Mr. Cupples, and stride on into the brothel, where he spends the night. Nor is it his sexual transgressions for which Alec feels remorse next day: convincingly enough, he laments only the shameful action he has committed in striking his friend, and it is this alone that brings about the revulsion necessary before he can promise to change his ways.

And again the morning after, Mr. Cupples lays no stress on Alec's whoring: Alec must "gie ower" not only "the drink" but "the lave o' yer ill gaits" (the rest of your bad habits), but this is all that is ever said again about that side of his derelictions. Finally, with a sure touch, Mac-Donald refrains from inflicting on Alec Forbes what Victorian moralists would have thought a suitable punishment: Alec does not become diseased; he does not feel himself an outcast from society; when later he falls in love with Annie, his wicked past is never mentioned: he has consorted with light women, learned his lesson from the blow he struck Mr. Cupples, and reformed; that is all. So far as we learn, Alec does not even "wiss he hadna." [37] We may cavil at the distorted form that the news of Alec's sins takes in the mind and speech of the little girl in Glamerton who has overheard them mentioned, and we may protest that she can hardly have understood so much without understanding all. Her conceit that prostitutes are really men in women's clothing starts trains of thought in twentieth-century minds that MacDonald can hardly have intended. Though phallic women were not known to him by that name, they were none the less part of his fantasy. But his straightforward, pungent, handling of the episode as a whole amounts to a triumph.

Nor does MacDonald leave us wondering why Cupples, the gentle scholar and Alec's good angel, had taken to drink in the first place. In one of his efforts to keep Alec from the bottle, Cupples tells him his story: we shall find it a familiar one. As a youth, he had just arrived in a great house in the north, where he had been employed to catalogue the library. A most beautiful girl came in without seeing him, and, as she was on the point of selecting a

book by " 'Some hermaphrodeet cratur that had no respec'
for man or woman, an' whase neck sud hae been thrawn
by the midwife,' " Cupples had stopped her. She told him
that she had been looking for a book to help her learn
Gaelic. Their first interview led to many others, and soon
Cupples was hopelessly in love. The girl

> "was a wee body, wi' muckle black een, that lay
> quaiet in her face, and never cam' oot till they war
> wantit, an' a body gimp and sma', but roon' and weel
> proportioned throughoot. Her hand and her fit war
> jist past expression bonny."

One night

> my een war suddenly dazed wi' the glimmer o' some-
> thing white. I thocht the first minute that I had seen
> a ghost, and the neist that I was a ghost mysel'. For
> there she was in a fluffy cloud o' whiteness, wi' her
> bonny bare shouthers and airms, and jist ae white
> rose in her black hair, and deil a diamond or ruby
> aboot her!
>
> "It's so hot," said she, "in the drawing-room! And
> they're talking such nonsense there! There's nobody
> speaks sense to me but you, Mr. Cupples."
>
> "Deed, mem," says I, "I dinna ken whaur it's to
> come frae the nicht. For I hae nae sense left but ane,
> and that's nearhan' 'wi' excess o' brichtness blind.'
> Auld Spenser says something like that, doesna he,
> mem," I added, seein' that she luikit some grave.
> But what she micht hae said or dune I dinna ken;
> for I sweir to ye, bantam, I know nothing that hap-
> pent after, till I cam' to mysel' at the soun' o' a lauch
> frae outside the door. I kenned it well eneuch, though

it was a licht flutterin' lauch. . . . I sprang to my feet, but the place reeled roon', and I fell. It was the lauch that killed me. What for sud she lauch?—And sic a ane as her that was no licht-heidit lassie, but cud read and unnderstan' wi' the best?

Cupples is smitten with delirium, and comes to long after at home in his mother's cottage. At Aberdeen he experiments with a bottle of whiskey sent him by a friend as a present. After his first drinks, he says to himself with pride: " 'My leddy canna, wi' a' her breedin' and her bonnie skin, haud Cosmo Cupples frae lo'ein' her.' " He is launched on his drunken course. Nor when Alec suggests that he give it up—Alec hears the story before he has taken to drink himself—can Cupples at this time yet bear to contemplate it:

"The verra attemp'—an' dinna ye think that I haena made it— aich. What for sud I gang to hell afore my time? The deils themselves complain o' that. Na, na. Ance ye hae learned to drink, ye *canna* do wantin' it, Man, dinna touch't. For God's sake, for yer mither's sake, for *ony* sake, dinna lat a drap o' the hell-broth gang ower yer thrapple—or ye're damned like me forever and ever. It's as guid's singin' awa' yer sowl wi' yer ain han' and yer ain blude."

Mr. Cupples lifted his glass, emptied it, and, setting it down on the table with a gesture of hatred, proceeded to fill it yet again.[38]

All the more do we feel the force of his renunciation of drink, when finally he undertakes it in order to save Alec. Here, in what is probably the most powerful short story in Scotch between Scott's *Wandering Willie's Tale* (1832) and Stevenson's *Thrawn Janet* (1887), George MacDonald tries once more to exorcise the devils of that youthful summer of 1842. For the first time, in all the attempts he has made to tell the story, he makes it happen, not to the hero—the young farmer of "A Hidden Life," Anodos of *Phantastes*, Campbell of *The Portent*, Sutherland of *David Elginbrod*, all of whom, like Alec Forbes, represent MacDonald himself—but to Mr. Cupples, a secondary character, who, for all the affection with which his creator regarded him, could never be mistaken for himself. Small and weazened, ashamed of his physical inadequacy, ready to admit that he had been a "gowk" to aspire to the lady, full of respect for the great house instead of rebellious distaste for the rich, Mr. Cupples differs completely from George MacDonald. The shocking flirtation, MacDonald is saying, did not happen to me but to someone else: at last it had become so remote in his own past youth that the pain had died down, and he could turn the episode into art.

The lady we recognize instantly: she looks like Euphra and, we assume, like his own enchantress: small, slender, well-proportioned, with beautiful hands and feet, dark, clever, and heartless. A single laugh at her triumph over poor Cupples is all her villainy. There is no flirtation, no kiss, no love affair. Yet somewhere Cupples has learned much:

> "Man, ye had better lay han's upon a torpedo, or a galvanic battery, nor upo' a woman—I mean a woman that ye hae ony attraction till—for she'll gar ye dirl till ye dinna ken yer thumb frae yer muckle tae."

MacDonald makes Cupples himself reveal the girl's false-
ness without realizing it: is it not unlikely that an intelligent and well-educated young woman would *un*inten-
tionally reach for a wicked book on the library shelf?
Rather, are we not supposed to realize something that
Cupples himself has never realized: the corrupt girl came
to the library, unaware of the presence of the librarian,
to find the book by the "hermaphrodeet cratur," and when
Cupples saw what she was doing she produced the excuse
that she was looking for a book that would help her learn
Gaelic? We may even conjecture that the author of the
book she actually began to touch was Sterne, whom
MacDonald hated.[39]

During Alec's illness after Kate's death, Mr. Cupples
comes to Glamerton to visit him. There he helps disgrace
Robert Bruce by exposing him as a thief before his fellow
Missionars. Restored to health by his own abstinence, Mr.
Cupples becomes a friend of Crann's, and takes his own
place among the Glamerton people. Mrs. Forbes herself
realizes the groundlessness of her earlier prejudices
against him. Annie, who is helping nurse Alec, enters the
sickroom just at the moment of his recovery; she inter-
cepts the glance of mutual affection between the patient
and his friend Mr. Cupples, and sees the love on the face
of Mrs. Forbes, who is also in the room. It strikes her with
the force of a revelation. The love she has seen she knows
is God. She realizes that God has been with her all the
time:

> "He gie'ed me my father, and sent Broonie [the cow]
> to tak' care o' me, an' Dooie [Dow, her father's farm-
> hand and her loyal friend], and Thomas Crann, and
> Mrs. Forbes, and Alec. And He sent the cat when

I gaed till Him aboot the rottans. An' He's been wi'
me I kenna hoo lang, an' He's wi' me noo. . . ." [40]

Alec too has had his revelation in the loneliness of a
Greenland winter. Miraculously, at the deepest moment
of his depression, when all his shipmates have gone on
ahead, to perish, the thought of God has come to him,
and, soon afterward, rescue. Thomas Crann had always
predicted it for Alec, and now MacDonald makes it happen. His hero and heroine come together and agree to
marry only after each has come to the full knowledge of
George MacDonald's ever-present and all-loving Father
through what Crann and MacDonald would agree was a
glimpse of His face.

III

Third and last of the major Scotch novels, *Robert
Falconer* (1868) has sometimes challenged comparison
with *Alec Forbes*. MacDonald himself, when asked which
of his novels he thought the best, answered: "I had most
models before me in *Robert Falconer*." Ronald Mac-
Donald remarks that his father was "well into his stride"
in *Alec Forbes* but "fully extended" in *Robert Falconer*,
and Greville calls *Robert Falconer* "nearer his genius." [41]
But too many of the old faults creep back. As in *David
Elginbrod*, the action is sharply divided into a Scotch
and an English portion, so that the book falls apart.
Whereas in *Alec Forbes* MacDonald skillfully subordi-
nated most of his preaching to his narrative, enhancing
its interest by making it relevant to the development of
characters in whom the reader is interested, in *Robert
Falconer* he introduces long sermons for their own sake,

often delaying the action intolerably and making the
reader lose interest. *Alec Forbes* for long stretches reads
like an idyll of Scotch town and country life, and emphasizes its joys, but *Robert Falconer* emphasizes the
dullness, the sombreness, and the intellectual and emotional poverty of Falconer's youth, and the severity of the
old faith that tortures his days. Moreover, the main theme
of the novel, though deeply interesting for the student
of MacDonald's own psychology, seems forced, unreal,
uncomfortable.

Robert Falconer we have met, in *David Elginbrod,* as
the tireless and beloved independent social worker among
the London poor, who helps Hugh Sutherland track
down the wicked mesmerist Funkelstein and introduces
him to the preaching of F. D. Maurice. In this new novel
Falconer is the protagonist, fourteen years old at the opening of the story, living with his grandmother in the Scotch
town of Rothieden, as much Huntly as Glamerton in
Alec Forbes. Robert's

> mother had been dead for so many years that he had
> only the vaguest recollections of her tenderness, and
> none of her person. All he was told of his father was
> that he had gone abroad. His grandmother would
> never talk about him, although he was her own son.
> When the boy ventured to ask a question about
> where he was, or when he would return, she always
> replied, "Bairns sud haud their tongues."

At night, Robert hears his grandmother praying in anguish, crying out to God because of her lost son and the
eternal damnation she fears he has met:

> "To think o' my bairnie that I carriet, i' my ain body,
> that sookit my breists, and leuch in my face—to

think o' 'im bein' a reprobate! O Lord! cudna he be
eleckit yet? Is there *nae* turnin' o' thy decrees? Na,
na; that wadna do at a'. But while there's life there's
houp. But wha kens whether he be alive or no?
Naebody can tell. Glaidly wad I luik upon's dead
face gin I cud believe that his sould wasna amang
the lost. But eh! the torments o' that place! and the
reik that gangs up forever and ever, smorin' the
stars. And my Andrew doon i' the hert o' 't cryin'! And
me no able to win till him! O Lord! I *canna* say thy
will be done. But dinna lay 't to my charge; for gin
ye was a mither yersel' ye wadna pit him there . . . .
it's a' drink, drink and ill company. . . ."

Mrs. Falconer's love for her lost son wars agonizingly
with her uncompromising Calvinist certainty of his fate
—if indeed he is dead. In Mrs. Falconer, MacDonald was
portraying his own grandmother, one of whose sons had
also absconded in disgrace.

Robert tries to soften his grandmother's views, but she
can only urge that he pray constantly for his father. On
the sabbath, Robert prays:

"Oh Lord! save my father. . . ."
"If it be thy will," suggested his grandmother. . . .
"I'm tryin'," grandmother, . . . but I canna say 't.
I daurna say an *if* aboot it. It wad be like giein' in
till's damnation. We *maun hae* him saved, grannie!"
"Laddie! Laddie! haud yer tongue. . . . O Lord,
forgie 'm. He's young, and disna know better yet.
He canna unnerstan' thy ways, nor, for that matter,
can I prenten' to unnerstan' them mysel'. . . . But
O Lord, if it wad please thee to hear oor prayer . . .
eh! hoo we wad praise thee! . . ."

Now comes news that Andrew Falconer has vanished in India and must be supposed dead.

Grandmother summons Robert home from school to announce that henceforth they must omit Andrew from their prayers. Robert refuses, since God himself has not told him that his father is truly dead. But it is clear that Robert really believes the news:

> His favorite employment . . . had hitherto been to imagine how he would grow a great man, and set out to seek his father, and find him, and stand by him, and be his son and servant. Oh! to have the man stroke his head and pat his cheek, and love him! One moment he imagined himself his indignant defender, the next he would be climbing on his knee, as if he were still a little child, and laying his head on his shoulder. For he had no fondling his life long, and his heart yearned for it. But all this was gone now. A dreary time lay before him, with nobody to please, nobody to serve; with nobody to praise him. Grannie never praised him. She must have thought praise something wicked. . . .

The search for the lost father: here is the theme of *Robert Falconer*.[42]

Even as expressed in this passage, it makes us feel slightly queasy. For MacDonald is playing a curious game. He himself had lacked and wanted tenderness and physical affection all the years of his childhood. But he was *not* brought up by a stern grandmother missing the fondling of an affectionate father. He was brought up by a stern (but kind) father and missed the fondling of an affectionate mother. For Robert Falconer's story Mac-Donald has reversed the sexes and shifted the generations of his own youthful condition, and he has further obscured matters by faithfully portraying in Mrs. Falconer his own actual grandmother, who did *not* bring him up.

But Robert Falconer, like George MacDonald, longed deeply for a mother. What does Robert do immediately after he has heard the news of his father's death? He does just what Anodos did in *Phantastes:* he goes at once to the garret and begins to explore the bundles of paper on the shelves:

> What were they all about? He understood that they were his father's; now that he was dead, it would be no sacrilege to look at them. Nobody cared about them. He would see at least what they were. It would be something to do in this dreariness. Bills and receipts and everything ephemeral . . . met his view. Bundle after bundle he tried, with no better success. But as he drew near the middle of the second shelf, upon which they lay several rows deep, he saw something dark behind, hurriedly displaced the packets between, and drew forth a small work-box. His heart beat like that of the prince in the fairy-tale, when he comes to the door of the Sleeping Beauty. This at least must have been hers.[43]

MacDonald has not told us, nor has Robert Falconer told himself that he was looking for anything of "hers." Falconer told himself, and MacDonald told us, only that it would pass the time to search in the dead father's private belongings. But the mounting excitement told Falconer, told MacDonald, and now tells us what it was that he was looking for, and found.

Like Anodos, who searched the secret compartment of his father's escritoire and found there the tiny fairy ancestress for whom he felt such ambivalent longings—a miniature woman—Robert Falconer, when he opens the work-box, comes upon a miniature of his mother, a charming portrait set in pearls, which he puts on a thread and hangs about his neck under his clothes. Also in the box is a bit of paper with a hymn and the words " 'O Lord! my heart is very sore.' " His mother had been grieving for her profligate husband. While Anodos could pursue the vision of his mother across fairyland until he found the earth-goddess in the cottage on the island, Falconer, like MacDonald, lived in the real world, and their mothers were dead. Falconer's father, however, is only *reported* dead; so the son can continue to search for him to "be his son and servant."

Here again we touch on something very close to MacDonald's fantasy. In *If I Had a Father* and in the destroyed *Seekers and Finders,* the neglectful fathers had disguised themselves as servants to the sons. In *Robert Falconer* the son yearns to be a servant to the neglectful father. Can one escape the implication that MacDonald felt a burden of guilt? His own father had been deeply kind but could never be a mother; the boy had felt the ordinary resentment and rebelliousness which he could not own to himself and which he disguised as love, but he reproached himself for feeling: hence the preoccupation with fatherhood and sonship and mutual service; hence his theological certainty—so often reiterated—of God's benevolent fatherhood; hence the frequent comparison of earthly and heavenly fathers.

MacDonald heightens the drama: Robert has discovered his grandfather's violin, but his grandmother confiscates it. In her absence he finds it once more and begins to practice surreptitiously in a deserted thread factory that once formed part of the family linen business. There one day, Mary St. John, a kind neighbor, who knows of his secret love for music, discovers him lying on the floor with his head wounded. When he comes to, he calls out " 'Father, father,' " but will never tell how he got his wound. To the heavy indictment against the lost father this blow is now added, though we do not yet learn what the father was doing in the factory or why he knocked down his son.

Through long years packed with incident—a university career at Aberdeen, travel abroad, medical studies, the acquisition of wealth from a kind benefactor—the main thread of the narrative runs, though sometimes it is almost lost. Long after his initial discovery of his mother's work-box, Robert finds a lower compartment in it, containing a sealed letter addressed to his father: to deliver it un-broken will be "the first duty of his manhood." But the search is postponed until some clue can be found.

Then, in London, Robert meets by chance a female tramp from Rothieden, who tells him only that she has seen his father the night before. Hope revives:

> God 'ill gie me my father some time, grannie; for what man can do, wantin' a father? Human bein' canna win at the hert o' things, canna ken a' the oots an' ins, a' the sides o' love, excep' he has a father amo' the lave to love; an' I hae had nane, grannie. An' that God knows." [44]

The program of social work among the London poor begins, and everywhere Falconer spreads the word that his father, Andrew, lives somewhere among them. Once he glimpses him in a flash of lightning but is too busy saving a girl from suicide to pursue him and loses the track. But finally Robert's friends in the slums find Andrew, unconscious, a victim of drink and drugs, a thief who has robbed his own mother of the deeds to the property on which the factory stood so that he can sell the fabric of it (that is what he was doing there when he knocked Robert down), a total reprobate.

At first, faced with the unconscious derelict, Falconer feels that "romance had suddenly deserted his life, and it lay bare and helpless." But he straightway buckles down to the task of rehabilitation: as he undresses the helpless old man and puts him to bed, the sight of a pin in his clothes shows that some final instinct toward decency still remains. Falconer's own tears flow, and he begins to play the violin quietly to his father as he lies unconscious.

> Was it a fact or a fancy of Robert's eager heart? Did the man really say:—"Play that again, father. It's bonnie, that! I aye likit the *Floo'ers o' the Forest*. Play awa'. I hae had a frichtsome dream. I thocht I was i' the ill place. I doobt I'm no weel. But yer fiddle aye did me gude. Play awa', father?" [45]

The sodden father reverts to childhood and remembers his own father's playing. But, in fact, it is his son. The roles have been reversed with a vengeance: the son is father to his own father. It is the final triumph, the realization of the child's wish that as he grows large his parents may grow small.

When he judges the time ripe, Robert gives his father the sealed letter found in his mother's work-box, and identifies himself as their son. The letter is a long appeal to Andrew to abandon drink and join his wife in heaven. After long theological discussions by way of preparation, Robert brings Andrew back to Rothieden in time for grannie to know before she dies that her son has been found and has repented, and that her prayers have been answered. In floods of tears, father and son embrace over her deathbed. Soon afterward, they set out on a voyage to India, and are drowned when the steamer sinks.

The dedication of Falconer's life makes it impossible for him to love normally. Mary St. John, a beautiful Englishwoman ten years older than Robert, lives in the large house formerly owned by Robert's parents, attached to the small one that belongs to old Mrs. Falconer. One night by candlelight, she inadvertently opens a door between the houses, and appears to Robert on the stairs in her night clothes looking like an angel. But they do not meet until he is seeking a place to practice the violin safe from his grandmother, and Mary lets him cross her garden as a short cut to the deserted factory. She tends his wound after his father has knocked him down, kisses him on the forehead after he has lost his violin, and gives him piano lessons secretly in her own room, which he reaches clandestinely through the door that still connects the two houses. Robert's first sight of Mary's bedroom opens the doors to paradise:

> All before him was elegance, richness, mystery. Womanhood radiated from everything. A fire blazed in the chimney. A rug of long white wool lay before it. A little way off stood the piano. Ornaments sparkled and shone upon the dressing-table. The door of a wardrobe had swung a little open, and discovered the sombre shimmer of a black silk dress. Something gorgeously red, a Chinese crape shawl, hung glowingly beyond it. He dared not gaze any longer. He had already been guilty of an immodesty.

As Miss St. John comes into the room, she finds him in a reverie, and hears "him murmur the one word *Mamma!*" *It is the room he was born in.*

Thus the obvious sexual attraction of Miss St. John for Robert is overlaid, at the very moment when he comes to realize it himself, by his need to have her play the role of mother. MacDonald has already told us that Mary St. John had "met with a disappointment, and concluded herself dead to the world," so she will not fall in love with Robert either. He thinks of her first as beautiful woman, then as mother, and then, as the taboos begin to operate, as something still more forbidden and un-sexual:

> . . . she was just, like the type of womankind, a virgin mother. She saw the nobility of his nature through its homely garments, and had been, indeed, sent to carry on the work from which his mother had been too early taken away.

The emphasis is now on her virginity and inaccessibility. He shows her his mother's miniature and gives her his mother's thimble; she teaches him to play the piano, smoothes his manners, and helps make a gentleman of him. But grannie discovers what is going on, and without a word has the door between the houses walled up: she is implacably determined not to allow the possible sinfulness of music to corrupt her grandson. When Falconer feels the smooth plaster where the bolt to the door had formerly been, "It was to his hands the living tomb of his mother's vicar on earth." [46] He is too shy to ring the bell at the street door; since the clandestine lessons must stop, there can for a time be no contact at all.

But later he resumes the music lessons during his vacations and kisses Mary's hand; and still later, he tells his grandmother that they are practicing together. Scenting love, she says this time—for Robert is much older now— "'Weel, she's a fine lass, Miss St. John; and if ye tak' to ane anither ye canna do better.'" But Robert ". . . did not even suspect what she meant. He no more dreamed of marrying Miss St. John than of marrying his forbidden grandmother." Here is the old incest taboo, of which the fairy had reminded Anodos when she took on human stature, and he reached to embrace her: "'. . . a man must not fall in love with his grandmother, you know,'" to which one must add, *especially* when she is really a mother-surrogate like Anodos' fairy or Falconer's Miss St. John.

Yet MacDonald immediately manages to have things both ways:

> Robert, however, notwithstanding the pedestal upon which Miss St. John stood in his worshipping regard, began to be aware that his feeling toward her was losing something of its placid flow. . . .
>
> Possibly also Miss St. John may have had to confess to herself that had she not had her history already, and been ten years his senior, she might have found no little attraction in the noble bearing and handsome face of young Falconer. . . .

One evening, needing her help in a village emergency, he knocks on her door, and, thinking it is her maid, she bids him enter. She is brushing her hair; he is "seized with awe, and his limbs trembled." Instead of talking the English he has now learned, "the dim vision of Mary's lovely face between the masses of her hair, and the lavender odor that filled the room,—perhaps also a faint suspicion of impropriety. . . ."—all this drives him to talk

Scotch. Now Robert's state of heart toward Mary is confused indeed:

> But although she now *possessed* him, although at
> times he knew only himself as loving her, there was
> such a mountain air of calm about her, such an out-
> going divinity of peace, such a largely moulded
> harmony of being, that he could not love her other-
> wise than grandly.[47]

From mother-surrogate Mary is on the way to becoming
once again a possible object of sexual love.

But another influence at once supervenes. This is Falconer's friend Eric Ericson,[48] a poor tubercular student,
a sceptic, whom Robert yearns to redeem. Ericson thinks
himself in love with Mysie Lindsay, a charming empty-
headed sixteen-year-old girl, but he and Robert and Mary
St. John—marooned after a coach accident—spend a
night in a deserted mansion near the roadside. Instantly
Mary's "noble stately womanhood" impresses Ericson,
and as he prays,

> "O God . . . if thou art, why dost thou not speak?
> . . . . There can be no God or he would hear."
>
> "God has heard me!" said a full-toned voice of
> feminine tenderness somewhere in the air. Looking
> up, Ericson saw the dim form of Mary St. John half-
> way up the side of the lofty hall. The same moment
> she vanished—trembling at the sound of her own
> voice.
>
> Thus to Ericson as to Robert had she appeared as
> an angel.

Mary becomes his nurse; they fall in love. Though she
cannot convert him, she is lost to Falconer, who over-

hears Ericson on his deathbed say to Mary "'Perhaps a kiss in heaven may be as good as being married on earth.'" [49] (In heaven the golden key will no longer be necessary.) Long after, when he is engaged in his good works in London, he meets Mary St. John again, as a sister of mercy, living a life similar to his own; and he regularly leaves to her care the female derelicts whom he rescues.

The saccharine sentimentality of these episodes affects us more unpleasantly than it did MacDonald's contemporaries. MacDonald, who often succeeds in creating a living woman character, has failed with Mary St. John; she remains only an angelic dummy, partly because Robert Falconer from the first must lose her: he cannot have a happy love affair or marriage with any woman because MacDonald has made him a half-mad devotee of the new gospel of fatherhood. Falconer scolds a proud society girl who is rather in love with him. He enlists her in his program of rendering the poor "the justice the nation denies them." When she catches a fever and dies, Falconer weeps as he leaves her deathbed, and we surmise that, had things been otherwise, he might have been attracted to her. MacDonald himself sensed that he would not convince his readers that the physical and spiritual rescue of an aged confirmed drunkard and thief was worth the sacrifices that Robert Falconer had to make as a man, although that drunkard was his own father, and at the very end of the novel MacDonald argues that the conversion of Andrew had supreme value. But even contemporaries found it hard to accept the main theme of the novel, or its implications as a sermon.

If *Robert Falconer* fails, its reminiscences of Huntly lend it strength. Three of its other characters, the shoe-

maker, the waif, and the grandmother, complete our ap-
prehension of MacDonald's native town. Alexander Alexander, the shoemaker, called Elshender Elshender or
Dooble Sanny, is also the town drummer, a drunkard who
mistreats his wife. But he has a passion for music, and a
violin of his own. He gives Robert his first lessons:

> ". . . dinna han'le her as gin she war an egg-box.
> Tak' haud o' her as gin she war a leevin' crater. Ye
> maun jist straik her canny, an' wile the music oot
> o' her; for she's like ither women: gin ye be rouch
> wi' her, ye winna get a word oot o' her. . . . Come
> to me, my bonny leddy. Ye'll tell me yer story, winna
> ye, my dauty?"

Sanny manages to substitute his own inferior violin "the
auld wife," for Robert's violin, "the bonny leddy." Robert
sneaks into the shoemaker's house at night, and recovers
his own, but he has to leave his shoes behind, and this
later proves his undoing. On Sanny's deathbed Robert is
able to speed his repentance; the minister's reading of the
parable of the prodigal son does the rest: Sanny jubilantly
promises the Lord "I'll never lat taste o' whuskey intil my
mou', nor smell o' whuskey intil my nose, if sae be as I
can help it . . ." and Robert, who is having his own severe
religious troubles, notices ironically—and with imagery
taken from *Pilgrim's Progress*—that "Dooble Sanny, the
drinking, ranting, swearing shoemaker, was inside the
wicket-gate, and he was left outside for all his prayers,
with the arrows from the castle of Beelzebub sticking in
his back." [50]

The waif, Shargar ("a word of Gaelic origin, applied,
with some sense of the ridiculous, to a thin, wasted, dried-
up creature"), abandoned by his mother, a female tramp,

is the illegitimate son of the local wicked lord, the Marquis of Boarshead, and so half brother to the Marquis' heir, the even wickeder Lord Rothie. Without letting his grandmother know, Robert smuggles Shargar into the garret, and steals food for him from the table; he protects him at school, and turns him into a devoted friend. Suspicious that Robert is keeping animals in the garret, his grandmother searches in the dark; Shargar escapes, but because he is wearing a kilt, she thinks he is a woman. Horrified, Mrs. Falconer is convinced that Robert is depraved, a victim of the family curse that has ruined his father, her son Andrew. But when her mistake is cleared up, grannie takes Shargar into the house.

Poor Shargar: he finds himself in precisely the situation that would plague his American counterpart, Huck Finn, when sixteen years later his adventures would first see the light:

> . . . in bed, clean, and, for the first time in his life, between a pair of linen sheets,—not altogether to his satisfaction, for mere order and comfort were substituted for adventure and success.

> But greater trials awaited him. In the morning he was visited by Brodie, the tailor, and Elshender, the shoemaker, both of whom he held in awe as his superiors in the social scale, and by them handled and measured from head to feet . . . not only was he uncomfortable in his new clothes . . . but he was liable to be sent for at any moment by the awful sovereignty in whose dominions he found himself, and which, of course, proceeded to instruct him . . . in his own religious duties. . . . His past life of cold and neglect, and hunger and blows, and homelessness

and rags, began to glimmer as in the distance of a
vaporous sunset, and the loveless freedom he had
then enjoyed gave it a bloom, as of summer-roses.[51]

When Shargar and Robert find the confiscated fiddle
in old Mrs. Falconer's bed, they take the violin out of its
case and replace it with Boston's *Fourfold State,* that
sombre Calvinist work which we have already examined
in David Elginbrod's mother's library, "the torment of
Shargar's life on . . . Sunday evenings . . . ." Remembering his own youthful hatred of this book, MacDonald
playfully refers to the boys' trick as "the entombment of
Boston in a fifthfold state." [52] When Robert goes off to
Aberdeen, Shargar joins him. Robert's benefactor, Dr.
Anderson, takes Shargar in and pays for his education.
Both Robert and Dr. Anderson encourage Shargar to
think he can be a gentleman, Robert in particular advis-
ing him to defend his mother's honor if it should ever be
impugned.

By emphasizing the natural qualities of bravery and
gentlemanliness in the bastard Shargar, and by contrasting them with the villainy of his legitimate half-brother,
Lord Rothie, MacDonald is making one of his usual
vigorous comments on Victorian social standards in
general and on the profligacy of the aristocracy in particular. Lord Rothie has seduced a Rothieden cottar's daughter, in whose father's tiny cot Robert Falconer had found
The Arabian Nights and *The Tempest,* which had opened
the world of books to him, and lightened the dreariness
of his grandmother's regime. Having fled with her baby
to Aberdeen, the girl meets Robert and warns him that
Rothie now intends to run off to the continent with Mysie
Lindsay, the silly girl with whom Ericson had been in

love. By boarding the Antwerp packet with Shargar's help, and smuggling a letter to Mysie, and (somewhat incredibly) by climbing the tower of Antwerp cathedral and playing Scotch tunes on the cathedral bells, Robert warns the girl. The Belgian police put him in jail for a few days; so the reader does not hear how his efforts succeeded until many years and several hundred pages later.

India and the army do wonders for Shargar:

> The drawling walk had vanished, and a firm step and soldierly stride had taken its place; his bearing was free, yet dignified; his high descent came out in the ease of his carriage and manners; there could be no doubt that at last Shargar was a gentleman.

On leave in London, Shargar encounters his mother (the very tramp from whom Robert would hear about Andrew Falconer), and before Robert's own eyes thrashes a cabman who speaks roughly to her, thus putting the final proof to the proposition that he has become a gentleman. Robert Falconer, who had himself taught Shargar this principle, stands by delighted as his pupil practices it; and George MacDonald, who created them both, impresses upon his reader how thoroughly aristocratic his standards of gentlemanly conduct were, especially for one who so often protested against these standards.

When Falconer meets the girl whom Shargar wants to marry, a Miss Hamilton, he recognizes her at once as Mysie Lindsay. She tells him that years ago, in her foolish girlhood, she had indeed been saved by Falconer's playing on the Antwerp bells, and had taken refuge from Lord Rothie with a kindly Scotch lady at the inn in Antwerp. Not only had she reached home intact, but a rich childless relative had made her his heir on condition

that she take his name. While she is telling Falconer her
story, Rothie, now Marquis of Boarshead, enters; when
Mysie refuses to see him alone he proposes marriage to
her in the presence of Robert and Shargar. She refuses
him thus publicly, and he refers to his own past effort to
seduce her:

> "You are aware, madam . . . that your reputation
> lies in the hand I offer you?"
>
> "The worse for it, my lord . . . . But your lord-
> ship's brother will protect it."
>
> "My brother! . . . . What do you mean? I have
> no brother!"
>
> "Ye hae mair brithers than ye ken o', Lord Sandy,
> and I'm ane o' them," said Shargar.
>
> "You are either a liar or a bastard, then . . . ."
>
> ". . . No liar, my lord, but a bastard, thank
> heaven . . . . If I had been ain brither to you, my
> Lord, God only knows what a rascal I micht hae
> been." [53]

Boarshead reaches for his whip; Falconer throws him
across the room, where he falls over an ottoman; and the
servants are instructed to show him out. Exit the villain
in a burst of melodrama. Shargar marries Mysie; they
take his mother's other bastard, the little girl, out to India
with them.

The happy marriage of Mysie to Shargar ran counter to
any number of literary conventions. The Victorian public
did not believe that army officers were gentlemen by
definition or that bastards could become so. Nor could a
girl who had gone off alone with a man for several days
hope to regain her social position, even though by a miracle she had managed to protect her virginity from his

wickedness and her own folly. We cannot believe in MacDonald's treatment of the problems of Shargar and Mysie. As for Rothie, he is nothing but the standard villainous seducer, no more motivated than his exact counterpart, Beauchamp, in *Alec Forbes*, who makes love to Kate in order to spite Alec. To be a nobleman by birth is for MacDonald to be half condemned already. So long as Shargar is a child in the Falconer household, faced with adjusting to Calvinism, he rings true. When he grows up, and the problem of becoming a gentleman rears its head, and as nature's nobleman he has to be contrasted implicitly and explicitly with his own noble but wicked half-brother, he becomes only a puppet.

But even Dooble Sanny and Shargar are centers of minor interest by contrast to Mrs. Falconer and her religion, and its impact upon Robert, a theme almost as important as his search for his lost father. In her muslin cap, with its black ribbon, seated in her small horsehair-and-mahogany-furnished parlor, the formidable grannie rules her household with a hand of iron. " 'Noo, be quiet,' " is her greeting to Robert whenever he comes into the room, even after a long absence. In her way she loves him, but will not or cannot show it. Some of her books we have had a chance to examine in the small library left to David Elginbrod by his mother. Now we encounter them again, with additions. Part of Shargar's discomfort at being domesticated arose from the stifling religious atmosphere the books created:

And now the Shorter Catechism seemed likely to be changed into the Longer Catechism, for he had it Sundays as well as Saturdays, besides Alleine's "Alarm to the Unconverted," Baxter's "Saint's Rest,"

Erskine's "Gospel Sonnets," and other books of a like
kind. Nor was it any relief to Shargar that the gloom
was broken by the incomparable "Pilgrim's Progress" and the "Holy War," for he cared for none of
these things.

No wonder that it is Shargar who takes the lead in hiding
Boston's *Fourfold State* in the fiddle case.

> Tormented by fears of Hell, Robert himself made
> many frantic efforts to believe that he believed; took
> to keeping the Sabbath very carefully,—that is, by
> going to church three times, and to Sunday school
> as well; by never walking a step save to or from
> church; by never saying a word upon any subject
> unconnected with religion, chiefly theoretical; by
> never reading any but religious books; by never
> whistling; . . . all the time feeling that God was
> ready to pounce on him if he failed once; till again
> and again the intensity of his efforts utterly defeated
> their object. . . . But through the horrible vapors
> of these vain endeavors, which denied God alto-
> gether as the maker of the world, and the former of
> his soul and heart and brain, and sought to worship
> him as a capricious demon, there broke a little light
> . . . from the dim windows of such literature as
> came his way. Besides the "Pilgrim's Progress,"
> . . . . strange to say, was Defoe's "Religious Court-
> ship," and . . . Young's "Night Thoughts." [54]

Even more important was Klopstock's *Messiah*, where
Robert encountered the angel Abaddon, who repented
his rebellion. Did he get back to heaven? Klopstock did
not say. Until Robert finds the *Arabian Nights* and *Tem-*

pest, these are all the books he has: grandmother drops his copy of *The Lady of the Lake* behind the skirting board in the kitchen for the mice to eat.

Turning over Abaddon's case in his mind, Robert comes to his grandmother with "a plan for almost emptying hell." Those in heaven, he explains, seated at the supper of the Lamb, washed white, will hardly enjoy themselves when every now and then they hear the wailing of the damned and smell the burning flesh. He intends to work steadily to get to heaven himself, he says; and his grandmother gives him the usual counsel: " 'Strive and pray. Resist the deevil. Walk i' the licht. Lippen [trust] not to yersel' but trust in Christ and his salvation.' " But these clichés no longer serve. Robert Falconer has his own motive for working to get to heaven. He intends, with Christ's permission, to rise at table on his first night in heaven, and say:

". . . it's jist ruggin' an' rivin' at my hert to think o' them 'at's doon there. . . . Noo, we hae nae merit, an' they hae nae merit, an' what for are we here and them there? But we're washed clean an' innocent noo; and noo, whan there's no wyte lying upo' oursel's, it seems to me that we micht beir some o' the sins o' them 'at hae ower mony. I call upo' ilk' ane o' ye 'at has a frien' or a neebor doon yonner, to rise up an' taste nor bite nor sup mair till we gang up a'thegither to the fut o' the throne, and pray the Lord to lat's gang an' du as the Maister did afore's, and beir their griefs, and cairry their sorrows doon in hell there; if it may be that they may repent an' get remission of their sins, an' come up here wi' us at the lang last, an' sit doon wi' 's at this table a' throu'

the merits o' oor Saviour Jesus Christ at the heid o'
the table there."

Having propounded his plan, Robert bursts into tears
and runs from the room.

Startled by this bit of practical Christianity, Mrs. Falconer feels it somehow blasphemous, and knows that
Robert ought not to meddle with such matters. However,
her thoughts of her own lost son make her more sympathetic to the proposal than she otherwise would have
been. She has no real answer to the plan for emptying
hell, except the old one, and this she gives, while she
comforts him and wipes his tears:

> "Ye ken as weel's I du that them 'at gangs *there* their
> doom is fixed, and naething *can* alter 't. An' we're
> not to alloo oor ain fancies to cairry's ayont the
> Scripter. We hae oor ain salvation to work oot wi'
> fear an' trim'lin'. We hae naething to do wi' what's
> hidden. Luik ye till't 'at ye win in yersel'. That's
> eneuch for ye to min'."

The overpowering reality of heaven and hell to grandmother and grandson, and the humanity of both, she in
her conviction and he in his doubts, make this interchange
a moving one. MacDonald always was obsessed by the
emotional impact of Calvinism upon children, and this is
one of his most effective uses of the theme.

Yet Annie Anderson, in *Alec Forbes,* worried about her
own salvation and that of her friend and protector Alec,
convinces us and therefore moves us more than Robert
Falconer trying to empty hell by getting the saved to
work to free the damned. Annie is a child in trouble;
Robert is MacDonald the minister speaking effectively

through a fictional character. The plan itself simply expands that old cry of MacDonald's own, which he so often puts into the mouths of those in his novels of whom he approves: " 'I dinna care for Him to love me if He doesna love ilkabody,' " and we are not surprised to find Falconer himself uttering the thought in precisely these terms. It is natural too that when he come to read *Paradise Lost,* Robert sympathizes with Satan, and finds God "pompous, scarcely reasonable and somewhat revengeful." [55]

But although for special reasons Mrs. Falconer comforts Robert in this extremity, and although she does indeed truly love him, and we believe in her love, she remains an appalling tyrant. Suspicious because she has detected Shargar bringing home a perfectly good pair of Robert's shoes from the shoemaker (the ones he has had to leave behind when stealing his own violin back), Mrs. Falconer proceeds to interrogate Dooble Sanny, who gives her a mocking account of how the shoes came into his shop:

> "The de'il brocht them in ae day in a lang tangs; and says he, 'Elshender, men' the shune for puir Robby Faulkner; and dooble-sole them for the life o' ye; for that auld luckie minnie (grandmother) o' his 'ill sune hae him doon oor gait, and the grun's het i' the noo; an' I dinna want to be ower sair upon him; for he's a fine chield, an' 'll mak' a fine fiddler gin he live lang eneuch.' "

Laughingly Sanny then strikes up "The De'il's i' the Women," but he has unwittingly given Mrs. Falconer the clue she needed merely by referring to Robert as a fiddler. She goes home, and finds the fiddle gone from its case in her bed, and Boston's book in its place. Robert returns from school:

> As he entered his grandmother's parlor, a strange odor greeted his sense. A moment more, and he stood rooted with horror, and his hair began to rise on his head. His violin lay on its back on the fire, and a yellow tongue of flame was licking the red lips of a hole in its belly. All its strings were shrivelled up save one, which burst as he gazed. And beside, stern as a Druidess, sat his grandmother, in her chair, feeding her eyes with grim satisfaction on the detestable sacrifice. At length the rigidity of Robert's whole being relaxed in an involuntary howl like that of a wild beast, and he turned and rushed from the house in a helpless agony of horror.

His terrible grandmother has denied to him his music, the one resource that had kept "the finer faculties of the mind awake, wonder alive, and the interest above mere eating and drinking. . . ." [56] She completes her work and throws him altogether back upon the dreariness of his life when soon afterward she walls up the door that has taken him to Mary St. John.

Readers who dismiss such torture of a child as improbable need consult, for example, only the autobiography of Augustus Hare, and read the ghastly story of the way in which he suffered at the age of eight when his pet cat was deliberately hanged on the order of a relative, only because it gave him pleasure.[57] Having read it, let the student reflect that the order was given not by a retrograde Scotch Calvinist of the old school like Mrs. Falconer, but by the sister of that very Frederick Denison Maurice whom MacDonald so admired: this atrocity took place in precisely that milieu which he felt to be so superior to the Calvinism of his fellow Scots. Falconer, of course is not eight, but sixteen. After his first anguish at the death of the "bonny leddy," his violin, he confronts his grandmother, with fierce opposition:

> "She had nae blude to cry for vengeance; but the snappin' o' her strings an' the crackin' o' her banes may hae made a cry to gang far eneuch notwithstandin'." [58]

MacDonald makes Falconer the spokesman for his own views on repentance. He tells his father:

> ". . . you've got to repent; and God won't let you off; and you needn't think it. You'll have to repent some day."
>
> "In hell, Robert," said Andrew. . . .
>
> "Yes. Either on earth or in hell. Would it not be better on earth?"
>
> "But it will be no use in hell," he murmered.

In those few words lay the germ of the preference for hell of poor souls enfeebled by wickedness. They will not have to *do* anything there,—only to moan and cry and suffer forever, they think. It is effort, the outgoing of the living will that they dread. The sorrow, the remorse of repentance, they do not so much regard; it is the action it involves; it is the having to turn, be different, and do differently, that they shrink from; and they have been taught to believe that this will not be required of them there—in that awful refuge of the willless . . . . But tell them that the fire of God without and within them will compel them to bethink themselves; that the vision of an

open door beyond the smoke and the flames will
ever urge them to call up the ice-bound will, that
it may obey; that the torturing spirit of God in them
will keep their consciences awake, not to remind
them of what they ought to have done, but to tell
them what they *must* do now, and hell will no
longer fascinate them. . . .

"Father, it *will* be of use in hell," said Robert,
"God will give you no rest even there. . . ."

Will it be credible to my reader—that Andrew
interrupted his son with the words:—

"Robert, it is dreadful to hear you talk like that.
Why, you don't believe in the Bible!"

His words will be startling to one who has never
heard the lips of a hoary old sinner drivel out
religion.

Nor of course can Robert ever accept his grandmother's
view of God. As he grows older, he grows to be an ever-
more vocal defender of the MacDonald doctrine of a
loving God, and expresses it to his grandmother, in his
manhood, in no uncertain terms:

". . . ye speyk aboot him as if he was a puir, prood,
bailie-like body, fu' o' his ain importance, an' ready
to be doon upo' onybody 'at didna ca' him by name
o' 's office—aye think-thinkin' aboot's ain glory; in
place o' the quaiet, michty, gran', self-forgettin'
a'-creatin', a'-uphaudin', eternal bein', wha took the
form o' man in Christ Jesus, jist that he micht hae
't in's pooer to beir and be humblet for oor sakes.
. . . Whatever's no like Christ is no like God."

"But, laddie, he cam' to satisfee God's justice by
sufferin' the punishment due to oor sins; to turn

aside his wrath an' curse; to reconcile him to us. Sae he cudna be *a'thegither* like God."

"He did naething o' the kin', grannie. It's a' a lee that. He cam' to satisfee God's justice by giein' him back his bairns; by garrin' them see that God was just; by sendin' them greetin' hame to fa' at his feet, an' grip his knees an' say 'Father, ye're i' the richt.' . . . He took oor sins upo' him . . . by no sleicht o' han', by no quibblin' o' the lawyers, aboot imputin' his richteousness to us, an' sic like . . . but he took them, and took them awa'. . . ." [59]

As a man, Falconer has thought things through and become so convinced of his own point of view that he can tell his grandmother that the basis of Calvinist theology is "all a lie." This MacDonald deeply believed, and we must note to his great credit that he has given us in old Mrs. Falconer, as in Thomas Crann, a Calvinist who arouses our pity for the torments that true believers themselves must suffer, while she inflicts suffering on all around her.

IV

But the occasional portrait of a sympathetic Calvinist did not assuage the wrath of those contemporaries to whom MacDonald's onslaught was an affront. An anonymous writer in 1869, examining in alarm all of MacDonald's published work to date, expresses grave fears of his influence. Just because MacDonald's style is "seldom surpassed for natural ease and graceful flow," his writings present all the greater danger, especially to young ladies:

Heretical talk, under the rose, is fashionable in some most carefully guarded homes, and Mr. MacDonald's novels bring fresh food for those who would fain share in the freethinking of which they can only get whispers from the outside; and they supply, too, specious answers to many of the deep and terrible questions which more thoughtful young readers are not yet wise enough to leave in the hands of a Higher than they.

Specifically, the critic finds very offensive the "flippant" tone with which MacDonald characterizes the books in David Elginbrod's library—Boston, Erskine, and the rest. It is true, he admits, that the books are out of fashion, but

They were real and strong in their day, and at all events do not pretend, like some of those before us [i.e. those of MacDonald himself] to an inspiration superior to that of the Bible. A decent respect for opinion divergent from his own . . . would . . . have caused the writer to expunge so crudely juvenile a passage. But everywhere we find the strong revulsion against extreme Calvinism breaking all bounds, and including in its bitter scorn much that is among the most precious articles of belief.

The concept that one may repent in hell and so qualify for redemption creates a "Protestant purgatory," where we are to have a body, "there will be snowdrops and sunsets," and we shall see our friends again. MacDonald's view, that the truly hardened sinner may as well get to hell as quickly as possible and begin the repentance that he has shunned on earth, stimulates his critic to declare that this disposes of all arguments against capital punishment, and justifies the Sicilian Vespers and the Massacres of St. Bartholomew's Day.

Note the real anger with which the critic attacked: MacDonald flicked his opponents on the raw. This particular reviewer was not above using the snide snobbery of the day as a weapon. He criticizes MacDonald's allegedly poor punctuation as reflecting his "want of early education," and remarks that one can understand why MacDonald prefers the poorer members of society "for it is not so easy to preach to our equals or superiors either in age, knowledge, or station; and to talk or write is with Mr. MacDonald necessarily to preach." [60]

Another opponent, George McCrie, writing in 1875, couples MacDonald with George Eliot and complains that a novel is no longer what it used to be and ought to be: instead of entertaining and relaxing, novelists now preach. The right way to start a new religion, he protests, is by an elaborate work of demonstration, not by a novel, which, because of its popularity, is "not a fair way of propagating religious views." Specifically, McCrie disapproves of MacDonald's attacks on the Shorter Catechism, finds the reformation of Alec Forbes and Mr. Cupples "ludicrous," and disbelieves in the power of love alone to work such a change in human beings as that which MacDonald has portrayed in Murdoch Malison. MacDonald, he feels, ignores the entire meaning and implications of sin.

Moreover, McCrie declares, in the "mawkish Wordsworthian sentimentality" of Margaret Elginbrod, "sacred matters are brought into grotesque connection with things of a lighter character," and are "dwarfed down into insignificance and contempt. . . . There is a de-

ceptive appearance of great profoundness in the importance" attached to a "religion showing itself in the
department of the childish and the small . . . such as
finds God in the sough of fir trees." MacDonald must be
held responsible for "the tendency to substitute the
shallows of natural religion for the glorious mysteries
and depths of evangelical theology." Also it is "unfair"
to portray in David Elginbrod a splendid example of the
old Scotch rural stock, who has adopted MacDonald's
"lax heresies." In real life, such a man as David *would
not be* a heretic. The worst of MacDonald, according to
McCrie, is that he combines with his perversity impos-
ing moral qualities. But

> when he hoists his tight-rope of daring theological
> speculation, and proceeds to mount it, that he may
> show how nimbly he can walk over it, our admira-
> tion is at an end; and when we see him stretch it
> above a gulf infinitely more fearful than that into
> which the Niagara Falls descend, and cross and re-
> cross it, balancing himself with Denison Maurice's
> pole, we not only condemn him, but cannot hold the
> community which goes out to see him guiltless.[61]

Though few modern critics will share McCrie's theology, many will agree with some of his strictures: David
Elginbrod *is* incredible, MacDonald *does* cavalierly push
aside tough theological and philosophical questions; he
is ungovernably sentimental; emotion rules, not intellect;
indeed, MacDonald glories in the defeat of intellect and
the sovereignty of emotion, as if the processes of reason
were in themselves disgraceful. In one way McCrie still
seems quite right: MacDonald was not fair.

But twenty-odd years later, the tone of the opponents

had greatly softened. To Thomas Gunn Selby, writing in 1897 from the same point of view as the earlier critics, but far more in sorrow than in anger, George MacDonald no longer seemed the menace he had seemed in the sixties and seventies. Now other and greater dangers threatened: Thomas Hardy with what Selby calls his "pits of night-soil," and other novelists who were victims of the current "epidemic of feverish eroticism." By contrast MacDonald is "sweet in ethical temper," although often theologically unsound. Reproachfully, Selby objects to Falconer's characterization of his grandmother's God (as a "puir, prood, bailie-like body, fu' o' his ain importance") in the speech quoted above: the

> righteousness which is the ruling note in the old evangelical theology certainly deserves a more reverent description than that of a mere court etiquette, and is not truly or fittingly treated when made an antithesis to the goodwill of the divine Fatherhood

Though we may listen sympathetically to David Elginbrod when he expounds his doctrine of imputed righteousness—

> "That man only is justifeed wha pits himsel' into the Lord's hands to sanctifee him. Noo! An' that'll no' be dune by pittin' a robe o' richteousness upo' him afore he's gotten a clean skin aneath it."—

we should realize that MacDonald has gone to the other extreme and fallen into the opposite danger:

> The past peril consisted in making the doctrine of justification overshadow that of regeneration; the peril of the moment is lest we should reverse the

process, and forget the equal importance and the in-
separable connexion of the two parts of man's salvation.

Selby notes with some disapproval MacDonald's "be-
nign determinism," his emphasis on the heart and moral
sense rather than on the mind and understanding, his
Wordsworthian pantheism.

> Perhaps the optimism of George MacDonald . . .
> takes insufficient account of the facts of human life
> and character. . . .

Moreover,

> He ignores the scientific interpretation of Nature,
> and never attempts to adjust it to his rosy Words-
> worthian aestheticism. These may be some of the
> reasons why his influence outside Christian circles
> is scarcely appreciable. The course of thought has
> grown more bitterly pessimistic in spite of the voice
> of hope he has uplifted in the wilderness. And yet,
> if the optimism is dreamy and exaggerated, his
> view is at least nearer the truth than its opposite.

Here Selby enables us to record the great change in the
thirty years since *Robert Falconer* had appeared. The
critic of 1869—the year after its publication—would
have been shocked at the very thought that there might
exist "circles" other than Christian. He attacked Mac-
Donald as a heretic. But in 1897, though deploring his
intellectual softness, Selby welcomes him as an ally
against the new enemy: pessimistic scepticism deriving
from scientific thinking.

As for the doctrine of divine fatherhood, in which the

heavenly father is constantly likened to an earthly father, Selby vigorously objects to its sentimentality. He admits —as the vigorous Calvinists of the 60's and 70's would not—that since the Reformation the concept of God had been far too one-sidedly harsh and gloomy, and welcomes the softening that comes with the new emphasis on Christ's benignity and love. But MacDonald again has gone to the other extreme. He is

> inclined to interpret the divine Fatherhood from a sentimental standpoint and to make domestic emotions a scale by which to measure God and the principles of His government.

This is to overlook the fact that God has more than one child, and that

> When paternal love has two or more children to deal with, it must take the scales of justice into one hand and the sword into the other, and become august and unswerving righteousness.

MacDonald recognizes only that theology that derives from

> that facile surface emotion for the offspring which is shared by eagle and tiger in common with man, and which does not send its roots deep into those deep, broad, sacred qualities of human nature which constitute its supreme distinction.

Selby scornfully sums up MacDonald's belief

> the ultimate analysis of the ethical mystery behind human life, and of the theological expressions assumed by that mystery, is to be found in a sweet and effeminate type of domestic love.[62]

Here Selby cuts close to the bone. His use of the terms
sweet and *effeminate* shows that his reflections on Mac-
Donald's views had brought him by a different road to
the same point that we had reached in our own examination and analysis of *Robert Falconer*. MacDonald tried
to transform the role of the father in the family into the
role of the mother; like Robert Falconer he had had no
fondling in his life. His confusion made him uncertain
what he sought: in *Phantastes* Anodos openly seeks a
mother; but Robert Falconer, though ostensibly seeking
a father and finding him, is concealing (and unsuccess-
fully) his true yearning for a mother. So, too, the
paternal God, who ostensibly loves all His children like
a father, actually loves them instead like MacDonald's
own rather sickly conception of the mother. "Sweet and
effeminate": one must admit that Selby has hit the mark.

He does not cite, but we may now do so once again,
the lament of old Mrs. Falconer for her son Andrew already quoted above. Addressing God, she says He would
not put Andrew in hell *"gin ye was a mither yersel'."*
And, we may note, God does *not* put Andrew in hell.
He acts exactly as if he *was* a mither himsel'. The "gin
ye was a mither yersel'" formula is, we see, only a
version of the Elginbrod epitaph, but the substitution of
"mither" is all-important. This is the real trouble with
Robert Falconer and with George MacDonald: they had
to put up with earthly and heavenly fathers when what
they wanted was an earthly mother. They wanted fathers
to be as much like mothers as possible. Lacking a mother,
they attributed to the heavenly father what they long-
ingly imagined to be her qualities.

Selby rightly finds that the Elginbrod epitaph sums
up MacDonald's creed. Irritated, he calls it, and what

it represents, "a grotesque mixture of the boldness of
faith and of the irreverent Gnosticism which is puffed up
with the conviction that it can solve all mysteries." If
you read MacDonald, he adds, you might think there
was nothing in the New Testament except the Sermon
on the Mount and the parable of the prodigal son.
Human fathers simply are *not* divine, nor is the divine
one simply human: He is *God* the Father as well as God
the *Father*. MacDonald has simply blinked the doctrine
of the atonement: it was after all Christ's death that
made the forgiveness of sin possible. Selby would maintain that what Mrs. Falconer said to Robert was after
all true, and not "all a lie":

> "But, laddie, he cam' to satisfee God's justice by
> sufferin' the punishment due to oor sins; to turn
> aside his wrath an' curse; to reconcile him to us."

Moreover, although MacDonald proclaims his opposition to Calvinism, he has, unwittingly, because he is too
ignorant to realize it, retained a form of its theory of
volition: he has replaced the elect and the reprobate
divisions of mankind with an elect and a later elect:

> George MacDonald is a determinist, but his deter-
> minism is gracious, amiable, and smile-wreathed,
> leaving no member of the human race unsaved at
> last. . . . He takes little account of the part played
> by the human will in resisting the righteousness of
> God, and of the sinister potentialities of that will.
> The will of a bad man in the MacDonald philosophy
> is simply inactive; it is not deliberately and desper-
> ately set upon evil. Sin is simply an unhappy fit of
> somnambulism [a shrewd dig at Euphra]. Depravity

is not so much enmity toward God and resentfulness of virtue and its demands, as a stubborn indisposition to exercise the power of choice.

No wonder such simple and unreal depravity can be cured in hell. MacDonald, Selby maintains, ignores the fact that the choice of evil implies the refusal of good, and indeed the whole idea that human beings *have* a choice. The trouble with the doctrine that in the end everybody will be saved is that it comforts "not those who mourn but those who are in the heyday of their frivolity and transgression, building them up into resolute indifference to spiritual things." [63]

Our fourth (and last) theological opponent of Mac-Donald, S. Law Wilson, writing in 1899, sounds similar notes. Like Selby, Wilson dismisses most "modern" novelists (Hardy, Gissing, Grant Allen) as "cloacal," and welcomes MacDonald's "rich and delicate imagination, lofty moral thoughtfulness, splendid descriptive power, deep spiritual insight, a vast wealth of illustration, and a vivid character-painting scarcely surpassed by any of our living writers." But then he attacks MacDonald's "gallery of Calvinist cranks," and feels that his scorn for the worthies in Elginbrod's library is indiscriminate caricature. MacDonald's own piety he finds "maudlin" and "sentimental," his theology "perverse," and, for example, his notions of conversion "childish and even silly." Like Selby, he declares that MacDonald simply has not understood human depravity or the need for regeneration.

Undue emphasis is laid on the part played by natural influence in the process of man's salvation, and regenerating efficiency, which we had thought belonged exclusively to the Spirit of God, is freely attributed to such things as fiddles, kites, scenery, music, and the memorials of departed friends.

When Cupples and Alec Forbes take the pledge, it is only "the spirit of essential life and humanity" that is necessary; Murdoch Malison is reformed by pity and remorse; Alec Forbes, in the end, by the weather (in Greenland). Wilson dismisses this scornfully as "sentimental vaporing."

> . . . in the MacDonald theology . . . we are each of us blessed with a nature good enough from the beginning, and, once we cleanse away a trifle of rubbish that overlays or obscures it we "find ourselves," and very soon find our God.[64]

Most readers in the 1960's will probably find the theological differences between MacDonald and his opponents without much reality. Even in his own day, his master, A. J. Scott, and at least two leading Scotch ministers, John McLeod Campbell (1800–1872) and Norman Macleod (1812–1872), as well as the layman Thomas Erskine of Linlathen (1788–1861), believed in a theology approximating MacDonald's. So, within limits, did Maurice. But MacDonald allowed his personal history to determine the nature of his God. And he alone commanded a novelist's public.

By the time of his death he no longer seemed shocking. In 1906, indeed, only a year after his death, a critic could write

> To the liberal and emancipated thinkers of today there is nothing shudderingly irreverent in this demand upon the Creator to live at least up to a human standard of kindness; but to the stern up-

holder of the stern and wrathful God of Israel of
that time it seemed a very daring appeal.[65]

And not only daring but comforting. As an old friend
wrote when MacDonald died in 1905:

> It would be impossible to say how many souls, dis-
> tressed, troubled, perplexed by the Calvinism of
> thirty or forty years ago, found George MacDonald
> a refuge from the storm. I question whether any
> priest sitting in his confessional ever had so many
> hearts laid bare to him as he. Certainly no priest
> ever dealt with perplexed souls in a wiser way . . .
> he was a great gift of God to the latter half of the
> nineteenth century.[66]

Up to a point, then, the protests of his ministerial
critics simply show whose ox was gored. On the other
hand, nobody, even now, who takes seriously the problems of sin and regeneration can help but fear that, if
MacDonald's doctrine should be accepted, men would
rely on their own goodness and on the certainty of their
own eventual redemption: evil in this world might increase. MacDonald's lack of rigor in definition, his repudiation of the intellect, his visceral and emotional
response to the problems of human life, his bland self-
confidence, his reiteration of his own vague doctrines of
benevolent Fatherhood, go a long way toward justifying
—from the intellectual point of view alone—the harsh
strictures of his opponents. Even his own loving son
Ronald wrote in 1911:

> . . . he was at one time known most widely for his
> fight against the Calvinistic doctrines of election
> and eternity of punishment. Today, I think he might

be pained to see how base a sense of freedom from obligations has arisen as a by-product of a religious movement in which he took so influential a part.[67]

And when we ask a different question: whether the three major novels can survive as works of art under the weight of preaching with which he loaded them, we have to answer that *David Elginbrod* and *Robert Falconer* cannot. They vividly express the revolt of a mystic, influenced by his childhood circumstances, by his illness, and by the German romantics, against the harshness of early nineteenth-century Scotch Calvinist doctrine and its supporters. They engage our interest as social and psychological documents. But as art, with the exception of *Alec Forbes,* they fail.

CHAPTER 5

Wilfrid Cumbermede and Other Fiction

". . . a dominant form tends to attract to itself writers
whose talents would have fitted them much better for
other kinds of work. Thus . . . a mystic and natural
symbolist like George MacDonald is seduced into writing novels."

C. S. Lewis, *The Allegory of Love* *

I

After *Robert Falconer,* the novels poured out in a steady
stream. Novels sold: the public demanded more and
more. As George Smith had told MacDonald, "Nothing
but fiction pays." It was not MacDonald's choice; he
once remarked: "I like preaching best, then writing
poetry, then writing stories." But he needed the money
that novels earned him, and also felt a moral responsibility to preach his sermon to the largest possible audience. His son Ronald once asked him

why he did not, for change and variety, write a
story of mere human passion and artistic plot. He
replied that he would like to write it. I asked him
then further whether his highest literary quality was
not in a measure injured by what must to many
seem the monotony of his theme—referring to the

* New York: Oxford University Press, Galaxy Books, 1958, p.
232.

novels alone. He admitted that this was possible;
and went on to tell me that, having begun to do his
work as a Congregational minister, and having been
driven by causes here inconvenient to be stated, into
giving up that professional pulpit, he was no less
impelled than compelled to use unceasingly the new
platform, whence he had found that his voice could
carry so far. Through stories of everyday Scottish
and English life, whose plot, consisting in the conflict of a stereotyped theology with the simple human aspiration toward the divine, illustrated the
solvent power of orthodox Christianity, he found
himself touching the hearts and stimulating the consciences of a congregation never to be herded in
the largest and most comfortable of Bethels.[1]

With few exceptions, the twenty-three novels Mac-
Donald wrote in addition to the three we have already
examined at first glance seem simply to ring the changes
on one or more of his favorite themes. The preacher's
message varies little, although he may sometimes choose
a new or unusual text to preach upon or find an arresting new way to make his point. The "Scotch" novels
are by and large better than the "English" ones. The
poorer ones in each category sometimes seem perfunc-
tory. Yet we must bear in mind the incessant drudgery
necessary to produce so many: sometimes two or even
more were running simultaneously as serials in different
periodicals. With so vast, so steady an output the wonder is perhaps less that MacDonald should often have
descended to banality as that he should ever have risen
to writing that is still readable, and something more, almost a century later. Even the worst (sometimes espe-

cially the worst) of MacDonald's novels have their own peculiar interest.

Of them all by far the most arresting is *Wilfrid Cumbermede* (1872),[2] a *Bildungsroman* like *Alec Forbes* or *Robert Falconer,* set, like them, in the early nineteenth century but told in the first person. Long ago Greville MacDonald suggested that his father had written this novel under the influence of the emotions aroused in him by his involvement in John Ruskin's love affair with Rose La Touche. But Greville never pursued his own suggestion further, nor has anyone else apparently read *Wilfrid Cumbermede* with this in mind. Yet because it does indeed represent MacDonald's effort to make in fictional form a statement about the Ruskin affair, this novel takes on an interest all its own.

Its first fourteen chapters, about a third, move with economy and charm, and without preaching, but with certain ominous overtones not heard unless one listens for them. As a child, Wilfrid, an orphan, lives with his uncle, a well-educated farmer. Though the family seems of humble origin, there is a secret about Wilfrid, symbolized by an ancient sword that hangs on the wall, and by a splendid watch given him by his ninety-five-year-old great-grandmother, who lives upstairs, eager for death. During a great storm one night, the child overhears his uncle refusing the offer of a mysterious visitor to take him away and bring him up and pay for his education. Wilfrid feels great relief when his uncle rejects the plan.

But the whole episode has aroused feelings of guilt and terror. Some time before, Wilfrid had discovered in the lumber room a mechanical toy invented by an ancestor:

It had a kind of pendulum . . . my fancy concerning it was that if I could keep the pendulum wagging long enough, it would set [the] trees [outside the window] going too; and if I still kept it swinging, we should have such a storm of wind as no living man had ever felt or heard of. . . . I had not . . . had the courage to keep up the oscillations beyond ten or a dozen strokes; partly from fear of the trees, partly from a dim dread of exercising power whose source and extent were not within my knowledge. I kept the pendulum in the closet . . . and never spoke to any one of it.

On a hot windless afternoon sometime later, Wilfrid decides

I was nearly a man now; I would be afraid of things no more; I would get out my pendulum, and see whether that would not help me. Not this time would I flinch from what consequences might follow . . . I strode to the closet in which the awful instrument dwelt. . . . I set it in motion, and stood watching it. It swung slower and slower. It wanted to stop. It should not stop. I gave it another swing. On it went, at first somewhat distractedly, next more regularly, then with slowly retarding movement. But it should not stop. . . . I sat and watched it with growing awe, but growing determination as well. Once more it showed signs of refusal; once more the forefinger of my right hand administered impulse. Something gave a crack inside the creature: away went the pendulum swinging with a will. I sat and gazed almost horror-stricken. Ere many moments had passed, the feeling of terror had risen to such a

height that, for the very terror, I would have seized
the pendulum in a frantic grasp. I did not.

As it continues, the wind actually does rise and grows
steadily into a gale. Wilfrid decides he must stop the
pendulum: "I seized hold of the oscillating thing, and
stopped it; but to my amaze and consternation, the
moment I released it on it went again." He decides he
must take it to bed with him "and stifle its motions with
the bed-clothes." But, as a horseman gallops up outside,
it stops. This is the man who wants to take Wilfrid
away. Wilfrid is sure that his playing with the pendulum
has brought on the storm.

Can we doubt that we have been reading a description
of masturbation? Once we accustom ourselves to the
shock of thinking of it in this way, and contemplate the
possibility that MacDonald himself so thought of it, we
understand why he imagined and set down the episode.
MacDonald was Ruskin's confidant. Ruskin himself regarded his youthful masturbation as a dreadful sin, and
confessed it as such to Mrs. Cowper-Temple and Mac-
Donald. Tormented as he was by Ruskin's difficulties,
was not MacDonald, an experienced worker with symbols, trying to tell the story of an oversensitive and
deeply imaginative boy? At school, where Wilfrid is very
happy, he has a fantasy, "the family romance," as psychologists call it: "Aware of the humbleness of my birth,
and unrestrained by pride in my parents—I had lost
them so early—I would indulge in a daydream of what
I would gladly have been."

He tells stories to his friends:

My favourite invention, one for which my audience
was sure to call . . . and which I enlarged and

varied everytime I returned to it, was of a youth in humble life, who found at length that he was of far different origin than he had supposed. I did not know then that the fancy, not uncommon with boys, had its roots in the deepest instincts of our human nature. I need not add that I had not yet read Jean Paul's *Titan,* or *Hesperus,* or *Comet.*

But Wilfrid's uncle pledges him to try not to learn the secret until he is old enough, and meanwhile gives him for his own the great sword, overt symbol of a noble ancestry, but also a phallic symbol of manhood, like Mossy's golden key.

The housekeeper of a neighboring great house, Mold-warp Hall, which belongs to Sir Giles Brotherton, a Baronet, shows Wilfrid the great library there. Here he meets Clara, a charming girl of thirteen, a little older than he. On one of his visits to the Hall, he brings his sword to compare it with those in the collection there, and is invited to spend the night. He and Clara watch from the battlements as the guests arrive for a ball. The children are shut out on the roof; she gives him a kiss to help his courage, and he bravely climbs around a buttress and in at a window so that he can let her back into the house. During the night the sword is mysteriously taken from him. He has somehow been unmanned. Wilfrid discovers that Clara's father is an attorney, the very man who had offered to adopt him and caused his fright. His uncle now warns that this man is a former friend of Wilfrid's father, but "dangerous" and "worldly." Up to this point in the story, the Ruskin-character is Wilfrid himself.

Now, with the hero in his teens, the story enters a

new phase, in which struggle and passion predominate. Wilfrid goes off to school in Switzerland with a boy his own age, Charley Osborne, deeply sensitive, the son of a clergyman. Charley's father is "severe, pure, and irritable . . . an *Evangelical* of the most pure, honest, and narrow type," who is "overlaying and smothering" his son's life. As for Charley, "A tremulousness about the mouth betrayed a nervous temperament." At the first sight of the Jungfrau,

> "Oh, Charley!" was all I could say. Our hands met blindly and clasped each other. I burst into silent tears . . . His eyes too were full of tears, but some troubling contradiction prevented their flowing . . .

Here MacDonald quite explicitly introduces a new theme: the conflict between strict evangelical piety as embodied in Mr. Osborne, and the Wordsworthian pantheism that sees God in nature. Wilfrid tells us

> . . . I was coming in for my share in the spiritual influence of Nature, so largely poured on the heart and mind of my generation. The prophets of the new blessing, Wordsworth and Coleridge, I knew nothing of . . . Yet I was under the same spell . . . Nature was a power upon me. I was filled with the vague recognition of a present soul in Nature, with a sense of the humanity everywhere diffused through her and operating upon me.

For his part, Mr. Osborne, before taking his leave of the boys,

> . . . gave us a solemn admonishment on the danger of being led astray by what men called the beauties

of Nature—for the heart was so desperately wicked, that even of the things God had made *to show his power,* it would make snares for our destruction.

But the terrifying father now departs for the moment, and Charley begins to pick up:

It is a terrible thing when the father is the cloud and not the sun of his child's life . . . From his father he had inherited a conscience of abnormal sensibility; but he could not inherit the religious dogmas by means of which his father had partly deadened, partly distorted, his: and constant pressure and irritation had already generated a great soreness of surface.[3]

The Ruskin personality is now split, Wilfrid representing the attractions of Wordsworthian pantheism and Charley the unfortunate impact of evangelical narrowness on the spirit.

Wilfrid and Charley room together at the school. Their relationship leaves little doubt in our minds: they are lovers. Lost and wet through after an Alpine walk, Wilfrid takes refuge at a mountain inn, where the lady of the house and her daughter offer him the girl's clothes while his own are drying. They put her jewelry on him as well as her garments, and he himself asks them to comb his hair as much like the girl's as possible. "I was but a boy," he tells us, "and had no scruple concerning a bit of fun of which I might have been ashamed a few years later." " 'One girl may kiss another,' " he says, and does so. At first glance this disguise seems to help the plot: Clara and her father, who are travelling in Switzerland, happen in, and talk about Wilfrid without recognizing him as a Swiss girl, until he speaks up and lets them know who he is. But in fact nothing that they say is of any importance for the story, nor is there any particular reason why they should have appeared at that moment. Did not MacDonald wish his reader to see Wilfrid as effeminate?

When Wilfrid is sick, Charley nurses him "more like a woman than a boy," and he himself ". . . learned to love Charley Osborne more dearly. We renewed an affection resembling from afar that of Shakespeare for his nameless friend; we anticipated that informing *In Memoriam*." Wilfrid dreams that both are dead; in the dream, Charley urges him to take courage; Wilfrid begs Charley not to leave him, and finds himself "floating half reclined on the air. We met midway each in the other's arms." As the dream goes on, the boys find themselves in Mr. Osborne's rectory, and Charley disappears, while Wilfrid finds himself lying in the bed beside Mr. Osborne. He wakes up in fright: the terrifying but uncompromisingly masculine father has attracted him to his bed. Wilfrid never tells Charley his dream, for fear of overstimulating him, and ends the account, "Oh my Charley! if ever we meet in that land so vaguely shadowed in my dream, will you not know that I loved you heartily well?" The schoolmaster becomes suspicious of them because they are always alone together. Their schoolmates also dislike them for the same reason, one of them referring to the two as "a pair of sneaks." The schoolmaster whips Wilfrid for taking part in a fight that begins because of the two boys' unpopularity, and Charley weeps because he feels disgraced at not having rushed to Wilfrid's defense. The master will no longer

permit the two boys to sleep in the same room, "and
school was not what it had been to either of us."

When we turn from the published text of *Wilfrid
Cumbermede* to the original manuscript and examine
these episodes as MacDonald originally set them down
on paper, we find our impressions strengthened by words
that MacDonald wrote down and later expunged, either
from the manuscript itself or, presumably, from the
proofs. Wilfrid loves Charley "more as a sister than as
a brother loves. Certainly such was the fashion in which
he loved me." MacDonald expands the reference to *In
Memoriam,* and adds "Indeed had it not been for the
more athletic exertions to which Mr. Forest (the schoolmaster), in regard of our returning strength, gradually
accustomed us, there was even danger of [our mutual
affection for] and tenderness over each other [degener-
ating into an appearance of] begetting a sentimentality
[which would have been] not only mawkish in the eyes
of others but actually tending to undermine the love
itself." (Words within brackets crossed out in MS.) Later,
Wilfrid feels an irresistible impulse to throw his arms
around Charley's neck and kiss him, but resists it because, he reminds himself, he is not a girl.

At Oxford, the two meet again, with some embarrassment on Charley's part; he is now the friend of the
dissipated Geoffrey Brotherton, son of Sir Giles of the
Hall, who is unaccountably hostile and snobbish toward
Wilfrid. When Charley confesses that he has got a girl
pregnant and fears that he must marry her, Wilfrid saves
him by investigating and discovering that it is all a joke
played on the innocent Charley by Brotherton and his
dissolute friends. The old friendship resumes once more:

"When it was his turn to come to my rooms, I would watch for his arrival almost as a lover for his mistress." And when Charley moves to London to read for the bar, Wilfrid follows him and shares his rooms. Mr. Osborne is horrified to find him there and treats him with such cold hostility that Wilfrid has to leave. It is of course Wilfrid as narrator who tells us that what Mr. Osborne fears for Charley in Wilfrid is the influence of infidel views. To our way of thinking, the relationship had enough in it to alarm a father, regardless of Wilfrid's religious ideas.

It would be futile to debate the precise degree of Mac-Donald's awareness of homosexual relationships, or of his intention to portray one. But even if one sets aside as sentimental Victorian hyperbole the terms that the young men use about each other, one can hardly miss the implications of Wilfrid's dream or of his transvestitism. We must inevitably regard the boys as having a homosexual relationship, and we can easily understand the circumstances in Charley's and Wilfrid's lives that led to it.

MacDonald, like Ruskin, had himself experienced an Alpine revelation, but in middle age, not in youth, and long after he had already undergone great influence from Wordsworth. Wilfrid and Charley undergo the same emotional experiences, in that same, deliberately chosen, Swiss environment so conducive to discussions of the true relationships between God and Nature. But there is more in these episodes of *Wilfrid Cumbermede* than that. Ruskin's love for the beautiful young neurotic Rose La Touche had deeply involved the MacDonalds. Ruskin had "laughingly" told George MacDonald that he was not impotent and had explained away his failure to

consummate his first marriage. MacDonald had come
to believe that Ruskin's first wife, now Effie Millais, had
calumniated Ruskin in the warning letter she had written
to Rose's mother, Mrs. La Touche, which Mrs. La Touche
had shown to Rose. The MacDonalds took the grave
responsibility of arranging interviews between the ill-
assorted pair of lovers after Rose's parents had forbidden
them to meet, but a seeming return of happiness had cul-
minated in another bitter and disappointing separation.

MacDonald could not of course deal with the affair
directly or introduce into his novel recognizable portraits of the real personages. But, in his portrait of Mr.
Osborne, and in his account of Mr. Osborne's impact on
Charley, MacDonald was thinking of the tragedy that—
so he believed—evangelical Christianity had made of
Ruskin's life: first that of his over-possessive parents, and
then that of Mr. and Mrs. La Touche, one of whose
main objections to Ruskin was that in their narrow view
he was not a believer. MacDonald says of Charley:
"Gifted with the keenest perceptions, and a nature unusually responsive to the feelings of others, he was born
to be an artist." He is describing a nature precisely like
Ruskin's own. No doubt, he also wanted to use the hint
(or more) of sexual abnormality in the relations between
Wilfrid and Charley as a substitute for what he could not
possibly say about the peculiar sexual constitution of
Ruskin.[4]

In the final third of *Wilfrid Cumbermede*, MacDonald
shows himself unable to resolve simultaneously the two
sets of themes: that of a lost heir, and that of religious
and sexual tensions and abnormal passion. The book
collapses hopelessly. Sir Giles Brotherton offers Wilfrid
the chance of restoring the books in the library at Mold-

warp Hall. But, although Clara is often present, Mac-
Donald does not revert to his usual theme of love in the
library: indeed, Wilfrid, though attracted by Clara, keeps
from falling in love with her because he resents her
friendly conversations with Geoffrey Brotherton. Instead,
it is Charley Osborne who falls in love with Clara, while
Wilfrid is more and more attracted to Charley's sister,
Mary Osborne. Wilfrid has a dream about Mary, in
which she figures as his beloved "Athanasia," the death-
less one, a dream of love and death underground—like
Phantastes—and of the removal of a veil; just as Isis was
Rosebud in Novalis' fable, "the lifted veil of Athanasia
revealed ever and only the countenance of Mary Osborne."

An entry in a parish register records the marriage of
Wilfrid's great-grandfather, the proper heir to Moldwarp
Hall: if Wilfrid had his rights, he would be the heir.
Having known this for years, Mr. Coningham, Clara's
father, had wanted to marry her to Wilfrid, and so
profit when the time should come for Wilfrid to claim
his rights. But on second examination, the entry appears
to be a forgery; and Wilfrid now believes that his great-
grandparents did not marry until after his grandfather's
birth: he thinks his grandfather was illegitimate.

On one occasion, when he is spending the night at the
Hall, Wilfrid dreams of love and death and wakes to
find his own lost sword lying on the bed, restored to him
as mysteriously as years before it had been taken. Even
more astonishing and disturbing: Mary Osborne in all
her beauty is asleep on the neighboring pillow. The
sword lies between them (as between Tristram and
Iseult). At first Wilfrid plans to feign sleep, so that when
she wakes she can escape, thinking that he does not

know they have been in bed together. But "never before
or since have I found myself in a situation half so per-
plexing; and in a few moments I was seized with such
a trembling that I was compelled to turn my thoughts to
the only other possible plan." (In the original MS Mac-
Donald wrote "I feared the shaking of the bed would
arouse her.") Wilfrid steals out in the early morning,
clothes and sword in hand, without waking Mary or revealing to her the embarrassing position they are in.
We learn that the sword had been stolen long years ago
by the custodian of the armor collection at the Hall.
Clara had put it back: she hoped to cause a quarrel between Wilfrid and the Brothertons that would cause him
to claim his rights to the estate, so that her father might
give up his hope that she and Wilfrid may marry and
consent to her marrying Charley. But we never find out
—nor did Wilfrid—how in the world Mary had got into
his bed. Wilfrid is the narrator. Perhaps it was all an
hallucination.

But let us consider the obvious phallic significance of
Wilfrid's sword. After it had been stolen from him at the
Hall, we almost immediately saw him dressing in girls'
clothes and embarking on a love affair with a boy. It is
mysteriously returned to him at the Hall, and simultaneously the boy's sister, his true lady-love, is in bed
with him, and he is unbearably excited, but inhibited.
Soon after, a maid—knowing that the room was Wilfrid's
—brings him a ring left there; she assumes it is his. It
is, however, Mary's ring which she has left there; and
he accepts it to save her embarrassment, and then puts
it on the third finger of her left hand, begging her to ask
no questions. This is more than symbolic marriage; it is
to all intents and purposes marriage.

Charley secretly watches Clara confessing to Wilfrid her part in the restoration of the sword, and he sees the two embrace fraternally as Wilfrid forgives her. But Charley is sure that they have betrayed him. He goes home and commits suicide with a dagger belonging to Wilfrid. The relationship between Charley and Wilfrid has been so intimate that when Charley loves Clara he cannot dismiss the notion that she loves Wilfrid. In a final passage that suggests he was thinking of Ruskin's tragedy—compounded as it was by the hereditary taint of insanity—MacDonald sums up Charley's problem as one of faith: he had no resources but his friends.

> For, ever tortured by a sense of his own impotence, of the gulf to all appearance eternally fixed between his actions and his aspirations, and unable to lay hold of the Essential, the Causing Goodness, he had clung with the despair of a perishing man to the dim reflex of good he saw in her and me. If his faith in that was indeed destroyed, the last barrier must have given way, and the sea of madness, ever breaking against it, must have broken in and overwhelmed him . . . he inherited a strain of madness from his father, a madness which that father had developed by forcing upon him the false forms of a true religion.[5]

Shattered by the suicide, Wilfrid loses everything he loves to the hated Brotherton, who buys Wilfrid's favorite horse and retains possession of Wilfrid's Hall: for Wilfrid is after all the true heir, since Brotherton has forged the false entry in the register. Worse still, in order to avoid a lawsuit, Wilfrid has had to return the sword to Brotherton. He is unmanned again. So it is no wonder that Brotherton succeeds also in marrying Wilfrid's love, Mary Osborne. Just why this paragon of female virtue should have consented to marry a brutal and unfeeling rake, we do not learn. But Wilfrid's love for her prevents him from suing Brotherton for possession of the Hall. At the moment when Wilfrid discovers the forgery in the parish register, Brotherton and he fight, and Wilfrid is competently throttling his rival on the floor of the church, when Brotherton is saved by the intervention of . . . the horse, which nudges Wilfrid and reminds him of his Christian duty. At the very end of the book, Brotherton dies, Wilfrid claims the property, and we are left in doubt whether he will now propose to Mary.

If George MacDonald seldom wrote anything more effective on its own level than the first third of *Wilfrid Cumbermede,* he never wrote anything more ludicrously inept than the last third. He had set himself in the central third the problem of portraying deep emotional conflicts, and it defeated him. In real life, he helped Ruskin pursue the desperate courtship of Rose La Touche, but he never seems to have stopped to consider that, even if not impotent, Ruskin was at least peculiar: he had lived for years with a beautiful wife, whom he had certainly loved before his marriage to her, and he had refused with horror to consummate the marriage. Nor did it seem to trouble MacDonald that Ruskin was thirty years older than Rose; nor did he face the supreme irony that it was precisely those sexual relations of marriage which Ruskin insisted he could and would offer to Rose that horrified and repelled her: had Ruskin been willing to admit impotence or to agree to abstain from physical intimacy, he might well have won the girl. Like

the knight in his own *Phantastes* who can look on at
evil without recognizing it because his soul is so pure,
MacDonald failed to appreciate sexual abnormality, and
so helped to renew the agonizing relationships that
within a few years would drive Rose to death and
Ruskin to madness. *Wilfrid Cumbermede* is in part at
least his effort to try to deal in disguised form with the
forces that he saw at work in the affair of his friend. Its
failure as a novel therefore becomes almost irrelevant,
since it stands as a small and hitherto unnoticed monu-
ment to one of the most shocking human tragedies of
the entire century.

II

It would serve no purpose to give a detailed account
of all MacDonald's remaining novels. In this section we
shall pass them rapidly in review, singling out those
features that are of especial interest, taking the Scotch
novels first, and then moving to the English. This will
enable us, in a final section of this chapter, to generalize
about the attitudes which MacDonald's fiction reveals.

The series of Scotch novels opens with *Ranald Bannerman's Boyhood* (1871), a pleasant but unimportant children's story,[6] and continues with *Malcolm* (1875), a full-
length three-volume novel for adults, like its sequel, *The
Marquis of Lossie* (1877).[7] A twenty-year-old fisher boy
in the village of Portlossie, well-educated by the local
schoolmaster, Malcolm is generally believed to be the
grandson of the blind town piper, Duncan MacPhail, a
Highland immigrant, who cherishes a fanatical hatred
for all Campbells because of the horrors of the Glencoe
massacre. Malcolm wins the confidence of Florimel,

young daughter of the Marquis of Lossie, the great local nobleman, and becomes a sailor on his yacht. Deeply in love with Florimel, Malcolm fully realizes how far she is above him. Yet, on one occasion, in the library of Lossie House, among the books he loves so well, she asks him what he would do if he were an earl's son; and he declares his love for her, only to meet with her rebuff: like Hugh Sutherland, or Cosmo Cupples, or MacDonald himself. As the elaborate plot unravels, the preternaturally virtuous Malcolm proves to be the legitimate son of the Marquis, stolen by a malicious midwife. Florimel is illegitimate: her father had married her mother without knowing that his first wife was still alive. On his deathbed the Marquis reveals this to Malcolm, and as the first novel closes Malcolm determines to keep the secret from Florimel, who has succeeded to the title in her own right, and is Marchioness of Lossie.

So the old fantasy has here taken on new aspects. How can the humble fisher-lad properly aspire to the noblewoman? How can Curdie aspire to the princess? How can George MacDonald aspire to the girl in the library? Only, for men with aristocratic standards (like Malcolm and George MacDonald), by proving to have blood as noble. As Marquis of Lossie, however, Malcolm can no longer desire Florimel, because she is his half-sister. He transmutes his old passion into brotherly love, and becomes Florimel's groom. But he wants to see her happily married: not to Lord Liftore—one of MacDonald's typical brutal noblemen, who in *Malcolm* has ruthlessly seduced and abandoned a village girl—but to Mr. Lenorme, a painter. Florimel's pride will not permit her to become engaged to Lenorme, whom she really loves. Eventually Malcolm tells her the truth. Liftore will not want to marry her once he learns that she is not only not a Marchioness but herself illegitimate; the true lover, Lenorme, will not care. Florimel's pride is humbled to the earth, and Malcolm's virtue triumphs.

In *Malcolm* we encounter one of the most interesting of a series of idiots and deformed men of various kinds whom MacDonald introduces into many of his novels, presenting all of them sympathetically as somehow superior to ordinary people. This is the mad laird, Stephen Stewart, a hunchback, a wanderer who lives out of doors, visits the village school occasionally and is kindly cared for by one of the fishermen's daughters. He announces his arrival by chanting an eerie refrain: "I dinna ken whaur I come frae." He is fatherless, and his mother, horrified at his deformity, hates him, treats him cruelly, and continually plots to put him into an asylum. This has turned his head: now he cannot bear even to hear the word "mother," and falls into a fit if anybody says it in his presence. The poor mad laird believes himself to have no father at all, and when Malcolm tries to tell him about God ("The Father o' Lichts"), he answers, "like a scared animal," " 'I hae nae father. I hae only a wuman.' " The mad laird is an extreme variant of Robert Falconer's and George MacDonald's difficulty: instead of being motherless, like MacDonald, or motherless with a reprobate and absent father, like Robert, he is fatherless, but with a reprobate mother. The result is the collapse of his reason.

The interest in idiots and the conviction that somehow they represent a deep and true piety was based in part on actual experience. Louisa MacDonald once gave her last sixpence to an idiot boy in a London park, to help him buy a kite he wanted, because she had heard

him express his belief in a Father in Heaven. And
George MacDonald himself had in his childhood known
in Huntly an idiot who thought he was an army officer,
and who was obsessed with the notion that the bell in
the nearby ruined belfry of the church at Ruthven said
"Come hame, come hame" whenever it rang. Louisa
wrote the story of her encounter, and her husband later
retouched it. He in turn embodied his reminiscence in
a story of a pretty Scotch girl who defends the idiot from
the persecution of schoolboys, is disappointed in love,
dies, and is buried next to the idiot beneath the belfry.
MacDonald had included both stories in *Adela Cathcart*
(1864). As we know, he also leaves somewhat ambiguous
the question of young Diamond's sanity in *At the Back
of the North Wind*. But MacDonald's series of *real*
Wordsworthian idiots, those whose "life is hidden with
God," and whom "fathers and mothers of the lowest
class of society" (if not, of the highest) love and cherish,
begins with the mad laird.[8]

In *The Marquis of Lossie,* the painter Lenorme shows
Florimel a painting he has begun,

> . . . meant for the unveiling of Isis, as presented
> in a märchen of Novalis, introduced in *Die Lehrlinge
> zu Sais,* in which the goddess of Nature reveals to
> the eager and anxious gaze of the beholder the
> person of his Rosenblütchen. . . . But on the great
> pedestal where should have sat the goddess there
> was no gracious form visible. That part of the pic-
> ture was a blank. The youth stood below, gazing
> enraptured with parted lips and outstretched arms,
> as if he had already begun to suspect what had
> begun to dawn through the slowly thinning veil—

but to the eye of the beholder he gazed as yet only on vacancy.

Lenorme explains to Florimel that he has never found a suitable model for Isis-Rosebud and asks her to sit for him; she consents. Malcolm astonishes the painter by the profundity of his criticism of the finished painting: though the Isis-figure is in the very act of unveiling her mysteries, of making a revelation, she should remain enigmatic. Like Anodos singing before the marble lady and for a brief moment making her visible—naked— with his song, so Hyacinth stands before Rosebud in the picture MacDonald has imagined, and so—Malcolm feels—Lenorme should stand before his love, Florimel. Believing that a pure woman deserves a pure man, Malcolm secures from Lenorme an assurance that he is pure as Galahad and so deserves Florimel. Thus Mac-Donald uses Novalis' Hyacinth and Rosebud as the pretext for a little sermon on pre-marital chastity.[9]

To the usual long passages of broad Scotch in *Malcolm*, MacDonald added the many speeches of MacPhail, the blind Highland piper, whose true native tongue is Gaelic. The *Edinburgh Review* referred to *Malcolm* as a "masterpiece of popular philological discrimination," but many readers must have found this new dialect difficult and irritating: the piper uses the pronoun *she* to refer to himself, and the phonetics of his speech resemble Fluellen's in *Henry V*:

> Something will pe wrong, yes, put she'll not can tell where. No, her pody will not pe full of light! For town here in ta curset Lowlands, ta sight has peen almost cone from her, my son. It will now pe no more as a co creeping troo her, and she'll nefer

> see plain no more until she'll be cone pack to her
> own mountains.

The fierce clan loyalty which MacPhail exemplifies
reflects a whole society that had already almost disappeared in MacDonald's own childhood, the period in
which he sets the story. In the piper, he records his
nostalgic admiration for the old, passionately loyal, yet
never servile, bonds that bound the Highland clansman
to his chief. The chief is the genuine nobleman, as contrasted with the purse-proud, English titled gentry. When
Malcolm becomes Marquis, MacPhail—in deep distress
because his beloved adopted grandson has proved to be
part Campbell—goes off to Glencoe to die; but finds that

> . . . the clan-spirit was dying out, the family type
> of government all but extinct, the patriarchal vanish-
> ing in a low form of the feudal, itself already in ab-
> ject decay. The hour of the Celt was gone by. . . .

In misery, he returns to Portlossie, and is reunited forever with Malcolm:

> "My poy! My poy! Her nain son Malcolm! . . .
> You'll must pe forgifing her for coming pack to you.
> She cannot help lofing you, and you must forget tat
> you are a Cam'ell."

In MacDonald's gallery of Scotch portraits, the piper of
Portlossie, drawn in part from family stories of his own
great-grandfather, takes a major place.

The good schoolmaster, Alexander Graham, in *Malcolm*
is a "stickit" minister, and so the target of abuse from
the meaner spirits of the town, including the wicked
Rabelaisian midwife. Seeing Graham coming home from
a funeral with an elderly lady on his arm, she exclaims,

"Sic a couple's yon twasome wad mak' . . . Meg
Horn the auld kailrunt and Sanny Graham the
stickit minister. I wad like weel to be at the beddin'
o' them. Eh! the twa heids o' them upon ae bowster!"

But Graham himself informally preaches George Mac-
Donald's doctrines of a loving God to the villagers as
George MacDonald himself had done after his failure at
Arundel. And the doctrinaire Calvinist members of his
little conventicle suspect him of heresy and plot against
him. The presbytery dismisses him from the school, just
as MacDonald had been dismissed from his pulpit. And,
in *The Marquis of Lossie,* Mr. Graham appears in poverty in London, invited to preach from a congregational
pulpit, and like MacDonald eventually ousted from that
as well. He ends his days as a kind of resident chaplain
to Marquis Malcolm. Holy in his poverty, he represents
MacDonald's own ideal picture of what he himself
gloried in being.[10]

Next in order among the Scotch novels come *Sir Gibbie*
(1879), one of the better ones, and its sequel, *Donal
Grant* (1883), one of the worst.[11] "Sir Gibbie" is a
motherless waif in the streets of Aberdeen, the son of a
drunken cobbler named Galbraith, descendant of a line
of baronets, who has lost all his property, and who now
has a shoemaker's shop under the stairs of what was once
the ancestral townhouse. The cobbler-baronet loves his
little boy and spends each Sunday making a pair of
boots for him, but since he only works on them on Sundays, Gibbie outgrows each pair before he can wear
them, and his father sells them with the other shoes he
makes, and spends the proceeds in drink. Nightly at the

dram-shop, Gibbie patrols the streets until his father appears, and then escorts him home:

> Imagine a small boy with a gigantic top, which, six
> times his own size, he keeps erect on its peg, not by
> whipping it round, but by running round it himself,
> unfailingly applying at the very spot and at the very
> moment, the precise measure of impact necessary to
> counterbalance its perpetual tendency to fall in one
> direction or another . . . and you will have . . . a
> real likeness of Sir George attended, any midnight
> in the week, by his son Gilbert. Home the big one
> staggered, reeled, gyrated, and tumbled; round and
> round him went the little one, now behind, now be-
> fore, now on this side, now on that, his feet never
> more than touching the ground but dancing about it
> like those of a prizefighter, his little arms up and his
> hands well forward, like flying buttresses . . . They
> propped it here, they propped it there; with won-
> derful judgment and skill and gradation of force
> they applied themselves, and with perfect success.
> Not once . . . had the self-disabled mass fallen
> prostrate in the gutter, there to snore out the night.
>   . . . the twain went reeling and revolving along
> the street, much like a whirlwind that had forgotten
> the laws of gyration, until at length, it spun into the
> court, and up to the foot of the outside stair over the
> baronet's workshop. Then commenced the real strug-
> gle of the evening for Gibbie—and for his father
> too . . . All up the outside and the two inside stairs
> . . . Gibbie stuck to his business like a man . . .
> The house . . . was . . . filled with humble folk
> . . . if any of them were roused, . . . it was but to

recognize at once the cause of the tumult, with the remark "It's only wee Gibbie luggin' hame Sir George."

Gibbie pushes his father onto the bed and lifts his legs onto it, and then "In triumph he spread over his sleeping father his dead mother's old plaid of Gordon tartan," and creeps under it himself.

> Gibbie clings to his father with deep love: His heaven was his father's bosom, to which he clung as no infant yet ever clung to his mother's . . . He never said to himself "My father is a drunkard, but I must make the best of it; he is all I have." He clung to his one possession—only clung—; this was his father—all in all to him.

Here MacDonald has imagined still another variant of the situation in *Robert Falconer:* Gibbie has not, it is true, lost his father, and so he does not need to search for him; but out of pure joy and filial love he serves his father as Robert Falconer longed to serve his. Gibbie does not miss food or shoes but goes happily half-starved and barefoot about the streets; he does not miss his mother, so long as he has his father and can help him. This is perhaps the most extreme example of MacDonald's doctrine of the uniqueness and unique importance of fatherhood.

After Gibbie's father dies, he is left a waif indeed, but nobody can take him in: he is like Shargar or Huck Finn:

> There were some who would gladly have brought him within the bounds of an ordered life; he soon drove them to despair . . . for the streets had been

his nursery and nothing could keep him out of them
. . . however Gibbie's habits might shock the ladies
. . . who sought to civilize him, the boy was no
more about mischief in the street at midnight than
they were in their beds.

He witnesses a shocking murder and flees from the city,
far out into the countryside, hiding in barns, and living
off the land. Eventually he finds a cottar's hut, high on
a mountainside, where Janet, the wife of the cottar, feeds
him deliciously. At the foot of the mountain, he helps the
cottar's son, Donal Grant, a cowherd, watch the cattle.
MacDonald has shown us this delightful child laughing,
screaming, and, once, barking to imitate a dog. It is only
now that we realize he has misled us: for when Donal
Grant says to Gibbie " 'Canna ye speyk, man?' " Gibbie
shakes his head. He is dumb.

So Gibbie is the second in the series of deformed or
handicapped characters who appear in MacDonald's
later novels. He has a "luminous" face. At the very moment when he enters the cottar's hut, Janet has been
reading the New Testament passage, "Inasmuch as ye
have done it unto one of the least of these my brethren
ye have done it unto me." His enchanting smile had won
her so that for a moment she had thought it was the
Lord himself. Like Diamond, in *At the Back of the North
Wind,* Gibbie, we now realize, is Christ-like.

In the large farmhouse whose proprietor employs
Donal Grant, Gibbie plays the part of brownie, secretly
spending the nights in the barn, secretly creeping into
the kitchen in the early morning to clean it thoroughly,
and feeding the horses. The local laird, who has married
a Galbraith heiress and taken the name, deeply loathes

superstition: his theology was "entirely of the New England type of corrupted Calvinism, with which in Scotland they saddle the memory of great-souled, hard-hearted Calvin himself." The laird grows so angry when his little daughter comes to believe that there is a brownie on the tenant-farm that he sets a trap for Gibbie, catches him, and has him brought to "the house of his ancestors."

A brutal gamekeeper is ordered to strip and whip the boy. He almost kills Gibbie by two terrible blows, one horizontal, the other vertical. Saved from worse punishment only by the anguished intervention of the laird's little daughter, the crucified Gibbie flees stark naked to Janet in the cottar's cabin:

> It was the same child who had come and gone so strangely before! He held out his hands to her, and fell on his face at her feet like one dead. Then, with a horror of pitiful amazement, she saw a great cross marked in cruel stripes on his back . . . Could it be the Lord was still, child and man, suffering for his race?

Janet and her husband, who are Donal Grant's parents, take Gibbie in, and treat him as their own; she reads him the New Testament until

> . . . his whole soul was full of the man, of his doings, of his words, of his thoughts, of his life. Jesus Christ was in him—he was possessed by him. Almost before he knew, he was trying to fashion his life after that of his Master.

As he grows up, the little dumb Scotch waif is as nearly Christ-like in his life as MacDonald can make him.

His foster-parents teach him to read and to write on a slate; he performs prodigies of kindness and valor. The brutal gamekeeper who once whipped him falls into his power, but Gibbie spares him. A great flood sweeps the region, and Gibbie saves not only the laird's daughter and a favorite white horse, but the gamekeeper too. Gibbie inherits a fortune from a relative, and Mr. Sclater, the minister from Aberdeen, takes him back to the city and has him educated. He learns to talk on his fingers, and to wear town clothes, but he has a disconcerting habit of quoting the New Testament to Mr. and Mrs. Sclater whenever he thinks their conduct needs it—for example when they do not invite his old friend the dram-shop keeper to sit down at table with them. The minister's wife protests to her husband:

> You really must, Mr. Sclater, teach him the absurdity of attempting to fit every point of his behavior to—to—words which were of course quite suitable to the time when they were spoken, but which it is impossible to take literally nowadays.

Both Gibbie and his friend Donal Grant, now also a student in Aberdeen, fall in love with Ginevra, the daughter of the laird, who loses all his fortune in crooked speculations. Gibbie wins her in the end, though he tries to withdraw and help Donal's courtship in every way he can. He buys back the laird's (and his own) house in the country; and, after first breaking her of the habit of drink, he establishes his friend the landlady of the dram-shop as housekeeper in the old Galbraith town house, where his father had labored as a shoemaker. Throughout, the laird remains unbelievably brutal and violent.[12]

The later parts of *Sir Gibbie* drag. MacDonald's imagination could not rise to deal with the problem he had set
himself: what does the Christ-child do in the real world
when he grows up? Young Diamond, MacDonald had
killed off; the ancient child who is the Old Man of the
Fire in "The Golden Key," inhabited a myth. All that
Gibbie does (or can do) is settle down and become a
prosperous but virtuous landowner. The concept of the
hero of a novel as Christ proves effective only so long
as the hero is a child, or until he can die or be crucified.
This being so, why make Gibbie dumb? He would have
aroused just as much sympathy with the power of speech,
and we would have been spared the lapse in taste when
Ginevra proposes marriage to him on her fingers. But
MacDonald clings to the sanctity of deformities. Somehow, the faults in the book fade from the memory, and
Gibbie remains a kind of unrealized Scotch Myshkin.

Donal Grant, however, is a mere farrago of worn-out
themes from MacDonald's earlier books: somnambulism,
irrationally brutal noblemen, preposterous machinery.
After many trials, Donal wins the earl's niece, but she
dies almost at once, and he seems to prefer her dead:
as he puts it, in the very words of Campbell in *The
Portent,* "'I wait; I wait.'" At times, this novel ap-
proaches a solemn parody of itself.[13] *Castle Warlock*
(1882), written between *Sir Gibbie* and *Donal Grant,*
is a pleasant story of hidden treasure.[14] *What's Mine's
Mine* (1886) [15] contrasts the money-grubbing commer-
cial standards of a rich London distiller with the old
patriarchal clan-values of the Highlands, now in retreat,
a theme worked out in love affairs between the distiller's
daughters and two noble clansmen, brothers. One of the
minor characters is "Rob o' the angels," an idiot who

talks to the angels, the son of a deaf and dumb father,
to whom he is perfectly devoted:

> . . . was he not simplicity itself, truth, generosity,
> helpfulness? Did he not, when a child, all but lose
> his life in the rescue of an idiot from the swollen
> burn? Did he not, when a boy, fight a great golden
> eagle on its nest, thinking to deliver the lamb it had
> carried away? Knowing his father in want of a new
> bonnet, did not Rob with his bare hands seize an
> otter at the mouth of his hole, and carry it home,
> laughing merrily over the wounds it had given him?

Here MacDonald reduces to an absolute minimum the
element of civilization or intellection involved in human
relationships: between the deaf-mute father and the idiot
son in the wilderness there is nothing to interfere with
the pure emotion of paternal and filial love. Wordsworth
would not have approved of the converse with angels but
would have welcomed the "blessed mindlessness in nature" of the idiot.[16]

Three shorter and less ambitious works close the series
of Scotch novels. *The Elect Lady* (1888) simply reaffirms
the values that MacDonald had voiced as far back as
"The Hidden Life" more than thirty years earlier.[17] In
Heather and Snow (1893)[18] the frivolous laird, Francis
Gordon, truly loves the noble rustic maiden, Kirsty, despite the snobbish disapproval of his mother, who drinks
and wastes his substance. He tries to seduce a silly village
girl, whom Kirsty saves from his clutches; indeed, she
horsewhips him, and marries him herself, having first
saved his life in one of those tremendous snowstorms that
alternate with floods as MacDonald's catastrophes of
nature. Kirsty's brother, the least appealing of MacDon-

ald's idiots, calls himself "Dog-Steenie," and behaves like
a dog; he is in constant search for the "bonny man"
(Christ), who takes him at last during the snowstorm.
Salted With Fire (1897) was MacDonald's last book, published two years after *Lilith*. His faculties had in some
measure already given way, and the book should perhaps
claim immunity from criticism. Yet it rises well above his
lowest depths.[19]

Turning to the English novels, we find that *Annals of
a Quiet Neighbourhood* (1867), *The Seaboard Parish*
(1868), and *The Vicar's Daughter* (1872), all three-
deckers, follow the fortunes of the family of the Reverend
Mr. Walton, Vicar of Marshmallows. The first is pure
melodrama: the wicked seducer of a village girl wants to
marry the delightful heiress of the Hall, whose vicious
mother is trying to force the marriage, having already
in effect murdered her elder daughter for marrying a man
of her own choice. Though Mrs. Oldcastle of the Hall
reaches startling degrees of violence in her efforts, Mr.
Walton saves the heiress by marrying her himself. The
sequel introduces a painter much under the influence
of Ruskin, but the book consists largely of sermons. In
the third novel of the series two characters engage our
interest: Lady Bernard, drawn from Lady Byron, immensely charitable, and ready to reprove her servants
when they are rude to a gentleman; and Miss Clair, perhaps suggested by Octavia Hill, who performs prodigies
as a social worker in London.[20]

In *Guild Court* (1868),[21] MacDonald tried his hand
at imitating Dickens. In a little cul-de-sac in London lives
Mr. Kitely, the bookseller, who does not believe in God,
with his daughter, Mattie, a child who has her own devil
called Syne, continually refers to Christ as "Somebody,"

and calls Mr. Spelt the cobbler "Mother" because she already has one father. MacDonald obviously adored Mattie, but the modern reader will look far before finding a more revolting child in the entire range of Victorian fiction. In and out of *Guild Court,* there wanders the waif, Poppie, who is hit with a gin bottle at Mrs. Flanagan's tenement, takes refuge in Madame Tussaud's where she thinks the waxworks are all corpses, and hides under the pall on the bier of the Duke of Wellington. Mr. Spelt lures Poppie like a bird, with morsels of bread and sweets left temptingly on the street. The central love affair of the novel is that between Lucy Burton, the niece of a heartless rich merchant, and Tom Worboise, the weak and erring son of a heartless rich lawyer. MacDonald also introduces a family of rich sympathetic Jews named Morgenstern, quite probably ancestors of Marjorie Morningstar.

St. George and St. Michael (1876) is the only historical novel that MacDonald ever wrote, a typical Victorian costume piece.[22] In *Thomas Wingfold, Curate* (1876) and its sequel, *Paul Faber, Surgeon* (1879), he returned to contemporary England.[23] *Thomas Wingfold* has the doubtful distinction of being his only genuinely immoral novel. Helen Lingard, a gently-nurtured girl, hides from justice her half-Hindu half-brother Leopold, who has murdered his flirtatious sweetheart, daughter of a nouveau-riche manufacturer. Helen nurses him through interminable fevers of remorse and delirium to an edifying deathbed. The pious curate, Wingfold, in love with Helen, makes himself an accessory: he actually blackmails the mother of the murder victim into silence. She knows that it was Leopold who killed her daughter, but Wingfold keeps her quiet by threatening to reveal a damaging fact

in her own past, which he has accidentally learned. Mac-
Donald tries in several ways to cloud the issue: the victim,
Emmeline, he portrays as so heartless that she almost
deserved death; the murderer, in addition to being an
emotional half-oriental, takes drugs, and so has deadened
his conscience; Wingfold actually does advise Leopold
to confess, and succeeds in convincing him that he ought
to do so, but plot machinery prevents it.

Yet none of this really conceals that in this book Mac-
Donald, the preacher, was preaching evil. Helen Lingard
is not wholly moved by pure affection for her brother:
"We should be the talk of the county—of the whole country," she says. Nor can we share Wingfold's opinion when,
in answer to Helen's question, "You don't think very
badly of my poor brother, do you, Mr. Wingfold?" he answers "I think I never saw a lovelier disposition." When
Wingfold confronts the mother of the murdered girl, and
refers to Leopold as "the poor youth whom your daughter's behaviour made a murderer of," and the mother protests that "The villain took her precious life without giving her a moment to prepare for eternity," we feel that
the mother has much the better of the argument.[24]

In *Thomas Wingfold* MacDonald carried to their ultimate highly un-Christian extremes his convictions that
flirts deserve anything they may get, and that parvenus
are generally criminals. If he were just the ordinary writer
of Victorian sensation novels, one might not find this
worth comment. But *Thomas Wingfold* is also permeated
through and through with MacDonald's usual preaching:
Wingfold has doubts of his calling, exacerbated by an
agnostic cousin of Helen's, and allayed by a particularly
loathsome pair of pious hunchbacks named Polwarth,
uncle and niece, who are gatekeepers at a great house.

Against the background of violence and illegality, which MacDonald almost excuses, the sentimental vaporings of the curate and his deformed advisers about the study of Christ's life as an incentive to faith seem particularly offensive.

Paul Faber, Surgeon explores other aspects of sexual morality and its relationship to religious belief. Faber himself, the devoted doctor, with a genuine mission to heal and serve mankind, is an atheist. For him, death, "at worst," is "but a knock on the head and a longish snooze." He falls in love with Juliet Meredith, the beautiful, almost penniless orphan daughter of an army officer, whom he saves from death by giving her a massive (and quite fantastic) transfusion of his own blood. Gradually he causes her to question her own faith—she is not a very intelligent woman—and they marry. But she has not confessed to him a pre-marital affair with another man, and after marriage, though she does not believe that he has the absolute right to know about it, she none the less is miserable until she tells him. Faber, who has the loftiest possible ideals for women, is deeply shocked, and though Juliet hands him a whip and begs him to whip her and so purify her, he throws the whip away and leaves the room.

This is where his atheism causes him to fail as a man. Had he but truly accepted Christ, he "would have washed her clean with love and husband-power." As it is, she leaves the house, bent on suicide, and is saved only by the kindness of the daughter of the retired Congregational minister, Dorothy Drake, who hides her in an empty house. When Juliet's bonnet is found in the pond, it is believed that she has killed herself. Miserable, and dreadfully aged by his suffering, Faber, upon reflection, comes to sympathize with the poor wife he has driven away, the more so since he himself had years ago had an illegitimate child by a charming girl with whom he had lived in sin. Juliet is pregnant, and when she has a difficult time, Faber himself attends her, and without recognizing her, or only half-recognizing her, performs a second transfusion that saves her life. Her semi-conscious prayer to God brings him recognition of her and begins his conversion. They are reconciled, and their joy increased by the fact that Faber's illegitimate daughter is the very child whom the Congregational Minister, Mr. Drake, had years ago adopted and brought up as his own.

Thomas Wingfold and his wife, the sister of the murderer in the earlier novel, reappear, but without any mention of their dark past. Wingfold is represented as a near-saint: he even converts to Christianity the rector whose curate he is, and this by a single sermon! He and the hunchbacked Polwarths also bring their powers to bear on Faber and Juliet. Despite his atheism, Faber loves animals and deeply opposes vivisection; he drives from his house an assistant who has been experimenting on a dog.

Paul Faber shows how little of an absolute Victorian moralist George MacDonald was: in an age when a woman's loss of virginity before marriage was damning and nobody asked about a man's past, he had the courage to denounce the double standard, and to argue that only the pure man could demand or deserve the pure woman, as in the case of Lenorme and Florimel in *The Marquis of Lossie*. But here the point is made more explicitly, and is turned around: as the veteran of an illicit affair and the father of a bastard, Faber ought to sympathize with Juliet not repudiate her. By eventually reconciling them and giving them a happy marriage, MacDonald preaches that it is the Christian husband's duty to forgive any peccadilloes that a truly loving and repentant wife may confess to him. This was still radical doctrine for 1879, although not as violent as Wilkie Collins' plea for the reclaimed prostitute in *The New Magdalen* (1873).

In *Paul Faber* MacDonald included many reminiscences of the unhappy days when he had had the Congregational pulpit at Arundel. Here, better than in Greville MacDonald's biography of him, we get an intimate view of the petty-minded sanctimonious lower-middle-class tradesmen that made up the congregation, many of them cheats as well. Their taste in sermons rejected "mere edification in holiness" and insisted on "a large infusion of some polemic element." What they cared for was "not to grow in grace, but in social influence and regard." Trained in a college that placed all its emphasis on "pulpit-*success,* the lowest of all low successes, and the most wordly," their minister none the less delivers himself of mystical speculation in the pulpit:

> The love of the past, the desire of the future, and the enjoyment of the present, make an eternity, in which time is absorbed, its lapse lapses, and man partakes of the immortality of his Maker. In each present personal being, we have the whole past of our generation enclosed, to be re-developed with endless difference in each individuality. Hence perhaps it comes that every now and then, into our consciousness float strange odours of feeling, strange tones of by-gone affections, strange mental sensations of indescribable sort and texture. Friends, I should be a terror to myself, did I not believe that

> wherever my dim consciousness may come to itself,
> God is there.

Are we not reading the actual words of George MacDonald spoken from the Arundel pulpit more than a quarter of a century earlier? Instantly, as in real life at Arundel, the congregation in *Paul Faber* suspects its minister of *Germanism*. The sermon on the special blessedness of animals in *Paul Faber,* however—which was probably also his own at Arundel—MacDonald puts into the mouth not of the Dissenting minister but of the liberal Church of England curate, Thomas Wingfold. Perhaps it was the chance to repeat these early preachments in a widely-circulated novel and at the same time to satirize his former enemies at Arundel that made MacDonald regard *Paul Faber* as his best novel, a judgment which nobody else is likely to share.

MacDonald's experience at Arundel, viewed in fiction, resembles very closely the most famous Victorian fictional account of a ministry among the Dissenters, William Hale White's *Autobiography of Mark Rutherford.* Like Mac-Donald, Rutherford found his education for the ministry sadly inadequate, went to his first pulpit full of zeal, and instantly encountered the small-minded, falsely pious, intensely respectable lower-middle-class deacons and their families, without a spark of intellectual interest or spiritual fervor, ready to condemn anything they had not heard before as " 'German,' . . . a term of reproach signifying something very awful, although nobody knew exactly what it was." Like MacDonald, Rutherford found himself out of a job, and like MacDonald found his chief consolation in Wordsworth.[25]

The five remaining "English" novels, belonging to the

eighties and the nineties, three of them full-length three-
deckers, show a marked falling off in interest. *Mary
Marston* (1881) proclaims again the MacDonald doctrine that kind hearts are more than coronets: the heroine, a saintly young attendant in a village draper's shop,
is the daughter of one of the partners in the firm, a dea-
con in the local Baptist church. Naturally she comes in
for brutal snobbery not only from the county gentry and
the yeomanry but from churchgoing members of her own
class, and even from a houseful of typical MacDonald
London servants. Mary's view, through thick and thin,
is "What can it matter to me . . . whether they call me a
lady or not, so long as Jesus says *Daughter* to me?" This
sustains her through the vicissitudes of a dismal plot.[26]

In *Weighed and Wanting* (1882) [27] interest centers on
two children of the Raymount family: Hester, a pious
social worker among the poor who brightens their lives
by singing to them, and gives up her fiancé when he
objects to her low tastes; and Cornelius, a weak ne'er-do-
well, terrified of his father, who embezzles funds from the
bank and secretly marries a former maidservant. There
are two children's deathbeds, one of a poor child, one of
a rich. There is also a pathetic magic-lantern performance of *Pilgrim's Progress* by a drunken old ex-clergyman,
arousing Hester's pity and Cornelius' derision, which
MacDonald certainly meant as a sardonic reference to
his own family performance of the same play. MacDonald was not drunken, but he was an ex-clergyman and he
felt old and poor, and he loved *The Pilgrim's Progress;* so
that when he asks the question

> When the hall and the gas and the advertising were
> paid for, what would the poor old scrag-end of hu-

> manity, with his yellow-white neck-cloth knotted hard under his left ear, have over for his supper? [28]

he is almost surely thinking of himself. So too the novel's preoccupation with entertainment as an important, perhaps the pre-eminent, social service surely reflects his effort to answer the critics of the family theatrical enterprise.

Home Again (1887), a one-volume novel, reverts to *David Elginbrod* for its plot and characters. Once again, forty-five years after the events, MacDonald returns to worry the bone of his own youthful rejection. The naughty jilt, Lufa, looks and behaves exactly like her earlier prototype and almost homonym, Euphra; and in the end, the hero rediscovers the girl he has left behind. Like the hero of "A Hidden Life," written so many years ago, he returns to his father and his father's land and way of life:

> . . . you don't want to be a finer gentleman than your father. Stay at home and help him, and grow strong. Plough and cart, and do the work of a labouring-man. Nature will be your mate in her own workshop.[29]

There and Back (1891) [30] runs over the familiar materials for the last time: the worthy bookbinder, Richard Tuke, is in fact the heir to the baronetcy and finds love in the library, where he is only a humble workman. In *The Flight of the Shadow* (1891) [31] the idyllic love affair between the narrator-heroine and the hero is clouded by the savage wickedness of his mother, who shrinks from nothing in her efforts to stop the marriage, and who has also poisoned the youth of the heroine's beloved uncle

and his lost twin brother. With faint overtones of Hoffmann's *Elixiere des Teufels*, the story seems feebly motivated, although charmingly written.

III

The twenty-three novels here passed in review are all
sermons, more or less. Yet we have not found in them a
single new theological idea. By the time MacDonald
wrote *Robert Falconer*, in 1868, he had already fully
developed his conception of God and of God's relationships to mankind, of heaven and hell, rewards and punishments. Moreover, in these later novels, MacDonald
does not even revert to the theological arguments of the
earlier ones. Nowhere do we find a David Elginbrod denouncing the doctrine of justification by faith, an Annie
Anderson inquiring about salvation hoping to be among
the elect, a Robert Falconer fiercely denouncing the concept of eternal damnation. The critic of 1869, wishing to
attack MacDonald as a theologian, had already before
him all the essential texts available to the critic of 1897.

The failure to introduce new ideas one can easily explain on the supposition that MacDonald simply never
had any after 1868. Nor can one reasonably find fault
with this: if a man can develop his views satisfactorily by
the time he is forty-four, why should one expect him to
add to them or modify them during the decades that
follow? But it is much harder to explain MacDonald's
failure to continue in any sustained way to preach his old
doctrine. One can only conjecture that perhaps the critics
had stung him by their attacks, and that he was unwilling
to jeopardize the sales of his books and so decrease his
audience if its members could not accept his controversial

views. So, in the novels after 1868, the preaching is mostly
without theological content, conveying moral lessons,
often essential ones, and often put in beautiful or arresting language, but emotional, not intellectual. In *There
and Back* (1891), Richard Lestrange, the lover of literature, the bookbinder who reveres the contents of the
books he binds, goes to Oxford at last. But he ". . . gained
little distinction at his examinations. He did well enough,
but was too eager about real knowledge to care about
appearing to know." [32] Those who want real knowledge,
MacDonald says, are not those who do well on examinations: true knowledge is of the soul, not of the mind;
a little intellect goes a long way. It is better to do badly
on examinations than to do well.

From the very beginning, also, we have known that
MacDonald does not shrink from physical violence:
Julian Lamballa, in *Within and Without,* is casual as he
stabs the villain. But nothing in the earlier novels, not
even the brutal flogging by schoolmaster Murdoch Malison, in *Alec Forbes,* has prepared us for the number and
vividness of the whipping episodes in the later novels.
In *Sir Gibbie* when the wicked laird has caught the poor
little dumb child and ordered him beaten, and the gamekeeper has stripped him, MacDonald continues to describe the cruelty in detail:

> When the blow fell, the child shivered all over, his
> face turned white, and without uttering even a moan,
> he doubled up and dropped senseless. A swollen
> cincture, like a red snake, had risen all around his
> waist, and from one spot in it the blood was oozing.
> It looked as if the lash had cut him in two.
> The blow had stung his heart and it had ceased

to beat. But the gamekeeper understood vagrants! the young blackguard was only shamming!

"Up wi' ye, ye deevil, or I s'gar ye," he said from between his teeth, lifting the whip for a second blow.[33]

If this were the only such passage, one might well explain it away as designed to arouse sympathy with the wretched Christ-like Gibbie, and to make the reader feel that the child is being tortured as Christ was tortured.

But let us look at Juliet Faber's plea to her husband Paul after she has confessed her pre-marital affair; she has deliberately pulled her nightgown over her head and handed him a whip, and is now naked at his feet:

> "Do it, Paul; do it, husband. Make me clean that I may look women in the face. Do, Paul, take the whip and strike me. I long for my deserts at your hand. Do comfort me. I am wanting the sting of it, Paul, to know that you have forgiven me. If I should cry out, it will be for gladness . . . Will you not be my saviour and forgive me my sin? Oh, do not drive me mad. I am only clinging to my reason. Whip me, and I shall be well. Take me again, Paul. I will not, if you like, even fancy myself your wife any more. I will obey you to the very letter. Oh beat me and let me go."

Perhaps Juliet's very eagerness to arouse Paul's anger enough to get herself beaten has itself stimulated her confession. Her teasing wish to tell him about her earlier sin, which he does not suspect and will not otherwise discover, the twentieth-century reader will surely ascribe to a longing for punishment. But if Juliet is what we would call a masochist, Paul is not a sadist: he is too much of a gentleman; he throws the whip out of the window, drags "his foot rudely from her embrace," and leaves her naked on the floor.

The astonishing thing is that MacDonald condemns Faber for *not* whipping Juliet:

> Had he struck once, had he seen the purple streak rise in the snow, that instant his pride-frozen heart would have melted into a torrent of grief; he would have flung himself on the floor beside her, and in an agony of pity over her and horror at his own sacrilege, would have clasped her to his bosom and baptized her in the tears of remorse and repentance; from that moment they would have been married indeed.[34]

MacDonald is recommending an act of violence, an act that he himself calls sacrilege, in order to release the flood-gates of emotion: he prescribes an orgy of tears, combined—as he specifically hints—with an orgy of sex. How did MacDonald know that the sight of a single purple weal would so arouse Paul Faber? Did the thought of weals arouse MacDonald?

In *Weighed and Wanting*, Mr. Raymount, who has long been brooding on his disappointment in his son Cornelius, the embezzler, has had rather more to drink than is good for him, when he discovers Cornelius asleep in *his* study chair. He yields to the promptings of the devil (although nothing in Mr. Raymount's character, as we have come to know it through three long volumes, has prepared us to believe that he will act this way):

. . . when the poor creature looked up half awake, and saw his father standing over him with a heavy whip in his hand, he was filled with a terror that nearly paralyzed him. He sat and stared with white, trembling lips, red, projecting eyes, and a look that confirmed the belief of his father that he was drunk . . .

"Get out of there, you dog!" cried his father, and with one sweep of his powerful arm, half dragged, half hurled him from the chair. He fell on the floor, and in weakness mixed with cowardice lay where he fell . . . When Raymount saw the creature who had turned his hitherto happy life into a shame and a misery lying at his feet thus abject, he became instantly conscious of the whip in his hand, and without a moment's pause, a moment's thought, heaved his arm aloft, and brought it down with a fierce lash on the quivering flesh of his son . . . There was the poison of hate in the blow. He again raised his arm; but as it descended, the piercing shriek that broke from the youth startled even the possessing demon, and the violence of the blow was broken. But the lash of the whip found his face, and marked it for a time worse than the small-pox.

At this point, Cornelius' wife Amy bursts into the room from the garden; she throws herself on Cornelius to protect him, but Mr. Raymount, who does not know about their marriage, concludes that here was "some worthless girl that had drawn Cornelius into her toils, and ruined him and his family forever!" He lashes her too:

He heaved his whip, and . . . the blow fell. But instead of another and shriller shriek following the

lash, came nothing but a shudder and a silence and
the unquailing eye of the girl fixed like that of a
spectre upon her assailant. He struck her again.
Again came the shivering shudder and the silence;
. . . Cry she would not, if he killed her!

But she faints, and Mr. Raymount fears he may have
killed her indeed, and may have to stand trial for murder. Mrs. Raymount and Hester come to the rescue, and
when Hester picks up poor Amy,

> . . . she saw on Amy's neck a frightful upswollen
> wale. She looked at her father. There was the whip
> in his hand! "Oh, papa!" she screamed, and dropped
> her eyes for shame.

The morning after this frightful scene, Mr. Raymount
wakes feeling sorry; the devil has left him. He goes to
Cornelius' bedroom, finds Amy there, discovers that they
are married, and hears Amy's plea for his acceptance and
his forgiveness of Cornelius: He breaks down:

> "Forgive me, Amy!" he cried, stretching out his arms
> to her. "I have behaved like a brute! To strike my
> son's wife! I deserve to be hanged for it! I shall never
> forgive myself! But you must forgive me for Christ's
> sake."
>
> Long ere he had ended, Amy was in his arms,
> clinging to him—he holding her fast to his bosom.
> The strong man was now the weaker; the father and
> not the daughter wept.

She calls to Cornelius

> ". . . Out of your bed and down on your knees to
> your own blessed father, and confess your sins. Tell

him you're sorry for them and you'll never do them again."

. . . He got out of bed at once, went straight down on his knees, as she told him, and, though he did not speak, was presently weeping like a child. It was a strange group in the gray of the new morning . . . the girl in the arms of the elderly man, and the youth kneeling at their feet, both men weeping and the girl radiant.[35]

In *Weighed and Wanting,* then, MacDonald actually shows us the great orgy of tears and forgiveness which he would have liked to put into *Paul Faber* but could not, because Faber would not use the whip on Juliet.

Even Thomas Wingfold, MacDonald's ideal preacher, yields to precisely the same impulse of violence in punishing his beloved child, who has done "a mean thing."

"I told him I must whip him; that I could not bear doing it, but rather than he should be a damned, mean, contemptible little rascal, I would kill him and be hanged for it . . . Well, what do you think the little fellow said? 'Don't kill me, papa,' he cried. 'I will be good. Don't, please, be hanged for my naughtiness! Whip me, and that will make me good. . . .' I cried . . . The child took out his little pocket-handkerchief and dried my eyes, and then prepared himself for the whipping. And I whipped him as I never did before, and I hope in God I shall never have to do it again. The moment it was over, while my heart was like to burst, he flung his arms around my neck and began kissing me. 'I will never make you cry again, papa!' he said." [36]

This might pass as an ordinary case of parental discipline were it not for the extravagance of the remark about killing the child and being hanged for it. No wonder the boy preferred to be whipped! Nor can we fail to conclude that MacDonald's own fantasies, especially in the later years turned more and more often to whips and whipping. Kirsty Barclay's horsewhipping of her own lover, Francis Gordon, for making love to an innocent village girl, in *Heather and Snow*, is the only instance in which a woman lashes a man. But the men lash the women, each other, and their children.

Long ago, in *Alec Forbes*, in answer to the Catechism question, "What doth every sin deserve?", Annie Anderson had answered "A lickin'." Although MacDonald had then meant the little anecdote humorously, we find ourselves wondering, when faced with these outbursts of whipping in the later novels, whether MacDonald himself had not come to believe in Annie's answer. Surely we find rising to the surface now the violence he had long struggled to repress. Guilt now must be punished (or, in the case of Sir Gibbie, innocence outraged) by acts of extreme, often almost irrational, violence. MacDonald had long struggled to conquer his own aggressions by reiterating his emphasis upon earthly and heavenly love. It is clear that this was no longer enough, and that he now derived some satisfaction from contemplating both the infliction and the reception of blows.

In the light of all this later flogging we must reconsider "Murder" Malison, of whom MacDonald had said "I doubt whether the discovery of a boy's innocence was not a disappointment to him." MacDonald well knew that a man with the compulsion to punish does not readily relinquish it. Though he shows sympathy with Malison's plight as a "stickit" minister, and with his reform after the crippling of the little boy, Malison's sin too calls for punishment, and he must be drowned in order to atone. Without further comment, we may also quote here a passage from the *Reminiscences* of Greville MacDonald, the adoring, almost worshipping, son who wrote his father's biography:

> My father, in the education of his children, put duty before everything. In spite of his repudiation of Calvinism, he upheld passive obedience as essential in training the young . . . it made me look upon my father with some fear. He stood for the Inexorable. So that when appeal to an undeveloped moral sense failed, corporal punishment, sometimes severe, was inevitable. It compelled submission, but never made me repentant. Certainly it did not encourage my brains. But worse, it made an over-sensitive child craving for love, so truly afraid of his father that more than once I lied to him. He never spoke of himself as having been punished for, I think, it would have seemed like irreverence toward that noble character, who, as *David Elginbrod* in the novel thus named, represented my grandfather.[37]

With the beatings we must group the scatological punishments meted out to the servants in *The Princess and Curdie*. But perhaps the most phantasmagoric collection of cruelties in all of MacDonald's writing we find in the late story for children, *A Rough Shaking* (1891). A Christlike child resembling Diamond or Sir Gibbie, Clare Skymer, loses his mother in an earthquake in Italy; his father, a naval officer, believes him lost also. Clare also loses his foster-parents, a kind parson and his wife. Peo-

ple call him half-witted and girlish; bullies maltreat him;
the wife of a kind farmer drives him away; he preserves
the life of an abandoned baby, though starving himself,
and establishes himself and the child in an abandoned
house. Rats gnaw the flesh from the baby's toes. Clare's
employer kicks and beats him, the police take away the
baby and drive him from the house. When he gets a job
in a travelling menagerie, the owner's brother-in-law
lashes him with a whip, plots to cut his dog's throat, and
eventually tries to feed Clare to a hungry puma. When
he gets a job as a bank clerk, one of the other clerks
knocks him down and makes him black his boots. Locked
in a wild beast's cage, and shanghaied onto a naval vessel, he finally encounters his father. He might as well
have lived in Gwyntystorm.

A Rough Shaking is a nightmare. Together with *The
Princess and Curdie,* it reflects the older MacDonald's
hatred of mankind and his preference for animals. Clare
Skymer is first glimpsed as something of a St. Francis, an
elderly man with a miraculous horse named Memnon,
which obeys orders and does errands for him. Birds light
in Skymer's beard, and his dogs are talented and disciplined. As he tells the story of his life, we find him
as a child playing with pigs in their pen and fearlessly
entering a bull's stall, "a little brother of Jesus Christ
bringing a taste of his father's kingdom to his great dull
bull of a brother." Animals save him from people: the
bull, his dog, the puma in the circus; at the end it is a
panther tethered on the deck of his father's ship which
recognizes him as the child it had played with as a cub
long years before, and so makes it possible for Clare's
father in turn to recognize him. The beasts are better
than the human beings.[38] We now remember the kind

and helpful animals we have met in almost every novel, especially horses, such as Malcolm's spirited Kelpie, Old Diamond, and Wilfrid Cumbermede's Lilith, but also grandmother's hen, air-fish, pigeons, Lina, and the good beasts.[39]

Among human beings, only children are good, retaining their primal innocence. Not only the Christ-children, like Diamond, Gibbie, and Clare Skymer, but the more human children, both in the fairy-tales and in the novels, are kind and warm. Even the little realists, like Nanny the crossing-sweeper or the little thief that for a time shares Clare Skymer's wanderings, have qualities lost to the best of adults. Back to Vaughan, and more particularly to Wordsworth goes this admiration for the purity and delightful freshness of childhood, shared with Mac-Donald by many of his Victorian contemporaries, including his friend Lewis Carroll, who, however, concentrated his affections upon little girls. "He who will be a man," MacDonald once wrote, "and will not be a child, must—he cannot help himself—become a little man, a dwarf." [40]

George MacDonald's children are usually motherless. But when mothers exist they are seldom kind and loving: Mrs. Forbes, Alec's mother, and Little Diamond's mother are exceptions. Again and again MacDonald paints harsh, cruel mothers, who actually want to hurt or even kill their children. Mrs. Oldcastle of the hall in *Annals of A Quiet Neighbourhood,* has brought about the death of one daughter, and is barely prevented from killing a second. The mad laird's mother in *Malcolm* has reduced him to such a state that the very word "mother" drives him into fits. In *Heather and Snow* the frivolous, hard-drinking, haughty squire's mother squanders his substance and regards him as an impediment. In all these cases, social snobbery partly motivates the cruelty: the women either fear unsuitable marriages for their daughters or sons or want to enjoy the income from the estate unhindered, or both. Listen to John Day, in *The Flight of the Shadow,* describing the behavior of his mother, Lady Cairnedge, when he refuses to marry the girl she has chosen for him:

> "She was pale as a corpse; her very lips were colourless; her eyes—but I will not go on. 'Your father all over,' she snarled—yes, snarled, with an inarticulate cry of fiercest loathing. . . . If I do not quite think my mother, *at present,* would murder me, I do think she would do anything short of murder to gain her ends with me."

For this savagery we get only the explanation of the heroine's uncle, who has known Lady Cairnedge in her youth:

> "There are women, some of them of the most admired, who are slaves to a demoniacal love of power. The very pleasure of their consciousness consists in the knowledge that they have power—not power to do things, but power to make other people do things. It is an insanity, but a devilishly immoral and hateful insanity." [41]

These cruel, child-hating, child-killing mothers are all preparatory sketches for MacDonald's Lilith, whom we have yet to meet. But the explanation of their behavior and attitudes sounds remarkably like the explanation of the Alder-maiden that the lady in fairyland had given Anodos.[42] The difference is that the Alder-maiden was an active sexual jilt: she used her power to get men into her toils; she was a young man's female demon. The death-dealing mothers are Alder-maidens grown older: Lady Cairnedge in her youth had actually been an Alder-maiden, enslaving the twin brothers just in order to exercise her power. In her middle age, she is a harpy who conspires against her young. So the aging MacDonald broadens his attack, and his wicked women age with him. In his works of fancy and imagination again and again he can imagine the mother-goddess, all-loving and all-knowing; in his works of fiction, however, he shows his resentments, his aggressions, and his longings in just the opposite way.

If the surviving mothers are often devils, the heroes of MacDonald's fiction often lack virility. Though it arises from his concern with his love for God, it is Count Julian's neglect of his wife that leads to his domestic tragedy. The rustic hero of "A Hidden Life" withdraws to a farm and never speaks to his love. The hero of "The Broken Swords" is too introspective and effeminate for war and loses his girl also. The tearful Anodos, despite his eroticism, is doomed to sexual frustration. The indecisive Campbell, of *The Portent,* in the "sad" version of the story, passively "waits" for a reunion with his loved one in the hereafter; so does Donal Grant. In the "happy" version of *The Portent,* it is Lady Alice, brandishing the Malay creese, who saves herself and her lover too. Wilfrid Cumbermede is effete. Bursts of tears accompany the career even of Robert Falconer, the "ideal" hero. Though Hugh Sutherland is a pleasant enough young man, he does not appear especially masculine. Sir Gibbie is too delicate and too Christ-like to make his earthly love for Ginevra credible. Clare Skymer seems never to have had a wife, only pets. Diamond dies untimely. Alec Forbes,

Malcolm, Paul Faber, Mossy, and Curdie, however, are men. Accompanying the low level of masculinity in his heroes MacDonald shows a keen appreciation for and sympathy with girls and women. Margaret Elginbrod, or Annie Anderson or Margaret MacLean (*Salted With Fire*), are worth two of their lovers. Florimel, Mary Marston, and Hesper Redmain have high spirits and strong characters. Even the wicked flirts, like Euphra, Sepia, Lufa, Mr. Cupples' charmer, Alder-maidens all of them, are fully realized.

MacDonald never relented in his hatred for the upper classes. In reflecting upon it, we can think of several possible explanations. Scotch history is full of violence; down to the eighteenth century, the highlanders lived lives like those of the Albanian mountaineers, with their blood feuds and their willingness to extend to whole families, including the children, the vengeance they owed to a single member. The Glencoe massacre was a part of MacDonald's own family past. Huntly Castle, on the very edge of the town where he was born and passed his youth, had been the scene of a more than usually revolting incident, perhaps legendary, when the men of the Earl of Huntly brought to the castle 200 children of the Farquharson family, and kept them in the dungeon cells, feeding them publicly like pigs at a trough for the amusement of the castle guests. MacDonald knew this episode well and refers to it in *Alec Forbes*.[43] The descendants of the Marquises of Huntly in the Castle, the Dukes of Gordon, often behaved arrogantly and cruelly; they were the landlords of George MacDonald's father. Possibly these ancestral and childhood associations with a noble family that had in the past committed black deeds contributed to MacDonald's hatred of the nobility.

Surely, his class-feeling was exacerbated by the jilt in

the library, whom we have met so often, and by his poverty. His fantasy was always that he was himself noble: Malcolm is truly a marquis, Curdie of royal blood, Wilfrid Cumbermede the true heir to the Hall, Richard Tuke the bookbinder really Sir Richard Lestrange the Baronet. All earned their high-born ladies by proving to be equally high-born. MacDonald's own friends among the gentry, like Lady Byron, the Cowper-Temples, and Lady Caroline Charteris (daughter of the Earl of Wemyss), did not affect his hatred of their class: he regarded them only as honorable exceptions to the rule. Even the lesser gentry, the squires, and the Scotch lairds, are usually villains, as in *Sir Gibbie*, or stupid, as in *David Elginbrod*, or indecently haughty, as in *Wilfrid Cumbermede* or *Annals of a Quiet Neighbourhood* or *Mary Marston*. Poverty, however, ennobles even a gentleman: the penniless laird in *Castle Warlock* is truly a MacDonald hero; but the rich Lord Mergwain in the same novel is as repulsive as any of the wicked nobles, if more credible than some.

The Marquis of Lossie, Malcolm's father, occasionally behaves well, but this is at moments when the old sense of clan chieftainship and responsibility asserts itself strongly enough to predominate over his dissolute past, his new-fangled citified ways, and his natural coarseness and brutality. (He had been an intimate of the Prince Regent.) The MacRuadh, in *What's Mine's Mine*, in whom this clan leadership survives unimpaired, almost alone in the novels gives us MacDonald's idea of the good nobleman; and The MacRuadh is poor, and has fallen on evil days. Lady Bernard in *The Vicar's Daughter* is, of course, an exception, but MacDonald intended her in any case as a portrait of Lady Byron, his great benefactress.

True nobility resides in workmen: for example in shoe-

makers, like MacLean in *Salted With Fire* or Mr. Spelt in
Guild Court. In fact, we find so many good shoemakers
in MacDonald that we wonder whether he was consciously inspired by his love for the visionary cobbler
Jacob Boehme to try to associate mystical virtue with all
those of Boehme's trade. There is another in *Donal Grant*,
and still another in the story for children, *Gutta Percha
Willie*.[44] If some of them are drunkards, like Sir George
Galbraith, Sir Gibbie's father, or Dooble Sanny, even
this is not to their discredit: Sir George loves Gibbie and
is a true father to him; Dooble Sanny repents in the end,
and, as a musician, was always halfway to heaven anyhow. Together with MacDonald's noble carpenters, black-
smiths, stone-masons, bookbinders, with his great-hearted
paupers, like the acrobats in *Weighed and Wanting*, and
with the cripples and idiots, who are usually men of low
degree, the shoemakers suggest that simplicity itself is
sacred to MacDonald. He also greatly admired skill and
ingenuity of craftsmanship. Willie MacMichael, hero of
Gutta Percha Willie, becomes as a child a talented blacksmith, shoemaker, carpenter, and mechanic. He discovers
a medicinal spring in the garden of an ancient priory,
builds himself quarters in the ruins, a forge, and a tree-
house for his younger sister. When grown up and trained
as a doctor, he and his father turn the priority into a hospital, where patients benefit from the healing waters.

The very act of buying and selling MacDonald feels
to be evil in itself. Dishonest speculators abound: his
businessmen are apt to be crooked, whether it is George
Crawford in *The Elect Lady*, who learns his dishonest
ways in America, or the very rich Ferdinand Redmain
in *Mary Marston*, who has made his pile by methods better not described, or the purse-proud city-man in *The*

Vicar's Daughter, who is ruined. Redmain's middle name is Goldberg, but MacDonald never calls him a Jew, or joins the majority of Victorian novelists in regarding Jews as sharp practitioners in business: the only Jews in the whole range of the novels are the generous and noble Morgensterns of *Guild Court.* In *What's Mine's Mine* Mr. Palmer's money comes from whiskey and is therefore tainted in any case.

In a short story called "The Butcher's Bills," a well-to-do businessman who insists on accuracy in the household accounts almost drives his wife mad with resentment and remorse because she must report all her personal expenses and cannot make her books balance. Only after she has run away from home in a kind of mental collapse does the husband awaken to his own shortcomings.[45] But even when the merchants are only village butchers they are usually cheats. The son of Mr. Weir, the carpenter in *Annals of a Quiet Neighbourhood,* loses his job as a clerk in a shop because he will not overpraise his stock. After Arundel, the lower middle classes disgusted MacDonald. He strove to be fair: there is a good butcher in *Paul Faber* to offset the cheat, and a good draper in *Thomas Wingfold* to offset the many dishonest ones in other books. In the short story, "Stephen Archer," a solemn priggish but goodhearted stationer, who is a devout Dissenting Christian, is immeasurably broadened in his outlook by his love for a pure girl from the dregs of society, whose only aim in life is to keep her young brother out of bad company.[46] But by and large we may take Robert Bruce, the penny-pinching, mealy-mouthed storekeeper in *Alec Forbes,* as representing what MacDonald really thought about business and trade. Some of this may have derived from the disgrace of his uncle Charles and the

light-hearted optimism and financial failures of his specu-
lator-brother, also named Charles.

Servants share MacDonald's dislike with noblemen and
tradesmen. It is curious that he should have held the concept of service in such high esteem, and so bitterly detested professional servitors. No calling, he felt, could be
higher than for a son to serve a father, as in *Robert Falconer*, a father to serve a son, as in *Seekers and Finders*,
a brother to serve a sister, as in *The Marquis of Lossie*,
or a friend to serve a friend, as in *Mary Marston*. Yet in
MacDonald's view the practitioners rarely realized the
beauty of their calling. From the footman whom Hugh
Sutherland stares down in *David Elginbrod* to the insolent household of Lady Bernard which she rebukes in
The Vicar's Daughter and the incredibly disagreeable staff
of the Redmains in *Mary Marston*, the reader finds the
servants more snobbish and cruel than their masters.
Though the palace servants in *The Princess and Curdie*
are the worst, Florimel's maid tries to poison Malcolm,
and even the kind Mrs. Wilson in *Wilfrid Cumbermede*
turns spiteful: when the Brothertons employ Wilfrid to
restore the books in the library, she refuses to defend
his title to his sword. No doubt some of this reflected
MacDonald's own experience of snubs at servants' hands;
but the virulence with which he expresses his dislike none
the less arouses some wonder.

Members of all professions make their appearance in
the novels. The wordly Mr. Coningham of *Wilfrid Cumbermede* is the only lawyer to play much of a role: he is
not quite a villain, but almost. Professors receive warm
treatment in *Alec Forbes*, and the savage Murdoch Malison is balanced by Mr. Graham, the learned and inspiring
schoolmaster of Portlossie in *Malcolm*, and by Donal

Grant, who takes pupils. Doctors come off well. Robert Falconer's benefactor is a doctor; Paul Faber, despite his atheism, is presented as a disinterested servant of humanity; while Hester Raymount chooses to marry the charitable physician, Mr. Christopher, the healer in the slums. Percivale in *The Seaboard Parish* and *The Vicar's Daughter,* and Mr. Lenorme in *The Marquis of Lossie* show MacDonald's reverence for artists and his debt to Ruskin for his views on art. Duncan MacPhail the blind piper, Joseph Jasper the violinist-blacksmith (*Mary Marston*) and Robert Falconer and Dooble Sanny testify to his worship of music, and his feeling that musicians are divinely inspired. Mr. Raymount, of *Weighed and Wanting,* and Mr. Raymond, of *At the Back of the North Wind,* are the only authors. MacDonald shows a mild respect for his own calling but nothing more.

Among the clergy, it is remarkable that MacDonald never introduces a Catholic priest; indeed, Catholics make no appearance at all, despite the survival of the old faith in Scotland and its popularity as a subject in Victorian fiction. But he ranges widely among the Protestant clergy, as we have seen, from the Missionar Calvinists through Church of England priests of all sorts. He gives us smug country ministers, like Mr. Bevis in *Paul Faber,* to whom Wingfold teaches his Christian duty; fashionable city clergymen like the one in *David Elginbrod;* inspirational and devoted preachers modeled on Maurice; and humbler men who act as guides and friends to all their parishioners, like Wingfold, or the Vicar of Marshmallows, Mr. Walton.

The Dissenters appear seldom, but when they do they play a significant role, like Mr. Drake in *Paul Faber,* or the minister in *Annals of a Quiet Neighourhood.* In both cases the Church-of-England hero, Wingfold or Walton, shows complete tolerance, and even affection for the Dissenter; Walton insists that he not be forced to pay the tithe to the Church of England and saves him from having his furniture confiscated. Though MacDonald had bitter memories of the congregation at Arundel, and disapproved of the emphasis on accommodation that he felt permeated training for the Congregational ministry, he none the less pays eloquent fictional tribute to the fine human values he had found in the best of his dissenting colleagues. In every case he also emphasizes the cruel snobbery with which the gentry and the social climbers treat the Dissenters. No sectarian, MacDonald perhaps makes his point most dramatically in the contrast he draws in *Mary Marston* between the aggressive, hypocritical, climbing churchman, Turnbull, who is also dishonest, and his high-minded, scrupulously upright partner, Marston, who is a Baptist.

It is for social workers in the city and farmers in the countryside, however, that MacDonald reserves his real affection. Robert Falconer, quietly using the fortune he has inherited to help the poor, the weak, and the criminal, and searching for his father all the while, reaches heights of heroism scaled by no other MacDonald hero. Mary St. John, the woman he loves, also devotes herself to social work. Miss Clare, in *The Vicar's Daughter*, loved and admired by the roughest denizens of the teeming slums, among whom she lives by choice, is almost a saint. Hester Raymount, sensitive and strong-minded, makes social work her career because she hears a call to it as clear as that of any man to his profession; and she gives up her financé because he disapproves of her work and scorns the people among whom she does it. If one is a city-dweller, MacDonald is saying, the noblest thing to do is to alleviate for a little while some of the worst agonies that the poor suffer. In *Thomas Wingfold,* Mac-Donald declared, "When all men are Christians, the state will inevitably be communist, or perhaps cease to exist," [47] but he was not really a political or social radical. He regarded the social system as dreadful, and as needing constant mitigation at the hands of the kind saints among mankind, but as essentially irrelevant. In a world where the benevolent Father loves each of his children, and what appears to be the shape of evil is really the best good, how could it be otherwise?

The hero of "A Hidden Life," at the very beginning of MacDonald's literary career, chose to go back to his ancestral farm; but the only other alternative he considered was work among the poor of the city: the choice, posed so early, represented MacDonald's view that these were the two best things a man could do. So David Elginbrod joins the father of the hero of "A Hidden Life," and so, especially in the Scotch novels, David is joined by other intelligent, high-minded, hard-working, thoughtful, men who work their land. In the country, too, the poorest are the best: the humble cottars in whose house Robert Falconer discovers *The Arabian Nights* and Shakespeare, and Donal Grant's parents, also cottars, who take Sir Gibbie in and give him shelter and love. Near the very end of his career as a novelist, in *Home Again,* MacDonald drew an English farming father with all the virtues, and a son who in the end came home to farm again, like the hero in "A Hidden Life." Had MacDonald himself not been a preacher turned novelist, he would surely have gone among the poor in the streets of London or ploughed his father's acres in Aberdeenshire.

CHAPTER 6

Lilith

"This River has been a Terror to many, yea the
thoughts of it also have often frighted me."

The Pilgrim's Progress

I

FOR THE MACDONALDS, the eighties and nineties were
decades of trial. They named their house in Bordighera
"Casa Coraggio": MacDonald had long before discovered
that "Corage, God Mend Al," was an anagram of "George
MacDonald," and inscribed it on his book-plate, with
Blake's picture of the aged "man through death's door
going," who enters the tomb in weariness, and emerges
at the top young and vigorous, like Mossy after the bath
of the Old Man of the Sea, leaving "old Death behind." [1]
The huge household at Bordighera grew by the adoption
of two little girls and their mother, who had tuberculosis.
The summer migration to England for the playing of
Pilgrim's Progress took place each year until 1887. The
children, growing up, participated to an astonishing degree in all the family enterprises, the sisters sacrificing
their own interests to the care and education of the
adopted waifs, the brothers gradually leaving the household for their own professional training.

At Bordighera, on Wednesdays and Sundays, MacDonald would lecture on Dante or Shakespeare, or preach informally to as many as a hundred visitors at a time. An organ was added to the room, and music always formed a part of the ceremonies. At Christmas the family performed mediaeval *tableaux vivants*. The stuffier members of the English colony were disturbed at the MacDonalds' habit of inviting the Italian children of the place to come to the Christmas festivities, and appalled when the family put on a special concert for pay and used the money toward wiping out the debt on the new church—Catholic of course—in Bordighera. Greville, launched on a successful medical career, reports how his father somewhat impractically hoped that, "like some chief of a clan," he might in Italy gather again all his sons around him, and how his disappointment gave rise to "certain tragical misunderstandings that seemed insoluble."

A daughter, Grace, died of tuberculosis in 1884; and *her* small daughter of the same scourge in 1891. The MacDonald's eldest child, Lily (Lilia), who had given up her lover to remain a member of the family theatricals, now sacrificed her life to nurse a friend who was dying of tuberculosis and caught the disease herself, dying in 1891. In the face of her illness, MacDonald showed the most astonishing fortitude, constantly reassuring his wife that real life lay ahead, and that reunion with Lily would come soon for all of them: a "great good" was coming to them all. Greville's account of Lily's death is of almost intolerable pathos: she, who had been named after the Lilia of *Within and Without,* the child that died in MacDonald's first work of fiction, she, who had played Christiana to her father's Mr. Greatheart, now died in her father's arms, and disappeared into the Dark River. To maintain resignation, even joy, in the face of such calamity, took all the fortitude that even George MacDonald could summon up. He "could hardly leave the grave: he came back twice after all others had left, and it was with difficulty he was at last led away."

What we know of the years that follow is chiefly the reiteration of faith, voiced in letter after letter of sympathy to friends whose husbands or wives had died. MacDonald continued to write, *Heather and Snow* and *Salted With Fire*, as we have seen, both dating from the period after Lilia's death. He read much, returning to Boehme, and studied Spanish and Dutch. But his attention wandered, his brain relaxed; by degrees he stopped writing; he suffered from eczema and insomnia; he spoke seldom, and then almost never, and in 1897 sank into a kind of "constant waiting." Once, late in 1898, with a look of despair, he told his wife "I know you are all going away from me, and I'm going to be left in a strange house." Though she reassured him, he relapsed into silence, which lasted until his death. Greville MacDonald bought some land in Surrey, and there he built a house for his parents designed by an architect brother. Here the senior MacDonalds settled in 1900; Louisa MacDonald died in 1902, and her husband in 1905, nursed to the very end by loving daughters.[2]

But in the years before the final silence descended, MacDonald returned once more to the form of the visionary romance that he had created in *Phantastes*. In 1890, he wrote, almost without stopping, the first version of *Lilith*, only about one third the length of the version that was finally published in 1895. Three times, Greville MacDonald has discussed the composition and revision of his father's last important book. In 1924, he issued a new

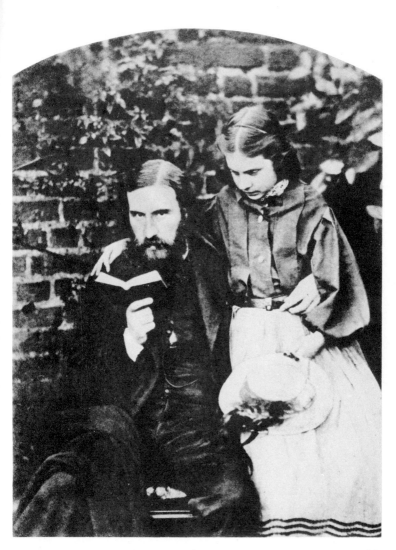

George MacDonald with his daughter Lilia (Lily) Scott MacDonald.
(Photograph by Lewis Carroll)

The Golden Wedding, 1901

edition of *Lilith*, with an interpretative introduction, and
a paraphrase of the manuscript of the earliest version.
In 1925, in his biography of his father, and in 1932, in his
own *Reminiscences*, he added new material to his earlier
accounts.

When MacDonald revised and expanded *Lilith* for
publication, he gave it to his wife to read. She, "less brave
than he in philosophic adventure, found the narrative
often distressing, its hidden meaning too obscure; and
she feared lest it should be taken as evidence of weaken-
ign power rather than the reverse . . . she wrote of it
to me as 'a terrible book, though portions, such as the
loveliness in death, and the grand ending are exquisitely
beautiful'; and she could not be happy over its publication." In their disagreement—the only one of their entire
married life—father and mother turned to Greville, who
was surprised to be selected as juror, and happy to read
the manuscript. He wrote his mother that he found it
the best of all his father's works, "the Revelation of St.
George the Divine," and it was published.[3]

In the British Museum manuscript collection, there survive no fewer than six pre-publication versions of *Lilith*,
packed in a wooden box as given by George MacDonald's daughter Winifred Louisa, Lady Troup. Examination of these reveals that all except the first are essentially
the version that was eventually published. Thus what
we may call *Lilith 1* survives in its original bound note-
book, dated March 28, 1890, and written on the right-
hand rectos of 161 consecutive lined leaves, the rest
remaining blank. *Lilith 2* is a typescript version, far nearer
the final published version than *Lilith 1; Lilith 3* is a
heavily revised typed copy, in three sub-divisions; *Lilith 4*
is the galley proof as printed from *Lilith 3*, itself heavily

marked and scored; *Lilith 5* is the first revise; and *Lilith 6*
a bound copy of the second revise, only very slightly
marked, but inscribed "Winifred Louisa MacDonald from
her father—to close the series of development. May,
1895." This differs only in trivial details from the final
book version. Scholars can follow the substantial revisions
from *Lilith 2* to *Lilith 6* and may one day produce a detailed account of MacDonald's methods of composition.[4]
But the major differences in structure are those between
Lilith 1, on the one hand, and *Lilith 2–6*, on the other.
The collection of manuscript materials shows us not the
stages of the transition between these two but only the
completed transition itself.

Lilith 1 begins as follows:

> My mother I had no memory of, and my father had
> become to me as a shadow, and an old shadow. But
> there were things told of him among the servants
> that kept alive in the hearts of some of us a vague
> sense of something we did not well know what to call
> it [sic]. For my part I could not tell whether I re-
> membered anything or not, though I must have seen
> him. The portrait of him hung in the entrance hall
> of the house. . . . There were persons in the house-
> hold who said that he was dead; there were others
> who said that all they were justified in saying was
> that he had disappeared: whether he was dead, espe-
> cially as what *dead* meant they could not tell, they
> did not know: one thing only was certain, that he was
> nowhere to be found. There was indeed one solemn
> old person, always draped in black as if he were
> always mourning his master's absence, who, as often
> as he was questioned, expressed himself as unspeak-
> ably shocked at the wickedness of thinking he was

dead, but would tell you things about him that made
you wish he were dead indeed—at least would have
made me wish he were dead but that I did not believe
what the butler told me about him. . . .

We at once recognize the situation here as resembling
that in *Robert Falconer:* the hero has only the vaguest
memories of his father, who is perhaps a reprobate. As in
Robert Falconer, the hero resolves upon the search:

My mind was filled with my determination to devote
my life to the finding of my father. Something in my
heart said that he was not dead, and I would not believe it until I despaired of finding any other place
in which to look for him. I felt that all my life hitherto had been but a preparation for setting out to
search after him.

When we turn to *Lilith 2,* this whole theme has become
a story within the story: it is no longer the way the book
begins, with the hero speaking in his own person, but a
story in a manuscript found by the hero, told *by* the
hero's father about his search for *his* father. In *Lilith 3*
even this aspect of the search is crossed out.[5] And in this
and all later versions, the search shrinks to nothing, since
the narrator finds his father, without having set out to
look for him, at the very beginning of his explorations
of the other world. Thus, *Lilith* apparently began as a
companion-piece to *Phantastes:* the search for a father
balancing the search for a mother. But even in *Lilith 1*
the voyages into the other world soon became so crowded
with episodes and so full of other symbolism that the
search for a father never took the central position an-
nounced for it. And in the later versions, the original
theme vanished altogether.

In addition to Greville MacDonald (surely a biased witness) and H. G. Wells (who chose for praise only one of its aspects), Harold Child and W. H. Auden have greatly admired *Lilith*. Child wrote of it:

> The story is so packed with meaning, so full of images of which the meanings seem inexhaustible, that it is marvellous to see how George MacDonald keeps it, as a story, moving, and is ever ready with some new and strange vehicle of a beautiful or grotesque or horrible imagination.

And Auden elaborated this point of view in some detail in his introduction to the 1954 reprint, praising the tightness of its allegorical structure.[6] Yet we shall have reason to disagree. Perhaps Louisa MacDonald was right in her instinctive feeling that it would have been better for her husband's reputation had *Lilith* not been printed. One might forgive its cruelty, its ugliness, its irresponsibility, its brooding depression, if one could feel with Child that the images had inexhaustible meaning, and that the author kept the story moving. Close reading of *Lilith* has convinced me instead that, despite powerful and occasionally moving passages, it is feeble, ambiguous, and inconsistent in its imagery, full of senile hatreds and resentments, and the most violent in its aggressions of all MacDonald's works. The consolations that it professes to offer seem to have lost their meaning for the author himself.

II

Lilith is the story of Mr. Vane (we never learn his first name), an orphan, just out of Oxford, heir to a large house

—which he has not seen since childhood—with a fine, many-roomed library, containing many books on the history of science and on metaphysics. One of its doors is covered with artificial book-backs, among which there sticks out half of a book, laid in across the top; Vane pries it open, he can see lines of manuscript; but since the other half is missing, he can make no sense out of it. He occasionally catches glimpses of the ghost of a former librarian, Mr. Raven, who had served his ancestors, and who now sometimes haunts the place. One day the vision leads him up a flight of stairs he has previously not known about into a garret, in the center of which he finds a small room with a large old mirror; he is looking at the sun's rays reflected in it when the reflection disappears; a landscape takes its place, and he steps through the mirror frame into another world.

Unlike Anodos in *Phantastes,* who stays in fairyland from beginning to end of his three-week dream, Mr. Vane in *Lilith* makes five trips back and forth to the other world, each time finding himself in his own house when the trip is over. The other world has certain features that mark it out as in many ways a higher realm than this one, but it has others that make it even less attractive: it is not in itself Limbo or Purgatory or the country at the back of the North Wind or—as a whole at least—any other way-station between earth and heaven, such as the realms of the Old Men of Sea, Earth, and Fire that Tangle passes through after death in "The Golden Key."

Its physical and mental laws vary from those of this world, but its moral laws, like those of all worlds, are the same. One's awareness of one's identity, even one's identity itself, fades away. It is, perhaps, another planet: MacDonald suggests this in several ways: it has several moons, rather than one, and Mr. Vane never comes to understand the law of their rising and setting; some of them move much faster than the earth's moon, and much of the action takes place in bright moonlight. Mr. Raven, also, when Vane has come to know him, once refers to the animals and the weather on Uranus, which he has recently visited; so that we know him to be an inter-planetary traveler. Vane's other world is, however, not Uranus, but it has some—not many—points of resemblance to the other planet in the first story that Anodos read in the library of the fairy palace.

Yet, although Vane's other world resembles another planet, it also occupies the same space as our own world and the same time. *Lilith 1* bore the subtitle "A Tale of the Seventh Dimension," and though MacDonald expunged this from *Lilith 2* and all later verisons, he kept the idea that had lain behind it. Following Boehme, he took as four more dimensions the four temperaments of man—the choleric, the sanguine, the phlegmatic, and the melancholic, each corresponding with one of the "humours," bile, blood, phlegm, and black bile, and with one of the "elements," fire, air, water, and earth. Those give man sustenance and emancipate him from the other three dimensions. So, Raven explains, a tree in the other world stands on the hearth of Vane's kitchen, and grows right up his chimney: if he walks to the other side of it he will walk through his housekeeper's niece who is practicing on the piano in his breakfast room, and then through the kitchen fire. The wild hyacinths growing in the fields of the other world are inside Vane's piano in this one, and lend sweetness to the music, while the quiver of near-by rose petals in the other world gives off the odor of Grieg's Wedding March as it is being played in this one.

MacDonald took as epigraph for all of *Lilith* a passage from Thoreau's "Walking":

I took a walk in Spaulding's Farm the other afternoon. I saw the setting sun lighting up the opposite side of a stately pine wood. Its golden rays straggled into the aisles of the wood as into some noble hall. I was impressed as if some ancient and altogether admirable and shining family had settled there in that part of the land called Concord, unknown to me,—to whom the sun was servant,—who had not gone into society in the village,—who had not been called on. I saw their park, their pleasure-ground, beyond through the wood, in Spaulding's cranberry-meadow. The pines furnished them with gables as they grew. Their house was not obvious to vision; their trees grew through it. I do not know whether I heard the sounds of a suppressed hilarity or not. They seemed to recline on the sunbeams. They have sons and daughters. They are quite well. The farmer's cart-path, which leads directly through their hall, does not in the least put them out,—as the muddy bottom of a pool is sometimes seen through the reflected skies. They never heard of Spaulding, and do not know that he is their neighbor,—notwithstanding I heard him whistle as he drove his team through the house. Nothing can equal the serenity of their lives. Their coat of arms is simply a lichen. I saw it painted on the pines and oaks. Their attics were in the tops of the trees. They are of no politics. There was no noise of labor. I did not perceive that they were weaving or spinning. Yet I did detect, when the wind lulled and hearing was done away,

the finest imaginable sweet musical hum,—as of
a distant hive in May, which perchance was the
sound of their thinking. They had no idle thoughts,
and no one without could see their work, for their
industry was not as in knots and excrescences em-
bayed.

But I find it difficult to remember them. They fade
irrevocably out of my mind even now while I speak
and endeavor to recall them, and recollect myself.
It is only after a long and serious effort to recollect
my best thoughts that I become again aware of their
cohabitancy. If it were not for such families as this,
I think I should move out of Concord.

This passage from Thoreau, quite innocent of Boehme-
ian metaphysics, suggests what MacDonald seems to have
had in mind as the essential relationship between the two
worlds of *Lilith* better than the cumbersome equation of
the four temperaments with four additional dimensions.
This no doubt explains why he dropped the original subtitle, and limited the clue given the reader in the published text of *Lilith* to a single statement by Mr. Raven
that Mr. Vane is now in the "region of seven dimensions."
As in MacDonald's earlier tales of fantasy, time is also
out of joint in the other world: on Vane's second trip,
summer turns to winter after what seems only half a day,
and Raven explains that "In your world you cannot pull
up the plumb-line you call gravitation, and let the world
spin round under your feet." In the other world, a familiar
situation prevails:

Every one . . . has a beast-self—and a bird-self, and
a stupid fish-self, ay, and a creeping serpent-self too
—which takes a good deal of crushing to kill! In

truth, he has also a tree-self and a crystal-self, and I don't know how many selves more—all to get into harmony. You can tell what sort a man is by his nature that comes oftener to the front.

The evolutionary aspect of the selves, so marked in "A Hidden Life," *The Princess and the Goblin,* and *The Princess and Curdie,* here disappears, and man has them all simultaneously.

The entrances to and exits from the other world are skillfully managed. The first trip seems almost an accident, although the Raven leads Vane upstairs to the mirror. But after a brief conversation with Raven in the other world, Vane walks into a pine wood, and sees something vaguely shining between two of the trunks; it disappears as he comes nearer, but when he walks between the trunks he has a slight shock, and is back in his garret: he has walked through the surface of the mirror in the other direction. On the second trip, a mere step into the garden with Raven is enough to make the transition: Vane had not wanted to go again, and after a disturbing experience he runs away, dashes through a door, and finds himself back in his library: he has opened from the other side the door with the artificial book-backs. Both of these trips have been brief; each has taught Vane only a little more about the other world and about mankind. After the second, he finds in his library a manuscript account by his father, describing how Mr. Raven had shown him also the way into the other world. Until "old Sir Upward," a remote ancestor of the Vanes, had shown it to him, Raven had not known there was a route into it through the Vane house. Now Raven sometimes uses the Vane mansion as a route home. The manuscript goes on

to describe the method more fully: the garret roof can
be made to revolve in such a way that at noon the sun's
rays fall on a mirror on the wall, and are thence reflected
into (but not out of) the other mirror that Vane has
already passed through once. This creates in the mirror
the image of the other world and the possibility of entrance.

Ashamed of his earlier flight, Vane now of his own
accord manipulates the mirrors and enters the other world
for a third time, a long visit, full of adventures, in which
he comes to know its inhabitants and its problems. Like
Anodos, he disregards an injunction; and so, against his
will this time, returns into our world. But after a brief
interlude, he travels in again through the mirror for a
fourth long visit. His moral and spiritual education and
preparation for eternity virtually completed, he none
the less, while dreaming, behaves in such a fashion that,
to his despair, he finds himself back in his house. But this
may well all be *part* of the dream. So may his fifth trip,
not accomplished by mechanical means, and his ostensible return from it. The book ends with Vane apparently
in this world, but only with ambiguity: he may only be
dreaming that he is back. H. G. Wells, preoccupied at the
same period with the same problem, wrote MacDonald:

> I have been reading your *Lilith* with exceptional in-
> terest. Curiously enough I have been at work on a
> book based on the same idea, namely that, assuming
> more than three dimensions, it follows that there
> must be wonderful worlds nearer to us than breath-
> ing and closer than hands and feet. I have wanted to
> get into such kindred worlds for the purposes of
> romance for several years, but I've been bothered

by the way. Your polarization and mirror business
struck me as neat in the extreme.

But though MacDonald devised this "neat" business, he
was too sure an artist to use it too often; there are other
ways into and out of his other world, and Vane himself
uses some of them. [7]

As Vane comes to know the topography and inhabitants
of the other world through experience, and through occasional explanations from Raven and others, we also
come to know them: the first visit is too short for more
than a brief metaphysical discussion about doors out and
doors in. It serves to disturb Vane and make him feel
the uncanniness of the other world. On the second, in-
voluntary visit, from the garden, Mr. Raven, who sometimes takes his human shape, sometimes that of the bird
whose name he bears, begins to teach and demonstrate:
he plunges his beak into the ground, and pulls out a red
worm: when he tosses it into the air, it spreads great
wings, "gorgeous in red and black" and soars aloft.
Though worms come from the earth, this one will never
return there: as we learned long ago in *David Elginbrod,*
"the caterpillar dies into the butterfly." Prayers from our
world—from living hearts—materialize as live pigeons
or as flowers in this other one. In the other world, Mr.
Raven is a sexton, in charge of a burial ground; and he
deliberately makes the parallel between this task and his
former earthly role as a librarian: "Except you are a true
sexton, books are but dead bodies to you, and a library
nothing but a catacomb."

On his second visit Mr. Raven takes Mr. Vane to his
cottage, surrounded by a churchyard, and Vane momentarily feels old, and that his life is over. Raven and his

beautiful wife invite Vane to join their legion of sleepers, whom they show him, after giving him the "perfect meal" of bread and wine (communion). Lying in long rows in an icy vault, on couches, the sleepers are at peace: none of them is dead yet; to die is to come alive, and some of them have only begun the process. When they are really dead, they come alive and leave the cemetery. Vane does not want to go to sleep: he wants first to find, or make, or invent or discover something; he cannot believe that sleep must precede any real action. He rebels at the cold in the vault and at taking the place reserved for him: his complaints—says Raven—bring the air of death into the chamber, and he runs away, and back to his library. Among those he has seen in the vault are a beautiful woman and a splendid man, side by side, the man with his hand half closed. Unable to understand the true nature of the sleep of the dead, Vane is not ready to die into life.

On his third, voluntary visit, therefore, Mr. Raven refuses to allow him to come to his house and sleep: he reveals that the man with the hand half closed is Vane's father, and that his ancestors are mostly there; but that Sir Upward has waked and left, and Vane's grandfather is still in the "Evil Wood, fighting the dead." Bitter at Raven's seeming inhospitality, Vane follows a firefly-like creature, whom Raven throws into the air to guide him. When he tries to grasp it, and it descends into his hand, its light goes out: "all was dark as pitch; a dead book with boards outspread lay cold and heavy in my hand." As plainly as possible MacDonald here voices the warning against the reason or the intellect: when it tries to grasp light it simply kills it, and turns it into book learning, dead-weight knowledge that no longer radiates inspiration, the age-old cry of the mystic against the rationalist. As Augustine says: "Let the voices of men be silent, and the reflections of men be stilled: let them stretch out not as if to grasp those things which cannot be grasped, but as if to take part in them." [8]

Vane passes through the "bad burrow," where dreadful creatures (perhaps the horrors of his imagination), a tiger, a worm, burst from the earth as he passes by, though the moonlight restrains them from attacking him. Here too a beautiful woman, with a dark spot on her left side, appears only to disintegrate: her arms and legs rush off as serpents, and "something flew up from her like a bat, and when I looked again she was gone." Next Vane crosses the "evil wood," where a mad ghostly battle between phantoms and skeletons rages; they fight on foot or on horseback as long as any two bones remain together, all urged on by the beautiful evil woman of the bad burrow.

> . . . skeleton jaws and phantom-throats swelled the deafening tumult with the war-cry of every opinion, bad or good, that had bred strife, injustice, cruelty in any world. The holiest words went with the most hating blow.

And the cry of the evil woman is " 'Ye are men: slay one another!' " This the place where, Raven has told Vane, his grandfather still fights the dead: it is where "those who will not sleep wake up at night, to kill their dead and bury them," presumably those who cannot relinquish even after death the principles they stood for in their combats and quarrels on earth: even "good" opinion, if it has bred strife on earth, must be abandoned, it would seem. The evil wood reminds one of Dante's *Inferno,* where the damned retain a passionate interest in what is going on in Italy and cling to their characters and opinions as they had been in life.

Vane now enters a forest, which is inhabited by two races. There are bad giants who live in wretched huts, the men almost indistinguishable from the women, "a sort of fungoid people with just enough mind to give them motion and the expressions of anger and greed," who capture Vane, and make him work for them, kicking him and feeding him on their abominable food. There are also charming children, the Little Ones, living on delicious fruit, who release him and play with him at times when the giants cannot catch them at it. Their leader is a tall grave girl named Lona, who finds a baby in the woods, which is the way, indeed, that all the children have come into being. Some of the children show signs of greed and selfishness; they begin to prefer the giants' food to their own; the others regard these signs with horror, since such children are on their way to developing into giants. In fact, all the giants were children once, and have grown into their present repulsiveness by exercising greed, sloth, and stupidity. In this world of the children and the giants there is no running water anywhere: former stream beds have dried up, although water may be heard running underground. So, too, nobody sheds tears: indeed the first water the children have seen is Vane's tears, wept at a pathetic song that one of the children sings. In Klingsohr's *Märchen* tears are truth; here, they, and the water, are something else. Vane senses that the growth of the children is somehow arrested despite their charm. They seem ignorant, "full of wisdom and empty of knowledge," and he wants to teach them things, since "knowledge no doubt made bad people worse but it must make good people better." But before he can embark on any such program he has to leave their forest, because the giants find out about his relations with the children and intend to kill him.

The giants are proud of being fat: as Vane remarks, "So they are in my world . . . only they do not say *fat* there, they say rich." Like the human rich, the giants care only for their own selfish pleasures. Those children that develop into them are clearly the fathers of the men they become. Yet the choice between developing the brutal mindless gluttony of the giants and remaining in the arrested innocence of the Little Ones is not a bright one: hence Vane surmises that it may be knowledge that the children need. We know MacDonald better than that. It is not knowledge the Little Ones need, but Mother-love. All the water—the essential maternal symbol—even the tears in their land, has dried up: the maternal affections are atrophied, for terrible reasons that we have yet to learn. The curse of the wicked witch in "The Light Princess" has here reached its ultimate. The finding of the babies in the wood is exactly what happens on the distant planet in the short story Anodos reads in the fairy library in *Phantastes*. But here, in the other world, the imagery is somewhat different: there are no babies on the couches in Mr. Raven's cemetery, although there are some children there. Perhaps the babies found in the wood are the babies who die in infancy on earth. Though the Little Ones exemplify MacDonald's familiar doctrine about the peculiar sanctity of childhood, their sentimentality is, as Auden remarked, "shy-making." Nor does the horrible baby-talk which MacDonald makes his Little Ones speak endear them to us: at the first sight of Vane's tears, one of them remarks to the other " 'Ou skeeze ze juice out of ze good giant's seeberries.' "

The children have told Vane of a Cat-Woman; they say she scratches, but Lona knows her to be good. They know also of another "giant-girl," who rules over a distant place, but who hates Little Ones and would like to kill them. Vane now passes the house of the Cat-Woman, Mara, on a rock in the midst of the desert. With her head and face muffled, she asks him in, and tells him something of the story of the other woman, who is "older than this world, and came to it from yours with a terrible history, which is not over yet." She had come to the city of Bulika, whose people had been simple farmers, and had taught them to dig for and sell diamonds and opals. When they killed a huge snake, she grew so enraged that she became "terrible to them," and declared herself their princess. Up till that time it had been The Land of Waters, but she

> "gathered what she could of the water over the whole country, closed it in an egg and carried it away. Her lap, however, would not hold more than half of it; and the instant she was gone, what she had not taken fled away underground, leaving the country as dry and dusty as her own heart."

No rain falls, and, were it not for the underground streams, everything and every person would have died. The wicked princess holds the people of Bulika in terror, and does what she can to prevent them from multiplying. Yet they

> "boast and believe themselves prosperous, and certainly are a self-satisfied people—good at bargaining and buying, and good at selling and cheating; holding well together for a common interest, and utterly treacherous where interests clash; proud of their prin-

cess and her power, and despising every one they
can get the better of; never doubting themselves the
most honourable of all nations, and each man count-
ing himself better than any other." [9]

The reader will have drawn his own conclusions by
this time: the beautiful woman with the spot on her side,
who dissolved into serpents and a bat in the bad burrow,
who cheered on the fight in the evil wood, who hates and
wants to kill children, who had stolen the water and rules
Bulika, is Lilith. Originally an Assyrian goddess of the
storm, and later because of a misunderstanding of her
name, a blood-sucking night spirit, she appears in the
Talmud with wings, seductive, preying on those who
sleep alone. She steals and kills children; one of her
symbols is the owl. Later in Jewish folklore she takes
her place as the first wife of Adam, made of dust like
him, and not taken from his rib as Eve had been. Unable
to live with Adam, she had vanished under water but
commands legions of demons.[10] Vane does not yet realize
that he has already seen her several times. As for Bulika-
city, it is just like the Gwyntystorm of *The Princess and
Curdie*, the city of the selfish money-worshipping men
MacDonald hated.

Mara also tells Vane of an ancient poem in the library
of Bulika which none of the citizens can read, but which
predicts that the Little Ones will eventually triumph
over the giants and fill the land. Mara's faithful messenger is a great white cat, a panther or (later) a leopardess.
Vane spends the night in her house; she feeds him on
delicious bread and water; he dreams he is sleeping on
the couch next to his father's in the cemetery. The next
morning she explains that nobody can stay more than one

night in her house and sends him on his way to perform a vague mission in Bulika. Mara, who weeps a good deal, is apparently the incarnate spirit of repentance, who can make others repent; she is, perhaps, the Magdalen. Though she is very beautiful, Vane feels no sexual longing for her; indeed, *Lilith,* by contrast with *Phantastes,* is an old man's book, and Vane, unlike Anodos, feels little or no desire for the women he meets.

Tortured by loneliness, Vane now crosses a desert and a forest, where he spends the night in an "ivy hall," like that which Thoreau glimpsed in the woods near Concord. Vane wakes to see a ghastly ball in which all the dancers have naked skulls as heads; again, the woman with the spot on her side watches scornfully. When she leaves, the clothes and flesh scale off of the dancers, and as skeletons they disappear. Vane encounters two skeletons in the ruins of an old coach and by their conversation learns that they had been man and wife on earth, he a neglectful husband, a dissipated nobleman, and she a quarrelsome selfish wife. Mr. Raven appears to comment for Vane on what he has seen: as the skeletons advance in truthfulness, they begin to develop bodies; the dancers were many centuries ahead of the two figures in the coach, and will eventually recover faces and flesh to clothe their skulls. In leaving him to continue his journey, Raven warns him never to trust a second time anybody who has once deceived him. If Vane forgets this rule, "some evil that is good for you will follow." If he remembers, "some evil that is not good for you will not follow."

By the roadside Vane now finds the emaciated naked body of a woman who seems dead but whom he hopes to revive. He warms her (without a touch of sexual attraction) in his arms all night, bathes her in the waters

of a hot stream that he discovers, and when he sees signs
that she is not dead, submerges her for hours during each
day in its waters. He makes a nest for her in a warm cave
and keeps her there. After a week he notes the discolora-
tion on her side. Though she is beautiful, he feels no love
for her, but realizes the need to be good to her simply for
his own sake. For three months he tends her; he makes
clothes for her, and discovers, as she grows stronger, that
a kind of leech is biting him in his sleep, and that he is
growing weaker.

Suddenly she wakes and claims to have warded off
from him a white leech six feet long. When she realizes
that he has nursed her all this time, she says, " 'You have
done me two worst of wrongs—compelled me to live,
and put me to shame: neither of them can I pardon.' " She
flings out her left hand, and he falls, hit on the forehead
by something ice cold. He follows her and begs to be her
slave; she treats him with blazing contempt, but when
he kneels down beside her she kisses him on the cheek,
and he feels severe pain: she has bitten him again. She
tells him that her people will stone him as a beggar if he
should follow her, and then she strips and turns into a
great spotted leopardess which rushes off toward Bulika,
pursued by a white leopardess.

Vane now encounters a woman who has saved her child
from the spotted leopardess by beating its foot with a
stone. She tells him more about Lilith, whom he had
involuntarily restored to life:

> If the princess hears of a baby, she sends her (the
> spotted leopardess) immediately to suck its blood,
> and then it either dies or grows up an idiot. . . .
> There is an old prophecy that a child will be the

death of her. That is why she will listen to no offer of marriage, they say. She does not care about her country. She sends witches around to teach the women spells that keep babies away, and give them horrible things to eat. Some say she is in league with the Shadows to put an end to the race.

Even now, Vane is not fully convinced of Lilith's evil character. He continues on to Bulika because

I must see, if but once more, the woman I had brought to life! I did not desire her society: she had waked in me frightful suspicions; and friendship, not to say love, was wildly impossible between us! But her presence had a strange influence upon me, and in her presence I must resist, and at the same time analyse that influence!

He further hopes somehow to learn to protect the Little Ones against this desperate enemy of children.

Bulika itself lives up to advance notice: Vane looks poor, and the people throw things at him and are rude: "to the people of Bulika, as to house-dogs, poverty was an offence." In the streets, he sees a white creature following a kind of shadow-man: "he cast no shadow, and was himself but a flat and superficial shadow, of two dimensions, . . . an opaque shadow, for he not merely darkened an object on the other side of him, but rendered it, in fact, invisible." A woman offers to take him home, but when she gets him there, she abandons him on an outside landing. The door of the house opens, and Mara appears and takes him in to rest. But a moaning disturbs him; the white leopardess appears with a newborn baby in its mouth; Vane makes her drop it; but Mara comes

and picks it up and pushes both Vane and the white
leopardess out of doors. Suddenly,

> A bulky object fell with a heavy squelch in the mid-
> dle of the street, a few yards from us. I ran to it,
> and found a pulpy mass, with just enough form left
> to show it the body of a woman. It must have been
> thrown from some neighbouring window.[11]

Like the people of Gwyntystorm, or of London, those
of Bulika are purse-proud savages. But the terror that
pervades the town is new and derives from Lilith's own
terror. No wonder, in the kaleidoscopic whirl of events
that surrounds him, that Vane has not realized the benevolence of the white leopardess, Mara's ally, who has
obviously been saving the newborn baby from the spotted
leopardess, one of Lilith's incarnations. The shadow, so
far from carrying any of the symbolic or allegorical con-
notations that Anodos' shadow carries in *Phantastes*,
seems to be no more than a devil, perhaps the devil himself, one of those with whom the woman has told Vane
Lilith is in league, to put an end to the race. Friend of
sterility, hater of children, murderess of women, Lilith is
a horror.

Like the fortifications of Gwyntystorm, those of the
city and palace of Bulika have fallen into semi-ruin from
neglect. In the central hall of the palace the spotted
leopardess sits in a great cage. Finally a servant consents
to take to Lilith Vane's message that "one who knows the
white leech" wants to see her. When she appears, Lilith
is loving and kind: she escorts Vane to a splendid bath,
feeds him with bread, milk, and wine, and tells him that
of all the many lovers who have sought her, he is the one
she wants. He is suspicious; he notes a large clumsy glove

on her left hand. Momentarily tempted by her advances, he is startled by a sudden roar, perhaps a warning from the white leopardess. Also, Lilith has given herself away by describing herself as "bounding" over a stream; he now realizes that she must at times be the spotted leopardess. Embarrassed, she now invites him to sleep, and when he wakes she is standing over him wiping his blood from her lips. She strikes him with a handkerchief, and he is momentarily blinded, but sees her leaving the room in the form of a spotted leopardess. Vane realizes that "I was a tame animal for her to feed upon; a human fountain for thirst demoniac."

More horror follows: Vane returns to the house where he had spent the previous night, and he is met by "the fall of something soft and heavy between me and the stair, and at my feet lay a body, frightfully blackened and crushed," the woman who had originally brought him there. The spotted leopardess comes downstairs with the baby in its mouth, and the white leopardess attacks her; she drops the child, and there is a great cat-fight, during which the spotted leopardess changes back into Lilith before Vane's eyes: she is wounded, and the white leopardess rescues the baby. Though Lilith lies to him about her wounds when he returns to the palace, and though he is now fully aware of her evil and deception, he yet feels pity for her. He therefore disregards Mr. Raven's warning not to trust a deceiver a second time, and when Lilith asks him to climb a tree to get her a flower to heal her wounds, and binds his feet with strips of cloth to help him climb, he accedes. No sooner does he reach the top of the tree than he finds himself drenched with water: he falls down through the column of water thrown up by the fountain on his own lawn in this world and lands in his own garden. He hears the Raven croaking "I told you so" in his ear.

III

Remorse and Raven's reproaches overcome him. Not only has he forgotten the advice about trusting a deceiver a second time, he has failed to do anything for the Little Ones, despite his wish to do so. He had left them instead of staying with them; not recognizing in time what his true work was. He had abandoned his work while actually doing it. We must conclude, I think, that in his old age and grief, MacDonald came to believe that he should have remained a minister: he had left his congregation (the children in an arrested state) in order to help them by being a writer (going into the world—Bulika—London): but now he was asking himself if he had not left his true work too soon. What could Vane have done for the Little Ones? He answers himself: it had occurred to him that their lack of development came from lack of water, and he might have dug through to the water he had so often heard underground and made it available to them. Here we remember the Light Princess, who like the Little Ones needed to cry before she could be a girl worth anything, and recall that her retardation also was closely connected with the drying up of the lake. However, in her story, sorrow over her prince brought its own tears; in *Lilith,* Vane ought to have dug for water: MacDonald should have poured forth his love upon his flock. Moreover, Vane ought not to have taught the children fear of the giants: had he been brave he might have reduced the giants and made them the Little Ones' slaves. The giants, we know, are the rich; is not MacDonald saying that, had he stayed with the poor and humble ones of the earth, he could have helped them combat the brutality and ignorance of the rich? Finally, Vane has not told Lilith how he hated her. All these things he might have avoided had he accepted Raven's initial invitation to sleep in the cemetery.

In fact, a blue Persian cat had emerged from the fountain together with Vane, and has now accompanied him and Raven to the library. Raven draws from the shelf the mutilated book; it is whole (the other half of it is inside Raven's own library, but he draws it through into this dimension), and from it reads a poem vaguely referring to Lilith's wickednesses. Cat-wails from the Persian cat accompany the poem; Raven prevents her flying up the chimney, and holds her on the hearth by drawing a pattern on the floor. The cat is Lilith; and Raven now identifies himself: he is Adam, her husband:

"Mr. Vane, when God created me . . . He brought me an angelic splendour to be my wife: there she lies! For her first thought was *power;* she counted it slavery to be one with me, and bear children for Him who gave her being. One child, indeed, she bore; then, puffed with the fancy that she had created her, would have me fall down and worship her! Finding, however, that I would but love and honour, never obey and worship her, she poured out her blood to escape me, fled to the army of Aliens, and soon had so ensnared the heart of the great Shadow that he became her slave, wrought her will, and made

> her queen of Hell. . . . The one child of her body
> she fears and hates, and would kill. . . ."

The child is Lona, leader of the Little Ones.

Lilith, when Vane had found her nearly dead, had been smitten while crossing the hot stream that divided her realm from the Little Ones' forest; she had been on her way to kill Lona. Unable to reach Lona in her own world, she had then plotted to follow Vane into this one, and so back through the mirrors in Vane's house, which would bring her out on the Little Ones' side of the stream. That was why she had bound Vane's feet with strips of cloth, and had followed him up the tree, and down the water column of the fountain. Vane had provided her with the first contact she had had with an inhabitant of our world of three dimensions. Lilith, Adam-Raven tells Vane, exults that Eve has borne to Adam "a countless race of miserables." But Adam and Eve have repented, and one day Lilith too must repent. Lona will be the instrument of her mother's redemption.

Listening on the hearth, the cat shrieks with jealousy at hearing Eve mentioned, turns into the spotted leopardess, and then into Lilith herself. She denies the existence of the spot on her side, maintaining that it belongs to the leopard and not to her. She declares that she will never repent, but will drink Lona's blood. Adam manages to transform her back into a cat and lock her in a closet, and he and Vane rush upstairs to hasten back through the mirror into the other world ahead of Lilith. Adam instructs Vane to go to Eve's cottage and get instructions there, but not to go directly back to the Little Ones. But Lilith, as the leopardess, bursts out of the closet and through the mirror into the other world ahead of them. The white leopardess of Mara hastens to head her off, and Adam and Vane follow.

Back in the other world for the fourth time, Vane resists Adam's advice to prepare for action by inaction, to sleep first in the cemetery as the right way to help the endangered Lona and the other children. Adam shows him the great horse he will have to ride next morning; but he cannot wait and mounts. He disregards Adam's assurances that if he yields to the temptation to seek out the Little Ones without first sleeping in the cemetery, he will bring mischief on the children. Though Adam reminds him that his past great mistake had been to refuse to join the dead in sleep, Vane cannot be moved, partly because he loves the horse so much and cannot resist putting him to the test. "Take the horse," Adam finally says, "and ride to failure! May it be to humility!" But after Vane has had a splendid brief ride on the mighty horse, across the bad burrow and down into the dry stream bed, the moon begins to behave queerly:

> We were near the middle of the many channels, my horse every other moment clearing one, sometimes two in his stride, and now and then gathering himself for a great bounding leap, when the moon reached the key-stone of her arch. Then came a wonder and a terror: she began to descend rolling like the nave of Fortune's wheel bowled by the gods, and went faster and faster. Like our own moon, this one had a human face, and now the broad forehead now the chin was uppermost as she rolled. I gazed aghast.
>
> Across the ravines came the howling of wolves. An ugly fear began to invade the hollow places of my

heart; my confidence was on the wane! The horse maintained his headlong swiftness, with ears pricked forward, and thirsty nostrils exulting in the wind his career created. But there was the moon jolting like an old chariot-wheel down the hill of heaven, with awful boding! She rolled at last over the horizon-edge and disappeared, carrying all her light with her.

The mighty steed was in the act of clearing a wide shallow channel when we were caught in the net of the darkness. His head dropped; its impetus carried his helpless bulk across, but he fell in a heap on the margin, and where he fell he lay. I got up, kneeled beside him, and felt him all over. Not a bone could I find broken, but he was a horse no more. I sat down on the body, and buried my face in my hands.

The behavior of the moon is like that in Emile Verhaeren's poem *La baie*, "La lune et tout le grand ciel d'or / Tournent et roulent vers leur mort," which his analyst, Baudouin, ascribes to the "tortured and tragical phase" of Verhaeren's life. Certainly, we must attribute *Lilith*, with its similar imagery in this striking passage, to a similar phase in MacDonald's life: the moon rolls downward toward terror and anguish.[12]

Wolves attack Vane, cats drive them off, but only to attack him themselves as he presses onward through the Evil Wood. On the other side of it, he falls for a second time into the hands of the giants. But this time, the Little Ones, mounted on miniature elephants, bears, horses, and other beasts, liberate him from the giants. They explain that they have built their nests in trees in the forest and can now sing like birds. A refugee among them is the woman of Bulika with her baby who had first told Vane

about Lilith. She has remembered the prophecy that
children will eventually prove Lilith's downfall, and she
now proposes that they mount an expedition against
Bulika. The white leopardess has driven off the spotted
one; so the children have been saved from Lilith by
Mara. By way of a preliminary training experiment, the
woman teaches the children to throw stones accurately,
and they succeed in defeating the giants, and driving
them from the forest.

Vane encourages the project of the attack on Bulika.
He has fallen in love with Lona, who

> was become almost a woman, but not one beauty of
> childhood had she outgrown. . . . To see her with
> any thoughtless, obstinate, or irritable little one, was
> to think of a tender grandmother. I seemed to have
> known her for ages—for always—from before time
> began. I hardly remembered my own mother, but
> in my mind's eye she looked like Lona; and if I
> imagined sister or child, invariably she had the face
> of Lona! My every imagination flew to her; she was
> my heart's wife.

Again we note the low level of Vane's sexual interest;
grandmother, mother, sister, and child all occur to him
before wife. Moreover, Vane's motives include a distinctly
worldly ambition: after the Little Ones shall have destroyed Lilith, he expects Lona to succeed as princess.
As Lona's husband, he will then have the opportunity to
develop "a noble state," and also to open up commerce
in precious stones between the two worlds. As MacDonald
sets them down, these ideas of Vane's have a distinctly
incongruous ring: Vane has never before manifested any
interest in political power or making money. Possibly

MacDonald intended to imply that such base longings would naturally creep into his mind because he had disobeyed Adam and had not yet slept.

In preparation for the journey, Vane tells the Little Ones that they had been brought to the forest when very young in order to save them from the cruelty of Lilith and that in Bulika their mothers await them. This kindles their longing to have mothers. Lona, too, who does not know that she is Lilith's daughter, says, " 'I would give my life to have my mother! She might kill me if she liked! I would just kiss her and die!' " Led by birds and insects and mounted on their miniature beasts, the army of children, with Lona, Vane, and the woman of Bulika at its head, advances on the city. The reception is what one might expect: when one of the children kisses a woman he has selected to be his mother, and a man begins to seize the child, the girls in the army have to stab him with their spears. The white leopardess has to join the group to help save one of the children whom one of the women of Bulika has thrown into a hole preparatory to handing him to Lilith. Another of the children is killed; but, fortunately, he is one whom Lona had been expecting to grow into a bad giant anyhow. Lona concludes that the people of Bulika are not worth delivering.

Vane reflects that the whole rash expedition had arisen out of his own obstinacy and failure to trust Adam. But we find utterly repulsive the situation of the innocent children, led under false pretenses on a kind of crusade against evil incarnate, and misled into expecting to find their mothers and to get motherly love from the Bulikans, whom Vane knows to be thoroughly depraved. Vane's behavior is either incredible or inexcusable. If MacDonald intended to paint the tragic consequences of Vane's irre-

sponsible failure to listen to good advice, he has certainly
succeeded; but only at the cost of depriving Vane of the
reader's sympathy. In the face of the mistreatment of the
children and the actual murder of one of them, what will
the reader care about Vane's silly and unconvincing ambitions to create and govern a noble state with large
foreign trade? MacDonald's art has failed him. It is at this
point in the narrative of *Lilith*, moreover, that one senses
most clearly the disillusionment with all humanity that
pervaded MacDonald. Without love, he was saying to the
human race, you condemn your children to stunted development or to destruction. To demonstrate this he
shrinks from no cruelty in his narrative: in fact, he seems
actually to enjoy the terrible. The squelching sound of
bodies as they drop on the streets of Bulika, and the grimness of the scenes there on this second visit outdo in their
sadism-masochism the lashings of the novels and the
brutality of *The Princess and Curdie*.

Terrified because she thinks the prophecy of her doom
at the hands of a child is about to be fulfilled, Lilith tries
to think her way out of the difficulty:

> Now what she called *thinking* required a clear con-
> sciousness of herself, not as she was, but as she chose
> to believe herself; and to aid her in the realization
> of this consciousness, she had suspended, a little way
> from and above her, itself invisible in the darkness
> of the hall, a mirror to receive the full sunlight re-
> flected from her person. For the resulting vision of
> herself in the splendour of her beauty, she sat wait-
> ing the meridional sun.

For a few moments at noon, the vision comes, but does
not help her; she must wait twenty-four hours more be-

fore it can come again, while the entire city quakes with
terror at the occupying army of beasts and armed children. Close "under the mirror stood the Shadow which
attended her walks, but self-occupied, him she did not
see." Returning to the instrument of the mirror, which
had preoccupied him in *Phantastes,* MacDonald here
makes, in passing, a profound judgment on human nature.
Narcissus at least was in love with the reflection of himself as he was, but Lilith's special form of narcissism is as
repulsive and complicated as her evil: in order to preserve
the illusion that she is as she believes herself to be, Lilith
must see herself reflected in the splendor of the noonday
sun. All the time, she cannot see the devil himself, her
attendant.

Vane and Lona and twelve of the strongest boys from
the army of Little Ones go to the palace next day, just
as the mirror has shown Lilith that the black spot on
her side has spread. Lona calls out "Mother" to Lilith,
who shivers and grows black with hate; as Lona rushes
to embrace her, Lilith dashes her to the marble floor.
Vane picks her up bleeding. She murmurs " 'Mother,
mother,' " and is "dead as earth." Lilith becomes withered,
as she had been when Vane had first found and rescued
her. The Little Ones (temporarily thwarted by the
Shadow) capture and bind her; they sling her on their
beasts, and take her off, retreating from Bulika with
Vane and the corpse of Lona, back towards Adam's house
through the scenery we have come to know: across the
hot stream, past the ivy hall where the dancers dance
with the children and the two skeletons are moving toward redemption through mutual dependence; and to the
children's nest-village in the forest, where Vane resettles
them, except for twelve who come along on the rest of

the journey. All the time, Lilith behaves like the monster
she is, biting one of the children who tries to feed her,
biting Vane and attacking him in the night. But in vain:
her time has come, and he is determined to take her to
Mara's house.

Though the children are frightened of Mara, Vane
reassures them. Solemnly, Mara greets the new arrivals:
she has been waiting thousands of years for the moment
of Lilith's defeat. Through a troubled night, in which the
sleeping children are disturbed by the howling of wind,
the fear of floods, and the crying of cats, Vane looks on as
Mara struggles with the recalcitrant Lilith to force repentance upon her. A "silvery slowworm" that has crept
into the fire and heated itself "white-hot, vivid as incan-
descent silver, the live heart of essential fire," emerges,
and enters the black spot in Lilith's side, penetrating to
"the thoughts and intents" of her heart. In a sweat, she
can see herself "afar in the hell of her self-consciousness."
Desperately resisting, Lilith will not let herself be re-
made. She refuses to try to open her clenched hand.
Though she stoutly calls herself "queen of Hell and mistress of the worlds," she has now by her own actions
undone God's own work of creation: the source of life,
which "had been with her every moment of her wicked
years," had now "withdrawn itself; all that was left her
of conscious being was the dregs of her dead and corrupted life." At the peak of Lilith's defiance,

> Her bodily eyes stood wide open, as if gazing into
> the heart of horror essential—her own indestructible
> evil. Her right hand also was clenched—upon exist-
> ent Nothing—her inheritance!

But with God all things are possible. He can save even the rich! [13]

Here we come face to face with George MacDonald's final full-length picture of the evil female: from the Alder-maiden of *Phantastes* through the various proud and vicious children-hating mothers of the novels to Lilith there is a natural and inevitable progression. But though Mac-Donald has made Lilith the most lovingly studied incarnation of wickedness of them all, he has got no further in explaining her motives than with any of the others: they are the way they are because they are the way they are. It is the measure of *Lilith*'s failure that, even in a fantasy, where the writer needs to be less careful of verisimilitude than in a novel, we cannot understand or believe in the protagonist. No mere prophecy of her death would produce the fatal hatred of a mother for an unoffending daughter. And George MacDonald's unsure taste was seldom more blatantly displayed than by his interjection of the final dig at the rich at this most solemn moment of Lilith's hour of trial. The remark is not apropos of anything: no rich persons are, or ever have been, characters in the story; no doubt MacDonald had reason, or thought he had reason, to hate the rich; and there is, of course, good New Testament evidence that a rich man enters the kingdom of heaven only with some difficulty. Yet this particular remark at this moment seems the gratuitous sneer of an old man who has lost control over his literary materials.

At the end of the struggle with Mara, Lilith consents to be taken to Adam, who will forgive and help her. Acknowledging that it is she rather than Mara who is the slave, Lilith now wants to die, and Mara tells her that she will die out of death into life. As Lilith weeps for the first time, the rain falls: soon, as Mara tells the twelve Little Ones, the waters under the earth will flow, and there will be rivers everywhere. Lilith's tears, the rain water, the water that Mara gives the children to drink— their first—is the symbol of maternal love; it makes the children feel so strong that one of them conjectures (with his usual bad taste) that it must be elephant juice. As the procession moves across the dry river bed from Mara's cottage toward Adam's, and on into the bad burrow, the monsters rise up from every side, reaching for Lilith. They are appropriately ghastly:

> Long-billed heads, horribly-jawed faces, knotty ten-
> tacles innumerable . . . . solitary bodiless head with
> frightful contortions of visage and a loathsome howl
> . . . . a dreadful head with fleshy tubes for hair
> . . . . a long neck, on the top of which, like the
> blossom of some Stygian lily, sat what seemed the
> head of a corpse, its mouth half open, and full of
> canine teeth . . . a shapeless jelly. . . .

Eve and Adam greet the advancing party, whom the white leopardess protects against the monsters. Eve, who calls Lilith "the mortal foe of my children," warns Mara against trusting her too soon, and Mara says to Eve:

> "But you will open to her the mirror of the Law of
> Liberty, mother, that she may go into it, and abide
> in it. She consents to open her hand and restore: will
> not the great Father restore her to inheritance with
> His other children?"

Here is another mirror, to add to the one through which Raven and Vane find passage between the worlds and the one that Lilith has hung in her hall to catch her reflection at noon. This is the first we have heard and the last we hear of "the mirror of the Law of Liberty." No sooner has he produced this new image than MacDonald abandons its, perhaps because it is confused and confusing: surely it is the law of liberty that Lilith is to abide in, not the mirror of the law, whatever that may have been?

Into Adam's cottage and down into the vaults of the cemetery goes the entire party, after a meal of bread and wine (communion) has been served to the children, but not to Lilith. Eve tells Lilith:

> "Your own daughter you have but sent into the loveliest sleep, for she was already a long time dead when you slew her. And now Death will be the atonemaker; you shall sleep together."

Here we see the pitfalls that inconsistency digs. If death *per se* is a good thing, then why should Lilith be blamed for killing Lona at all? But, in fact, the killing of the daughter by the mother is, and was intended to be, a shocking crime, and one for which Lilith is blamed. But at the very moment when Lilith killed her, we are now told, Lona had been a long time dead, in the special sense of wakening into life. But this too is puzzling: the way to wake into life is to sleep in the cemetery, and Lona has never yet done this. MacDonald has muddled his own symbols and clouded the entire cosmology that he has been trying to contsruct. In the punning "atonemaker," which is both "atone-maker and "at-one-maker," we find further confusion: Lilith still has to atone for killing Lona;

and yet Lona had already been dead when it happened.

Lilith takes the couch in the vault next to Lona. Adam reassures her that even the shadow will come there when his turn comes: that is, the devil himself will repent and be redeemed one day, the ultimate outcome of the Mac-Donald theology. Before she sleeps, Lilith must open her hand, but the fingers have grown through the palm, and she cannot do it. So Adam cuts off the deformed member with the sword "the angel gave me when he left the gate." A new hand begins to grow where the old one was, and Lilith goes to sleep. Each of the twelve Little Ones who were inexplicably chosen ahead of the others for this eternal experience (can they be the twelve apostles?) chooses a couch, two of them joining Lilith, the white leopardess, and Lona. Before Vane himself may lie down, he must venture out into the desert and bury Lilith's severed hand. He fulfills this mission and obeys his instructions not to speak to any of the tempting shadows that throng his path.

With the burial of the hand, the underground waters are at last released. Vane returns to Eve's cottage, and Lona invites him to join her in sleep: "I cannot rest until you are with me, gliding down the river to the great sea, and the beautiful dreamland. The sleepiness is full of lovely things; come and see them." Before Vane lies down, Adam tells him that the woman on the couch next to his father is his mother, and that she will be up and away before his father, "when she has come to the splendour of her beauty." He also explains that "women are coming faster" than men to sleep in the cemetery, MacDonald's final comment about the relative virtue of the sexes, despite all of Lilith's evil. In peace and cold, Vane goes to sleep.[14]

IV

And here *Lilith* ought to end. But MacDonald was facing a dilemma. Vane is the narrator; Vane is dead; how then can Vane have told his story? I believe that all the remainder of *Lilith* represents nothing but Mac-Donald's extrication of himself from this mechanical problem. W. H. Auden says,

> If *Lilith* is a more satisfactory book than *Phantastes*, one reason is that its allegorical structure is much tighter: there seems to be no particular reason, one feels, why Anodos should have just the number of adventures which he does have—they could equally be more or less—but Mr. Vane's experiences and his spiritual education exactly coincide.[15]

I would agree that *Phantastes* is loose in structure, but would argue that Auden is wrong about *Lilith:* we have in fact already reached the end of Vane's education, but *Lilith* goes on in order to enable MacDonald to find a device for ending the story.

On his couch Vane dreams, the dreams that come in the sleep of death, the dreams that aroused Hamlet's apprehensions; MacDonald calls this chapter "The dreams that come . . ." with *Hamlet* clearly in mind. Vane is naked on a snowy peak; white mists billow round him; he is Adam; he is not Adam but a "child in the bosom of a mother white with a radiant whiteness," a youth on horseback on his way to some blessed goal. He atones to all of those he has ever wronged: he confesses to his father that he had told him two lies; for one man he has wronged he builds a house, for another he makes a garden, for a third he trains horses; he writes poems and songs for them, makes them laugh with joy. Love possesses him. In the moonlight, he wakes to find his dead all gone; he rises to find Adam's cottage empty. Outside a delicious lake covers the heath, and the dry bed of the stream is flowing with a river. He is on a pilgrimage to find his living dead. In delight, he wades and swims ahead, and then encounters Adam.

Adam tells him that he is still dreaming on his couch, and at Adam's command he reaches out his hand, and takes that of Lona, on the next couch. So far he has seen only the shadow of the truth, but he will see it all. Adam warns him that trials lie ahead (one cannot help asking why? has he not met and surmounted the tests, and atoned for all the wrongs he had ever done?), and in his dream he longs to be awake. So he finds himself lying beside a pit, and remembers that in his childhood he could always wake from a dream by falling. In order to wake himself up, he rolls over the edge of the pit and falls in; and then wakes . . . in the garret of his house.

In frustration and despair he blames himself for having tried to end the dream; he tries the mirrors, but cannot make them work; he fears he has lost Lona forever, but on the fourth night in his own house he wakes in the cemetery, knowing that everything so far has still been part of his dream. Lona is beside him: "She fell asleep a girl; she awoke a woman, ripe with the loveliness of the life essential. I folded her in my arms, and knew that I lived indeed." Adam and Eve and Mara enter, and assure Vane and Lona that they have died into life. Vane's parents have departed; they are "up and away." Lona goes to Lilith's couch and kisses her. The sun rises. Adam and Eve and Mara looked at each other and smiled, and that smile went floating heavenward a three-petaled flower, the family's morning thanksgiving. From their mouths and their faces it spread over their bodies and shone through their garments. Ere I could say "Lo, they change!", Adam and Eve stood before me the angels of the resurrection, and Mara was the Magdalene with them at the sepulchre. The countenance of Adam was like lightning, and Eve held a napkin that flung flakes of splendour about the place.

With this Blake-ian passage, MacDonald seems launched on a description of the dawn of resurrection morning. Indeed, the golden cock that "Silent and motionless for millions of years has . . . stood on the clock of the universe" flaps his wings and begins to crow. The sound of the wings of the great shadow is heard, as he struggles to depart, and Mara says " 'The black bat is flown.' " The Little Ones awake.

But it is not yet the end, apparently. Adam says that the cock will be heard *"at intervals . . . until* the dawn of the day eternal" (italics mine). Why is this not that day? There is no apparent reason. Nor can Lilith or the white leopardess or the children asleep with them yet waken. But why should the innocent children have to stay on in the cemetery as long as the wicked princess and her counter-spirit? The party sallies forth from Eve's cottage, all peaceful and joyous, with "life a cosmic holiday." Vane is secure in the knowledge that life and truth are one, that "I lived and nothing could touch my life! My darling walked beside me, and we were on our way home to the Father!" But there are clear signs that the victory is only apparent. As they cross the lake that has

replaced the bad burrow, the beasts are all still beneath
the surface of the lake, not dead:

> Coiled in spires, folded in layers, knotted on them-
> selves, or "extended long and large," they weltered
> in motionless heaps—shapes more fantastic in ghoul-
> ish, blasting dismay, than ever wine-sodden brain
> of exhausted poet fevered into misbeing. He who
> dived into the swirling Maelstrom saw none to com-
> pare with them in horror: tentacular convulsions,
> timid bulges, glaring orbs of sepian deformity, would
> have looked to him innocence beside such incar-
> nations of hatefulness—every head the wicked flower
> that, bursting from an abominable stalk, perfected
> its evil significance. . . . So long as exist men and
> women of unwholesome mind, that lake will still be
> peopled with loathsomeness.

So it is not resurrection day. But must it not surely be
at least Vane's and Lona's and the Little Ones' own resurrection day, since the golden cock, silent for millions of
years, has actually crowed? What has made him crow? He
must have been celebrating something, must he not? If
so, then the sudden reappearance of the slumbering horrors at the bottom of the lake comes as a shock and a
smashing of the images of calm and joy. Why should
MacDonald feel it necessary to warn again of the vileness
of people with unwholesome minds, in the very moment
of the final triumph? Only, one is forced to conclude,
because he had lost control of his imagery.

In the beautiful dawn, the party crosses the river chan-
nels, and the one-time desert, now in blossom; the forest-
children climb the tree-tops. From the dark clouds around

a mountain they catch glimpses of a city. Flashes of lightning play about it, a gentle rain falls, they walk along a beautiful river, which flows down the mountain, up to the gate, and in to it. In one of the flashes "the beautifullest man" is heard by Lona (incredible but true) to say to the children " 'Ou's all mine, 'ickle ones; come along!' " As the party enters the city, angels carry off the children. One of the angels says, " 'These are the angels to take heaven itself by storm. I hear of a horde of black bats on the frontiers: these will make short work with such!' "

Where are we supposed to think the children are? Have they really got to heaven? Then why the reference to "taking heaven itself by storm"? And if it *is* really the heavenly city, then why the black bats on the frontiers? As we near the end, the imagery of *Lilith* breaks down completely. On the one hand MacDonald paints the picture of a triumphant resurrection. On the other, evil is all about, even on the "frontiers" of heaven itself. Even if one overlooks the revolting baby-talk of the "beautifullest man" (Christ, surely?), how can one regard the substance of these episodes as anything but bad mythology and bad art? And how can one avoid the suspicion that the Christian myth had worn thin for MacDonald himself?

The last brief episode does nothing to change this view. Without the children, Lona and Vane, now hand in hand alone, climb up the rocks on the far side of the city, through the clouds behind which stands the throne of the ancient of days. As they toil upwards, and Vane enters the deep folds of the cloud at the foot of God's own throne, a hand takes his, and draws him to a little door with a golden lock. The door opens, the hand pushes Vane through. He turns quickly and sees "the board of a large book in the act of closing behind me." He is alone in his library. Uncertain whether everything is part of his dream and whether he may not still be on the couch in Adam's cemetery, or whether he has waked too soon, not sure of the reality of what he has seen, Vane now waits. Lona is not with him, but Mara is, and has taught him much (what can this mean?). He will not again try to return to the other world through the mirror, since he has not sent back "by hand." The backs of the books in his library occasionally ripple, and he hears whisperings around him.

Like Campbell in the first version of *The Portent,* like Donal Grant, Vane says: "I wait; asleep or awake, I wait." And *Lilith* closes with Novalis' words, here given a slightly new translation, "Our life is no dream, but it should and will perhaps become one." This ending Mac-Donald did not add until *Lilith 4,* the galleys of the final edition.[16]

Though Anodos had met with frustrations in plenty, in the end he returned from his dream to believe in good. But Vane has been more cruelly frustrated than Anodos ever was: MacDonald has turned him back at the throne of the Lord Himself and thrust him out through a door entered by the golden keyhole, once the image of affirmation. Through the doorway through which Mossy was reunited with Tangle, Vane has been torn away from Lona and sent back to his lonely library here on earth—unless he is still dreaming. But if he is, why should he have been given the cruelly false dream of resurrection morn and the trip with Lona to the father that turned out in no trip to the father and no marriage with Lona? One cannot miss the implication that Vane's frustrations were to be final,

that something had gone wrong with Christianity, that
George MacDonald himself had found life's blows too
frequent and too heavy, that he could no longer strike
back, and that all that he could now do himself was wait
—wait.

Conclusion

We know that being weaned is a universal human experience, and we think we know something of its importance. Of George MacDonald we know that all his life he preserved the record of his weaning as his most precious and secret possession. He longed for a mother, and repressed the longing. He felt rebellion against his father, whom he also loved dearly, and this gave him deep feelings of guilt. Though his family was ancient, it was in humble circumstances, and he lived in a materialistic society that measured value by noble birth and financial means. He rebelled against the determinism of Calvinist theology, but he was a "stickit" minister, whose efforts in the priesthood had failed. He had tuberculosis and in agony had to watch it carry off many of the people he loved the most. These circumstances underlie the development of his fiction and help account for its main features as we have come to know them.

Longing for death as a means of ending his own torments and rejoining his lost mother, he discovered Novalis, whose own circumstances in life had in so many ways resembled his own. *Heinrich von Ofterdingen,* and the *Märchen* of Hyacinth and Rosebud in *Die Lehrlinge zu Sais* especially captured his imagination early, and held sway there, though sometimes in temporary eclipse, all his literary life. Novalis' comparison of human life to a dream ("Our life is no dream, but it ought to become one, and perhaps it will") closes *Lilith* in 1895 as it had closed *Phantastes* in 1858. Dreams offered a way of escape from life and enabled MacDonald to say things that he could not otherwise have said. Dreams play an important part even in his novels, notably in *Wilfrid Cumbermede*, and all his works of "fancy and imagination" are more or less pure dream-literature. So too, E.T.A. Hoffmann, who enthusiastically seconded Novalis' attack on the concept that dreams are mere froth, naturally attracted Mac-Donald, and, since Hoffmann had left behind works more numerous and varied than Novalis, MacDonald often turned to him too for themes and even for their treatment.

Again and again we have heard MacDonald echoing their attacks on realism and reality, and their defenses of poesy, imagination, and dream. Behind Hoffmann and Novalis stretched a line of literary and philosophical ancestors, of whom Jean Paul Richter was the most beloved and Jacob Boehme the most important for MacDonald. Although in his youth MacDonald knew Boehme chiefly at second hand, he admired him extravagantly even then, and in his old age turned to increasingly close study of his works. But Boehme is difficult and intractable at best, and one sees few direct traces of his ideas in MacDonald's fiction. The most important and most frequently recurring is the theory of evolution, shared by Swedenborg and Blake and adopted by Novalis before McDonald: man is the culmination of a process that begins with minerals and works up through vegetables and the lower animals. As he grew older, MacDonald played with this idea and invented two new processes of his own: that, as they become wicked, men revert to the self of the animal they most resemble; and that animals who have once been men may repent and evolve toward humanity once again. In moments of strong depression, disillusion, and aggressiveness, MacDonald preferred animals to people anyhow:

this love began in his childhood and played a direct part in his loss of his single pulpit: he seems to have preached a sermon predicting that animals might well have a place in heaven; he certainly believed it.

Surrounded in his youth by those who believed uncompromisingly in the doctrine of the elect, and so in eternal damnation for those who were not saved, as a mere boy he burst into tears, like one of his own tearful heroes, and declared that he did not want God to love him unless He loved everybody. Though at first sight one may see in this nothing but deep instinctive love of his fellow man, we find in MacDonald's writing so much hatred for mankind that we incline to attribute his wish rather to fear. Even as a child, MacDonald's active imagination could envision the probable sentiments of those frying in hell-fire for all eternity towards those enjoying the rewards of paradise through no merit of their own: Robert Falconer's plan for emptying hell is the most elaborate scheme for allaying the hostilities of the damned; but long before he had put it into his novel MacDonald had instinctively decided that he did not want the damned envying him his own place at the divine board. So they had to be saved. Therefore election and all its inexorable consequences were "all a lie." And for this and other reasons, something softer, more maternal, had to replace the terrible paternal Calvinist God. God was to act toward Martin Elginbrod as Martin Elginbrod would act toward God; God was to act as if He were a "mither himsel'." The Mother-God we have found incarnated in the long succession of grandmother-goddesses, earth-spirits, and wise women in the fairy-tales. In the fiction, God is effeminate.

Not so easily detected as the positive influence of the

German romantics and the negative influence of Calvinism, but none the less decisive, was the influence of Wordsworth. MacDonald has Wilfrid Cumbermede, ostensibly writing in 1820, say of himself, "I was coming in for my share in the spiritual influence of Nature, so largely poured on the heart and mind of my generation. . . . Nature was a power upon me. I was filled with the vague recognition of a present soul in Nature, with a sense of the humanity everywhere diffused through her and operating upon me." So Wilfrid's creator, George MacDonald, found Wordsworth a revelation and an inspiration at a much later time. Hugh Sutherland and Margaret Elginbrod in the fir wood find God in the soughing of the tree branches. MacDonald's God was everywhere in Nature, a loving God who would maternally look after all His-Her children, and, soon or late, redeem even the worst of them. Nothing that could happen was evil: it only seemed evil at the time; it was in truth the best good. We have much testimony to the comfort that these views gave to many victims of Calvinism. They were not in conflict with what Maurice preached (or seemed to be preaching).

Some, even some victims of Calvinism, refused to be comforted. Ruskin wrote MacDonald in 1866, "I have never known any person whose mind was of any accurately trained strength who could get the slightest help out of such thoughts," and "I suppose it is quite impossible for you dear good people, who think it your duty to believe whatever you like—and to expect always to get whatever is good for you, to enter into the minds of us poor, wicked people, who sternly think it our duty to believe nothing but what we know to be fact, and to expect nothing but what we've been used to get." Greville

MacDonald sorrowfully attributes this skepticism of Ruskin to a "tendency . . . to overvalue the fast-breeding facts of science," and suggests that he had forgotten "that Alpine revelation" which, as we know, he had shared with MacDonald and Wilfrid Cumbermede, and which itself stemmed directly from Wordsworth.[1] But we need not restrict Ruskin's "mind of any accurately trained strength" to the scientific mind. Ruskin had, in fact, posed the problem: was it to be reason or emotion, intellect or imagination that one trusted?

Again and again we have heard MacDonald answer this question in favor of the emotions, giving the same answer that Novalis and Hoffmann and Wordsworth had given. Little remains (and nothing important) of the work of intellect, the evil scribe, in Klingsohr's *märchen* in *Heinrich von Ofterdingen*. Serpentina and what she stands for triumph hands down over Veronica and what she stands for in *The Golden Pot*. In Wordsworth's "Poet's Epitaph," the Philosopher "would peep and botanize upon his mother's grave," and with the Moralist, the "intellectual All-in-all," receives perhaps the bitterest condemnation of any of all the despicable race of ordinary men; while the poet reserves his praise and love for the "weak . . ./ idler . . ./ Contented if he might enjoy / The things that others understand." In *Lilith*, Mr. Vane grasps—that is, he tries to understand, to comprehend— the light-giving firefly, and it turns into a dark dead book with boards outspread. Almost forty years earlier, Anodos had grasped—tried to understand, to comprehend—the maiden's singing crystal bowl and had broken it. "Let them stretch out not as if to grasp those things that cannot be grasped, as if to comprehend the incomprehensible, but let them stretch out as if to take part," as Augustine had put it.[2] So MacDonald repudiates the intellect, and joins forces with Wordsworth's "weak idler."

The repudiation of the intellect carried Wordsworth further. The hero of "The Poet's Epitaph" is identified not with man's life on earth, but with the world of eternity and man's life in eternity, and the poet invites him to "stretch thy body at full length;/ Or build thy house upon this grave." As David Ferry points out in his brilliant recent study of Wordsworth's major poems, the hero's "characteristic act is to stretch himself out as if in the grave, for his real world is the eternal and his fit companions are the eternally dead. Behind this poem and all those like it, in other words, is the paradox that he who would save his life must lose it."[3] Here, again, is MacDonald: the great good is coming, for Anodos; and, when they lose their beloved children, for MacDonald and his wife themselves. He waits; he waits, like Campbell, Donal Grant, and Mr. Vane. Mr. Vane's great fault comes in *not* stretching himself out on Adam's couch in the icy vault with his fit companions, the dead, in resisting the good sleep of death; had he accepted—and slept with the dead, and come alive—there would have been no *Lilith*. This is the death that North Wind is not cruel in bringing, the death that for Mossy is not "better than life," but "only more life," the death into which the caterpillar awakens when he becomes the butterfly, the death that is life itself, while life without it is death itself: " 'You will be dead,' " Adam tells Vane, " 'so long as you refuse to die.' "[4]

In "Lines Written in Early Spring," Wordsworth sees nature at play, in pleasure, enjoying the air, motion, the breeze; but man thinks, and can therefore take no pleasure in life. Just as the paradox is that to live you must die, so to be a true man you must repudiate man's characteristic power to think, and so approach the mindlessness and the pure enjoyment of trees, of birds, of nature. Here too MacDonald follows, with passion. His idiots are Wordsworthian idiots, blessed with mindlessness, Rob o' the Angels, Dog-Steenie, and the rest, who have the additional advantage over Wordsworth's idiots that MacDonald's motherly God is watching over them with special care, and they are already close to Him-Her. The slower the faculties the deeper the feelings, the more akin the human being is to Nature, the closer he is to MacDonald's God.

This current of attitudes that converges on MacDonald from Boehme and Novalis on the one hand, and from Blake and Wordsworth on the other, makes MacDonald a powerful spokesman for a point of view seldom voiced in Victorian England, where anti-intellectualism in itself was common enough but mysticism extremely rare. Carlyle's "Characteristics" began with the romantic preference for heart over mind, but ended with a return to Calvinist values. Maurice, Tennyson, and Carlyle proclaimed the writer as priest and prophet, but MacDonald *was* the writer as priest and prophet.[5] MacDonald is the only Victorian I know who makes his own the pure romantic doctrine of the uses of the imagination, and makes the Wordsworthian linkage between the rejection of the intellect and the acceptance of death as the way to life. This in itself helps explain MacDonald's strangeness: despite their obvious relationships to such other Victorian dream-romances as the *Alice* books and *Water Babies*, *Phantastes* and *Lilith* are unique. And despite their Victorian conventionality in form, their often shoddy style, their interminable sermonizing, their lack of invention, their clumsiness, and frequent absurdity in plotting, Mac-

Donald's novels strike one as off-key and somehow memorable.

Nor does the conflict between intellect and imagination lack relevance in our own day. MacDonald, it appears, was not merely voicing in a new way to a generation that no longer cared the romantic view of a question that had already lost its meaning and has not regained it. In a book called *Life Against Death, The Psychoanalytical Meaning of History* (1959), Norman O. Brown, after a thorough examination of Freud, repudiates the intellect and prescribes as the only salvation for sick mankind what he calls "polymorphous perverse" play, a theology of the resurrected body and a warm acceptance of death. He links Freud himself with this prescription, placing him in the tradition that began with Christ and St. Francis, and for modern times with Boehme, and that includes Blake and Novalis. Children aim only at pleasurable activity of their own bodies, and obtain therefrom pleasures closed off to the adult; normal adult sexuality is unnaturally restricting; play, as Boehme proclaimed, is the supreme good; "modern secular humanist intellectuals have in the main followed Plato and Descartes over the abyss into the insane illusion that the true essence of man lies in disembodied mental activity." Brown points to the cabbalistic interpretation of Genesis 1:27 to mean that God was both male and female, and underlines Boehme's acceptance of the view; this he links with Freud's discussion of the myth of the primal androgyne and declares that Eros strives to unify itself with its opposite, death, which man must cheerfully greet as part of life. Brown urges upon the psychoanalysts and the Christian theologians the study and revival and advance of the mystic ideas of Boehme and longs to obtain for humanity "the simple

health that animals enjoy, but not man" and the power to
speak once more the "sensual" language that animals still
speak but that man has forgotten.[6]

Here in the sixth decade of the twentieth century we
find a classicist and learned student of comparative mythology making all of George MacDonald's choices: not
intellect but pure emotion, not grown-ups but children,
not people but animals, a bi-sexual God, and the eager
welcoming of death as an essential part of life. It is not important that Brown does not know MacDonald, or that
he has apparently not read Novalis, or much of Boehme,
preferring to cite him indirectly, or even that he has tortured Freud. As a "modern secular humanist intellectual,"
I repudiate Brown's version (quoted above) of what
such people think. His book seems to me in large part
nonsense. Too weak to face twentieth-century life without
a rigid system (and disillusioned with Marxism), he has
striven to erect Freudianism into such a system. The result is certainly perverse (if not polymorphous). But this
too is not important, nor is it important that Lionel Trilling, who of all men should have known better, hailed
Brown's book as a major contribution to contemporary
thought.

What is important for us is that, in our own day, and
in their own modern, even ultramodern, dress, the ideas
that MacDonald held as the highest truths, that he got
from his own experience of life, and from Novalis and
Wordsworth, are being vigorously propounded once again
as the only possible salvation for man, the answers to all
his problems. Even if one dislikes these answers, as I do,
one must freely admit the continuing influence of the
school that gives them. And George MacDonald, alone
of his generation, gave them.

His advances repulsed by the flirt in the library, Mac-Donald nursed his grudge. Was not his ancestry as noble as hers, did not equally gentle blood run in his veins? What was it that made him ineligible? Only his lack of money. And so came the exhibitionism of the waistcoats with their gilt buttons, of the special white or scarlet suits, and more especially of the brilliant tartans that with great show called attention to the wearer, and simultaneously proclaimed the antiquity and purity of his line. To those who knew, the poor Scot had the truest nobility of all. And so, in the novels, we find the worn old tartans symbolizing the true aristocrat. In their sorry room, all that is left to them of the ancestral townhouse in Aberdeen, the drunken cobbler Sir George Galbraith and his poor dumb Christ-like waif of a son Sir Gibbie sleep under his mother's tartan—a Gordon tartan at that, the family of the oppressive lords of Huntly that were MacDonald's father's landlords. And the sadistic laird, who now occupies the old Galbraith country house and orders its true heir lashed, has acquired his wealth by trickery and speculation and his name by marriage. In this light we understand the nostalgia, in *Malcolm, The Marquis of Lossie,* and *What's Mine's Mine,* for the lost golden days of patriarchal clan loyalty: nothing pleased MacDonald more than to think of his father as the chief of a clan, or of his own authority over his children as that of a chief. So we understand the hatred for materialism, for the high value put on riches, for the rich, for commerce, and especially for those who, in Victorian England, made the most frequent, most superficial, and cruelest judgments of a man's station by external appearances: the domestic servants of the rich. And so we understand why Malcolm is really the Marquis, and why Curdie

has the blood royal, and the many other "family romances," that turn out to be true: MacDonald's whole
life was in some sense a family romance.

In his youthful idealism, MacDonald had taken the
pulpit in Arundel, sure that he could revivify the enthusi-
asm of his congregation by the brilliance and originality
and passion of his preaching. But brilliance, originality,
and passion were precisely what they wanted least and
suspected most. Like "Mark Rutherford," he found himself accused of "Germanism," which nobody could define
but all suspected, and was forced to resign. His pride,
perhaps his lack of self-confidence, made it impossible
for him to seek another pulpit. So, to his other resentments against the world was added the apparent failure
in his profession, the most sacred and portentous of all
professions. To the end, MacDonald liked preaching better than anything else, but could do it only indirectly,
through the pages of his books. And in the pages of *Lilith*
we have found him (in veiled terms) wondering whether
he had left his real work too soon. No longer sure, as he
had been when he created Anodos, that he had been
right in recognizing his own work as that of a squire and
not that of a knight, he doubted at the end of his life the
effectiveness of his entire career.

Finally let us consider the deaths of those near to him.
After his mother's death, in his childhood, they came
in two waves, separated by many years. His wife's mother
died in 1850, a brother in 1853, a half-sister in 1855, another brother and his father in 1858, and another half-
sister in 1859. Thereafter it was not until 1875 that tuberculosis began to rage among his children: his daughter
Mary Josephine died in 1878 (aged twenty-five, and for
three years before her death engaged to be married but

fighting a losing battle with the disease), a young son of fifteen in 1879, a second daughter in 1884 (aged thirty, the mother of a beloved granddaughter), and, in 1891 alone, this grandchild, a daughter-in-law, and the cherished eldest daughter Lilia. For sixteen years (1859–1875) between these two waves of disaster there was a respite; MacDonald's own disease was arrested, and he may well have let down his guard against the possibility that it would recur among his children. When the awful massacre began again, he was perhaps less well armed against it than he had been in his youth, when he had wished for death himself as a means of joining those who had gone before, and had expressed his grief in *Phantastes* and his resolution in "Love Me, Beloved."

If we suggest that the new wave of deaths profoundly disturbed the patterns of behavior and beliefs that he had made his own, and made it far more difficult to continue to insist on universal earthly and heavenly love while repressing the resentments and guilt that he actually felt, the suggestion fits with what we find in his writings. Except for "Murder" Malison, and Mrs. Oldcastle of the Hall in *Annals of a Quiet Neighbourhood,* we find few violent persons in the novels and fairy-tales written before the mid-1870's. But in 1875, the very year that tuberculosis reappeared in the family, the grandmother-goddess of *The Wise Woman* is impotent to cure the wicked children. The criminality of *Thomas Wingfold, Curate* follows (1876), and then the scatological punishment of the servants in *The Princess and Curdie* (first publication 1877) and grandmother's ultimate failure and disappearance. The apocalyptic destruction of Gwyntystorm ushers in the long series of whippings, irrational violence, and horror that we have found in so many of the later novels, beginning with *Sir Gibbie* (1879), and in *Lilith*. It is almost as if God had let MacDonald down and made it impossible any longer to repress his true feelings about mankind, which are often as savage as those of Teufelsbürst himself, the cruel painter of his early *fabliau*. Again and again he says that God is kind and that all men deserve eventual salvation, but increasingly he cannot help showing his true opinion of men, and, at the end, if I am right, in *Lilith*, his increasing inability to accept as good the seeming evils that have been piled upon him. The very reiteration of the assurances reveals the insecurity that underlay them.[7] MacDonald was not Job but God tried him as hard.

As George MacDonald withdraws into silence, and for his last five or six years of life, waits, like his own Campbell or Donal Grant, or Mr. Vane, one's heart goes out to him as a human being who fought bravely against the repeated blows and the profound sadness that life had meted out to him. With regard to his later work we may echo David Ferry's final judgment on Wordsworth's major poems, "His genius was his enmity for man, which he mistook for love, and his mistake led him into confusions which he could not bear." [8] Or, to put it another way, ". . . the optimism of the mystic, like all his qualities, is of a very special, a quite narrow variety. He assures us that the human spirit is capable of tremendous suffering in its progress toward a tremendous good; but he conducts his experiment under laboratory conditions from which all the situations that ordinarily baffle the human spirit, abundant enough in a sublunary realm, have been removed. 'The lie,' as Emerson said brilliantly of Jones Very's piety, 'the lie is in the detachment.'" [9]

Notes

1. E.M.W. Tillyard and C. S. Lewis, *The Personal Heresy. A Controversy* (London, New York, Toronto: Oxford University Press, 1939), 102–03.

2. Leon Edel, *Literary Biography* (New York: Doubleday Anchor Books, 1959), 91–122. Lionel Trilling, "Freud and Literature," *The Liberal Imagination* (New York: Doubleday Anchor Books, 1957), 37.

CHAPTER 1   The Beginnings

1. The chief source of information on MacDonald's life is the very full biography by his eldest son: Greville MacDonald, *George MacDonald and His Wife* (London: George Allen and Unwin, 1924), hereafter cited as *GMDW;* supplemented by the same author's own autobiography, *Reminiscences of a Specialist* (London: George Allen and Unwin, 1932), hereafter cited as *Rem.* The second son, Ronald MacDonald, contributed an affectionate briefer memoir, "George MacDonald, a Personal Note," to *From a Northern Window* (London: Nisbet, 1911), 55–113, a collection of essays on Scottish subjects edited by F. Watson. A useful bibliography of MacDonald's works is J. M. Bulloch, "A Bibliography of George MacDonald," *Aberdeen University Library Bulletin,* 5, 30 (February 1925), 679–747, especially valuable for the list of articles about MacDonald; hereafter cited as Bulloch. Joseph Johnson, *George MacDonald, A Biographical and Critical Appreciation* (London: Pitman, 1905) is useless.

2. *GMDW,* 342 ff, *Rem.,* 16 (Carroll); also see R. L. Green, ed., *The Diaries of Lewis Carroll* (London: Cassell, 1953), ɪ, 196, for *Alice,* and dozens of other references to his warm friendship for the whole MacDonald family. *Rem.,* 99 ff, Derrick Leon, *Ruskin, the Great Victorian* (London: Routledge and Kegan Paul, 1949), passim (Ruskin); see also below, Chapter 5, pp. 266–282. *GMDW,* 399 (Maurice); 355 ff (Edinburgh chair); 381 (Octavia Hill); 380 (Tennyson); 320, 393 (Thackeray); 275, 300 ff (Lady

Byron); 269, 271, 300 (feminists—also *Rem.*, 29); *"Phantastes*
. . . received a warm word—perhaps many warm words—from
Dickens": see W. B. Rands (Henry Holbeach), "George Mac-
Donald," *The Contemporary Review, 19* (December 1872), 43.
I have not located the passage—if it exists—in Dickens' printed
letters.

3. *GMDW,* 412 ff, 425 ff, 457 ff, 459, 455; *Rem.*, passim.

4. *GMDW,* 76, 435; Ronald MacDonald, *op. cit.*, 78–80 (appearance).

5. *GMDW,* 558 ff; *Rem.*, 330 ff, 346.

6. Louise Collier Willcox, "A Neglected Novelist," *North Amer-
ican Review, 183* (September 1906), 403; see also, for example,
W. Garrett Horder, "George MacDonald: A Nineteenth Century
Seer," *Review of Reviews, 32* (October 1905), 362. K. N. Colvile,
Fame's Twilight (London: P. Allan and Co., 1923, 237–38, pre-
dicted that it might be the twenty-second century before Mac-
Donald and other Victorians were read again.

7. Wells' letter printed in *Rem.*, 323–4; see also below, Chapter
6, pp. 338–339.

Chesterton's tributes respectively in the *Daily News,* September 23, 1905, p. 6, cited by Bulloch, 734 and by Horder, *op. cit.*,
356; in his introduction to *GMDW,* 14 f; and in *The Victorian Age
in Literature* (New York & London: Williams and Norgate, 1913),
152.

8. *Times Literary Supplement,* May 29, 1924, pp. 328–29; article identified as being by Harold Child in Bulloch, 735.

9. C. S. Lewis, *George MacDonald. An Anthology* (London:
Geoffrey Bles, The Centenary Press, 1946), 14, 16, 17, 20, 21;
Surprised by Joy, The Shape of My Early Life (London: Geoffrey
Bles, 1955), pp. 169, 202, 212. See also Chad Walsh, *C. S. Lewis:
Apostle to the Skeptics* (New York: Macmillan, 1949), passim,
for mentions of MacDonald's influence on Lewis.

10. *The Visionary Novels of George MacDonald,* ed. Anne
Fremantle, with an Introduction by W. H. Auden (New York:
The Noonday Press, 1954), v–vi. K. Wittig, *The Scottish Tradition
in Literature* (Edinburgh and London: Oliver and Boyd, 1958)
gives two sentences to MacDonald, both incorrect.

11. The very rare pamphlet is described by Bulloch, 723, who
knew of only one copy. He gives a reproduction of the front
wrapper. There is a complete copy in the Brander Library at
Huntly given by MacDonald's daughter, Lady Troup, and a copy
lacking outer wrappers, but with text complete, in the Houghton
Library at Harvard. A letter with it from Lady Troup to her

brother, Greville MacDonald, indicates that she had found it among the papers of their sister, Irene, Mrs. Cecil Brewer.

12. Bulloch apparently did not know of the 1873 edition, an 8-page pamphlet printed in double columns, with pages unnumbered, and bearing on its front outer wrapper a Christmas message and a word about Novalis signed by MacDonald and dated Christmas 1873. The Houghton Library at Harvard has a copy of this edition that came, with the earlier one, from Irene Mac-Donald Brewer's papers. It was surely this version that MacDonald sent to Ruskin after Rose La Touche died, and that Ruskin acknowledged in his last letter to MacDonald, written on June 2, 1875. (*Rem.*, 122–23.)

The 1873 version contains three songs (numbers VII, XIV, XV) that MacDonald had not included in his first effort. The later versions are to be found in *Exotics* (London: Strahan & Co., 1876), 1–36; and *Rampolli: Growths from a Long-planted Root* (London: Longmans, Green, 1897), 17–36, which includes all fifteen songs, not only six, as Bulloch wrongly says (p. 724).

13. *GMDW*, 183.

14. *GMDW*, 32–33.

15. *GMDW*, 31; 54; 34–35.

16. C. S. Lewis, *George MacDonald. An Anthology*, 10–11. This passage is also quoted by R. L. Green, *The Diaries of Lewis Carroll* (London: Cassell, 1953), I, 33, as a "corrective" to a Freudian approach to Carroll.

Contrast the following: "The more the son learns to 'idolize' his father, developing what Shand has called the 'conscience of the sentiment,' the more acute will become the tension of the inner attitude. It is such an attitude that can find relief in imaginative activity wherein both the love and the repressed hostility have play." Maud Bodkin, *Archetypal Patterns in Poetry* (London: Oxford University Press, 1951), 13–14.

I leave to students of Lewis the job of explaining his triumphal assertion of MacDonald's freedom from Freud, but recommend Alistair Cooke's review in *The New Republic* for April 24, 1944.

17. *GMDW*, 75, 82–83, 84, 85; 91, 92 ff, 113, 116.

18. *GMDW*, Book II, Chapter V to Book III, Chapter II (pp. 118–54).

19. Later included in the five-act drama, *Within and Without* (London: Longmans, 1855), Part IV, Scene i, pp. 109–11.

20. Novalis, *Schriften*, ed. Paul Kluckhohn (Leipzig: Bibliographisches Institut A. G., 1928)—hereafter *Schriften*—II, 17; III, 33; II, 17; III, 32.

21. *GMDW*, 191 ff.

22. Published in the *Monthly Christian Spectator*, 4 (October 1854), 633–40, signed "xxx," and reprinted in *Adela Cathcart* (London: Hurst & Blackett, 1864), II, 208–60. This seems to be the only fiction of this period that MacDonald later rescued for reprinting. Quotations from *Adela Cathcart*, II, 210, 211, 212, 213. R. R. Marett, "The Birth of Humility," *The Threshold of Religion*, 4th edition (London: Methuen, 1929), 199–200, refers to the importance of becoming a priest.

23. *Within and Without*, V, ii; p. 178.

24. *GMDW*, 224.

25. *Within and Without*, II, viii; p. 36.

26. *GMDW*, 223, 233, 240, 249, 252, 254.

27. *GMDW*, 247, 248, 251; 231, 234, 242, 235, 266 ff; 272, 281–282, 313, 505, 532.

28. *Poems* (London: Longman, Brown, Green, Longmans, and Roberts, 1857).

29. *Poems*, 4, 6, 13, 17, 18, 21, 25, 29, 30, 37, 45–46. MacDonald constantly revised the text of his poems, and, for example, "A Hidden Life," as it appears in *The Poetical Works of George MacDonald*, 2 volumes (London: Chatto & Windus, 1893), I, 133–168, differs very markedly in some instances from the version I am quoting here.

30. *Poetry and Prose of William Blake*, ed. Geoffrey Keynes, 4th edition (London: Nonesuch Press, 1939), 846–847, 345; see also *William Blake's Vala*, ed. H. N. Margoliouth (Oxford: Clarendon Press, 1956), 92; Novalis, *Schriften*, I, 357–58; III, 360; I, 247. Excellent discussion in Jacques Roos, *Aspects littéraires du mysticisme philosophique au début du romantisme: William Blake. Novalis. Balanchine* (Strasbourg: Éditions P. H. Heitz, 1951).

31. *Poems*, 36.

CHAPTER 2   *Phantastes,* The Dream Romance

1. *Phantastes* (London: Smith, Elder and Company, 1858)—all references that follow are to the first edition; Everyman's Library, number 732, frequently reprinted, with brief introduction by Greville MacDonald; *The Visionary Novels of George MacDonald*, edited by Anne Fremantle, with an Introduction by W. H. Auden (New York: The Noonday Press, 1954), includes *Lilith* and *Phantastes* in that order for reasons not clear to me. Quotations from *GMDW*, 288, 290.

2. Giles and Phineas Fletcher, *Poetical Works*, edited by Fred-

erick S. Boas (Cambridge: University Press, 1908), II, 79. The lines MacDonald used are Canto VI, 48, 1–2; the three stanzas quoted are VI, 46, 47, & 48. For the sources see A. B. Langdale, *Phineas Fletcher* (New York, 1937), 117, 146.

3. Printed consecutively in this fashion in the edition of Novalis which MacDonald used; *Novalis, Schriften,* edited by Ludwig Tieck and Fr. (Karl Wilhelm Friedrich) von Schlegel, 4th edition (Berlin, 1826), II, 170–71, in the second portion (*Aesthetik und Literatur*) of *Fragmenten vermischten Inhalt.* Recent scholarly editors have separated the fragments, which Novalis had in fact written down at different times, sometimes without the connectives that Tieck and Schlegel supplied. To find the actual original notes on which Tieck and Schlegel built the passage, the reader will need to look in the Kluckhohn edition already cited (Chapter 1, note 20), at III, 323, #286; 253, #987; 97, #238 in that order. But since our concern is with MacDonald, what is important here is the passage as he read it, not as Novalis originally jotted down the fragments of which it is composed. The only critic of *Phantastes* known to me who has paid attention to this passage from Novalis is E. S. Robertson, "A Literary Causerie: 'Phantastes,'" *Academy, 70* (March 31, 1906), 308, who rightly emphasizes its importance and expresses the wish that somebody would translate it.

4. See the correct form in *Schriften,* ed. Kluckhohn, III, 97, #238.

5. Schlegel may have been referring to the actual *Märchen* of Eros and Fable told by Klingsohr in *Heinrich von Ofterdingen,* or he may have meant to refer to Novalis' plan for the uncompleted portion of the work: see above, Chapter 1, p. 38. On the discussion of the *Märchen* as a literary form see Hermann Todsen, *Über die Entwicklung des romantischen Kunstmärchens* (Berlin, 1906), 18–20.

6. Thomas Haynes Bayly (1797–1839) wrote many comedies. *You Can't Marry Your Grandmother* is subtitled "An Original Petite Comedy in Two Acts." I have seen two editions, one published by Chapman and Hall, and the other "French's Acting Edition," neither dated. Lewis Carroll saw the play at the Olympic on April 12, 1858, the same season that *Phantastes* was published. *The Diaries of Lewis Carroll,* ed. R. L. Green (London: Cassell, 1953), I, 141. For the elemental spirits in the works of the German romantics, see Oswald Floeck, *Die Elementargeister bei Fouqué und andern Dichtern der romantischen und nachromantischen Zeit,* Jahres-Bericht des k.k. Staats-Gymnasiums in Bielitz fur das

Schuljahr 1908/1909 (part one) and 1909/1910 (part two); Fritz
Strich, *Die Mythologie in der deutschen Literatur von Klopstock
bis Wagner,* 2 vols. (Halle, 1910); Rudolf Buchmann, *Helden
und Mächte des romantischen Kunstmärchens* (Leipzig, 1910),
217–230. On Fouqué, see the recent work of Arno Schmidt,
Fouqué und einige Zeitgenossen (Stahlberg, 1958). George Smith
on *Undine, GMDW,* 318; MacDonald on *Undine,* quoted by Bulloch, 693. Paracelsus' treatise conveniently translated into English
with an introduction: "A Book on Nymphs, Sylphs, Pygmies, and
Salamanders, and on the Other Spirits," *Four Treatises of Theophrastus von Hohenheim called Paracelsus,* ed. Henry E. Sigerist
(Baltimore: Publications of the Institute of the History of Medi-
cine, The Johns Hopkins University, 1941), second series: Texts
and Documents, I, 215–253. The date of composition is unknown;
the date of the first printing was 1566; as early as 1836 an Italian
edition of *Undine* included a selection from Paracelsus (Sigerist,
222, note 10). Psellus' two works on demonology, "Timotheus;
or, Concerning the Daimons," and "What the Greeks teach about
the Daimons," ed. J. F. Boissonade, *Psellus* (Nuremberg, 1838),
and reprinted in J. P. Migne, *Patrologia Graeca, 122,* 817 ff and
875 ff; discussion in K. Svoboda, *La démonologie de Michel Psellos*
(Brno, 1927), Spisy Filosofické Fakulty Masarykovy University
v. Brne, no. 22. For Hoffmann, see P. Sucher, *Les sources du
merveilleux chez E.T.A. Hoffmann* (Paris, 1912), 4 and passim.
Montfaucon de Villars, *Comte de Gabalis ou entretiens sur les
sciences secrétes* (Amsterdam, 1725); there is an English translation: *Comte de Gabalis by the Abbé N. de Montfaucon de
Villars Rendered out of French into English with a Commentary*
(New York and London: The Brothers [i.e. of the Rosy Cross],
1914). My colleague, Professor Stuart Atkins, points out that
Anodos' grandmother-fairy is reminiscent also of Goethe's *neue
Melusine* in *Wilhelm Meisters Wanderjahre,* and of Eduard
Mörike's fairy in *Der Schatz* (1836).

7. For the passage see Novalis, *Schriften,* ed. Kluckhohn, I,
182–83.

8. Poe, *Marginalia* (Essay on dreams), *Works,* ed. E. C. Sted-
man and G. E. Woodberry (Chicago, 1896), VII, 312. For Hoffmann and the dream world see the discussion in H. W. Hewett-
Thayer, *Hoffmann: Author of the Tales* (Princeton, 1948), especially 180–181, and, for Schubert's influence, 119 ff and the
references listed 120, note 8. Novalis' passage in *Das allgemeine
Brouillon, Schriften,* ed. Kluckhohn, III, 98, #241. MacDonald
quoted this passage in a letter written to one of his sons, whose

wife had died, in 1891 (*GMDW,* 518); and he used it as the final words of *Lilith* (see below, p. 370).

9. *Phantastes,* 13, 35, 45, 46, 47, 48, 49, 50, 51.

10. Hyacinth and Rosebud, a very important influence on Mac-Donald elsewhere, in Novalis, *Schriften,* ed. Kluckhohn, I, 23–27. *The Golden Pot* best in E.T.A. Hoffmann, *Dichtungen und Schriften . . . Gesamtausgabe,* ed. W. Harich (Weimar, 1924) III, 3 ff; all future references to his works will be to this edition. For MacDonald's reading of *The Golden Pot, GMDW,* 259, 297–98. These passages are noted by Henry Zysltra, *E.T.A. Hoffmann in England and America* (unpublished Harvard University dissertation, 1940), 252 ff; but while he praises *Phantastes,* and points out the resemblance between Anodos' entrance into fairyland and the passage of Hoffmann's characters from one world to another, he mentions only *The Golden Pot,* confines his comparisons to this brief one, and seems not to have read *Phantastes* through: so many more parallels would have leapt to his eye had he done so.

11. *Within and Without,* IV, iii, pp. 113–14. Ovid *Metamorphoses,* II, 340–66; I, 548–67; VIII, 611–724; *Alastor* ll. 432–434; "Christabel," l. 42. For a discussion of "Nutting" see David Ferry, *The Limits of Mortality* (Middletown: Wesleyan University Press, 1959), 22 ff.

12. *Phantastes,* 60, *Alastor,* l. 209; *Phantastes,* 64, 71, 75, 76, 77, 78, 79, 81–82.

13. See his poem "A Story of the Sea-Shore," *Poetical Works* (London: Chatto and Windus, 1893), I, 173–74.

14. *Phantastes,* 90–91, 93–94, 97, 101, 102, 104.

15. *Peter Schlemihl* is available in many editions and translations. The best study of Chamisso is René Riegel, *Adalbert de Chamisso, sa vie et son oeuvre* (Paris, 1934). The shadow theme is discussed pp. 417 ff, but the discussion is mostly derived from the rather pedestrian articles he cites in his notes. Much better, and apparently unknown to Riegel, is the splendid article by Otto Rank, "Der Doppelgänger," *Imago,* 3, 2 (1914), 97–164. A suggestive essay is Denis de Rougemont, "Chamisso et le mythe de l'ombre perdue," *Cahiers du Sud,* Numéro Spécial 24 (May–June, 1937), 282–92. Stuart Atkins, "Peter Schlemihl in Relation to the Popular Novel of the Romantic Period," *Germanic Review,* 21 (1946), 191–208. Hoffmann, *Die Geschichte vom verlorenen Spiegelbild,* ed. Harich, VI, 27 ff; *Elixiere des Teufels,* IV: *Die Doppeltgänger,* VIII, 165 ff; *Kater Murr,* XII; *Prinzessin Brambilla,* III, 266 ff. For Goethe's experience, see *Dichtung und Wahrheit,*

III, book xi; for Maupassant's, see Rank, "Der Doppelgänger," 127. For the broken bowl, see P. J. Vinken, "Some Observations on the Symbolism of the Broken Pot in Art and Literature," *The American Imago, 15* (1958), 149–74.

16. *Phantastes,* 112, 114, 119, 120, 127.

17. Novalis, *Schriften,* ed., Kluckhohn, I, 154. For Werner, Roos, *op. cit.* (Chapter 1, note 30 above); Boehme, *Aurora, Sämtliche Werke,* ed. K. W. Schiebler (Leipzig, 1831–46), II, 112; compare Alexandre Koyré, *La Philosophie de Jacob Boehme* (Paris, 1929), 88 and elsewhere, which I find much the most helpful book on Boehme; see also H. H. Brinton, *The Mystic Will* (New York, 1930); Walter Feilchenfeld, *Der Einfluss Jacob Böhmes auf Novalis* (Berlin, 1922), 58 ff; and Edgar Ederheimer, *Jakob Boehme und die Romantiker* (Heidelberg, 1904). Novalis, *Lehrlinge zu Sais, Schriften,* I, 36. J. H. Buckley, *The Victorian Temper* (Cambridge, Mass., 1951), 97 ff, has an interesting discussion of water images among the Victorians, but his examples are baptismal and purificatory, not uterine. Much closer is Maud Bodkin, *Archetypal Patterns in Poetry,* 65 ff, where both Swinburne and Arnold are cited. For Goethe's Neptunism, cf. *Faust,* II, 7499, "Ohne Wasser ist kein Heil!" and passim.

18. Novalis, *Schriften,* ed. Kluckhohn, IV, 192 (Letter to Just, March 29, 1797); II, 389, #62 (*Neue Fragmentensammlung,* 1798); I, 28 (*Die Lehrlinge zu Sais*); III, 287–288, #39 (*Fragmente der letzten Jahren,* 1799–1800); the imagery of Klingsohr's *Märchen* discussed in Bruce Haywood, *Novalis: The Veil of Imagery* (Cambridge, Mass., 1959), 118 f. A psychoanalytic discussion of Hyacinth and Rosebud in E. F. Lorenz, in *Imago, 3* (1914), 260 ff, in an article primarily devoted to Hoffmann, cited below, note 23.

19. *Phantastes,* 136, 141, 141–42, 153, 156, 161–62, 169, 181.

20. Novalis, *Schriften,* I, 104 ff; Hoffmann's *Das verlorene Spiegelbild,* ed. Harich, VI, 27 ff; *Der Magnetiseur,* IX, 1 ff; *Der Elementargeist,* VI, 197 ff; *Der unheimliche Gast,* VI, 99 ff; *Das öde Haus,* IX, 133 ff; *Kater Murr,* XII. Hewett-Thayer, *Hoffmann,* 168, note 5, and 172; Sucher, *Les Sources . . . Hoffmann,* chapter II, deals fully with Hoffmann's sources for "animal magnetism."

21. *Phantastes,* 188, 196, 198–202, 205.

22. *Phantastes,* 208, 210, 211, 213.

23. E. F. Lorenz, "Die Geschichte des Bergmanns von Falun," *Imago, 3* (1914), 250–301; Novalis, *Schriften,* ed. Kluckhohn, I, 167; Tieck's *Runenberg* republished in *Phantasus,* I (1812), translated into English by Carlyle (1827) and by J. A. Froude and

J. C. Hare, *Tales from the Phantasus of Tieck* (London, 1845); Hoffmann, ed. Harich, IX, 179 ff, quotations, p. 189. It is a fascinating coincidence that Paracelsus himself on his travels had visited the mines at Falun in 1520. B. de Telepnes, *Paracelsus* (St. Gall, 1945), 36.

24. *Phantastes*, 221, 222–23, 225, 226, 227, 233, 229. *Alastor*, ll. 18, 22–23, 37–39, 41. Examples of praise by critics for "Alas how easily . . .": George Saintsbury, *Nation and Athenaeum, 36* (November 8, 1924), 218. "There were moments—and those neither brief, nor slight, nor few—when the possession of genius could without absurdity be assigned him. Large parts of 'Phantastes,' from the famous and exquisite 'Alas! how easily things go wrong' in verse, and many pieces of the prose, were good *sans phrase;* and very nearly if not quite great." See also J. A. Noble, *Academy, 44* (August 10, 1893), 147, who laments its omission from the collected *Poems* which he is reviewing, and calls it "the perfect little lyric"; E. A. Robertson, *op. cit.* (note 3 above), who says "Everybody knows it; even those who have never seen the book and know nothing else about it. . . . One must needs seek out the best in Shelley, or Keats, or Coleridge to surpass these lines. . . ."; Greville MacDonald (*Rem.*, 145) quotes the words of an acquaintance named McCorquodale as saying it was the most pathetic stanza in English, and "I can never repeat it aloud for fear I'll weep—hardened sinner that I am." For the dream of a British officer that he had fallen into the warm sea and had come to the surface to find a little boat, and its interpretation as rebirth, see Maud Bodkin, *Archetypal Patterns in Poetry*, 61; *Phantastes*, 240, 244, 248, 250. The "door of the Timeless" recalls the realm of the Mothers in *Faust*, II.

25. *Phantastes*, 257, 259, 266–67, 279, 283–84, 286, 287–88.

26. *Phantastes*, 303, 307–08, 308, 313, 314–15, 316, 319, 321, 322, 323.

CHAPTER 3   Fancy and Imagination

1. *Adela Cathcart*, 3 volumes (London: Hurst & Blackett, 1864) containing "The Light Princess," "The Cruel Painter," "The Giant's Heart," and "The Castle," as well as various other stories, not fairy-tales, mentioned elsewhere in this book; *Dealings with the Fairies* (London: Strahan, 1867), containing the first printings of "Cross Purposes," and "The Golden Key"; *Works of Fancy and Imagination*, 10 volumes (London: Strahan, 1871), containing first printings of the full text of "The Carasoyn" (the first

part of which had appeared as "The Fairy Fleet: An English Märchen" in *Argosy, 1* [April 1866], 417–32); "The Grey Wolf" and "Uncle Cornelius, His Story"; *At the Back of the North Wind* (London: Strahan, 1871), *The Princess and the Goblin* (London: Strahan, 1872)—despite the dates on the title-pages, each of these was published at the end of the preceding year; *The Wise Woman* (London: Strahan, 1875); *The Princess and Curdie* (London: Chatto & Windus, 1883), actually published as a book in 1882; "The History of Photogen and Nycteris: A Day and Night Märchen," *Gifts of the Child Christ,* 2 volumes (London: Sampson Low, Marston, Searle, & Rivington, 1882). For details see Bulloch under each title.

2. *GMDW,* passim. See also *Rem.,* 309. That experienced theatre-goer, Lewis Carroll, praises Lily's acting repeatedly and warmly; see *Diaries,* ed. Green, I, 219; II, 300, 382: he thought she was the only talented actor of the family. Other Victorian diarists and memorists often mention the performances.

3. *GMDW,* 295; *The Gifts of the Child Christ, and Other Tales,* 2 volumes (London, 1882); "If I Had a Father" is the last item in Volume II; reprinted in one volume as *Stephen Archer and Other Tales* (London, 1883); I have used an American reprint (New York: Routledge, no date).

4. *GMDW,* 319–20: "With much suggestive utterance, epigrammatic diction and knowledge of human nature in certain aspects, it is often theatrical in its presentation of characters, while its conversations are more like debates of some delegates in the audience-chamber of the writer's mind than real dialogue. Yet the book is wholly consistant with its writer's life-long convictions. Its central idea is not unlike that of *Within and Without,* though characters and narrative have nothing in common with that poem. Robert Falconer first appears here, though his own story is reserved for future telling. Like Julian, he stands for the prophet who primarily has vision of the truth always supreme to its concrete expression, while his antithesis, Aurelio, a young imaginative sculptor, finds in Beauty the manifestation of all Truth, and so seeks to idealize Form without any further concept of what Truth means. Then standing apart from each, is the idle young aristocrat with delicate and high-cultured feeling, who yet looks on Beauty as if manifested for its own and his own sake. Naturally he is the bad influence of the story; and his father, a melodramatic yet imaginatively conceived Bluebeard, with a chamber of horrors—not for wives, but for men and women whom he has hated and loved chiefly for the sake of injuring—is horri-

ble indeed. Yet it has many and great beauties. It reveals too the writer's intimacy with disreputable London—to which I think James Greenwood, the 'Amateur Casual,' may have introduced him."

5. *The Letters and Private Papers of William Makepeace Thackeray,* ed. Gordon N. Ray (Cambridge, Mass.: Harvard University Press, 1946), IV, 170.

6. *The Cornhill Magazine,* 2, 1 (July 1860), 83.

7. *The Portent: A Story of the Inner Vision of the Highlanders, Commonly called The Second Sight* (London: Smith, Elder and Co., 1864), 82–83, 107. Florence Becker Lennon, *Victoria Through the Looking Glass. The Life of Lewis Carroll* (New York: Simon & Schuster, 1945), 266, maintains that *The Portent* exactly parallels a cure of a post-traumatic amnesia reported many years later, and credits MacDonald with "a distinct intuition for psychological truths that were not officially uncovered till after his death." But the repetition of past experiences that brings about the cure of Lady Alice in the second version of *The Portent,* no matter how clinically useful, none the less makes bad fiction. Mrs. Lennon does not know much about MacDonald anyway: she calls him (260) a "full-fledged Church of England" parson, when of course he was nothing of the kind; she has read, apparently, only *The Portent* and *At the Back of the North Wind;* and she says (266) that MacDonald "shows no injury to his personality and no hardships in his environment."

8. *Adela Cathcart,* I, 123–33; quotations from 170–71, 189, 215, 139–40. The moral is added in this version only, 224; in versions printed separately, the conversation of the audience, possible in *Adela Cathcart,* had to be omitted. Hoffmann, *Die Prinzessin Brambilla,* ed. Harich, III, 322 ff, for the *Märchen. GMDW,* 324–25. The manuscript of "The Light Princess" is now in the Houghton Library at Harvard. Lewis Carroll accompanied MacDonald to the printer on the day he turned it in for publication: *Diaries,* ed. Green, I, 184. In *Adela Cathcart,* MacDonald has the teller of the story of "The Cruel Painter" gum his manuscript together in the same way (III, 173).

9. *Adela Cathcart,* III, 173–254; quotations from 186, 196, 219, 238, 239, 254; Hoffmann, *Der Artushof,* ed. Harich, VIII, 3 ff. Henry More, *An Antidote against Atheism,* A Collection of Several Philosophical Writings of Dr. Henry More (London, 1662), chapter IX, 114 ff, contains the story of "Johannes Cuntius," which MacDonald re-Germanifies as Kunz, as taken by More from "Relations of *Martinus Weinrichius,* a *Silesian* Physician and Philoso-

pher, which by way of Preface are prefixt to *Picus Mirandola* his *Strix* or *De ludificatione Daemonum. . . ."* (p. 111). MacDonald takes over the episode of a black cat scratching at the "dead" man's face and bolster in an effort to take him away, and summarizes Kunz's various tricks after death; it is MacDonald who makes Kunz a vampire. Since MacDonald himself obviously did not consult either Weinreich or Pico, I have not done so either. C. O. Parsons, "George MacDonald and Henry More," *Notes and Queries, 188,* 9 (May 5, 1945), 180–83, deals with this borrowing in some detail. He notes that More distrusted MacDonald's favorite, Boehme, for trusting too much to imagination and not enough to reason, but adds that both More and MacDonald opposed materialism.

10. *Adela Cathcart,* iii, 38–63, with a good many variations from the many later reprintings; quotations from 48, 83, 84–85. Hoffmann, *Die Königsbraut,* ed. Harich, vii, 243 ff. Stith Thompson, *Motif Index of Folk Literature* (Bloomington, Indiana, 1956), ii, 493, classified under "E 710," "External Soul." Type 302, *The Ogre's (Devil's) Heart in the Egg,* in Antti Arne and Stith Thompson, *The Types of the Folk Tale* (New York, 1905), 118 ff; two Highland versions (quite remote from MacDonald's treatment) in J. G. McKay, *More West Highland Tales* (Edinburgh and London, 1940), 23 ff and 45 ff; references to the theme in all the folklores of the world in J. Bolte and G. Polivka, *Anmerkungen zu den Kinder- und Hausmärchen der Brüder Grimm* (Leipzig, 1918), iii, 434 ff, on Grimm #197. The two versions closest to MacDonald, in G. W. Dasent, *Popular Tales from the Norse* (Edinburgh, 1859), 47 ff (several times reprinted), translations from Asbjörnsen and Moe, *Norske Folkeeventyr;* and Benjamin Thorpe, *Yule-Tide Stories. A Collection of Scandinavian and North German Popular Tales and Traditions* (London, 1853), 435 ff. On an Irish version, current among story-tellers as late as 1937, see R. Th. Christiansen, " 'Displaced' Folktales," *Humaniora: Essays in Literature-Folklore-Bibliography Honoring Archer Taylor on his Seventieth Birthday* (Locust Valley, New York: J. J. Augustin, 1960), 168–170.

11. "The Castle: A Parable." *Adela Cathcart,* iii, 283–314; quotation from 283.

12. "Cross Purposes," *Dealings with the Fairies* (London: Strahan, 1867), quotations from 209, 210–11. Of "The Grey Wolf" and "Uncle Cornelius His Story" (*Works,* 1871, x, 227–44, 247–308) the first is a werewolf story set on the Shetlands, and the second a ghost story in which a youthful experience with a

revenant launches the narrator on a lifetime of study of the supernatural. The interest of "The Grey Wolf" lies in the fact that the werewolf, a young girl, is obviously deeply unhappy at her fate, and does not enjoy performing the actions required of her by her animal nature. At the end, she is left in despair, still a victim of whatever enchantment has enslaved her. "Uncle Cornelius" has as its sole interesting feature the fact that the ghost (female) seems to have transmitted her chief trait—parsimony and over-meticulousness about household accounts—to a remote descendant, with whom the narrator is briefly in love: the suggestion is that character as well as appearance can be passed on through the generations.

13. "The Fairy Fleet: an English Mährchen," *Argosy*, 1 (April 1866), 417–32; quotations from 424–25, 431, 434.

14. "The Carasoyn," *Works* (1871), ix, 125–223; quotations from 200, 216.

15. "The Golden Key," *Dealings with the Fairies*, 248–308; quotations from 254, 258–59, 266, 267, 272, 275.

16. See Chapter 1, p. 38.

17. "The Golden Key," 278, 281, 293, 294–95, 297, 302, 305, 306.

18. *Faust*, ii, 6259, 6222–23. C. G. Jung, *Contributions to Analytical Psychology*, tr. H. S. and C. F. Baynes (London: Kegan Paul, 1928), 38–40; cf. Bodkin, *Archetypal Patterns*, 52. On childhood, compare MacDonald's sermon, "The Child in the Midst," *Unspoken Sermons* (London: Strahan, 1867), 1–26, published in the same year as "The Golden Key." The text is Mark 9:33–37. On this point in general, see the remarks of William Empson, *English Pastoral Poetry* (New York: W. W. Norton, 1938), 260 ff.

19. "The Golden Key," 299, 296.

20. *At the Back of the North Wind* (London: Strahan, 1871), previously serialized in *Good Words for the Young*, running from November 1868 to October 1869; quotations from 112, 115; *The Poems of James Hogg, The Ettrick Shepherd*, ed. William Wallace (London: Isbister and Co., 1903), 122–23; "Kilmeny" is the last poem in "Night the Second" of "The Queen's Wake."

21. "The Shadows," *Adela Cathcart*, ii, 80–149. According to Bulloch (719), "The germinal idea of this fairy story occurs in a collection of manuscripts written by the Powell family for their father on his seventy-first birthday, describing, in Mrs. MacDonald's handwriting, the first Christmas spent at Huntly Cottage, Hastings, 1857."

22. *At the Back of the North Wind,* 359–60, 358, 59, 364, 186–87, 8, 32, 254, 51, 184.

23. "The History of Photogen and Nycteris; a day and night Mährchen," first published in the *Graphic, 20* (Christmas, 1879), 4–5, 8–9; in book form in *The Gifts of the Child Christ and Other Tales, 2* volumes (London: Sampson, Low, Marston, Rivington, & Searle, 1882); often re-issued; I have used an American reprint (New York: Routledge, no date).

24. *The Princess and the Goblin* (London: Strahan, 1872); serial publication in *Good Words for the Young,* running from November 1870 to June 1871, and often reprinted. I have used an American reprint (Philadelphia: David McKay, 1920); quotations from 79, 80, 96, 103, 148–49, 87–88. *GMDW,* 412. It is interesting to note that when Maud Bodkin was examining her own response to the cavern images in "Kubla Khan" she remembered real cellars and wells from her childhood, and "also, fused with these, images of caverns and underground castle vaults, goblin-tenanted, which I gathered from an absorbed reading of fairy tales" (*Archetypal Patterns in Poetry,* 114). I would bet heavily that she was thinking of *The Princess and the Goblin.*

25. *The Wise Woman* (London: Strahan, 1875), previously serialized in *Good Things,* running from December 5, 1874 to July 3, 1875, under the title "A Double Story"; quotations from 85–86, 26.

26. *The Princess and Curdie* (London: Chatto & Windus, 1883), but issued late in 1882; first published serially in *Good Things,* between January and June, 1877. Why the book publication was so long delayed I do not know. I have used a reprint (London: Blackie, no date, but 1891); quotations from 3–4, 25, 27, 71, 73, 102, 103, 113, 180, 206, 217, 254–55, 51, 159, 54. For passages from Novalis and Hoffmann on the beauties underground, see above, Chapter 2, 88 and 89.

CHAPTER 4   Three Theological Novels

1. John Dyer, "The New Novelist," *The Penn Monthly Magazine, 1,* 6 (June 1870), 217, 219, 221.

2. *David Elginbrod,* 3 volumes (London: Hurst & Blackett, 1863). For the epitaph see *GMDW,* 320–21. A treatment of the theme of the epitaph with parallels from German, French, and Indian literature was written by F. Max Müller, under the title "Coincidences," *Athenaeum,* No. 3107 (May 14, 1887),

640–41. For other instances and references see J. M. Bulloch "The Elginbrod Epitaph," *Aberdeen University Review*, *12* (1924), 40–43.

3. *David Elginbrod*, I, 41, 49, 74, 160–61, 97.

4. *Ibid.*, I, 157–58.

5. Of many editions of the *Fourfold State*, I have examined the Fourth (Edinburgh, 1747).

6. I have used the edition published by Penniman and Bliss (Lansingburgh, 1806). Twenty-four editions were published in the forty years after Erskine's death in 1754. See A. R. MacEwen, *The Erskines* (Edinburgh & London, 1900), 150.

7. Erskine, 87; MacEwen, 150.

8. I have used the twenty-first edition (London, 1776).

9. I have used an edition revised by the Rev. John Carslaw (Dumfries, 1835); life of Peden on pp. 378–89.

10. 2 volumes (Edinburgh, 1802), first published in 1755; quotation from p. ix.

11. Twenty-sixth edition, 3 volumes (London, 1829).

12. Edited by James Moir (Edinburgh and London, 1889), p. xxiii.

13. *David Elginbrod*, I, 163–64, 165–66, 101.

14. *Ibid.*, I, 93–94, 98, 95–96.

15. *Ibid.*, I, 170–71.

16. *Ibid.*, I, 233; II, 2.

17. *Ibid.*, I, 319, 253, 298–99; II, 45, 47.

18. *Ibid.*, II, 236. *GMDW*, 302 reveals that Funkelstein was in part inspired by a Pole named Zamoyski who was giving exhibitions of "electrobiology" in England at the time.

19. *Ibid.*, II, 198.

20. MacDonald mentions Falconer first in a casual way, long before the reader has ever seen or heard of him, in commenting on Hugh's shallow love for Euphra: "His love was not a high one, not such as thine, my Falconer" (III, 6). No reader could have known what this meant. In another place MacDonald says ". . . I have attempted to tell a great deal about Robert Falconer and his pursuits elsewhere" (III, 137). Here MacDonald is referring to the novel *Seekers and Finders*, eventually destroyed, which, at the time he wrote *David Elginbrod*, he apparently still thought he would publish. He cannot mean his own later novel *Robert Falconer*, not yet even contemplated. He told Lewis Carroll that Falconer was an "ideal character" (*Diaries*, ed. Green, I, 192; February 10, 1863).

21. *David Elginbrod*, III, 6, 137, 175, 173, 212.

22. *Ibid.*, III, 158, 161.

23. *Ibid.*, III, 296; *Athenaeum,* January 17, 1863, 80.

24. *Ibid.*, II, 92–93, 101, 97.

25. *Ibid.*, III, 182, 183, 184.

26. *Ibid.*, III, 196, 200–01, 203; *GMDW,* 323, 398; Augustus J. C. Hare, *The Story of My Life* (London, 1895) I, 72; Ruskin, *Praeterita* (London: Rupert Hart-Davis, 1949), 451–52; the others quoted in Amy Cruse, *The Victorians and Their Books* (London: George Allen and Unwin, 1935), 111; on Maurice as a synthesizer see Walter E. Houghton *The Victorian Frame of Mind* (New Haven: Yale University Press, 1957), 178.

27. *David Elginbrod,* III, 184; *GMDW,* 85.

28. *Alec Forbes of Howglen,* 3 volumes (London: Hurst and Blackett, 1865); I have used an American reprint in one volume (Boston: D. Lothrop and Company, no date, but 1886).

29. *GMDW,* 19, note 1.

30. *Alec Forbes,* 2, 27, 31, 46.

31. *Ibid.,* 87.

32. *Ibid.,* 117–18.

33. *Ibid.,* 129–30, 130.

34. *Ibid.,* 135, 136–37, 56.

35. *Ibid.,* 33, 125, 142, 270. See below, Chapter 5.

36. *Ibid.,* 341–42, 359, 361, 370, 370–71, 377, 373, 382–83.

37. *Ibid.,* 371. For a discussion of sexual transgressions as treated in the Victorian novel see Patricia Thomson, *The Victorian Heroine. A Changing Ideal. 1827–1873.* (London: Oxford University Press, 1956).

38. *Alec Forbes,* 345–53.

39. Elsewhere in *Alec Forbes* (p. 124) Mr. Cupples says of *Tristram Shandy:* "A pailace of dirt and impidence and speeritual stink. The clever deevil had his entrails in his breast and his hert in his belly, and regairdet neither God nor his ain mither. His lauchter's no like the cracklin' o' thorns unner a pot, but like the nichterin' o' a de'il ahin' the wainscot. Lat him sit and rot there." Compare *Adela Cathcart,* II, 285.

40. *Alec Forbes,* 397.

41. *Robert Falconer,* 3 volumes (London: Hurst & Blackett, 1868). MacDonald's own comment in W. Garrett Horder, "George MacDonald: A Nineteenth-Century Seer," *Review of Reviews, 32* (October 1905), 362; Ronald MacDonald, in *From a Northern Window* (see Chapter 1, note 1), 94–95; *GMDW,* 353.

42. *Robert Falconer,* I, 7, 87–88, 167–68, 176.

43. *Ibid.,* I, 177–78.

44. *Ibid.,* ɪɪ, 221; ɪɪɪ, 22, 75–76.

45. *Ibid.,* ɪɪɪ, 215, 221–22.

46. *Ibid.,* ɪ, 319, 320, 309, 321, 326.

47. *Ibid.,* ɪɪ, 212; *Phantastes,* see above, Chapter 2, p. 46; *Robert Falconer,* ɪɪ, 213–14, 236–37, 242.

48. MacDonald intended Ericson as a portrait of his own brother, John Hill MacDonald, who actually wrote the poems scattered through *Robert Falconer* and attributed to Ericson. *GMDW,* 164.

49. *Robert Falconer,* ɪɪ, 202, 204–05, 256–57, 292.

50. *Ibid.,* ɪɪɪ, 79; ɪ, 131; ɪɪ, 33, 35.

51. *Ibid.,* ɪ, 25, 126, 127, 128. *Huckleberry Finn* was first published in 1884, sixteen years after *Robert Falconer,* and Mark Twain was an admirer and friend of MacDonald: "The two writers were very intimate, and had discussed co-operation on a novel together, so as to secure copyright on both sides of the Atlantic" (*GMDW,* 457). After their meeting in the United States, Mark Twain visited the MacDonalds in England in 1873 or 1874 (*GMDW,* 465). But I do not mean to suggest that Shargar's response to Mrs. Falconer's "civilization" helped inspire Huck to respond the same way to the efforts of the Widow Douglas and Aunt Sally: only to point out that the two responses were identical.

52. *Robert Falconer,* ɪ, 211, 212, 259–60.

53. *Ibid.,* ɪɪɪ, 38, 152–53. In *GMDW,* 346–47, there is a letter from George to Louisa MacDonald written from Antwerp in the summer of 1865 describing his delight in this cathedral tower: "Just think of a man being able to sit at a finger-and-pedal-board 250 feet from the ground and play any time he liked on 40 bells yet higher—play to the whole city spread below!"

54. *Ibid.,* ɪ, 108–09, 127, 154–55. The works referred to, in addition to *Pilgrim's Progress* and Erskine's *Gospel Sonnets* (see above, note 6), already encountered in David Elginbrod's library, are Joseph Alleine (1634–1668), *Alarm to Unconverted Sinners, In a serious treatise shewing what conversion is not and correcting some mistakes about it;* Richard Baxter (1615–1691), *The Saints Everlasting Rest: or, a treatise of the blessed state of the saints in their enjoyment of God in glory;* John Bunyan (1638–1688), *The Holy War made by Shaddai upon Diabolus, for the regaining of the world, or The losing and taking again of the town of Mansoul;* Daniel Defoe (1661–1731), *Religious Courtship: being historical discourses on the necessity of marrying religious husbands and wives only;* and Edward Young (1683–1765), *The Complaint: or, Night Thoughts on Life, Death, and*

Immortality. Of these only the last seems to merit a further word here: Young's morbidity made his poem immensely popular among the German romantics, who in turn influenced Mac-Donald directly; it is interesting to note that he had read Young in his childhood, and worth remarking that there was much to attract him in Young's melancholy: "I wish we were all dead," MacDonald's youthful slogan, is perhaps enough to show the connection.

55. *Robert Falconer*, ɪ, 162–63, 164; ɪɪ, 8 (compare above, text, and note 32); ɪ, 185.

56. *Ibid.*, ɪ, 300, 301, 148–49.

57. Augustus J. C. Hare, *The Story of My Life* (London, 1896), ɪ, 178 ff, with the grim climax on p. 186.

58. *Robert Falconer*, ɪ, 305.

59. *Ibid.*, ɪɪɪ, 251, 252, 253, 68, 69, 70.

60. "George MacDonald as a Teacher of Religion," *London Quarterly Review*, 31 (January 1862), 403, 408, 423, 425, 402, 416.

61. George McCrie, "A Word to George Eliot and George MacDonald," *The Religion of Our Literature* (London: Hodder and Stoughton, 1875), 307–08, 298, 301, 307, 303, 313–14.

62. T. G. Selby, "George MacDonald and the Scottish School," *The Theology of Modern Fiction* (London: C. H. Kelly, 1897), 131, 135, *bis*, 140, *bis*, 141, *bis*, 142, *bis*.

63. Selby, 143, 154, 164.

64. S. Law Wilson, *The Theology of Modern Fiction* (Edinburgh: T. and T. Clark, 1899), 28, 271–72, 282, 283–84, 285, 288.

65. See W. E. Houghton, *The Victorian Frame of Mind*, 49–50, and note 73, and the essays on McLeod Campbell and MacLeod in *Fathers of the Kirk*, edited by R. S. Wright (London: Oxford University Press, 1960); quotation from Louise Collier Willcox, "A Neglected Novelist," *The North American Review*, 183 (September 1906), 397–98.

66. Rev. W. Garrett Horder, "George MacDonald: A Nine-teenth-Century Seer," *Review of Reviews*, 32 (October 1905), 358.

67. In *From a Northern Window*, 72.

CHAPTER 5   *Wilfrid Cumbermede* and Other Fiction

1. *GMDW*, 318; W. Garrett Horder, "George MacDonald: A Nineteenth-Century Seer," *Review of Reviews*, 32 (October 1905), 358; Ronald MacDonald, "George MacDonald, A Personal Note," *From a Northern Window* (London, 1911), 66–67.

2. *Wilfrid Cumbermede,* 3 volumes (London: Hurst & Blackett, 1872); serialized in *St. Paul's* during 1870–71. I have used an American reprint in one volume (New York: George Routledge & Sons, no date).

3. *Wilfrid Cumbermede,* 11, 20–21, 23, 73, 128, 129, 130, 132, 127, 134, 135. Derrick Leon, *Ruskin, The Great Victorian* (London: Routledge and Kegan Paul, 1949), 409–411. For corroboration of my theory about the pendulum, see *The Diaries of John Ruskin,* selected and edited by Joan Evans and John Howard Whitehouse (Oxford: Clarendon Press, 1958), ii, 644, entry for March 9, 1868, for a most revealing dream; and Phyllis Greenacre, *Swift and Carroll: A Psychoanalytic Study of Two Lives* (New York: International Universities Press, 1955), 100, note 9.

4. *Wilfrid Cumbermede,* 147, 165, 172, 178, 183, 200, 135. The manuscript of *Wilfrid Cumbermede* is in the Houghton Library at Harvard (Ms Eng 1112.1); quotations from pp. 118, 124. For MacDonald and Ruskin, see *GMDW,* 328–42 and passim; also *Rem.,* 99–123, with many new bits of information; also Leon, *Ruskin,* passim.

5. *Wilfrid Cumbermede,* 423, 428–29.

6. *Ranald Bannerman's Boyhood* (London: Strahan & Co., 1871), serialized in *Good Words for the Young* during 1869–70. In this agreeable account of a Scotch childhood, the children of a widowed doctor conspire to play pranks on the disagreeable housekeeper whom their father engages to take charge of the household. In the end, she proves to be dishonest and is dismissed. Both Ranald and a much older friend love a little girl who dies; and Ranald leaves his boyhood behind in making the discovery that, while he has loved the girl as a child, his friend has loved her as a man. To its original audience the story must have had a very considerable appeal, though a modern reader who comes to it after *Alec Forbes* or *Robert Falconer* finds the childhood episodes already familiar and senses MacDonald's own discomfort at being unable to write his dialogue in Scotch for English children: he repeatedly and clumsily apologizes for introducing so much as a single word of his favorite dialect.

7. *Malcolm,* 3 volumes (London: Henry S. King & Co., 1875), serialized in *The Glasgow Weekly Herald* during 1871, four years earlier. *The Marquis of Lossie,* 3 volumes (London: Hurst & Blackett, 1877), serialized in the *Glasgow Weekly Mail* and in *Lippincott's Magazine* in the United States. Bulloch, 705.

8. *Malcolm,* i, 280; *Adela Cathcart,* i, 73 ff; 241 ff. MacDonald's story *The Bell* was printed first in *Good Words,* 5 (February

1864), 153–59; after its appearance in *Adela Cathcart* it appeared as "The Wow o'Rivven," published separately by Strahan in 1868 for the Royal Albert Idiot Asylum of Lancaster, and in *Works* (1871), x, 129–65. For the personal experiences see *GMDW*, 261 and 521. Also *Adela Cathcart*, I, 277–278, where the narrator explains that his grandmother (i.e. old Mrs. MacDonald) had been kind to the idiot, who called her "Auntie." For Wordsworth's words see David Ferry, *The Limits of Mortality* (Middletown: Wesleyan University Press, 1959), 96–97.

9. *The Marquis of Lossie;* I have used an American reprint in one volume (Boston: D. Lothrop, no date, but 1886); 49–50 and 121.

10. *Malcolm,* III, 284; I, ch. xv. *Marquis of Lossie,* 261, 280; "Recent Scotch Novels," *Edinburgh Review, 143* (1876), 348–49.

11. *Sir Gibbie,* 3 volumes (London: Hurst & Blackett, 1879); *Donal Grant,* 3 volumes (London: Kegan Paul, Trench & Co., 1883).

12. *Sir Gibbie,* I, 58, 59, 60, 62, 90, 205, 251–52, 304–05; II, 17; III, 59.

13. *Donal Grant,* III, 306. When the wicked earl returns to find that he has not succeeded in murdering his niece by walling her up in an old chapel, but that she after all has remodelled the old chapel instead, and installed an organ, she says to him:

> "Don't be frightened, uncle . . . I am not dead. You left me to die; but see the place of death has become the place of praise; the sepulchre was always the only resurrection-house. Here I am alive. Oh Uncle! I thank God."
>
> The earl stood motionless. His eyes were fixed upon her. His lips moved tremulously once or twice, but no word came. How much he took in of what she was saying, who can tell! At last he turned from her, glanced round the place, and said, "This is a great improvement." (III, 244–45)

14. *Castle Warlock,* 3 volumes (London: Sampson Low, Marston, Searle & Rivington, 1882). An impoverished but proud widowed laird, lives with his beloved son Cosmo in a bare stone castle. The worldly and brutally discourteous English peer, Lord Mergwain, travelling with his daughter Joan, takes shelter there from a snowstorm. Mergwain, whose father long ago killed an ancestor of the Warlocks, literally drinks himself to death on their premises. The bleakness of the house, the aging Scots maidservant, Grizzie, the greedy local landowner eager to seize the Warlocks' property—all add character to the simple narrative. In a country

that "produced more barley than wheat, more oats than barley, more heather than oats, more boulders than trees, and more snow than anything," MacDonald makes successful use of his favorite themes of perfect love between father and son and fierce family pride. As in *Malcolm,* the language is fresh and vigorous—"I'd as soon go to bed with the devil's grandmother as stop another half-hour in this abominable old lime-kiln," says Lord Mergwain ungraciously—and the rhyming talisman that in the end proves the clue to the treasure has a certain antique charm:

> Catch yer naig an' pu' his tail;
> In his hin' heel caw a nail;
> Rug his lugs frae ane anither—
> Stan' up, an' ca' the king yer brither.

When Cosmo finally locates the toy horse in the castle wall, and follows these directions, the horse falls apart, and the diamonds come showering down. (Quotations from 1, 2, 97.)

15. *What's Mine's Mine,* 3 volumes (London: Kegan Paul, Trench & Co., 1886).

16. *What's Mine's Mine,* ii, 31–32; Ferry, *The Limits of Mortality,* 97.

17. *The Elect Lady* (London: Kegan Paul, Trench & Co., 1883); I have used an American reprint (New York: Appleton, 1888). Alexa Fordyce, daughter of a miserly laird, a dreadful snob, has to give up the man she regards as eligible because he becomes a hardened crooked business man. When she humbles her pride and herself proposes to Andrew Ingram, a noble, learned rustic, who reads Milton and Vaughan and has written a book, Andrew rejects her. Instead, he marries his childhood sweetheart, daughter of a cottar, his female counterpart: it is she who tries to persuade the laird to give up a Cellini cup he has acquired by dubious means, and she who is falsely accused of stealing it.

18. *Heather and Snow,* 2 volumes (London: Chatto & Windus, 1893); I have used the American edition in one volume (New York: Harper & Brothers, 1893).

19. *Salted with Fire* (London: Hurst & Blackett, 1897); I have used the American edition (New York: Dodd Mead & Co., 1897). James Blatherwick, a divinity student who has seduced Isy, a charming girl, returns to his native village to be its minister and falls in love with Margaret MacLean, the saintly daughter of the saintly local shoemaker, who has found and rescued the abandoned baby who is the fruit of Blatherwick's sin. She refuses Blatherwick because she is not sure he loves God enough. Blather-

wick confesses his sin, marries Isy, and leaves the ministry, but only temporarily. The moral: repentance is all. The fate of Abaddon, the repentant angel in Klopstock's *Messiah,* remained uncertain, but when MacDonald characters repent heaven promptly reopens its doors to them.

20. *Annals of a Quiet Neighbourhood,* 3 volumes (London: Hurst & Blackett, 1867), serial publication in 1865–66 in *The Sunday Magazine; The Seaboard Parish,* 3 volumes (London: Tinsley Brothers, 1868); *The Vicar's Daughter,* 3 volumes (London: Tinsley Brothers, 1872); I have used an American reprint of the last (Boston: D. Lothrop, no date, but 1886).

21. *Guild Court,* 3 volumes (London: Hurst & Blackett, 1868), serialized during 1867 in *Good Words.*

22. *St. George and St. Michael,* 3 volumes (London: Henry S. King, 1876), serialized in *The Graphic,* in 1874–75. It tells the story of Dorothy Vaughan, a girl with cavalier sympathies, and her lover, Richard Heywood, a roundhead. She was born on St. George's day, and her slogan is "St. George for Merry England"; while he was born on St. Michael's, and his slogan is "St. Michael for the truth." MacDonald follows their adventures through the first five years of the civil wars, in a novel that is still remembered affectionately by those who read it as children. The chief interest of *St. George and St. Michael* derives from the portraits Mac-Donald paints of the Marquis of Worcester and his inventive son, Lord Herbert, later Earl of Glamorgan, who experimented with steam engines and other remarkable mechanical devices.

23. *Thomas Wingfold, Curate,* 3 volumes (London: Hurst & Blackett, 1876), serialized in *Day of Rest* during 1876; I have used an American reprint (New York: George Routledge, no date); *Paul Faber, Surgeon,* 3 volumes (London: Hurst & Blackett, 1879).

24. *Thomas Wingfold, Curate,* 408, 367, 592.

25. *Paul Faber, Surgeon,* I, 7; II, 255; I, 109, 112; II, 203–04, 84 ff; *GMDW,* 353. (William Hale White), *The Autobiography of Mark Rutherford, edited by his friend Reuben Shapcott* (New York: Scribner and Welford, 1889), first edition London, 1881, passim; quotation from p. 14. The anti-vivisection in *Paul Faber* represents a curiously popular literary theme of the 1870's and 1880's. Lewis Carroll, Wilkie Collins, and Ouida all wrote passionately on the subject. There is room here for an investigation.

26. *Mary Marston,* 3 volumes (London: Sampson Low, Marston, Searle & Rivington, 1881). Quotations: I, 50–51; II, 73 ff. Mac-Donald reintroduces some of his favorite types: a vicious Euphra-

like woman of the world named Sepia, a would-be poisoner (whose flirtation with an empty-headed young married man causes him to neglect his wife and let their baby starve); Sepia's former lover, a sinister Georgian count, who steals a ring, like Funkelstein, but is no mesmerist; and a noble untutored violin-playing blacksmith, whom Mary eventually marries. Students of the psychopathology of the Victorian novel will find themselves rewarded when they examine Mary's reasons for entering the service of the haughty Hesper Redmain.

27. *Weighed and Wanting*, 3 volumes (London: Sampson Low, Marston, Searle & Rivington, 1882).

28. *Weighed and Wanting*, I, 45.

29. *Home Again* (London: Kegan Paul, Trench & Co., 1887), 306.

30. *There and Back*, 3 volumes (London: Kegan Paul, Trench, Trübner & Co., 1891).

31. *The Flight of the Shadow* (London: Kegan Paul, Trench, Trübner & Co., 1891). I have used a "new edition" by the same publishers, no date, in their Indian and Colonial Series.

32. *There and Back*, III, 160.

33. *Sir Gibbie*, I, 283.

34. *Paul Faber, Surgeon*, II, 244–45, 246.

35. *Weighed and Wanting*, III, 248–49, 251, 254, 269–70.

36. *There and Back*, II, 235–36. Wingfold reappears in this novel.

37. *Rem.*, 27.

38. *A Rough Shaking* (London: Blackie, 1891); quotation from p. 69.

39. C. O. Parsons, "The Progenitors of *Black Beauty* in Humanitarian Literature," *Notes and Queries*, 192, 8 (April 19, 1947), discusses *At the Back of the North Wind* as a precursor of *Black Beauty*, and mentions Kelpie in *The Marquis of Lossie*, but not *A Rough Shaking*, or MacDonald's other horses. Nor does he apprehend MacDonald's preference for animals over human beings.

40. Bulloch, 693.

41. *The Flight of the Shadow*, 182, 279.

42. See above, Chapter 2, p. 58.

43. *Alec Forbes*, 250.

44. *Gutta Percha Willie, the Working Genius* (London: H. S. King, 1873), previously serialized in *Good Words for the Young* during 1872.

45. "The Butcher's Bills," *The Gifts of the Child Christ*, 2 vol-

umes (London: Sampson Low, Marston, Rivington & Searle, 1882);
I have used the American reprint, *Stephen Archer* (New York:
Routledge, n.d.).

46. "Stephen Archer," *ibid.*

47. Quoted in *GMDW*, 402.

CHAPTER 6 *Lilith*

1. *GMDW*, 554, quoting Blake's "Autumn Song."

2. *GMDW*, passim. Quotations: *Rem.*, 178, 303; *GMDW*, 526;
Rem., 335.

3. *Lilith. A Romance* (London: Chatto & Windus, 1895); *Lilith.
A Romance, With Introductory Key, a Paraphrase of an earlier
manuscript version, and explanation of notes by Greville Mac-
Donald* (London: George Allen and Unwin, 1924); *GMDW*,
546–55; *Rem.*, 320–24, 330–31; quotations from 320, 321.

4. BM Add. Mss. 46187. Labeled "MSS of LILITH by George
MacDonald (published in 1895)," and lettered "A" through "H."
What I have called *Lilith 3* is given the letters C, D, and E.

5. *Lilith 1* (A), 1–3, 7; *Lilith 2* (B), 38; crossed out in *Lilith 3*
(C), 72.

6. Child in *Times Literary Supplement*, May 29, 1924, p. 329;
Auden in Introduction to *The Visionary Novels of George Mac-
Donald*, ed. Fremantle (1954).

7. *Lilith* (1895 edition—note 3 above), v–vi, 25, 32, 37; *Rem.*,
323; for gravity, see above, Chapter 3 on *The Light Princess*, and
A. L. Taylor, *The White Knight: A Study of C. L. Dodgson*
(Lewis Carroll) (Edinburgh and London: Oliver and Boyd, 1952),
passim.

8. *Lilith*, 23, 37, 63. Augustine, quoted from the *Enarrationes
in Psalmos*, in Erich Auerbach, *Mimesis* (New York: Doubleday
Anchor Books, 1957), 135; translation mine.

9. *Lilith*, 66, 71, 72, 77, 92, 89; Auden in *The Visionary Novels*,
ed. Fremantle, v; *Lilith*, 85, 101, 102.

10. L. Ginzberg, *The Legend of the Jews* (Philadelphia: The
Jewish Publication Society of America, 1909) I, 65–66; III, 87–88.

11. *Lilith*, 129, 147, 157, 160–61, 162, 163, 170.

12. *Lilith*, 184, 186, 204–05, 215–20; C. Baudouin, *Psycho-
analysis and Aesthetics*, translated by E. and C. Paul (London:
Allen and Unwin, 1924), 115–16; cf. Maud Bodkin, *Archetypal
Patterns in Poetry*, 49.

13. *Lilith*, 240, 245, 254, 257, 279, 286, 297.

14. *Lilith*, 294–95, 296, 298, 314, 317.

15. Auden in Introduction to *The Visionary Novels,* ed. Fremantle, vi.

16. *Lilith,* 320, 330, 333, 334, 338, 339, 344, 348, 351.

Conclusion

1. *GMDW,* 334–35; compare the passage from Ruskin on his religious doubts quoted by W. E. Houghton, *The Victorian Frame of Mind,* 83.

2. See above, Chapter 6, pp. 340–41.

3. Ferry, *The Limits of Mortality,* 60.

4. *Lilith,* 217.

5. Houghton, 130, 150–51, 152–54.

6. Norman O. Brown, *Life against Death, The Psychoanalytical Meaning of History* (New York: Modern Library Paperbacks, Random House, 1959), passim; quotations from 34, 311. Houghton, 202, note 24, calls attention to the androgynous God described in the closing passage of Thomas Hughes' *Tom Brown's School Days.* But Hughes comes right out and says that God has motherly and sisterly, as well as fatherly and brotherly, aspects; MacDonald constantly proclaims God's fatherhood alone, while making Him motherly.

7. Somewhat as in the case of Browning or Thomas Arnold. See Houghton, 159–60, and the article by R. D. Altick there cited.

8. Ferry, 173.

9. Mark Schorer, *William Blake. The Politics of Vision* (New York: Henry Holt and Company, 1946), 91.

Index

(Italicized references indicate major discussion.)

treatment in "The Carasoyn," 132–33; grandmother-goddess, compared with her predecessors, 166; evolutionary theory in, 167–68; social comment in, 168; MacDonald's own view of the story, 168

Psellus, Michael, and elemental spirits, 48

Rampolli (1897), 389

Ranald Bannerman's Boyhood (1871), 282, 465

Rand, W. B., cited, 380

Rank, Otto, cited, 393

Richter, Jean Paul, 373; *Titan*, 66, 271; quoted in *David Elginbrod*, 195; *Hesperus, Comet*, 271

Riegel, René, cited, 393

Robert Falconer (1868), 8, 182, 227–253, 265, 266, 268, 331; its gloom and anguish, 228; the search for the lost father, really a search for a mother, 230–32; social work among the poor, 233; the impossibility of normal love, 235–39; the shoemaker, the waif, 239–40, 240–45; the portrait of the grandmother, 245–57; the plan for emptying hell, 247–49; the burning of the fiddle, 249–51; the doctrine of the loving God, 251–53

Robertson, E. A., cited, 391, 395

Robinson, Crabb, 5

Roos, Jacques, cited, 390, 394

Rougemont, Denis de, cited, 393

Rough Shaking, A (1891), its violence, animals in, 313–15

Royal Albert Idiot Asylum, Lancaster, 406

Ruskin, John, 5, 32, 296; makes MacDonald his confidant, 4; on F. D. Maurice, 205; and

Wilfrid Cumbermede, 268, 273, 276; his affair with Rose La Touche, his first marriage, and George MacDonald, 276–77, 280; cannot accept MacDonald's view of religion, 375–76; last letter to MacDonald, 389; cited, 402; *Diaries*, cited, 405

St. George and St. Michael (1876), 297, 408

Saintsbury, George, cited, 395

Salted with Fire (1857), 296, 328, 407–08; noble shoemaker in, 319–20

Schiller, Friedrich, 45; quoted by MacDonald, 31

Schlegel, A. W. von, 45

Schlegel, K.W.F. von, 44, 391

Schmidt, Arn, cited, 392

Schorer, Mark, cited, 411

Schubert, G. H., *Symbolism of the Dream* (1814), 50; *Aspects of the Night-side of the Natural Sciences* (1808), 50, 88

Scotsman, The, quoted in *Within and Without*, 29–30

Scott, A. S., 23, 263

Scott, Sir Walter, 181, 190; *Wandering Willie's Tale* (1832), 225

Seaboard Parish, The (1868), 296

Seekers and Finders, unpublished work, later destroyed, 113, 232

Selby, Thomas Gunn, criticizes MacDonald's theology, 256–62; cited, 404

"Shadows, The," as preliminary sketch for parts of *At the Back of the North Wind*, 152–53

Shelley, P. B., *Alastor*, and *Phantastes*, 46, 55, 86, 92, 94

Sigerist, H. E., cited, 392